Advance praise fc

Tom Foley has had a long and dis   ublic service. This new book offers a th   with the unique and highly effective combination of the biographer's narrative joined with Tom's own personal observations. *Honor in the House* not only provides insights about one of our nation's most decent and respected public leaders, it also provides a very useful guide to the fascinating course of American politics, especially congressional politics, from the 1960s to the 1990s.

Walter F. Mondale
Former Vice President of the United States and Ambassador to Japan

Former Speaker of the House and now Ambassador Tom Foley and his former press secretary Jeff Biggs have combined their extraordinary talents in a unique way to write a most interesting and objective account of Tom Foley's sojourn through the hurley-burley of political life.

At a time when there is so much cynicism about politics in general and the Congress in particular, it is good to read about one who epitomizes the ideal model for public service. This account of Tom Foley's most distinguished service in the Congress from 1964 through 1994 is a great textbook on what politics is all about. Tom very eloquently explains the ins and outs, the dos and don'ts of the everyday life of a congressman, and his rise through the Democratic leadership. The authors chronicle the legislative agenda during Tom's tenure, and candidly examine each of his campaigns for election.

I had the privilege of serving as the Republican leader for fourteen years at the same time Tom was advancing through the Democratic leadership ranks to ultimately become Speaker of the House. We obviously got to know each other well and became good friends. Moreover, we deeply respected one another as political adversaries, with never an ill word spoken between us. We had a mutual trust in each other that was not only good for us as leaders, but also wholesome for the institution we both loved.

Robert H. Michel
Former Minority Leader, U.S. House of Representatives

This is a vital book, combining a solid narrative of an important governmental career with delightful, candid personal comments by the subject of the biography, Tom Foley. The gentleman from Washington, who served for thirty years in the House of Representatives and became its Speaker, is a model legislator-politician—modest, funny, conscientious, and able. By his life and words, he restores respect to the battered reputation of the House—and points the way to the revival of its reputation.

David S. Broder
The Washington Post

It was a distinct privilege for me to have served with Tom Foley during his entire thirty years in the House. He will, without doubt, go down as one of the great lawmakers of the modern Congress. I cannot recall another Member who has enjoyed a similar depth of respect. A master of the legislative process, he understood fully the important role that the Congress plays in managing conflict and softening tension in a great, big, marvelously diverse country. He has carried out his many responsibilities with integrity, thoughtful deliberation, and dignity.

This excellent book helps to chronicle the many influences and developments in his remarkable life. It has Jeff Biggs's clearly written narration interspersed with Tom's comments and stories that reveal both his wit and warmth. The book produces marvelous insights into the role of the Congress in the nation and its inner operations. Tom Foley represents all that is the best in public service, and this book contains important lessons for us all.

Lee H. Hamilton
Former Member of Congress

Tom Foley is a rarity in the ranks of political leadership. He does his leading by example and quiet discourse. This book is a well-told story of how and why he operates that way. History will be very kind to Tom Foley. Here is an opportunity to get a pre-historian view of why.

Jim Lehrer
The News Hour with Jim Lehrer

Tom Foley's House service encompassed a period of momentous change in Congress and in the U.S. A participant in much of this history, he shows himself in this book to be a keen observer and analyst as well. He and his co-author—Jeff Biggs, who served as Foley's press secretary and thus can contribute first-hand observation as well—have produced a book that anyone interested in the Congress or in questions of representation should read.

An ingenious hybrid of third-person biography by Biggs interspersed with reflections by Foley, their account illuminates how much and in what ways the House has changed and how this has affected majority party leadership and the legislative process. It is also a fascinating account of a smart and decent man's highly successful political career, of his involvement in the movement to reform the House, his rise up the political ladder, his attempt as Speaker to maintain old norms of civility in an increasingly partisan chamber, and his ultimate failure to win reelection. In both guises, the book is informative, perceptive, and sometimes very funny. Foley is a great raconteur.

Barbara Sinclair
Marvin Hoffenberg Professor of American Politics, UCLA

Tom Foley was a rare leader in the turbulent politics of the American twentieth century. He led a fractious House of Representatives with dignity and a quiet strength not always appreciated by irascible members. He was an unusually civil politician in an increasingly uncivil arena. Tom not only recognized the importance of serving his constituency, but on occasion cast votes which he strongly felt were right yet knew were not popular with his constituents. He writes in the book, "If I hadn't taken at least one vote a term that jeopardized my job, then I was maybe going down the slippery slope." Many of today's politicians who precede every major decision with polling don't understand this fundamental test of political leadership.

Graceful in defeat, Tom Foley refused to either retire or reap the financial rewards of the private sector. He became U.S. Ambassador to Japan, and in doing so continued a lifetime of public service. Tom Foley helps restore the term "politician" to its meaning, "a student of the art and science of government."

Daniel J. Evans
Former U.S. Senator and Governor of Washington

HONOR
IN THE HOUSE

Speaker of the U.S. House of Representatives, Thomas S. Foley. *Courtesy House Photographer/ Jeffrey Biggs.*

HONOR
IN THE HOUSE

Speaker Tom Foley

Jeffrey R. Biggs
Thomas S. Foley

Foreword by Mike Mansfield

Washington State University Press
Pullman, Washington

Washington State University Press
P.O. Box 645910
Pullman, Washington 99164-5910
Phone: 800-354-7360   FAX: 509-335-8568
© 1999 by the Board of Regents of Washington State University
All rights reserved
First printing 1999

Cover illustration: Davis Buckley, AIA, artistic advisor
                        Frank Wright, artist
The painting is Thomas S. Foley's official portrait as Speaker of the U.S. House of Representatives. It hangs in the Speaker's Lobby in the Capitol with those of all other Speakers, and is the only one with a "pastoral" background in the nature of eighteenth century British portraiture.

Library of Congress Cataloging-in-Publication Data

Biggs, Jeffrey R., 1941–
     Honor in the House : Speaker Tom Foley / Jeffrey R. Biggs, Thomas
S. Foley ; foreword by Mike Mansfield.
        p.   cm.
     Includes index.
     ISBN 0-87422-172-2 (cloth : acid-free paper). — ISBN
0-87422-173-0 (paper : acid-free paper)
     1. Foley, Thomas S. 2. Legislators—United States—Biography.
3. United States. Congress. House—Speaker Biography. 4. United
States—Politics and government—1945–1989. 5. United States—
Politics and government—1989–   I. Foley, Thomas S.   II. Title.
E840.8.F65B54   1999
328.73'092—dc21
     [B]   99-12845
                                                              CIP

Contents

Tom Foley, Interior Committee Special Counsel for Washington's Senator Henry Jackson, gets a briefing from Montana's United States Senate Majority Leader Mike Mansfield, c. 1963. *Washington State University Libraries*

Foreword

A T THIS STAGE IN LIFE, I have learned to avoid taking on any more additional burdens than are absolutely necessary. But the opportunity to write a foreword for this book represented a pleasure, not a burden. I have admired Tom Foley's political—and now diplomatic—career for years.

Tom Foley's Fifth Congressional District of eastern Washington has more in common with the Montana I represented in the Senate than it does with the more urban Washington west of the Cascade mountains. Our two areas still have their empty vistas and vast expanses of wheatland. In the nineteenth century the land felt the impact of railroad workers, miners, and ranchers, influences still evident. There are no truly "safe" political seats in these areas, and any successful elected politician can ill afford to be parochial in his or her representation. This area represents an independent political spirit, and the voters have never been shy about voting long-term influential members of their congressional delegations out of office.

Both Tom and I came from Irish immigrant stock, which probably meant we were destined to be Democrats. But the legacy also meant we had to see more than one side to any argument. I could feel right at home with former Speaker of the House Tip O'Neill's comment that Tom Foley could always see "three sides to every argument."

When I entered Congress in 1942, and extending to Tom's first term in 1965, there were a number of traditions which set the tone for the way work was done. Among these older traditions were a concentration on the legislative work of congressional committees rather than public visibility of national issues through the media, a level of courtesy or comity among members which extended across party lines, a somewhat undefined period of apprenticeship for new members in deference to seniority, and a sense of patriotism about Congress which meant you had a lot fewer candidates running against the institution.

Although Tom and I were both involved in the congressional reforms which began in the 1960s and extended through the Legislative Reorganization Act into the mid-1970s, I had retired before the impact of a number of these reforms came to full bloom. Today's Congress is a far more open and decentralized body than in the 1950s, with power and decision-making authority far more diffuse. This book provides the reader with considerable color about what it was like to be Speaker of the House in an era of televised floor proceedings, daily press conferences, investigative journalism, and an almost all-pervasive media scrutiny.

This new style of Congress also required a different type of leadership. Tom was a former chairman of the House Agriculture Committee and a major architect of the Food Stamp Program, and no one questioned whether he had parliamentary skills when Speaker O'Neill appointed him Majority Whip in 1981. There were, however, some colleagues who questioned whether Tom was hard-nosed enough to be the point man for the Democratic majority.

Over the course of his next fourteen years in House leadership positions, Tom Foley proved he could be hard-nosed when required. But he was always civil, and always a gentleman. On Tom's last day as Speaker of the House, Republican Leader Bob Michel of Illinois rose to bid him farewell. He spoke of the virtues the departing Speaker had for so long typified: integrity, decency, and a commitment to crafting reasoned solutions to difficult problems. What struck me in the highly partisan world of today was that these qualities were being highlighted by the leader of the opposition. Although Tom could certainly rise to the challenge of being a solid Democrat, he did not believe in treating the Republican minority in a confrontational or hostile manner. Tom appreciated the fact that treating the minority with fairness and decency helps establish the basis for consensus which often has to transcend party lines. I think Tom would have called it governance. As Speaker, he rejected the argument of those colleagues who urged him to adopt a policy of constant attack against recently elected President George Bush. "I think if you want a daily partisan battle," Foley said in an interview, "and are not interested in getting anything more than the political embarrassment of the opposition . . . that's not for me. And if you have to have that as a requirement for the Speaker, then I think that I'm in the wrong job."

Following the 1992 elections, Tom found himself as Speaker of the House with a congressional majority and a Democratic President. He had to face the same kind of inflated expectations of a unified government that I did as Senate Majority Leader under President Lyndon Johnson. In the Senate in the 1960s, there were some Democrats who privately questioned whether my seemingly gentler approach would be successful in enacting a Democratic President's legislative agenda. It was akin to Tom's reaction to those conservative House Democrats who failed to support the one-vote victory for President Bill Clinton's 1993 budget. "We get a majority the old-fashioned way," Tom said. "We prevail upon conscience and judgment. We do not punish." For both of us, there was a certain virtue in letting Congress work its will through the collective judgment of individual members who were elected to represent their own constituents in their own right.

Tom represented his constituents well for thirty years. Yet he never shied away from voting his conscience, even if that occasionally went against the will of a majority in his district. Coming from the West, both Tom and I represented parts of the country where most pick-up trucks had a rack on the back window for a deer rifle or fishing rod. Gun control was always a very sensitive political issue. Tom had been a longtime opponent of gun control until 1994 when a psychiatric patient killed and wounded a number of people at Spokane's Fairchild Air Force Base. Tom's support of an assault weapons ban was regarded as a major factor in his 1994 reelection defeat. He was well aware of the risks he was taking in changing his position, but it was a matter of conscience and, as he would have said, if there was one vote he wanted to get, it was his own.

Throughout both of our congressional careers, Tom and I had a sustained engagement with the countries of the Pacific Rim. We both have always considered Japan as a Pacific power and have rejected any kind of isolationism. Also importantly, we have both regarded public service as a noble career. Maybe it was not surprising that, after leaving the Congress, we were both honored to have been offered the role of U.S. Ambassador to Japan. For both of us, this represented the beginning of a new career.

Tom Foley has a lot to tell the nation about public life and politics. We can all learn from his reflections. In this book, his views are presented in a most unusual, but very effective, way. What follows is neither biography nor autobiography. It is an innovative hybrid. Jeff Biggs, after twenty-one years in the Foreign Service and seven years serving on Tom's staff as press secretary/spokesman, has written the traditional third-person biography. Tom has injected his own first-person observations.

When I was elected to represent Montana in the 1940s, there were few staff members doing the work Jeff performed for Speaker Foley. This was before C-SPAN televised congressional proceedings, before the press had grown to its current dimensions, and before the legislative branch became as refreshingly open to the public as it is today. By the late 1980s, a press spokesman was about as close to the source as a congressional staff member could get. A history written by the spokesman and the principal is a rare and illuminating route to learn what the life of a congressman is like. Jeff and Tom make the collaboration work well.

If there is a bottom line to a story such as this, I think it is that the chronicle Tom Foley and Jeff Biggs have provided is one of optimism about politics and public service. In an era when both have been frequently pummeled and when the public too frequently is presented with an extremely cynical view of Congress, this is a story about the institution and about a congressional leader who tries to right the balance. It makes a good case as to why politics and public service can be ennobling. I hope it is not the last book of its kind.

Mike Mansfield

Foley's paternal grandfather had originally come to Spokane as an employee of the Great Northern railroad. A group of Great Northern employees are here photographed in downtown Spokane in the early 1900s. *Washington State University Libraries.*

🏛

CHAPTER ONE

Western Roots

I lived in a Republican neighborhood, where to some extent the many friends we had treated the Democratic allegiance of our family as one might treat a strange religion.
—Thomas S. Foley, 1989

At the Center of Change Over Thirty Years

I T WAS A STANDING-ROOM ONLY OCCASION. Swept in by the Lyndon Baines Johnson presidential landslide victory over Barry Goldwater in 1964, seventy-one newly elected members of the U.S. House of Representatives were gathered for their "freshman orientation" before a handful of senior House members. Senior Appropriations Committee member Representative Michael Kirwan warned the class to avoid the greatest mistake a new member could make. Was it an ethics question wondered Thomas S. Foley from eastern Washington. No. The mistake, Mr. Kirwan gravely emphasized, was "thinking for yourself." Foley, an idealist, was outraged. He had campaigned on change, on educational and health issues, and had come to Washington, D.C., to legislate new programs. Congress in the 1960s was a seniority-dominated body led by its chairmen. Nobody asked Foley's opinion. Mr. Kirwan was giving some tips. The new members would be well advised to follow the advice of the leadership.

The agenda Foley encountered in 1965 was that program he had campaigned on—LBJ's "Great Society" program with its emphasis on Medicare, aid to education, and support for urban programs. Thirty years later, in 1994, the Democrats lost fifty-two seats in the most disastrous congressional loss for a first-term president since Herbert Hoover in 1930. Members of the first Republican majority in forty years had also campaigned on change. They embraced the minimalist conception of government underlying the "Reagan revolution" of 1980 and committed themselves to dismantling the legacy of "Great Society" programs.

When Foley had entered the U.S. House of Representatives in 1965, legislative power was concentrated among predominantly conservative southern committee chairmen. These "lords proprietors of Congress" could exclude the press from their committee hearings, declare junior committee members legislatively "dead" if they proved too independent, and thwart the more liberal instincts of the leadership, including the Speaker. This culture led Foley into the Democratic Study Group and the democratizing reforms of the 1970s.

The Democratic reforms of the '70s gave the rank-and-file majority party membership, and the Speaker, significantly new influence over the selection of committee chairmen. Foley's successor as Speaker following the elections of 1994, Republican Newt Gingrich, instituted his own rule. There would be no "old barons" to challenge him or his own hand-picked committee chairmen. The GOP majority endorsed Gingrich's views and were willing, if not eager, to increase his leverage over committee chairmen. Where Speaker Foley frequently had to cobble together majorities from among disparate liberal, moderate, and conservative Democratic factions, Speaker Gingrich encountered few dissenters among House Republicans.

Representative and later Speaker Foley arrived and departed the U.S. House of Representatives an institutionalist with a deep respect for "the people's" legislative body as a deliberative forum requiring civility and respect on both sides of the aisle to keep the partisanship from becoming destructively personal. Representative Gingrich, the same driving force that had persuaded moderate and conservative Republicans in the early 1980s to adopt a confrontational stance toward Democratic management of the House, became the pivotal figure in consolidating power in the Speakership. Civility and bipartisanship, however, were frequently victims to this new leadership power.

Where Foley had built a reputation for bipartisanship and an ability to work with Republican presidents Reagan and Bush, Gingrich's "Contract with America" sought to replace the President as the nation's agenda-setter. Unlike any recent Speaker before or since, Foley had been a Democrat representing a marginally Republican district. The son of a judge, he was raised in an atmosphere of judiciousness. As his political career progressed, he survived by bridging, not accentuating, political differences.

Foley's 1964 electoral contest was so civil, respectful, even congenial, that it attracted media attention. The young lawyer had challenged conventional wisdom by running against a Republican incumbent with twenty-two years in the House, and won. It would be inconceivable today to imagine his campaign. He made his decision to run one day before the filing deadline with nothing in the way of staff, funds, or plans.

Despite the initial advice of his veteran campaign adviser Ed Rollins that "nobody beats a Speaker," in 1994 lawyer George Nethercutt ran what he called a "Foley-like" campaign and unseated a Speaker for the first time in more than a hundred years. Nethercutt successfully challenged the benefits a fifteen-term, thirty-year, incumbent could bring to his constituents with his campaign slogan: what the Fifth District of eastern Washington needs is "a listener, not a Speaker."

In 1964, the voters of eastern Washington's Fifth District unseated their twenty-two-year incumbent Republican congressman and replaced him with a young, liberal, native son. Thirty years later that same district "sent a message to the Capitol" and defeated their congressman at the acme of his influence as Speaker of the House. They defeated their Speaker and helped usher in the first Republican majority in the U.S. House of Representatives in forty years. This is the story of that native son, that Speaker, and that head of the defeated Democratic majority—Thomas Stephen Foley.

The Landscape of Eastern Washington

Seattle is the closest major American city to the Orient, a setting that has spawned an innovative, white-collar, foreign trade-oriented economy whose growth is driven not only by the big enterprises of the past—the Kaisers, the Weyerhaeusers, and the Boeings—but also more recent corporations with national visibility—including Bill Gates's Microsoft, Starbuck's Coffee, and Nordstroms. The Washington of the 1940s was liberal on economic issues and the Puget Sound area gave big majorities to Franklin Delano Roosevelt. Its mainstream Democrats, senators Warren Magnuson and Henry Jackson, who together represented the state in Congress for a total of eighty-seven years, believed in an active and compassionate federal government that fostered research and health care, nurtured a sustainable environment, built dams and hydroelectric projects, aluminum plants, and the nuclear-energy Hanford Works at home, and pursued an internationalist anti-Communist foreign policy abroad. State Republican loyalists had a simpler view of Magnuson and Jackson. They spent, they taxed, and, despite the occasional close call, they seemed invincible.

In contrast to the Seattle-driven western slope of the Cascade mountains, eastern Washington is a land of great rivers and bare parched land, where the Columbia, Spokane, and Snake rivers wind among vast plateaus, bringing water to the desert. If the state's plentiful timber once led to the belief it would never be exhausted, and its mineral deposits generated early gold and silver booms, both were surpassed by water. Grand Coulee Dam and the Columbia Basin Irrigation Project unlocked the agricultural potential east of the Cascades, transforming eastern Washington bunchgrass into fields of wheat.[1]

Spokane, the state's second largest city, was founded at the falls of the Spokane River. By the 1890s, it had become "an oasis of culture and refinement." Its Auditorium Theatre presented the latest productions from New York and London. The Spokane Gun Club became one of the Northwest's most active skeet shooting sites.[2] But the pride of Spokane came in 1914 with the opening of the twelve-story Florentine-style Davenport Hotel. With its Corinthian-columned "Isabella Room," its "Marie Antoinette Ballroom," its "Chinese Buffet," and its lobby fountain with water spurting from the mouth of a dolphin carried by a child, the Davenport brought prestige to the city.[3] A city which recorded a population of 350 in 1880 had grown to 104,000 by 1910 and numbered fifty men whose combined wealth equaled $50 million, based largely on holdings in mines, railroads, banks, and real estate in what locals called "the Inland Empire."[4]

Spokane today serves as the banking, marketing, and medical center of the "Inland Empire" or "Inland Northwest." It is now the West's largest city north of Salt Lake City and Denver between Minneapolis-St. Paul in the East and Seattle in the West. The area's Fifth Congressional District covers eleven counties and a two-hundred mile span extending north from the Oregon border to British Columbia. In this easternmost segment of the state, two-thirds of the people live in the greater-Spokane area, a city of some 170,000 characterized by large pockets of Irish Roman Catholic neighborhoods— comprising 15-20 percent of the city's population—and generational loyalties. Set in a pine-covered valley near the Idaho border, Spokane harbors a remote quality, a spot of inter-mountain "Middle America" set off by itself. It has traditionally been among the most conservative of America's larger cities. Outside Spokane's city limits, the vast remainder of the district is even more conservative and Republican, "but the rural voters are quick to turn against any administration in hard times."[5]

Judge's Son

For most of the twentieth century, the name Foley has been prominent in Spokane. Thomas Stephen Foley was born March 6, 1929 in Spokane, the only son of Ralph E. and Helen Marie (Higgins) Foley. In 1934 the Foleys had a daughter, Maureen. Tom frequently called his father, a legendary figure in Spokane who died in April 1985, the dominant influence in his life.

Born November 25, 1900, in Barnesville, Minnesota, Ralph Foley came to Washington in 1907 when his father, Cornelius F. Foley, a Great Northern Railroad boiler shop foreman, transferred to the railroad's boiler repair shops at Hillyard.

> My grandfather was a tough, old style Irish boss in the days when there wasn't much of a grievance committee through the brotherhoods. The family story is that he would fire a man for even a small dereliction of responsibility. The man's wife would then visit my grandmother, who took the grievance to my grandfather, and the man would be hired back.[6]

Harry Ellis "Bing" Crosby was one of Ralph Foley's early classmates at the Webster School in Spokane. A talented semi-pro baseball player, Ralph Foley went on to earn his B.A. at Gonzaga University in 1923 and his LL.B. in 1927, and for many years thereafter served as a part-time member of the law school faculty. He began his forty-seven years of public service in the Spokane County prosecuting attorney's office where he worked for seven years before being elected county prosecutor in 1934.[7] Ralph Foley was a Democrat in a community where most of the leading citizens were staunch Republicans.

> I grew up believing that Franklin D. Roosevelt saved the country, and that the Democratic Party stood for a sense of social justice and opportunity.
>
> I lived in a Republican neighborhood where, to some extent, the many friends we had treated the Democratic allegiance of our family as one might treat a strange religion. I learned at an early age that most of my friends were Republicans, but I had a fierce determination to defend the Democratic cause.[8]

Appointed by Governor Clarence D. Martin to the Superior Court bench April 2, 1940 and then elected on his own that November, Ralph Foley became the longest-sitting judge in the state's history with thirty-five years on the Superior Court. Judge Foley was recognized as the founder of the family court system in Washington, which he fostered in the belief that strong family ties and a child's need for affection were major elements in character formation.[9]

Ralph and Helen and their family lived in Spokane's prosperous South Hill neighborhood which, along with the earlier Browne's Addition, had housed the wealthy families of Spokane since the late 1800s.[10] The Spokane River divided the city. To the north around Gonzaga University the communities were more blue-collar, Democratic, and Irish Catholic, and to the south, more Protestant and Republican. South Hill was relatively untouched by the Great Depression which, along with much of the country, had hit Spokane hard. Already dizzy from the effects of a depression in agriculture, "business and industry reeled as banks closed their doors, stores closed or went into voluntary bankruptcy, sawmills ceased to operate, and mines curtailed production when silver and lead prices hit new lows."[11] Bread lines formed, and panhandling on city streets increased. Men stood in front of employment offices hopelessly looking for jobs that did not exist.

The senior Foley went out of his way to insure that his son was not blinded by any comfortable isolation of the family's relative prosperity.

> It was a constant effort to show me the circumstances of people less comfortable than ourselves. If he hadn't made these efforts, I can understand how people lose total touch with the circumstances of others.[12]

The image of the Depression never left Tom Foley, and fostered his political view of the federal government's responsibilities. Over the years he frequently spoke of the distress he felt over the growing underclass in U.S. society, "the alienation and separation of economic classes in this country. I would really like to bring about some amelioration of that. If it continues to grow, it could weaken the fabric of American society." His later role in the development of the Food Stamp program was a reflection of that concern.

As a boy the thirties were a time of very comfortable economic circumstances. I remember it seemed to me, more so than later in my life, that my parents were well enough off to entertain a lot, and I recall as a child also being somewhat resentful, that's the wrong word, somewhat questioning, as to why we couldn't have a cabin cruiser the way our friends next door had a cabin cruiser. . . . My father, on the other hand, drove me around to show me some of the shantytowns that had built up in the city, explained to me what the depression was about, pointed out the long lines of mostly unemployed and homeless men that waited every day behind the Sacred Heart Hospital for the handout from the nuns of a sandwich and coffee.

You knew, in an intellectual way, that there were a lot of people who were unemployed and that there was a lot of economic suffering, but there really was an invisibility about the broader economic distress in the country when people such as my family lived in Spokane in relatively comfortable neighborhoods. It was the Michael Harrington notion of "The Other America." A lot of people would drive from these neighborhoods to their office buildings and go to work, and drive back home and out to the country club to play golf, and this kind of thing was simply beyond their immediate experience, that anybody was having any great economic struggle or difficulty.

I remember having been struck by the fact that we were an unusual family, politically, and that the family's affection for Franklin Roosevelt and the Democratic Party was not shared, to put it mildly, by the neighbors. My good friend, Jimmy Pence, told me that his father, who was president of the bar association and the chairman of the Republican Party in Spokane County, had forbidden anyone in the family to mention Franklin Roosevelt's name in the house. When I was a little kid, maybe five or six, I remember playing this kind of mime game which was in response to the Republican neighborhood kids ridiculing the Works Progress Administration (WPA). They would do a very slow mime-like shovel, pretending to dig at a snail's pace, and pronounce that as WPA, and then energetically shovel and say that was free enterprise. So, taking up the challenge, I would reverse the order and do the slow-paced shovel and call that free enterprise, and then speed it up and call that WPA.

Even at a very young age I could sense the tremendous hostility that many people had about Franklin Roosevelt and, particularly in the relatively comfortable neighborhood in which we lived, the notion that Roosevelt was a kind of traitor to fundamental economic principles was pretty widespread, not just among the rich, but among people who lived in a middle-class environment. The maids were for Roosevelt, but they kept quiet about it.

My mother, I remember, took the little National Recovery Administration pennant and discreetly hung it on the back door of the house, rather than the front door, as a concession to the neighbors. Like so many families, particularly Democratic families, the Roosevelt radio speeches were a matter of enormous attention and respect, if not reverence. So when Franklin Roosevelt came to Spokane in 1936, my father, as the Prosecuting Attorney, was one of the leading Democratic officials in town and took me down to the train and I got introduced to President Roosevelt. One of the lingering memories of my life is watching the pilot train come into the station, with the soldiers lined up along the rail side all shouldering their rifles, and the opportunity to go on to the car and be introduced to Franklin Roosevelt.

From age five, when his father became Spokane County prosecutor, Foley grew up in a political but judicial environment. To attorney Jack R. Dean, Judge Foley was "the ultimate perfect gentleman. I would guess I tried something like 25 to 50 cases before him; it was always a pleasant experience—win, lose or draw." "Everyone loved Judge Foley, even some of those to whom he gave stiff sentences," said Federal District Court Judge Justin ("Bud") Quackenbush, whose father had been a deputy prosecutor under Ralph Foley. "He was a compassionate man, but in appropriate cases, he imposed strict sentences; in child-abuse cases, for instance, he was a tough sentencer. Even in that type of case, however, he always would orally reflect on some good in the defendant, even though the accused had done something of which the judge could never approve."[13]

"Tom is the great resolver," said Quackenbush. "I think that's a trait inherited from Judge Foley. He was the kind of person who really thought disputes should be resolved by mutual agreement. He was renowned for attempting to get people to compromise and settle their differences even in the middle of a trial. Those of us who practiced in front of Judge Foley would sometimes become a little impatient because we knew he was going to call us into his chambers and ask if we had pursued every avenue in an effort to resolve the matter without the necessity of having a winner and loser."[14]

Bud Quackenbush and Tom Foley took their bar exams together, and briefly served side by side as deputy prosecutors. Until Quackenbush went on the federal bench in 1979, he was Foley's first and continuing campaign manager. The Quackenbush family was prominent in Spokane's Masonic circles and the affiliation helped Foley overcome the anti-Catholic vote. Foley was the first Catholic from eastern Washington elected to Congress. "I see a lot of Judge Foley in Tom," Quackenbush said in an interview.[15] The Ralph Foley legacy included a fixed judiciousness mixed with compassion.

As long as I can remember, my father was in public life. He was a Deputy Prosecutor when I was born [and later] . . . became a Superior Court Judge. . . . My father served until well into my congressional career. He retired in 1975 and was then, in terms of service, the senior trial judge in the state. . . . So, all of my recollections of the official side of my father's life were associated with the law and the courts. I remember an early birthday party, I think at the age of six, where the premier event of the party was that all of my guests and I were taken to the county jail, fitted out with numbers, and photographed and finger-printed like common criminals. I mean it couldn't have been a greater success or a more marvelous experience. The kids were talking about it for weeks. At other people's birthday parties they put on funny hats and blew whistles. At mine they went to jail.

I have very early memories of going to political picnics and campaigns and my father shaking hands and handing out cards. It used to be a big thing at the time to hand out political campaign cards that had your message on them, and I was engaged at an early age to run around parks handing out my father's campaign cards, which people thought was terribly cute. I was considered, I guess, to be a handsome little boy. I had come in second or third in some kind of a baby photography contest. . . .

The legacy of my father is that he represented for me, then and now, a sense of public responsibility, performance and integrity that I've always thought was of a high standard. His reputation was extraordinary. Again, I grew up under both the encouragement and, I guess one would say, the shadow of having a father who, not only in that community, but around the state, was well known and highly respected. It became a kind of staple of my experience for somebody to say, "Are you Ralph Foley's son? Well, I have the greatest respect for your father." Year after year when he was judge, it was a non-partisan but elective office in Washington, he would lead the ticket. He would come out at the top of the ticket with more votes than Franklin Roosevelt. This was a kind of happy experience. On the other hand, I was always told that I had a tremendous responsibility to the family and the family name, that I could never do anything that would bring disrepute or bad reputation on the family, that I would get noticed more, and problems would be magnified if I ever got into any trouble. So I always felt a bit of pressure.

I remember one time when I was sixteen, and had just gotten my driver's license, I was driving my mother's car and was stopped by a police officer for speeding. He asked me for my license and I produced it, and he immediately asked whether I was any relation to Judge Foley. And I said, "yes, he's my father." Well, instead of giving me a ticket, he ordered me to follow him down to the police station. I followed him down and went into the police station and, in a couple of minutes, I was ushered into the presence of Clifford Payne, Chief of Police of the City of Spokane, whereupon I got a stern lecture about how my father would be unhappy, to say the least, disappointed, and embarrassed, to learn that I had been violating the speeding law which was but one of the many laws my father was sworn to uphold. Finally, after this long lecture, the chief proposed a bargain that if I promised never to speed again, and to observe all the traffic laws scrupulously, he wouldn't one, give me a ticket, or two, report the matter to my father. I signed up for that deal, and the first thing my father said when he got home was, "Tom, Chief Payne called and told me that Officer Jones stopped you for speeding." I thought to myself, there is no honor among chiefs of police.

Again, without exaggerating too much, my father was not only highly regarded, but almost famous for his patience, for his courtesy, and for his judicial nature. . . . I know later on, when I was a lawyer, how many lawyers appreciated the concern he had not only for presiding impartially over the court, but helping young lawyers who had made a mistake or two, perhaps in the pleadings. There were a couple of other very good judges who were impatient with any lapses on the part of young attorneys and would announce in court, very loudly, "Where is the distribution order? You know, Mr. Jones, you have to have a distribution order before final disposition." Very embarrassing. My father would call up the counsel and say, "You know, I'll make an excuse here, and continue the matter over until you get the distribution order." That was appreciated.

I remember being very impressed by a letter that Carl Maxey, a leading black lawyer in Spokane, sent to my father when he retired. Carl wrote that in all the years he'd practiced in his court he thought my father had dispensed justice with absolute integrity and impartiality, both as to him as counsel and to his clients.

The Foley roots were deeply planted in the Fifth Congressional District of eastern Washington. On the maternal side, Helen Foley's father, Stephen Higgins, was an Irish-immigrant railroad worker who eventually settled in Hartline, a bend-in-the-road wheat town of less than a hundred people about ninety miles west of Spokane. Stephen Higgins became a principal shareholder in a grain-elevator company and owner of considerable wheat land. Foley tells a story about going to the annual Lincoln County Fair in Davenport, west of Spokane, one Sunday early in his first congressional campaign and being introduced by the county Democratic chairman. "'This is Tom Foley,' he said. 'He's out of Spokane.' In Lincoln County, it's not best to be from Spokane." The longer the introduction went on, Foley recounts, the more it seemed to be falling on deaf ears. Frustrated, the county chairman eventually mentioned that Foley's mother had been born in Davenport,

> One of the farmers said, "Your mother was born in Davenport?"
> I said, "Yes sir."
> He said, "What was her name?"
> I said, "Helen Higgins."
> "Helen Higgins was your mother?"
> I said, "Yes sir."
> "Shorty Higgins your uncle?"
> I said, "Yes sir."
> He said, "Steve and Annie Higgins your grandfolks?"
> "Yes sir."
> He said, "You come with me."
> He took me up to some microphone somewhere and announced that this is Tom Foley, and he's Steve and Annie Higgins' grandson and so forth and so on. I either won Lincoln County or barely lost it, and I won it nearly every time since. It taught me that in politics there are things more important than party or even where you stand on the issues.

One of a half-dozen children of Irish immigrants Stephen and Anne Higgins, pioneer residents of Hartline, Helen Higgins attended Holy Names Academy in Spokane. In 1926, she was a school teacher in Mansfield when she married Ralph Foley, who was attending Gonzaga University School of Law. When Thomas Foley became Speaker in 1989, most national writers would comment on two of Foley's personality traits, a judicial temperament, and a fondness for "the finer things in life" such as classical music, art, and gourmet food. "Tom Foley got the temperament from his father, but the love of art, music and food from his mother," said cousin Henry Higgins.[16]

Native Son

> I grew up with a lot of cousins. There were six children in my Grandfather and Grandmother Foley's family, and six children in my Grandfather and Grandmother Higgins' family, and although several of them were childless, just those who had children produced a number of cousins. We used to gather at Liberty Lake in the summertime, and I'd divide my summer between going to Camp Reed, the YMCA camp, and spending several weeks at Liberty Lake. The closest of these cousins, in terms of both proximity—living in Spokane—and age, was Hank Higgins. He used to come into Spokane from Hartline, Washington, the tiny family town of my mother and her brothers and sister. Hank was the son of Harold and Mabel Higgins. Harold was the most financially successful

member of the family. He had two strikes against him as a boy growing up. He was enormously overweight and he had a speech impediment. A third blow came when he developed a severe problem with alcohol. He became an alcoholic. So the combination of being obese, alcoholic, and having a speech impediment was a remarkable series of things to overcome, but he became quite successful. He succeeded my grandfather as head of the Farmers' Union Grain Company, a grain elevator company that my grandfather had founded. He was also successful in the insurance and real estate businesses.

Hank was my "country cousin." He would come into town with his sister Rose Marie and mother, Mabel Higgins, and, while mother and daughter went shopping in Spokane for several days, Hank and I, at age eight or nine, used to be given something like twenty dollars by Uncle Harold [Harold "Shorty" Higgins] to amuse ourselves. Twenty dollars in 1937, when movies were ten cents, comic books were five, Cokes were five, and steak dinners cost fifty cents, was a lot of money, and that could keep us going for a good week seeing every movie in Spokane that was not prohibited. There were a couple of movie theaters that were off-limits to us, which we always wanted to go into but never had the guts. We developed a fast friendship, more like brothers than cousins.

We used to argue all night about everything, so it was very natural later on in life that Hank, in addition to being one of my best friends, was one of my severest critics. He had a very strong sense of what was right and wrong in public life—abuses of authority, callousness in government, a lack of responsiveness of Congress, and government justice in general. He also tested my father's patience by inveighing against the arrogance of judges and the insensitivity of the judicial system. Quick to judge, he was also a tremendously warm-hearted and generous individual. If you needed a friend, you couldn't do better than Hank Higgins. He might criticize the hell out of you, but if you had a problem, he was the first one there.

For the thirty years of his political life, Foley was supported by the early and continuing friendship of such people as Hank Higgins, Justin "Bud" Quackenbush, Gonzaga Prep classmate and for many years a Foley campaign treasurer Dave Robinson, and Spokane attorney Scott Lukins, who was a Foley friend of some fifty years and longtime campaign manager. They were among the friends who played key roles in Foley's electoral efforts and formed the bedrock of his ties to eastern Washington. They were never displaced by friends in the nation's capitol where enduring friendships were somewhat harder to develop.

I think it's probably not atypical of people in Congress. Two things happen. Friendships never really develop in the same way, as easily anyway, in

Washington, D.C., as they do at home. That's what really defines home I guess. I suppose it's true of most people that friendships are bonded more when you're growing up with your schoolmates, with people you go to college, with your family, and so on, than they are later in your professional life. But I think there's a particular problem with being in some areas of public life. You're everybody's friend and nobody's friend. You've got an unlimited number of friends and very few real ones. I don't want to exaggerate it, but the nature of serving in the Congress is to have a lot of people who are of your acquaintance and linked with you in some kind of a political or public way, but it's not quite the same thing as it is with the kind of real, italicized real, friends with whom one grows up.

There's a certain amount of sham on both sides in Washington, D.C. The politician, who's a candidate, who's everybody's friend, and the people who are your friend while you're in office. Not that those are exclusionary terms, but when you leave office, especially if you lose an election, you find out very quickly that there are some people, different time, different circumstance, that aren't there any more. If you don't expect some of this then you are very, very, unrealistic, and I think some people who lose or leave office get disappointed and hurt because they assume that when they were the chairman of the committee, or they were the president of the commission, or whatever they were, everybody loved them for themselves and not for their office, and they find out that there are people who would walk across the street just for the chance of saying "hello" to them before, and who will just keep walking after they leave. It's not a reason to feel bitter, it's just human nature. But there are also some people who are there just as much or more than they ever were.

A Jesuit Education

Longtime Foley childhood friend David Robinson recalls Foley as tall, gangly, and uncoordinated. "He was a superb scholar but a poor student. . . . He wasn't interested in grades, but he had tremendous depth." At Gonzaga High School, Spokane's Jesuit high school, Foley took the honors classical curriculum which included four years of Latin and two of Greek. He recalls having had a "checkered academic career," flunking algebra, and attending classes where discipline was reinforced with the wooden "hack paddle." "I didn't have to hack him or even call on him very much because I only called on the kids who didn't know the answer," said Father Victor Zehnder, Foley's 1946 high school physics teacher.[17]

Nicknamed "the Senator" by his classmates, Foley worked on the school newspaper, was in the Latin Club, and became a state debating champion with good friend Peter de Roetth. As one reporter later reflected, "Peter de Roetth and

Tom Foley were a winning duo. . . . As brainy teenagers, the South Hill twosome read Winston Churchill speeches aloud to each other." In 1946 the pair proved unbeatable through seventy-five debates.[18] In that same state tournament, remembers Scott Lukins, Foley won the one-on-one Lincoln-Douglas debate competition. But, in Foley's mind, the single most important school honor was his election to the service club, "Knights of the Leash." Wearing their white sweaters with a blue knight's crest, the Knights were given authority by the school to help enforce discipline with their "hack paddles." The somewhat "nerdish" Foley found himself in the prestigious company of thirty juniors and seniors, many of them athletic lettermen. He felt he had it made although, flushed with too much success, he was temporarily suspended as a senior when his grade average fell below the required minimum.

During summer vacations he worked for the state highway department in Metaline Falls, as a delivery boy for a downtown Spokane pharmacy; a counselor at the nearby YMCA camp; or at Hartline's Farmers Union Grain Company during the harvest season. Later, while at Gonzaga University, he worked in the local Kaiser Aluminum Company's Trentwood rolling mill. He still credits that experience with instilling an enduring sensitivity to blue-collar concerns.

In his junior year at Gonzaga University, having reentered "one of my cycles of mediocre scholarship," a discussion with the dean over academic attitudes led Foley to transfer to the University of Washington in Seattle. In leaving Gonzaga, however, Foley carried with him a sense of gratitude, affection, and debt for the intellectual training both Gonzaga Preparatory and the Gonzaga University provided him. Talking with a reporter thirty years later, Foley observed:

> I joke sometimes that the word "Jesuit" in the dictionary is defined as "a member of the Society of Jesus, a Roman Catholic religious order for men established by Ignatius Loyola." The next word in some dictionaries is "Jesuitical: sly, crafty, deceitful to some length."

As the reporter noted, Foley added quickly, with a laugh, "as if the shadow of some cleric is looking over his shoulder":

> . . . the pride of Jesuit teaching was to teach people to think, to analyze and to question.[19]

> When I was in school, I'd thought for a long time that I wanted to go to law school, but wondered whether this was really something I wanted to do or something I wanted to please my family by doing, and so I went back and forth. I got a draft deferment to go to law school and applied to Harvard Law School and found out I'd applied too late and so I went to the University of Washington. For some reason, I'm not really sure why, I got very turned off by the opening lecture of the assistant dean who, in effect, was saying "put out of your mind any glorious notions of the practice of law, this is a business as well as a profession." Anyway, he

so sufficiently cooled my idealistic ardor that I marched out and applied to go to the Graduate School of Far Eastern and Russian Studies which I did for a couple of years, and then returned to the notion I'd originally had of going to law school. I decided that's what I really wanted to do, and after a short stint in private practice I had an opportunity to go into the prosecuting attorney's office which was, in a sense, following in my father's footsteps. . . . In fact, the then prosecutor had been one of my father's deputies. I sort of imagined that I'd follow his career and at some time in the future I might get the chance to become the prosecuting attorney and later a judge.

Scott Lukins remembers Foley as a bibliophile who ordered books from Blackwell's of Oxford and for whom classes were secondary to reading. Lukins also remembers Foley as having operated part-time as a kind of freelance defender of down-and-out clients to the point that he received a letter from conservative Democratic state senator Davey Cower warning Foley of the dangers of involvement with the liberal-radical-communist fringe. While in law school, Foley also worked nights at the juvenile court.

Early Career

Foley had intended to follow in his father's footsteps. He practiced law briefly with his cousin Hank Higgins in Lincoln County. "The truth is most law students are educated to be, more than anything else, supreme court justices," Foley recalled in an interview. "[In school] they don't give you the foggiest notion, for example, of how to petition for a name change, and the first real, honest-to-God client I had was a couple who wanted to change their name." Deciding there wasn't enough business for his partner and himself, in 1958 he accepted a $500-a-month position as Spokane deputy prosecutor which, even four decades later, he would describe as "the most powerful job I ever had . . . I'd just sign a piece of paper and a man went to jail.[20] Foley insisted that lessons learned while a deputy prosecutor—lessons about not making decisions in the heat of anger and the pointlessness of revenge—guided him throughout his political career.[21]

From the county prosecutor's office Foley moved on to be Assistant Attorney General for Washington State. In 1961 he failed to secure the support of Senator Warren Magnuson for a position as U.S. Attorney in eastern Washington. The senator, Foley learned, had a personal minimum age for nomination, and Foley was too young at thirty-two. As a fallback, Foley went to Washington, D.C., to work as a special counsel on Senator Henry Jackson's Interior and Insular Affairs Committee for three years (1961-64). Before his death, Jackson's administrative assistant, Sterling Munro, recalled Foley as a Jackson protégé who was "shy, easy-going, capable, not aggressive, boisterous, or a tremendous workaholic." Four decades later, Helen Jackson, widow of the senator, said she always thought of Foley as being in the Jackson tradition: "He's so right for the job of Speaker, because like Scoop . . . he's very fair-minded and can persuade people who may be . . . on the opposite side politically to support positions he thinks are just. You don't feel there's this great ego out there, seeking out the TV cameras. He's just there doing his job and loving it for the sheer challenge of governing."[22]

"Scoop" was close to being almost a European Social Democrat. He believed that government had a social responsibility to provide a kind of safety net for people, to give strong support for education, to have a strong voice for the protection of the environment. He believed passionately in things like Medicare which were reflective of his own background when he had been taught a vigorous work ethic about personal responsibility—hard work and no nonsense. Getting up and doing the job every day was fundamentally part of Scoop Jackson's make-up. On the other hand, he was outraged that people who had worked hard all their lives, as he saw them, had to spend themselves into poverty and penury when health care costs had risen to the point where they had no means of taking care of themselves. When he would speak on those questions he was very convincing because he was obviously really motivated, and deeply committed. That was part of Jackson's unusual combination of being very liberal, very progressive, on domestic issues, and conservative on foreign and military policy. . . .

I used to be a little frustrated when business people in Spokane would occasionally complain to Scoop that I was voting "too liberal," which had nothing to do with foreign and military policy. They were talking about domestic policy. They had convinced themselves, just by lack of information, that Jackson must be as "conservative" on these issues of domestic policy as he was on foreign and military policy. I was actually much more moderate in many cases than Scoop was on these questions. I can remember one time I somewhat disingenuously turned it to my advantage in a political situation when I was attacked by an opponent as having a low grade on the score of the National Taxpayers Union and accused, therefore, of being sort of un-American. I've forgotten what the charge was, but it was damning. So I marched out in front of the press and said that "you know who has the worst record in Congress according to this organization? At the absolute bottom? That's Henry Jackson. And any organization that ranks Henry Jackson at the bottom of its list can be judged accordingly."

As a bachelor, one of Foley's after-hours responsibilities was driving Jackson to various receptions and fundraising events. A fringe benefit was that it amounted to a moveable seminar in practical politics in which, among other lessons, Foley learned an underlying rule to survival in Congress: no detail in the home state is ever so unimportant that it can be overlooked. "Scoop always did pay great attention to issues," Foley recalled.[23]

He was tremendously attentive to the individual problems of constituents. Each time he'd come back from Washington state, he'd call in the staff one-by-one and, in our particular area of responsibility, give us an assignment from notes written on the back of a match book, a scrap of paper, or a parking lot receipt, that Mrs. Jones had talked to him about this matter, or Mr. Smith about that, and he wanted to make sure we'd follow up on their concerns.

One anecdote probably illustrates how far Scoop's constituent concerns went. Sterling Munro tells a story about the time he was in the service serving in some remote military outpost. They watched as the sergeant's jeep came roaring up the side of the mountain one day. The sergeant demanded that anybody by the name of Munro get into the jeep immediately and come with him to see the colonel at headquarters. When Sterling was admitted into the presence of the colonel, the colonel informed him that he had received a call that morning from a United States Senator, and that he hadn't enjoyed it very much. He'd never spoken to a United States Senator before on the telephone. Sterling said he knew how he felt because he'd never spoken to a full colonel before. The colonel said that apparently Senator Jackson, the senator from Sterling's home state of Washington, had run into Sterling's mother in Bellingham, Washington, a couple of days previously, and [she] had confided to him that Sterling had not written home recently. Senator Jackson had called the colonel and asked him to talk to young Munro to see that he wrote to his mother.

Whereupon the colonel said, "Munro, will you do me a blankety-blank favor and write your blankety-blank mother?" Later on, when Sterling was standing review and the colonel passed by, he whispered something in his ear. All of his buddies wanted to know what it was the colonel had said. Sterling delighted in keeping them in the dark. What the colonel had really said was, "Munro, how's your mother?"

It revealed two or three things about Senator Jackson's way of dealing with things. One was that no issue was too small, no constituent interest too insignificant. Two, that the best way to handle it was to go right to the point of influence or decision in the government. And three, that the most efficient method of communication was the telephone.

Interviewed at the time of Senator Jackson's death in 1983, Judge Ralph Foley regarded Jackson's influence on his son as "simply tremendous. More than anyone else he [Jackson] impressed him [Tom Foley] with the dedication of someone who is representing other people."[24]

A Reluctant Candidate

In the spring of 1963, Jackson suggested to Foley that he think about running for Congress and that the first step should be joining a Spokane law firm. Although Foley was unresponsive then, he later recalled bringing up the subject himself in March 1964 with an inconclusive outcome. Early that summer, Fifth District Democrats were in their biennial quest for someone to run against Walt Horan, the Republican incumbent who had served in Congress for twenty-two years. Spokane had the state's largest Catholic minority, and three prominent Irish-Catholic lawyers—Robert Dellwo, Thomas Delaney, and Bernard Gallagher—had all run against Horan previously and lost decisively. The conventional wisdom was that Gallagher might try another run.[25] At this point an episode took place, indicative of Foley's entire career, in which he found himself a major player almost in spite of himself. Foley was not, in his words, a "Type A" personality who plotted out his career in advance.

> Some people are long-term planners, or think they are, and can sit around and make great speculations about the future. But, I'm convinced that there are so many accidents in professional and political life, as well as one's personal life, that it's really hard to do that in any meaningful way, other than to think "if something happens, perhaps I would do this or that." There are just enough of the "A types," the people that decide when they're seventeen years old, Bill Clinton, that they want to be President, or, when they're seven years old, that they want to be governor. There are people who testify that they wanted to be an astronaut, they wanted to be a great financial wizard, or they wanted to be an author, whatever, and from an early age they planned and worked for that, and it happened. And, I don't disparage the reality that some people have been able to do what they set out to do. I'm just not one of them.

On July 16th, the day before the filing deadline, Foley went for lunch at the Spokane Club, the city's premier social club, where he ran into some fellow Democrats including Joseph Drumheller, a local kingmaker of sorts and major fundraiser for Democratic candidates.

> In the middle of July, a few days before the end of the July 17 filing period for congressional candidates, I was in Spokane on Jackson's Senate Interior Committee business. I went to see Bernie Gallagher, who had been the candidate for Congress two elections before, and he said "yes, I am going to run." He said he'd sent a letter of intent and a check for the filing fee to the Superintendent of Elections in Olympia.
>
> I had gone to lunch at the Spokane Club which had a membership that was practically 90 percent Republican and 10 percent Democratic, and maybe a third of the Democratic members were sitting at one table.

I sat down and the subject of the congressional race came up, and I informed them I was going to run in 1966, two years hence, and that I hadn't made any plans to run this year, and didn't have any money, and wasn't organized, and all the rest of it. At that point Joe Drumheller, who was a leading businessman in the city, came in and sat down. He was a well-known Democrat and son of a pioneer Washington family. The Drumheller Airport is now Spokane's airport. Anyway, he was close to Magnuson and Jackson, but particularly close to "Maggie." He was his volunteer, unpaid, representative in Spokane. He sat down, and we started to talk, and as soon as I told him what I was planning to do, he dismissed it, and said, "Well, you won't do it." And I said, "Yes, I'm really thinking about doing it, Joe." He said, "No you won't." And I said, "Well, I really think I will." He said, "You're like all young people, Tom, you think that the party's going to come to you with a Tiffany tray, and an engraved card, and say, 'Please, we humbly beg you to run for Congress.' That isn't the way it happens. People get to Congress by wanting to run for Congress, and you've just told me you don't want to run for Congress, therefore, you're not going to go to Congress. And you've got excuses this year, and you'll have excuses next year, and the year after."

Well, it made me angry, and I said, "I'm not talking about money contributions, but I'd just be interested to know if I'd have your support because if I ran this year, I'd have a primary against Bernie Gallagher. I just talked to him and he's going to run." He said, "You'd have my support in the primary, and you'd have my support in the general, because you'd beat Bernie Gallagher. You could be the next congressman from this district, but you've just told me you're not interested, so we ought to talk about something else."

At that point I remember I got up, and excused myself, and walked across the club lobby, and walked over toward the library of the club, and into a phone booth. I called Western Union and dictated a telegram to be sent to Scoop Jackson in Seattle at the office, the office in Washington, D.C., and his residence in Washington, D.C., resigning my job, thanking him for all his support, and informing him that I was going to Olympia to file for Congress the next day. It just came over me, "what have I got to lose?" I also called my bank, the Northwest Bank in Spokane, and found that I was $325 overdrawn. I immediately called my cousin, Hank Higgins, and asked if I could borrow some money.

Foley later recalled the filing process:

It was a mad scheme. I set off for Seattle and met a host of friends who helped me celebrate my decision until about 3 a.m. We were to meet at 7 a.m. in the coffee shop of the Olympic Hotel and drive to Olympia to file. Deadline was 5 p.m. Nobody showed until 10:30. We finally got started about noon. We stopped for lunch. Then a tire blew out and we had to hitchhike to a service station to get it repaired. That was about 3:30. About 4:15 we were approaching the outskirts of Olympia and we ran out of gas. . . But the four of us pushed the car up a hill and we coasted into town. I filed at 4:45 p.m., 15 minutes before the deadline.[26]

After arriving in Olympia, I remember the Superintendent of Elections, Ken Stewart, turning to a Republican filer who had decided to run against Julia Butler Hansen, then our only Democratic member, and saying, "Just some advice." The superintendent said, "Don't think you're going to beat Julia Butler Hansen. Don't mortgage the house. You're a good candidate, and you'll be a fine representative of the Republican Party, but don't get carried away. I've seen people carried away, gotten into debt, and done all kinds of things, when everybody but the candidate knew that he was going to lose." So, we were all sort of smiling at the embarrassment of our fellow filer. And then the superintendent turned to me and said, "And, Tom, the same goes for you. Don't get carried away and think you can beat Walt Horan. He's an institution in this state. He's an institution in eastern Washington. He's got a lot of friends, and you're going to find that a lot of those friends are Democrats who will be nice to you, but they'll vote for Walt."

I finally reached Scoop the next day in Washington and he was very effusive. "I'll help you all I can. It's late, but I think you can do this," and so forth and so on. "Now," he said, "don't take any money from so-and-so," and I said, "Okay." "And," he said, "don't take any money from 'X.' And don't take any money from 'Y.'" And finally he said, "and don't take any money from 'Z.'" And I said, "Okay, Scoop." And I was waiting to hear the list of whom I should take money from, and he said, "I'll talk to you next week."

He was tremendously helpful though in terms not only of support and endorsements, but he also literally arranged for about a third or more of my total campaign effort, in terms of money. I spent, it might have been about $60,000, which was a lot of money then. To put it into perspective, I don't think any Democratic candidate had spent more than $22 or $23,000 in the past. So this was a big boost. And I would get letters from strange places. Long Island, the south of France, other places. The letters would sometimes say things like, "I've been a longtime supporter of Senator Henry M. Jackson, and I try, from time to time, when he runs for Congress, to be helpful to his election campaign. I have enormous admiration for him. He has told me this time he would prefer that, rather than help him, I should contribute to your campaign. And on his advice, with my best wishes, I'm enclosing a check for a thousand dollars." A thousand dollars in 1964 was what would get you admitted to The President's Club. A hundred dollar contribution was a respectable contribution, as it is now. But a thousand dollars was much more like $6 or $7,000 would be today.

So, he was as good as his word. Better. And he would even use his own campaign time, television time, reworking some of his ads in the eastern part of the state by going on camera and saying, "This is Senator Henry M. Jackson. I urge you to vote for Tom Foley for Congress."

I think it would be extremely difficult to begin a career in Congress now with the kind of campaign that I started in 1964. The whole idea of making the decision to run the day before the filing deadline would be absurd. In today's environment even the best financed and best planned campaigns are often political adventures against the odds. Nothing like the haphazard, last-minute, jump-into-the-race, that I did in 1964 is possible today.

CHAPTER TWO

Congress in the 1960s

Unseating a Twenty-two Year Republican Incumbent

FOLEY SURPRISED NEARLY EVERYONE by winning the Fifth District congressional seat in 1964 by a close margin of 12,000 votes, thanks to fundraising help from senators Jackson and Magnuson and a ride on Senator Jackson's coattails that proved to be even more important to Foley than Lyndon Johnson's landslide victory over Senator Barry Goldwater for President. The election was a family affair with Judge Ralph E. Foley gaining more votes than any other candidate on the ballot.[1] That Fifth District congressional campaign is still remembered for its lack of meanness or negativity. In an interview, Foley's mother said it had been wonderful having both a husband and son on the ballot, but "as a mother, my greatest thrill was the fact that Tom conducted the campaign on such a high plane, only on the main issues."[2] As was to become a hallmark of his campaign style, Foley ran what was described as "an unusually genteel campaign, refusing to attack Horan and even occasionally praising him" for what he had done for the district.[3]

One of the things that was interesting about it was that I had really found Walt and Sally Horan to be truly delightful people. Walt was a very warm and generous personality. When I worked in Washington, D.C., they obviously knew I was connected with the Jackson office, yet there was always a sense of warm, more than civil, treatment of me by the Horans. And so, it was true, what Ken Stewart, the Supervisor of Elections, had said. I mean, I found out, quite immediately, that Walt and Sally had an enormous number of friends, including a lot of Democrats. In fact, if you had somebody tell you, "Well, you know, we were in

Washington's Fifth Congressional District

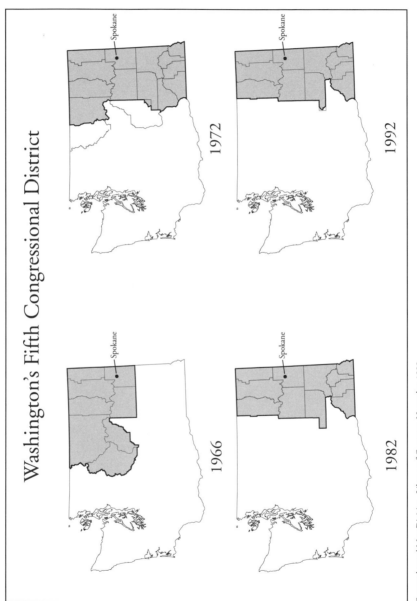

1966

1972

1982

1992

Spokane

Geography and Map Division, Library of Congress, November 1998.

Washington, D.C., five years ago, and the Horans took us to lunch," for-get it. Gone. That was a vote you weren't going to get. Thank you very much, nice to see you. But, you sort of prepared for a number of things, when you'd go around and talk to people like, "Hello, my name is Tom Foley and I'm running for Congress." "Why you doing that? We've got a congressman. Walt Horan's back there." And I'd say, "Yes, sir, I know. I'm running against Walt Horan." "Well, why you doing that?" It was not altogether an easy entry.

Horan was better at shaking hands and clapping backs. "Tom isn't comfort-able with that side of politics," cousin Hank Higgins recalled. Foley scored heavily in talking about issues, illustrating, for example, that he knew a great deal about the district's agricultural problems. A campaign aide at the time described what would be a typical scene over the next three decades: Foley met voters in the rural northern part of the state wearing a dark blue suit. "Do you think you're maybe overdressed?" the aide asked. "These people aren't voting for president of the Rotary Club," Foley responded. "I don't believe anyone wants to be repre-sented by someone who doesn't look and act the part of a member of Congress."[4] Throughout his career, Foley was careful about his clothes, changing them as many as three times a day during a hectic campaign. "Dressing down" generally meant going from a gray pinstripe suit to a blue blazer and gray slacks, each jacket with a neatly folded white handkerchief appearing from the breast pocket. William F. Mullan, a professor at Washington State University in Pullman who served as a county campaign coordinator for Foley during the '80s, underscored Foley's longtime campaign style. "In the past, I've suggested that he loosen up and go hunting, fishing, or pose [for photographs] with a cow, but he's always a three-piece-suit kind of guy out here too." Even at town meetings, Foley found it hard to be an enthusiastic glad-hander. "He doesn't like to ask people to vote for him," said Mullan. "He prefers talking issues."[5]

This was my first experience. I'd campaigned for other people, but it's easier, at least for me, to campaign for someone other than yourself. I fi-nally decided that I would say what I felt. This was not a race to discredit a very popular, and deservedly popular, congressman who had served the district well. It was a race about an argument that, after twenty-two years of good service, the time had finally come for a change. So, I praised Walt Horan's record, which I thought was praise-worthy, and pointed out some differences. It was, largely, a very positive campaign. He, in turn, said he'd known me, and my family, my father and mother, and that I was a fine young man. Of course the message was that when the time came for him to lay down his responsibilities that, if not me, he was sure some other fine young man would be around to carry on. But, not now.

Fundamentally, it was a campaign unusual to the point that UPI sent a reporter up from San Francisco to write about it. That the two candidates of different parties were carrying on this civilized and unusually mutually praising campaign. During the course of the campaign, a lot of people came to me with stories about Walt's drinking, and alleging that they had information that Walt had a serious problem with alcohol. I told the people on the campaign that we were going to stay a mile away from this, and we were not only going to stay away from it, we were really going to stay away from it, so that we weren't going to be hinting darkly about . . . we weren't going to degrade this campaign by personal references to Walt Horan.

Three days before the election, Walt Horan did a very unusual and, I think, a generous but politically unwise thing. He issued a public statement that this had been the cleanest campaign in which he'd ever been involved in twenty-two years of public life. It was a good statement, a nice statement, and I think it was probably true, but it would have been smarter to have said it at 8:01 p.m. on election day after the polls had closed. Because, for a lot of Walt's many friends, while it wasn't an endorsement of me, I think it was almost taken as permissive, that he wouldn't be as angry if people had voted for me that year, as he might have been in other campaigns. At any rate, it was a little too premature I think.

At some point on election day, although I don't think it was public until after the polls had closed, Walt went into the hospital with some slight heart problem . . . within almost a year after the election he made a trip to the Philippines to see his daughter who was married to an American officer on duty there. He apparently made the trip against medical advice, and died in the Philippines. I remember being struck by a story, I don't know if it was true or not, but I was told that in his last illness during which he had been comatose part of the time, Walt told someone he thought he heard the bells of the House calling members to vote.

I didn't think we were going to win, but I thought we were going to come close enough that this would be seen as an important showing and might secure a front-runner position for me in the next election. Perhaps by then Walt would have retired. As the election got closer and closer I became more and more confident that we might actually get more votes than Walt. I remember being prepared, and I think my father tried to prepare me, not to become overly optimistic. I know my mother, like all mothers, was convinced I was going to win. My father was convinced I was going to lose and, as a much more experienced hand on political realities, was very concerned that I was going to get thrown for a loop by overly optimistic expectations. I actually remember thinking I'm going to get more votes than Walt, but I think he's going to take me out with the absentees. We hadn't worked the absentee voters at all and Washington state counts the absentees after the election. . . . I was told there were some 12,000 absentees and I thought we'd probably lose them two-to-one. I was right. We did lose them two-to-one. But, by the time the final election tally was tabulated, before the absentees, I was ahead by some 17,000 votes.

There is no election like the first one, at least in my experience. Scoop had called me from Seattle and told me KING television had awarded me the election by nine o'clock on election night. I was then working against the even greater possibility of disappointment as this might get snatched out of my hands by the absentees. . . . I went to bed late, staying at Spokane's Ridpath Hotel, and I can remember getting up several times during the night and calling the all-night AP office in Seattle, disguising my voice so that I would not be discovered as the same person who had called only two hours before, and being told, "Yes, Foley's won the election over in Spokane." "No mistake?" "No, no mistake." Still I worried there was going to be some 5,000 vote error. . . . I got up the next morning at 6 a.m. and called Seattle, for the third time, and was assured that, yes, I had won.

"I follow an incumbent of many years who has served with dignity and honor," the victorious Foley told *The Spokesman-Review*, "and I wish to extend to him my high regards and best wishes." According to his administrative assistant, Congressman Horan was in Deaconess Hospital in Wenatchee for needed rest on election day, but had not suffered a heart attack as the press had earlier reported. Horan issued a statement saying, in part, "to our new man in Congress, Tom Foley, goes my sincere congratulations and best wishes for a successful session of Congress.[6] In a gracious personal gesture that became another Foley trademark, he held a reception in Horan's honor after the election.

When I went back to Washington, D.C., a couple of things stand out. The Jackson and Magnuson offices offered me all sorts of help. . . . I was sworn in on the 4th of January 1965, and Walt came on the floor, which was quite unusual, and took me into both the Republican and Democratic cloakrooms and introduced me as his successor as if we were members of the same party. People were flabbergasted by it. I learned something interesting about Congress. I was received with greater equanimity in the Republican Cloakroom than by some of the Democrats. People like Democrat John Rooney of Brooklyn, who had come to Congress with Walt, and served with him on the Appropriations Committee, viewed me as an enemy of his friend, and therefore, as his enemy. As I remember, Walt leaned down to this crusty, bald-headed, tough-minded,

Irish pol from Brooklyn, and, I heard him whisper, "John, it's all right." But it was never all right with John who never really accepted me. . . . When I think back on it now, it was an act of loyalty to his friend.

We also had a reception for the Horans, inviting the members of Congress to come say good-bye to Walt, and so forth. I remember Eddie Hebert, who was a powerful member of Congress and chairman of the Armed Services Committee, came in and said, "What is this love feast? I hate my opponent before, during, and especially after the election." But there was generally a broad sense of good will in the House for Walt and Sally Horan. . . . I know they would have preferred to have voluntarily retired which I understood he had been planning to do after the next election. But I think if he had retired, or if his health had overwhelmed him, there would have been an enormous number of people in the race. And because the district, at least based on recent presidential races, was prevailingly Republican, it would probably have been very difficult to win.

I think these things are guided as much by chance, almost accident and timing, as they are by effort and desire.

It was a fitting initiation for Foley, whose temperament and tactics led him throughout his career to shun confrontation and seek consensus. Looking back on his first campaign from the vantage point of some three decades in elective politics, and having subsequently suffered through his own exposure to personal attacks, Foley was clearly dismayed by the pervasiveness of mean-spiritedness in politics that had arisen over the years. "[Today] there is almost a Roman games spirit abroad. You pick up the front page and see who has been devoured by the lions."[7]

An LBJ Freshman

One of seventy-one Democratic freshmen elected to the House in Johnson's 1964 landslide, Foley supported almost all of the administration's landmark Great Society programs. As a recognized protégé of Magnuson and Jackson, those few Great Society issues he opposed tended to stand out, such as his growing opposition to expanding American involvement in the Vietnam War.

My first year I had a pretty high record of support for the Great Society programs based on the fact that most of us who were elected in 1964 had campaigned on the major elements of the Great Society such as Medicare, providing aid to education, support for urban programs. But, as we got into the second year, the number and speed of new ideas coming up from the White House increased, and I started to back away from sort of automatic support, and I think in the second year of my first term

I had barely over a 50 percent record of support for those issues the President had singled out.

In my first year, for example, I felt that a proposal for rent supplements, a program to subsidize rents for certain categories of low-income people, was initiating a new and perhaps ill-examined entitlement program. I was to be, that year and beyond, a strong supporter of Food Stamps and nutrition assistance, but suddenly rushing into a whole new category of assistance on rents seemed to me to be dangerous. So out of a very close vote in the House which passed rent supplements 208 to 204, I was on the 204 side. Shortly after that, by the way, the bill was brought to the Senate and never heard from again.

Right after that vote was cast in the House, Senator Magnuson, the senior senator from the state, and Senator Jackson, and Julia Butler Hansen, the previously lone member of Congress from the Democratic side, took us down to the White House, four of us newly elected members (Brock Adams, Lloyd Meeds, Floyd Hicks, and me) to visit President Johnson. No particular business, just a courtesy call. We weren't even put on the President's schedule to avoid questions about what the business was. We just went down to be formally and properly introduced to the President as the new members of the state delegation.

LBJ was sitting in the Kennedy rocking chair in the Oval Office and in front of him was a large coffee table with a call-director telephone system with innumerable buttons on it, and next to that a red phone which we all thought was the direct line to SAC [Strategic Air Command]. He was, apparently, in a pretty jovial mood, but suddenly turned very serious. He said he wanted, before we went any further, to thank the Washington delegation for its support for the rents supplement bill. And then turning his gaze directly on me, and sort of locking-me-in that intense Johnson look, he said, "I can't imagine why any damn fool would vote against that bill. It was one of the most sensible and needed pieces of legislation that Congress is going to consider this entire session." He said, "it was supported, by the way, by the mortgage bankers, by the Association of General Contractors, by labor, and by every group concerned about the elderly, and senior citizens, and the disabled in this country. And you'd have to be a hard-hearted, insensitive, fool to vote against that bill."

I thought to myself, while all my colleagues were smiling and accepting the compliments because they all voted for the program, that perhaps I ought to disclose that I'd voted against it. Then suddenly I thought again, there's no need, this is a direct communication from Lyndon Johnson to me that he knew about my vote, and he didn't like it.

Foley's congressional assignments to district-sensitive committees aided his future election campaigns: the Committee on Agriculture with subcommittees on Forests, Wheat, and Domestic Marketing and Consumer Relations, and the Committee on Interior and Insular Affairs with subcommittees on Territorial and Insular Affairs, Irrigation and Reclamation, and Mines and Mining.

At the time I came to Congress both parties had their own "Committee on Committees" as there is today. The Democratic committee was made up of the Democratic members of the Ways and Means Committee who were apportioned geographically. Once on the committee they tended to serve forever, but if, for example, someone from the Northwestern states retired, then somebody else from the Northwest would be picked. It wouldn't be somebody from South Carolina or New York. The member from your region, or zone, on the Ways and Means Committee, was the person you had to apply to for membership on a committee. You went to see him and asked for his help in nominating you for the Committee on Agriculture, in my case.

I went to see Congressman Al Ullman of Oregon who was my zone member on the Ways and Means Committee, and asked him to intercede to have me appointed to the Interior and Insular Affairs Committee because I had served on the Senate staff when Senator Jackson was Chairman. I got a call back from Ullman a couple of days later. He said he thought it would be better if he put me on the Agriculture Committee. He noted that there wasn't any Northwest Democratic member on the committee. Washington's Congresswoman Catherine May was on the committee, but she was a Republican and he thought we needed to have our own party representation. So, he thought, if I didn't mind, he'd like to substitute Agriculture for Interior.

I was a little bit presumptuous, thank God I was, and asked him if I could be on both. He hemmed and hawed and said that was going to be pretty heavy in a year when Congress had over sixty new Democratic members, several times the normal sized class. But he said he'd try. He succeeded and I got appointed to the Agriculture Committee, a major committee, and the Interior as a minor committee. You could be on two minors or a major and a minor, but not two majors.

As a combination, they were very good assignments, and my luck got even better. When we were selected by seniority for the Agriculture Committee the eleven new Democrats represented a very large group. I was given the number two assignment out of the eleven, which I attributed to my innate worth and dignity and Senate experience and so forth. I was appointed directly behind a former Georgia state senator who made no bones about wanting to serve a single House term and then retire. In essence I found myself at the head of my class. I then heard that, all my assumptions of merit aside, our names had actually been drawn out of a hat to determine the pecking order. In fact, determining the seniority of freshmen members is still made by drawing their names out of a hat.

Foley's introduction to unified government with Congress and the White House in the hands of Democrats came with all the advantages of the time. There was a broad-based public consensus to increase the power and responsibility of government, large congressional Democratic majorities, and an aggressive, impatient president with a clear agenda. As Texas Congressman Jim Wright, the future Speaker, described President Lyndon Baines Johnson, he was "bigger than life, a compulsive overachiever, always racing both the clock and the calendar to nail 'another coonskin on the wall.'"[8] As Foley had already discovered, even the most inadvertent brush with LBJ left its mark.

During my first year in office I struggled to get back to the state just as often as I could. Sometimes, after long sessions, the only way to do that was to fly to Seattle from Dulles Airport and then arrive early in the morning, and then turn around and fly 300 miles back to Spokane. So I was at Dulles Airport one night, I think I'd only been in office a couple of months, in the spring of 1965, and I was sitting in one of the mobile lounges that go back-and-forth to the plane, and waiting for us to depart for Seattle. While I was waiting there a young United Airlines agent came rushing up to the mobile lounge and announced in a very loud voice, "Is there a Congressman Thomas Foley on board?" And I raised my hand. And he said, "Thomas Foley of Washington?" And I said, "Yes." And he said, "Congressman Thomas S. Foley?" And I said, "Yes." And he said, again in a very loud, commanding, voice, to which everyone in the lounge was forced to listen, "Mr. Congressman, would you come with me immediately. President Johnson is on the telephone and urgently calling." I think everybody was quite impressed, none more than I because, while I'd been introduced to him, I'd never, to that point, actually spoken to the President that I could remember. And all the way down the concourse of the terminal, the United agent was sort of pushing people out of the way to make way for us. And through my mind was racing, "What is he calling me about? Is he going to offer me some kind of appointment? Is he going to ask me to do him some sort of favor? Support some kind of position?" And so on. It must be very unusual, I thought, for him to be calling a freshman member directly.

We got into the United office, where there were a couple of people working, and the agent made them all leave. And then he sort of bowed out the door himself, leaving me alone at a desk with the telephone off the hook. I picked it up, and the voice on the other end said, "Congressman Foley?" And I said, "Yes." "Congressman Thomas S. Foley?" "Yes." "Congressman Thomas S. Foley of Washington?" I said, "Yes, yes, I am." And the voice on the other end said, "Congressman, this is the White House Switchboard, would you please hold now for the President?" I said, "Yes, of course."

And, in a few seconds, a familiar Texas voice came on the line and said, "John?" And I said, "No, Mr. President, Tom Foley." There was a pause of a couple of seconds and then a loud string of very difficult to repeat oaths starting with a two-syllable pronunciation of "SHEEE-IT!" A long pause, and then "that stupid fool," and so on. "I wanted John Fogarty of Rhode Island." John Fogarty being a senior member of the Appropriations Committee.

There was not anything like, "Tom, I'm sorry, I think there's been a wrong number here" or "I hope we didn't bring you away from anything unnecessarily." No polite chitchat. Just a "God damnit" and a slammed receiver. It was, I think, the most seriously depressed moment in my congressional career up to that point if not beyond. I sat there rather shaken by the experience, and then suddenly I thought to myself, well, nobody else knows. Just the President, me, and one telephone operator who was probably hearing about it as I sat there. So, gathering my confidence, I squared my jaw and walked out of the office.

The agent immediately approached me and said, "Did you finish your conversation with the President?" I could truthfully report that I had finished my conversation with President Johnson. He escorted me back to the lounge, insisted on riding out to the airplane with me, and told the flight attendant that I should be immediately upgraded from tourist to first class, at the convenience of the airline, and that I had just finished a very significant and important conversation with the President of the United States.

I used to say, in those days, that's what a wrong number from the President could get you.

The Independence of the Washington Voter

Washington state has traditionally been fiercely independent in its politics, with a strong tradition of ticket-splitting harkening back to the nineteenth-century Grange and Populist movements. There is a strong sense that people matter, but political parties are suspect. It is also a state where voters do not register by party affiliation. Foley had surprised the Fifth District Democratic establishment with his 1964 victory. Most assumed he would be yet one more in the line of high-minded Gonzaga-bred Irish Catholics "who had broken their picks trying to upend Walt Horan."[9]

For the rest of the '60s and well into the '70s—similar to the wheat areas in Montana, Colorado, and Wyoming—eastern Washington, more an extension of its Rocky Mountain neighbors than the western part of the state, became part of the growing GOP strength.[10] Foley's 1966 reelection race against Dorothy Powers, a popular columnist with the Spokane *Spokesman-Review* in an excellent GOP year, was a major test and put in place a style of campaigning which would hold throughout his future campaigns.

The Powers campaign had adopted the National Republican Committee's tactic of making President Johnson the scapegoat of the fall elections. Announcing that he would run for reelection strictly on his two-year congressional record, Foley had to immediately respond to charges that he had amounted to little more than a Democratic "rubber-stamp" for the Johnson administration. His 1965 high support rating, he argued, was the result of having campaigned on issues which had been presented earlier by President Kennedy. In his second year he had voted against President Johnson on sixteen key issues and ended up with a 56 percent support rating.[11]

> In 1966, when the Republican campaign was "rubber-stamp Congress," the theme was reinforced to some degree by President Johnson's attitude toward the Congress. He once referred to the Congress, at least according to Republican legend, as "my Congress." I remember Richard Nixon going around the country and asking, "What's wrong with saying 'my Congress?' I'll tell you what's wrong, ladies and gentlemen, the Congress doesn't belong to any one man, and certainly not to any one party." And then he slipped in a comment that I found very useful later on during Republican presidencies. Former Vice President Nixon said, "and, ladies and gentlemen, the finest and most productive times in our history have been those times when the Congress and the Presidency were in the hands of different parties."
>
> But, in 1966, the "rubber-stamp campaign" was demonstrated by huge, papier mâché copies of rubber stamps being driven around in the back of trucks and the slogan of "the rubber-stamp Congress" being spread everywhere. Tactics were urged upon Republican candidates to collect as many old rubber stamps as they could, and dump them on the doorstep of incumbent Democratic members of Congress. The idea being that the people had elected a Lyndon Johnson protégé, a Lyndon Johnson corporal, rather than an independent member of Congress. I think in some cases it hurt the reelection chances of members.

To bolster his argument of independence, Foley used an incumbent's advantage of government-provided franked mail and sent his voting record to Fifth District residents. The Powers campaign used the Foley record to highlight his support of costly federal programs including foreign aid and Great Society poverty programs. "This is true with so many government functions," his opponent charged, "a good example being the fact that Rep. Foley sends out campaign material at taxpayers' expense."[12] "I believe that anyone who represents the people in Congress," Foley responded, "has a duty to engage in a full and frank discussion of the issues before the widest possible audience."[13]

National issues played a role in the 1966 campaign, but were quickly subordinated to local and regional concerns. Foley did not deal at length with congressional discussions of a possible tax increase. "I would not support any tax increase unless the money was used to balance the budget," he said. "If a tax increase is coupled with reduced federal spending, I would support it. But along with this we do need restraint in federal spending, as well as restraint in state and local spending and I would include restraint in private business on a voluntary basis." While recognizing a "real need to improve schools in large metropolitan areas where a racial problem exists," he voiced reservations of school busing to achieve a racial balance.[14]

Crisscrossing the district, Foley returned to his first campaign tactic, a tactic that would re-emerge in future races, of challenging the reluctant Dorothy Powers to debate the issues "so that the thousands of voters in the 5th District would have the benefit of complete information as to where each candidate stands."[15] Targeting long-standing regional concerns, which he would do throughout his political career, Foley greeted shift workers at Boundary Dam and the Metaline mines and noted that it had taken the combined efforts of the Pacific Northwest congressional delegations to prevent efforts that year to divert Columbia River water to Southwestern states.[16] In the southern part of the district, Foley organized a "Wheat Growers for Foley Committee" under the chairmanship of Lincoln County wheat grower and president of Western Wheat Associates, Gene Moos of Edwall, who would later join his Washington, D.C., congressional staff. Moos emphasized Foley's expertise gained as a member of the Wheat Subcommittee of the House Agriculture Committee and his role in the development of wheat export opportunities.[17]

Although Dorothy Powers ran a well-organized and well-financed race, Foley won with 57 percent of the vote.[18] For much of the decade thereafter, Foley's victory margins increased and his opponents grew steadily weaker. Most of them had neither money, experience, nor a gift for campaigning. In his 1968 reelection race against Republican Richard M. Bond, there were once again two Foleys on the ballot with Judge Foley running for reelection to the Superior Court. Many of the same issues arose in that congressional race, including Foley's being a "rubber-stamp" for President Johnson. Foley's response would remain a constant throughout his career:

> The members of Congress must be independent. The Congress is designed to be a separate entity from the President, not to be the instrument of presidential power, but to be a separate check and balance to the

President, not to oppose him all the time, not to support him all the time, but to have a different viewpoint.

Now, I would go to Congress again as I have in the past, if the people of this district give me their confidence and support, with the idea of exercising my judgment, doing honestly what I think is in their interest, and not merely to support or oppose a president.

I think that is heart and kernel of the difference between Mr. Bond and myself. He wants to go to Congress to be a supporter of Mr. Nixon if he's elected, or an opponent of Mr. Humphrey if he's elected. I go to Congress to help where I think I can, to support the programs that are wise for this district, and to oppose those that I think are not.[19]

Foley's record on agricultural issues remained an incumbent advantage, but he was forced to explain his votes on gun control and crime legislation. He had opposed the Senate version of the Omnibus Crime Bill because, he explained, he was opposed to the provision which permitted emergency wire tapping by police for forty-eight hours without a court order. Noting that "I've been opposed ever since I've been in Congress to the registration and licensing of guns," Foley noted that the House Gun Control Act did not require such registration and he supported the legislation because "I think it has value to limit the mail order sale of weapons. We can limit the sale of guns to minors."[20] It was a civilized race in which each candidate complimented the other for campaigning on important issues, and along with every Republican and Democratic incumbent in the Washington congressional delegation, Foley was reelected.[21]

Democratic Foley Builds A Republican Constituency

In 1970—as the senior northern Democrat, ranking sixth of the nineteen on the House Agriculture Committee—Foley beat George Gamble, the local staff coordinator for the conservative John Birch Society, with 67 percent of the vote. Once again, Foley campaigned on his record and what he regarded as the major issues facing the country. "How can we keep our society together and avoid extremes of far left and far right?" he asked. Reflecting the unrest on U.S. college campuses, crime was again a major theme. "We must effectively cope with the problems of crime and terroristic activities." In opposition to his opponent's assertion that "the American republic is being attacked from within by trained, organized agitators," Foley argued that college and university administrators should take action against illegal actions by students, but that law enforcement was primarily a local responsibility, with the federal role essentially to provide technical and financial assistance.[22] "I look to see the next Congress to be conservative minded if it is to reflect the mood of the voters yesterday," said Foley of his victory, "as there is no question in my mind that the people are deeply troubled about both economic conditions and violence. They will insist on effective legislation in both of those areas."[23]

The consensus was that Foley was building a personal following, considered strong enough to repel most Republican attacks. He was winning with some Republican support and there was the sense that "if he were not the Democratic nominee, the Republicans would have an excellent chance to pick up the seat."[24] His popularity with his constituents reached its peak in the 1972 election when he captured 81 percent of the vote against Clarice Privette, a tombstone saleswoman who was said to have sold her washing machine to pay the filing fee. With President Nixon's lopsided victory over Senator George S. McGovern and a 20 percent turnover in the U.S. House of Representatives, Foley praised the independence of eastern Washington voters. "Party loyalty is a thing of the past," he argued.[25]

In its first Foley electoral endorsement, *The Spokesman-Review* specifically differentiated his national versus local role. The paper judged the recent Ralph Nader report on individual congressmen as a fair enough summation that "Foley's voting record is most consistently liberal in the area of civil rights and is conservative on the issue of the Vietnam war and defense spending. He represents his district's interests on farm issues and has been a supporter of the federal farm program." Acknowledging that he was more liberal than the district he represented, the paper observed that "it must also be noted that he has proved highly effective in representing this district in the nonpolitical chores that have been given him to manage." While recognizing his excellent relations with the state's two Democratic senators, his rising seniority on the Agriculture (third among Democrats) and Interior committees (sixth) and his success in securing federal funding for Spokane's "Expo '74" World's Fair, the editors struck a balance on Foley. "This newspaper is not, in the current phrase, 1000 percent for Rep. Foley in the votes he has cast on national issues. Something like 50 per cent might be a better estimate, but in the present circumstances, the informed voter, it seems to us, would clearly have to support Rep. Foley if he wants the effective teamwork that has done much for the Fifth district to be continued."[26]

Although his 1974 margin of reelection victory against Gary G. Gage, a member of Spokane's chapter of the John Birch Society, declined to 64 percent, he would, by the mid-'70s, be considered statewide material capable of a run for the Senate.

Political Culture in the Congress

The fifty years from approximately 1920 through 1970 have been characterized as an era of committee government in the House of Representatives. As two authors deeply involved in the 1973-74 "Select Committee on Committees" or Bolling Committee effort to reform the congressional committee structure observed, "behind the seeming majesty of presidential leadership or the solemnity of judicial decision making," lay "the hoary precedents and creaky structures" of the congressional effort "to knit together the disparate purposes of 535 legislators. . . . Lacking the strong centripetal force of powerful leaders or disciplined parties, the House has become ever more fractionalized and unmanageable." Despite the defects, most members believed the committee system was the most important component of the legislative process. Committees performed the essential tasks of developing public policies, winnowing important proposals from the unimportant, modifying or presenting alternatives to executive branch recommendations, and reviewing governmental agency implementation of public laws.[27]

> Many committees had no written rules, they were run by the chairman, at his pleasure, in the manner he saw fit. There was no practical appeal from the chairman's rulings. There were no parliamentary rules of any particular application in the committees. The agenda was determined by the chairman. The process of committee hearings and recognition was determined by the chairman. Stronger by far than the Speaker in the overall House was the chairman and his committee, and so the agenda items that many members of Congress wished to advance through various committees of jurisdiction were blocked, often almost permanently, by the strong will of powerful chairmen.

> For example, Mr. [Wayne] Aspinall, the chairman of the Committee on Interior and Insular Affairs, had a distaste for what he thought were the wild imaginings of environmentalists. He considered himself, fundamentally, a conservationist. As far as organized efforts to pass wilderness bills or undertake the typical agenda of the environmental movement today, he had no interest in advancing such an agenda. He created, as it was possible to do through his own will and making, a new subcommittee entitled the Subcommittee on the Environment to which he assigned all bills which he did not intend any further action should be taken. It was a place of detention, a deep, dark, dungeon for the bills which he most disliked. His assignment of a bill indicated whether it had any chance of passage, but the unwritten sign above the Subcommittee on the Environment was "abandon all hope ye who are referred here."

The committees were charged with the formulation of legislation, majority-party leaders with the coordination and construction of floor majorities.[28] Even in that context, however, the Speaker in the mid-1960s was described as "something like a feudal king—he is first in the land; he receives elaborate homage and respect."[29] The "to get along, go along" spirit of former Speaker Sam Rayburn continued undiluted with Speaker John McCormack, and Foley's freshman orientation made clear the limits of new members' independent judgment.

Freshmen were to turn to the well-established hierarchy—their committee chairmen and the leadership—for direction on when to speak and how to vote.

In my day we didn't have much to do with the selection of the new officers of the House. That was taken care of by seniority and tradition. As new members, our "orientation" to Congress was limited to just two speeches, as I can remember them. One was by John McCormack, the then Speaker, who remarked that, "Sam Rayburn always said a Member of Congress can be elected by accident, but seldom reelected by accident." The message was subtle, but clear: if you come back in two years time after you've been, hopefully, reelected, we'll begin to take you seriously. But don't expect now that we're going to assume that you've been elected because of your abilities or because of your political skills.

The second speech was given by a very senior member of the Appropriations Committee, Michael Kirwan. He said he had come to warn us about the single greatest danger that could occur to a new Member of Congress beginning his or her political career. And he wanted to particularly warn us about this danger.

We thought it was a kind of ethical problem, and we leaned forward to hear what it was. He said, "That great danger, above all else, is . . . thinking for yourselves." He said, "For heaven's sake, don't do that. Maybe, if it's a matter of parochial concern in your own congressional district that doesn't have much to do about anything else, well, then, it's okay, maybe, to think for yourselves. Otherwise," he said, "follow the subcommittee chairman. Follow the committee chairman. Follow the Democratic Chairman of the Caucus. Follow the Democratic Whip. Follow the Majority Leader. And," he said, "especially, above all else, follow and support the Speaker."

I remember being flabbergasted at the speech. I had been elected to do something about the problems of the country in the '60s and '70s, and here I was having a senior member of my party suggesting I shouldn't think for myself, that I should just subcontract my judgment to the leaders of the party. To make matters worse, Kirwan said that he thought more people had gotten into trouble, as he put it, by thinking for themselves, than by stealing money. That was the final outrage. I remember being angry for the rest of that morning thinking that, if this was the attitude of our party leaders, how in the world can we be expected to have any confidence in them.

After about twenty-five years in the Congress, it became my honor to have been a subcommittee chairman, a committee chairman, the Chairman of the Democratic Caucus, the Democratic Whip, the Majority Leader, and finally, the Speaker.

I used to say to various groups that, as I was standing there on June 6th 1989 taking the oath of office as Speaker of the House, the wise words of Mr. Kirwan came echoing across a generation. How right he was. Members of Congress should support and follow the Speaker.

But today members in both parties have a tendency to think for themselves. And thank God for it.

Reform Votes and Tough Votes

From the 1920s into the 1970s, the committee chair possessed enormous powers and resources. The chairman controlled the committee's agenda, organization, budget, and staff. The chair decided which bills the committee would consider and in what order. The chair determined the committee's subcommittee structure and appointed its subcommittee chairs. Because committee chairmanships were attained purely on the basis of seniority, they were independent positions of influence. Neither the party leaders nor the members had any practical means of removing a chairman. Consequently, in the exercise of their powers, chairs were not constrained by a need to be responsive to any internal party constituency in order to retain their positions.[30]

On the first day in the Agriculture Committee I remember we were all pumped up. The chairman of the Agriculture Committee was Harold Cooley of North Carolina, a large husky man who wore egregiously expensive suits and custom-made shirts. The suits were almost too well tailored; they fit him like a glove. His custom shirts were fitted with very large and very expensive cuff links. He made an expensive and impressive appearance as chairman.

He strode out, took his chair at the head of the dais, rapped the gavel several times, and announced that he wanted to say a few words to the new members. "I hate and detest, hate and detest, to hear senior members of this committee, of either party, interrupted by junior members of this committee, of either party," he said. "You new members in particular will find that you will require some time, some of you months, others of you regrettably probably years, before you develop sufficient knowledge and experience to contribute constructively to our work. In the meantime, silence and attention," rapping the gavel for emphasis, "silence and attention is the rule for new members of this committee."

Sitting next to me was Kika de la Garza of Texas, and next to him was a new member from New York named Joe Resnik. Joe Resnik had made a very large fortune with his brother in organizing a company called Channelmaster Television which was, I think, the largest manufacturer of radio and television antennas in the country, if not the world. He was a self-made man, very confident and very successful. He leaned over to me and said, "No southern stuffed-shirt sonofabitch is going to shut me up." To which I responded, "Joe, please shut up or talk to the person on your right."

If my reaction sounds a little intimidated, it probably was because in those days the committee chairman, while he's important today, was in many cases virtually omnipotent in the House. The once enormous power of the Speaker, when it was relaxed, and reduced, and diminished at the time of Joe Cannon [1903-1911] was spread to the committees, and the committee chairmen took their new powers with both hands.

One committee chairman I served with, I believe it was Cooley of Agriculture, once described a junior member as being dead. He said, "You can come and sit in your chair. You can attend the meetings, but I'm not going to recognize you to speak. And you won't be able to amend any bills in the committee. On the floor you won't be given any time to speak in general debate, and I'll oppose any amendment you offer. And you won't be allowed to travel anywhere. And nothing you want to do for your district will come out of this committee. Soon as I find out it's you who wants it, it will be stopped. Let me give you some advice. Get off the committee. You're a zombie on this committee. You're a walking, living, dead man."

Well, later on, he reluctantly brought the member back to life after suitable apologies were made.

Just as it had once been considered the right of the crown to cut off the heads of those who were denounced as treasonous, it was the right of a committee chairman to make the life of any member of the committee, particularly any junior member, either productive and useful and profitable, or the opposite.

During the '60s, aided by significant Democratic congressional losses in the elections of 1966 and 1968, Foley rose to become Chairman of the Subcommittee on Domestic Marketing and at the end of the decade he ranked eighth in seniority among Democrats on the Agriculture Committee. He was a principal author of the 1967 Meat Inspection Act (the Smith-Foley amendment) which provided federal funds for states to use in imposing strict inspection standards on the interstate meat packing industry. As an urban committee member with close ties to liberal Democrats and to organized labor, Foley often had a special role to play in the Agriculture Committee's work. He had to maintain fragile alliances between the committee's southern majority and the northern liberals who tended to be skeptical of costly federal help for farmers.

In the first place I think I was seen by northern liberals, both inside and outside the Congress, as being sympathetic and supportive. I had been elected with strong labor help. I had high scores from organized labor, from the ADA [Americans for Democratic Action] and other progressive groups, and I was clearly identified on both sides as a progressive or, in those days, a liberal member of Congress. My appointment to the Agriculture Committee was not unique, but it was unusual. Most of the Democrats who served on the Agriculture Committee came from southern, border state, or sometimes from midwestern states when there had been an unusual election of a Democrat from the Midwest, but overwhelmingly the committee was southern and border states on the Democratic side, and midwestern or New England on the Republican side.

By the very nature of my political geography and demography, I stood out. I think I was in a better position than most people to approach members and plead the needs of Democrats from rural areas to have support, or at least not the opposition, of the progressive elements of the Congress. My strong support for nutrition programs, increasing the minimum wage, including agricultural workers in the minimum wage, being interested in rural development programs that would be helpful to small rural communities, all gave me an opportunity to talk to others in the Congress and outside the Congress about the need for support for wheat, feed grains, cotton, peanuts, dairy, and other traditional price-support programs.

On Interior, Foley was almost immediately involved in what became a career-long fight against diversion of water from the Columbia River to California and Arizona.

During this early period Foley cast one of the most difficult votes of his career with his decision to oppose an anti-crime bill enacted by the House in 1968 in response to the assassinations of the Reverend Martin Luther King, Jr. and Senator Robert F. Kennedy and to the widespread rioting in the primarily black inner cities. One of only a handful of members to vote against the bill, Foley was particularly disturbed by its provision granting broad new wiretapping authority to all levels of government.

It was difficult to vote against the Safe Streets and Crime Control Act. It was emotional and one of the truly popular issues of the day. I think the vote in the House was something like 360 in favor and 41 opposed. I voted among the 41 because I felt the wiretapping provisions were too loose and subject to abuse. My staff thought it might be a so-called "killer" vote for me because it was in an election year and I was facing a pretty stiff challenge. I thought it was inevitable that, from time to time, you had to cast some risky votes. If your votes were always comfortable, always in line with the dominant attitudes of the day, then you ought to start worrying about whether you were accommodating too much, or simply adjusting your own mental attitudes to conform with popular opinion.

I only learned later that, unbeknownst to me, there was, in the bowels of the bill, a mail-order restriction on hand-gun sales which became famous among the anti-gun control community, including in eastern Washington. I couldn't understand why my opponent wasn't raising the issue of my voting against the Safe Streets and Crime Control Act, and he couldn't figure out why I wasn't boasting about it.

I think almost every Congress has issues where you know that this vote is not going to be easy to persuade your constituents to agree with, or even to accept. On those tough issues, I often thought the aim should be to get people to acquiesce in your judgment even though they might not agree with you.

For a long time in my district, for example, there was no significant minority presence of either African Americans or Hispanics. The minority presence is higher now primarily because of the increased Hispanic population. For a long time attitudes on issues of civil rights, or anything touching on race, were very traditional. You'd travel into the counties north of Spokane and you'd hardly ever see an African American. A friend once said to me, "In this part of the country, every black knows every other," there are so few in the population. So, while the Voting Rights Act was never a problem in Washington state, when it came to issues such as open housing, it was a different matter. Although I wasn't in Congress for the fundamental legislation in 1964 on public accommodations, it was a vote I would have obviously cast in favor. It would, however, have been hard to get everyone to accept.

Foley's Standing After a Decade in Office

In the late '60s some people began to talk about Foley possibly running for a Washington state seat in the U.S. Senate if one opened up.

Well, in the first place, we had two United States Senators who were not only Democrats but were considered to be enormous assets for the state by many in both parties. Warren Magnuson and Henry Jackson were consistently voted to be the two most powerful, the two most effective senators. Magnuson had been Chairman of the Commerce Committee, ranking member of the Appropriations Committee, later became President Pro Tempore of the Senate, and Chairman of the Appropriations Committee. Scoop had been Chairman of what is now the Energy Committee, then called Interior, was ranking member of the Armed Services Committee, and was a member of the Government Operations Committee. So, between the two of them, they not only had complimentary coverage of a variety of legislative concerns to the state, but they were natural leaders. But, in this context, there was speculation that, at some time in the future, when either might retire or do some other thing in the government, that there would be a fight, most likely, it was argued, between [Representative] Brock Adams and me over who would be the successor.

I think the only time it got to be a close possibility was in 1969 after Richard Nixon had been elected President in a close 1968 election over Hubert Humphrey. There was open speculation, factually correct, that Nixon was going to offer the Secretary of Defense position to Senator Jackson. When Scoop was asked about it by the press he said he hadn't heard anything, but it would be very difficult for him to ever consider leaving the Senate because Republican Governor Dan Evans would, of course, be expected to appoint a Republican replacement in the Senate. When this matter came to Governor Evans' attention, as I recall, he said he had informed President Nixon that, if it would help the President get the cabinet he wanted, he would be willing to appoint, not just anybody that Jackson wanted, but someone who would be legitimately considered a Democrat.

For other reasons, Jackson declined to be considered, and the matter came to an end, but not before there was press speculation that if Jackson had accepted the Defense position, it was probable that Evans would have appointed me. The logic was that my congressional district was the most conservative held by a Democrat in the state, and if I were appointed to fill out an unexpired Jackson term, there would be a special election to fill the Fifth District and the chances were pretty good that a Republican would win. So, after the hypothetical appointment there would still be two Democratic Senators, but there would be four, not five, House Democrats, and three House Republicans. The net effect would have been to pick up a House seat. Whether that's true or not, I don't know, but that was the speculation at the time.

But, when I became a committee chairman in 1974, the whole idea of going to the Senate became much less attractive. I was, at the time, the youngest major committee chairman in decades, perhaps in this century. It was not something I was prepared to trade for being a junior senator at the bottom of the seniority list.

Marriage

If conventional wisdom argued that an ambitious young lawyer-politician should have married a Spokane girl, Foley, once again, defied it. In 1968, at the age of thirty-nine, he married Heather Strachan. Heather was born September 25, 1940 in Detroit, Michigan, where her father, Alan, worked for the United

Auto Workers. British by birth, her father left school at age fourteen, came to the U.S. seeking work, and apprenticed in an aircraft factory. In Detroit he met Heather's mother, Evelyn Berglund, a secretary. Evelyn's Finnish father came to the U.S. when he was seven and worked as a lumberjack.

Alan Strachan joined the United States Agency for International Development (USAID) in 1947 and moved the family to Greece where he worked in labor relations for some six years until Heather was thirteen. She attended grade school at what became the Anglo-American School. By the time the family returned to Alexandria, Virginia, for seven years (1953-59), Heather had a sister, Jill Penelope, nine years her junior. Over the next few years, Heather's father worked short periods for USAID in Korea and Latin America. Heather graduated from St. Agnes Episcopal School in 1957 and went on to university at Pembroke, the all-women sister school to all-male Brown, where she majored in international relations. Heather spent her junior year abroad in Pakistan where her father was head of USAID for West Pakistan. Living at home with her parents and sister, Heather studied math and economics at Presbyterian-supported Forman Christian College and, in the evenings, international law and European history at the University of the Punjab where almost all the students were Muslim and she was the only woman in any of her classes.

Heather graduated from Pembroke, now part of Brown University, in 1961 and returned to Pakistan for a year-and-a-half where she taught math at the American School. She remained behind for several months when her family returned to the U.S. in 1962 to complete the school year and travel in East Pakistan, Kashmir, and India. Her father had been reassigned to Cairo, Egypt. She lived for about half-a-year with her family in Egypt where she taught tenth and eleventh grade English and journalism at the international Cairo-American College. Once she acquired an Egyptian boyfriend, she remembers, her parents encouraged her to return to the U.S. Her interest in politics all but insured she would head for Washington, D.C. where she found an apartment on Rhode Island Avenue and got a job on Senator Jackson's staff.

Heather Strachan met Tom Foley her first day on the job when they were both working for Scoop Jackson. She was twenty-three and he thirty-four. They married five years later, December 21, 1968, while Heather was in her final year at George Washington University Law School and Foley had just been reelected to his third term in Congress. The wedding was in Ceylon (now Sri Lanka) where Heather's father was Director of the International Colombo Plan which coordinated assistance from twenty-one countries to Ceylon. It was not a traditional eastern Washington wedding, instead having "dancers dressed in scarlet cloth swathed into voluminous pantaloons and their chests adorned with multicolored beaded breastplates . . . as drummers beat a ritual tattoo." Witnesses, at suburban St. Mary's Roman Catholic Church, included the Speaker of the Ceylonese House of Representatives, Shirley Corea, and U.S. Ambassador Andrew V. Corry.[31]

It was assumed when they married that Heather would also work. "I am not going to waste three years of law school—I intend to use it," Heather was quoted in the *Spokane Daily Chronicle*. "After graduation I hope for some trial experience in court."[32] She finished her last semester of law school studying in her husband's congressional office. She gradually became involved in congressional staff work and in 1970 began working full-time for her husband. "Slowly, almost insidiously, day by day, found her working in her husband's office until she earned the title of administrative assistant—without pay," wrote Spokane reporter Rick Bonino in a Heather profile.[33]

For the rest of Foley's career, Heather worked as an unpaid administrative assistant, later chief-of-staff. Foley had been co-sponsor of an anti-nepotism statute that forbade government officials putting their relatives on the federal payroll. But he liked having her in the office on an unpaid basis and discouraged her periodic efforts to look for non-congressional work. Heather was, from the beginning, her own woman. His taste in dress was almost invariably formal in contrast to her preference for the informal. She also had her own independent political views and, over the years, came to be regarded as probably the single most powerful House staffer, a target of hard-edged partisan political comment and media scrutiny during the vitriolic '90s.

In a February 1990 *Christian Science Monitor* interview, Foley said he didn't think politics had been tough on their marriage "because Heather has been very much involved in my work, for over 20 years. . . . I can't really imagine how I could have been successful without her."

Over the course of her husband's career, Heather filled a distinct gap in Foley's managerial talents. No one can ever remember Foley sitting at a desk. He had said that he wasn't elected "to sign permits." As Speaker, he invariably signed enrolled bills on his lap or on a coffee table. From his time as subcommittee chairman through the Speakership, Heather ran the offices, hired the staff, set their salaries, resolved internal personnel disputes, and made sure the paper flowed. In the absence of children of their own ("sometimes these things work out that way, we just weren't lucky enough"), the Foley staff became almost a surrogate.[34] "I consider myself to have two bosses," said Werner Brandt, veteran Foley staffer and later executive assistant and House Sergeant-at-Arms when Foley became Speaker.[35]

"I had to work my way up," Heather once observed about her long staff career. Heather acquired the title of administrative assistant, still unpaid, in the mid-'70s. "He doesn't like administration. We have to figure out what he wants. He lets you know by indirection or by complaining. Life is never dull. The job keeps changing."[36]

As Foley rose in seniority Heather's range and influence increased proportionately. In addition to presiding over the House and related legislative duties, the Speaker has extensive administrative responsibilities: from "landlord on the

House side of the Capitol" responsible for assigning office space to approving contracts; from the appointment of experts to various commissions to overseeing member travel; from working with the Capitol Architect on the exterior and interior appearance of the Capitol to refurbishing the Liberty Statue on the Capitol dome. Among the Speaker's administrative tasks, Heather was seen as the "power behind the throne." During her husband's reelection campaigns, Heather would move out to Spokane for a number of weeks to work. Until their age made it difficult, Heather took her parents out as campaign volunteers.

As Foley absorbed a commitment to public service from his father, Heather's resolute commitment to simply being a "behind the scenes" staff member was rooted in her own family's notion of public service. Regardless of how senior her father became in the Agency for International Development, there was always an ambassador who was the public representative of the U.S. government. Everyone else was expected to be a less prominent member of "the country team," and generally the less visible the better. Even as her influence increased, she steadfastly refused interview requests to protect her privacy and individuality from a Washington, D.C., media inclined to pigeon-hole public figures.

Her intent was occasionally thwarted as "personality profiles" were written without her participation or any first-person comment. They gave rise to exaggerated early descriptions of her no-frills attire as an "old flower-child" or "Madonna." As she would explain, she'd worn sandals since a child in Pakistan and felt nothing in common with the "flower children" of the 1960s. The higher visibility of operating out of the Speaker's office suddenly brought the entire staff into more critical focus. Heather's preference for cotton dresses, sandals, and ponytails and braids gave rise to a dose of ridicule and invited a media search for anecdote. Once Dan Rostenkowski, Democratic Chairman of the Ways and Means Committee, had quipped when Heather interrupted a meeting to deliver a message to her husband, "Who was that? Pocahontas?" The story gained little circulation until Foley became Speaker.[37]

As the spouse of the Speaker, she also became the target for indirect shots at her husband. In 1992, Heather's name surfaced in connection with what became a Department of Justice criminal probe into alleged theft and embezzlement in the House post office. By innuendo, rather than fact, Heather was portrayed as playing a role in the investigation after she appeared as a witness before a grand jury. Never a target or subject of the investigation itself, Heather was caught up in the whirlwind of press attention which ultimately led to indictments against and subsequent convictions of the House Postmaster, a number of his staff, and several current and former members of Congress including Rostenkowski of Illinois.

Negative press in the capital has historically been unattributed by name and usually begins with such phrases as "a favorite story making the rounds on the Hill." It tended to underscore that "the spouse working for a [House] member has to strive not to become a surrogate member," as Gretchen White, chief of staff to Washington Republican Representative Sid Morrison, observed. "When you're on staff, you always have to remind people they're talking to you, and not to the member. That must be doubly difficult in the case of a spouse."[38] Heather occasionally won points with the press when she eliminated separate press and staff seating in the dining room or provided pizza during late night budget summit meetings, but gracious gestures seldom make news.[39]

President Jimmy Carter greets Ralph and Tom Foley. *Washington State University Libraries.*

CHAPTER THREE

🏛

The 1970s:

Prelude to House Leadership

The new theory of the Democratic Study Group was that reform, like salami, is best served cold and thinly sliced. Too much heat and too large a portion of reform inevitably produced a negative reaction within the Congress.

—Thomas S. Foley, 1996

Eastern Washington Strength

I N THE EARLY 1970s conventional wisdom held that Foley had built a personal following in his district strong enough to attract needed Republican votes and repel opposition.

Obviously incumbents had an advantage, as they do today, of press releases on your activities in Congress and official appearances in the district for discussions of public policy. Even opponents, sometimes especially opponents, would also want to attend a luncheon or dinner meeting or county fair wherever an incumbent was going to appear.

Secondly, you had the ability to provide constituent services. Frankly I don't remember what the occasion was, but I think it was a request to assist in a military service case involving the son of a motel owner in the central Washington town of Wilbur. I ultimately became the object of his perennial support. I think he was a Republican. An old political rule is don't help the parents, help the children and you win both. As a result, he used to flash up on his huge billboard before elections, "This is Tom Foley Country," and after the elections, "And it still is!"

The caveats to Foley's apparent strength were less stated but no less clear. If he were not the Democratic nominee, the Republicans would have had an excellent chance of picking up the seat, and, in the early '70s, he had yet to face a well-financed, moderate Republican with good credentials and political savvy. In 1972, following a court-appointed draft, the Republican-controlled Washington state legislature reconfigured the Fifth District. Foley lost the westernmost counties, including part of the remote Okanogan County bordering Canada (he eventually lost all of it in the '80s), and acquired the more reliably Republican Walla Walla area. In addition to votes, Okanogan had been the source of some of his best self-effacing humor.

In 1966 or 1967, I was invited to be the Grand Marshall of the Omak Stampede. The Omak Stampede is one of the premier rodeos in the West along with Calgary, Pendleton, Cheyenne, and other major events of this kind which mark the celebration of the skills of the Old West that still continue today. I was very honored by the invitation and I was promptly told that there would be a car, a convertible, for me to ride in. I protested that I should ride a horse at the Stampede, and my host-to-be said, "Well, we'll see." When I arrived in Omak, with my latest western outfit—slim jeans, a work shirt, a five-gallon hat, and newly bought boots—I was greeted with a white Oldsmobile convertible. I reminded my hosts that I thought I was going to ride a horse. They said, "That comes later, at the Stampede. First, we do the parade and lunch."

So there was a parade, and I rode on the back of the convertible, with the band playing, and waved my five-gallon, and then we had lunch. Over at the Stampede grounds, I found a beautiful, sorrel, quarter-horse with a silver-studded saddle and bridle, which was to be my horse for the day. I was introduced to a beautiful, young, eighteen-year-old Omak Stampede Queen, dressed in western clothes, riding a Palomino gelding, and a similarly very-attractive young woman in beaded buckskins from the Colville Indian Reservation, riding bareback on a piebald pony. I got on the back of my horse, rode around looking, in my mind, just like Tom Mix, Roy Rogers, or Gene Autry. We got up to the gate, and I thought we were going to walk around the rodeo arena a couple of times.

Instead, a gun went off, and the two women took off, in full gallop, riding around the rodeo ring, doing all kinds of tricks. Standing on the back of the horse, waving under the horse's girth, riding backwards, while I loped along behind them, looking pretty ungainly. But, I got through it, and I thought to myself, "God, I'm glad that's over."

Then they brought up fifty riders representing the Omak-Okanogan Sheriff's Posse, all carrying American flags, and I thought "this has got to be slow!" I was told that we were going to go around the ring a couple of more times with this very large cavalry. Instead, they all went off again at full gallop. I got caught up in the group. Suddenly, I found my horse going counter-clockwise to a general clockwise direction of the posse, resulting from my horse having shied from a flag in its face. And suddenly, I'm out there all alone. The posse had disappeared through the chute. I'm struggling to get control of one rein that's been lost and a stirrup that's somehow disappeared under the horse's belly. Suddenly, along with all the other guests, I heard the western announcer's voice booming over the loudspeakers: "Well folks, I guess we can all see that our good congressman, Tom Foley, hasn't been wasting his time and money back in Washington, D.C., takin' ridin' lessons." There was a general guffawing, and hooting, and applauding, and so on.

I wanted to leave town by the first available transportation. Dick Larsen, who was then my Administrative Assistant told me, after I had gotten back in the stands, "that was wonderful." "What do you mean wonderful? I made a fool of myself." "Exactly," he said. "That's exactly what you did, and it's just terrific. People up here learn to ride at the age of three, like they learn to ski in Norway, when they're toddlers, and if you'd come here and ridden around the ring like a western rodeo star, and reared the horse, and waved your hat, they would have hated you as a show-off that was, at most, pretty good at what they do very well." He said, "You proved that you were from Spokane, that you couldn't ride worth a damn, but you got out there and made them feel good about the fact that they could. You'll win this county, I predict it." And I did.

Foley's Growing Congressional Strength During the Nixon Years

By 1972 Foley had risen to be the sixth-ranking Democrat on Interior and his rise on Agriculture was even more rapid. With three senior southern Democratic retirements and two defeats, forty-three-year-old Foley now ranked third in seniority behind seventy-five-year-old W.R. Poage of Texas and sixty-seven-year-old Frank Stubblefield of Kentucky, and was Chairman of the Subcommittee on Livestock and Grains. In 1973 he managed the controversial food stamp section of the omnibus farm bill. The bill needed the liberal food stamp provisions to gain support from the AFL-CIO, but Republicans sought to add an amendment barring food stamps for strikers. Along with Agriculture Chairman Poage, Foley managed to get the bill through a diverse coalition of southerners, rural Midwest Democrats, and a slim majority of labor-oriented members.

By this time we were writing into the title "The Omnibus Food and Agricultural Act of 1973" or some such language which aimed to link assistance and support to farmers in the traditional, strict sense, along with assistance to consumers, those who use agricultural products. The new consumer programs were aimed especially at those who were the beneficiaries of special federal nutrition programs. The consumer interest, of course, was reflected in the interests and concerns of organized labor, the Consumer Federation of America and other consumer groups, and the more progressive wing of the Democratic Party generally. Northern liberal Democrats traditionally had a certain skepticism, to put it mildly, about the relatively large costs of the federal farm programs that were often associated with conservative southern and border state Democrats and Midwest Republicans.

I made it my personal mission to plead with the urban constituencies and liberal wing of the party about how important it was to have their support for these programs. I argued that we had advanced beyond anything in the past in the way of true assistance to people who were suffering from malnutrition and other vulnerable constituencies including the elderly, handicapped, and people who came from low-income parts of the country. Without liberal support for this bill, the disadvantaged would be denied. Liberal Democrats had become used to focusing on what they thought was the unnecessary support for "rich" or large-scale farmers. I was pleading with them to see the other side of the picture.

Any help we got from these members was useful because in the past their antipathy had been focused on the chairman of the committee, Bob Poage, whom I liked and respected. Mr. Poage had a bark that was much worse than his bite, and an image that was much more conservative and unfriendly than the reality of his performance as committee chairman. But getting over the attitudes of prejudgment and hostile views of a lot of the liberal members to the committee and its leadership was a big problem.

There was also an element of retribution among liberal Democrats. Urban members rankled at the fact that southern and border state Democratic members would not support minimum wage increases, labor legislation, traditional Democratic urban issues. They were always aligning themselves with Republicans, claiming that their districts would not support that kind of voting record. So they were always looking, in a legislative way, for a vulnerable spot to repay this lack of support in the party from their colleagues in a way that might hurt them.

Managing the bill was an early example of Foley's consensus-building talents. Characteristically, he would give much of the credit elsewhere, in this case to the Nixon administration for having advanced the anti-hunger fight in the U.S. "You get in trouble if you say a good word about Richard Nixon in Democratic circles, but that is the truth."[1]

Among his key votes in the 93rd Congress (1973-74) were issues he would support throughout his career: busing to aid desegregation, funding for public television, the highway trust fund dedicated to the national infrastructure, consumer protection legislation, and disclosure of corporate campaign contributions as well as individual candidate political campaign disclosures. Among his key opposition votes were strip mining, limits on farm subsidies, bombing in Cambodia, and a constitutional amendment supporting school prayer.

A Rung on the Leadership Ladder and the Reforms of the '70s

As Foley had risen in the Democratic ranks, he developed a reputation as a sharp parliamentarian. In 1974 he rose out of the pack when he replaced Iowa Representative John Culver as chair of the Democratic Study Group (DSG). The DSG was the strategy and research arm of liberal and moderate Democrats and was in the vanguard of the effort to limit the authority of the domineering committee chairmen.

This was a pivotal position for Foley at a particularly critical juncture in the House of Representatives. A majority of House members felt the benefits of the committee system outweighed the costs by enabling them to vote for district constituent interests and giving them the opportunity to ascend the seniority ladder to committee power. For more junior liberal Democrats, the calculus was less attractive because the powerful committee chairmen were largely conservative southerners and they, not the party leaders, set the policy agenda, determined legislative substance, and managed to thwart most liberal policy goals. The ideological split between northern and southern Democrats persisted even as the Democratic majority margin in the House grew from an average 52.4 percent of the seats from 1951 through 1958 to 60.8 percent from 1959 through 1970. The divisions among Democrats intensified as the legislative agenda expanded into Kennedy-Johnson social-welfare and civil liberty issues of the 1960s and found southern Democrats considerably closer to Republicans than to their northern party colleagues.[2]

Democratic liberals tended to blame conservative control of the major committees for their own policy impotence, and, late in 1959, in the first session of the 86th Congress, they had formed the Democratic Study Group. While its initial purpose was to provide information and coordination for liberal policy efforts, it became the driving force behind the internal reform of the House in the 1960s and 1970s.[3]

A major DSG focus was the meager opportunity the system allowed for rank-and-file members' participation in the legislative process. Reformers believed it was necessary to broaden participation in legislative decisions, to make the committees and their chairs more accountable to the full Democratic Caucus, and to enhance the capacity of the party's only central agent—the party leadership—to advance the majority's legislative objectives. Two vehicles the Democratic Study Group recommended in 1970 were regular monthly meetings of the Democratic Caucus to discuss policy and strategy, and secondly, creation of a caucus-formed panel to study and recommend possible reforms in House operations. The panel, in its early years called the Hansen committee after its first chair, Democratic Representative Julia Butler Hansen of Washington, was technically the Committee on Organization, Study and Review (OSR).[4]

The reform movement coincided with an underlying transformation in the larger U.S. political system. The power of political parties to control congressional nominations had given way almost entirely to an open electoral arena in which autonomous and sometimes inexperienced politicians won nomination through direct primaries. These new politicians were a different breed from their predecessors: better educated, more oriented toward public policy, and unwilling to take a back seat to their more senior colleagues. The result of these changes was to introduce a new era in the history of the House of Representatives in which its predominant characteristics would become equality of members' rights, diffusion of power, and a more open process of deliberation.[5]

The unquestioned leader of the reform movement was liberal Democratic Representative Phil Burton of San Francisco, who had won a special election to fill a vacancy in the House in 1964 and arrived just ten months ahead of Foley. Described as brilliant, passionate, obsessive, and given to abusing even his friends when they did not go along with him, Burton was "a San Francisco version of Lyndon Johnson. . . . He can be as clear as the four letter words that dot his speech, or as obscure as a Delphic oracle."[6] "He's got the personality of a Brillo pad," Democratic Representative Morris Udall of Arizona once said, "but he gets a lot done."[7] For much of his career, both in the California state legislature and in Washington, Burton's concerns were identified with traditional liberal causes and organized labor. He knew most members' districts as well as or better than they did, and was the mastermind behind the 1980s California redistricting that furthered Democratic Party interests. "Phil Burton was not subject to the oft-spoken criticism of liberals that they would rather be righteously prophetic in their stands than get something accomplished." He looked for vulnerabilities and strengths in members to know when and where it was necessary to compromise.[8] In the view of fellow reformer Ralph Nader, Burton "was the strategic networker par excellence."[9]

Burton, a former chairman of the Democratic Study Group, was a Foley mentor who persuaded him to run for the chairmanship of the DSG. After Foley took over the DSG, Burton said to Common Cause President Fred Wertheimer, "I will keep him [Foley] close to me. He is the one person capable of being Speaker, other than me."[10] Years later, after the fires of reform of the '70s had been banked, Speaker Foley would be criticized for not sufficiently pursuing further reforms; for not continuing to carry the Burton banner long after most of the troops had mustered out.

In my congressional experience, among the three co-equal branches of government, Congress has been the most accessible to the public, most adaptable to a changing environment, and the most self-critical of the way it goes about its business. There is always some level of internal reform taking place. There was a clear era which began at the end of the 1950s before I came to Congress, which was spearheaded by the Democratic Study Group in the late '60s and early '70s, and reached something of a crescendo when a large block of new Democratic freshmen arrived with the 1974 elections. Efforts in the '50s were frustrated by a reaction against too much, too fast. The strategy, revised beginning in the mid-1960s [with the DSG] was that reform, like salami, is best served cold and thinly sliced. Too much heat and too large a portion of reform inevitably produced a negative reaction within the Congress.

It was a calculated decision to hold back and, year-by-year, meaning Congress-by-Congress, offer a few, well-chosen, well-organized, well-researched, and well-prepared reforms which the caucus could digest without dyspepsia. This was a real contrast to the earlier efforts in which sweeping manifestos of change had met with massive resistance, and nothing was accomplished. Under the new approach, a lot was accomplished.

Committees were required to publish their procedural rules and open their meetings to the press and the public. The Democratic Steering and Policy Committee, an arm of the leadership, became the new "Committee on Committees," replacing what was felt to be the unwarranted power formerly given to the Ways and Means Committee to make committee assignments. Seniority was no longer the single, decisive factor. There was now a requirement that committee chairmen and some selective subcommittee chairmen be elected by the full caucus through secret ballot. There was a broad-based democratization spirit which drew power from the committee chairmen and dispersed it down toward subcommittee chairmen and the overall membership.

Less noticed by the press and public, there was also a dispersion of committee chairmen's influence with an enhancement of the Speaker's power. The Speaker, for example, was given the power of multiple referral of bills, providing for influence over legislation at the beginning and end of the process. Of particular importance, the Speaker was granted exclusive control over the selection of Democratic members of the Rules Committee.

A good deal of the thinking behind these reforms had been done informally at the DSG office, which had become Burton's personal lair. A group of us who had been involved in the reform movement for a number of years including Phil Burton, Executive Director Dick Conlon, Jim

O'Hara of Michigan, Don Fraser of Minnesota, Abner Mikva of Illinois, and I would meet at the end of the day and kick around ideas and strategy. We spent hours, for example, discussing how to work with the leadership. Many senior Democrats, including Speakers [Carl] Albert and [Tip] O'Neill, for example, were almost viscerally suspicious of Phil Burton and identified him with all manner of imagined plots and strategies.

During this period of congressional reform, Foley clearly emerged as a reformer, not a radical. With the arrival of the new Democratic freshmen class of '74, he also emerged as an intermediary between the Democratic Study Group and the group of new entrepreneurs who pressed for wholesale change.

> The major distinction in the area of reform is that the radical wants to fundamentally change the structure of the system either totally redistributing power or reordering or restructuring the organization, whereas the reformer takes the organization and the distribution of power, to some extent, as a given and wants to improve it on the margins and make it more effective, more equitable, fairer, and more distributive.

The Class of '74

Representing a net gain of forty-three seats, the seventy-five newly elected post-Watergate freshmen Democrats in the 94th Congress were a new entrepreneurial phenomenon in Congress. They had raised their own campaign funds, depended less on the party structure or congressional leadership, and arrived with a reformist spirit more than a researched agenda. The new freshman class served notice early that it was no ordinary group when it opened its own office two blocks from the Capitol and hired its own staff. Over four days in mid-January, every committee chairman was invited to address the class.[11]

Joe Crapa, staff director of the new members' caucus, concluded that the most important thing about what came to be known as the "Watergate Babies," because of their election in the public revulsion over Watergate, was their conviction that they were reformers. "They had a sense that the people had elected a different kind of Congress. Their reputation as a class was therefore to do things differently. . . . For the most part, they were not party people, but outsiders. . . . Many had won their races via the media, so they were fairly sophisticated about using television. . . . They were suburban, well educated in good schools. . . They were clannish and self supportive and not dependent on anyone."[12] They provided the new bodies for the last major assault on the old rules. Many believed afterward that they overturned the seniority system all by themselves, but the mechanism was carefully designed years earlier in Burton's DSG offices.[13]

> With the sudden appearance of this unexpectedly large Democratic class, we saw the opportunity to move more aggressively on those reforms

which had been held back and presented to the caucus a bit at a time. But we also had to contend with new members who had their own ideas about what to do and started out with a skeptical attitude toward the existing establishment. While the DSG veterans were primarily concerned about putting new procedures in place and constraining the abuses of power by some committee chairmen, this new class evinced more of an instinct for the jugular. Changing the process was fine, but they wanted some trophies on the hunting lodge wall in the form of some chairmen's heads.

Among the most significant of the final doses of reform, rivaling Burton's election as chairman of the Democratic Caucus, was Speaker Carl Albert's reluctant support for transferring responsibility for making Democratic committee assignments from Ways and Means to the leadership's Steering and Policy Committee. When the twenty-four-member committee convened on January 15, 1975 to vote on chairmen, Majority Leader Tip O'Neill moved that all of them be nominated by voice vote. But new rules required separate votes on each chairman, which the committee proceeded to do alphabetically. Common Cause had added to the volatile atmosphere by issuing a well-timed major report on House chairmen. Using three standards—compliance with House, caucus, and committee rules, use of power, and fairness—the report concluded that F. Edward Hebert of Armed Services, George H. Mahon of Appropriations, W.R. Poage of Agriculture, and Wayne Hays of Administration all "show a pattern of serious abuse."[14]

As Chairman of the Democratic Study Group in 1974, Foley had helped spearhead the drive to open up committee proceedings and weaken the seniority system. While he backed the change in House rules that allowed secret-ballot elections of committee chairmen, Foley refused to become involved in the effort to oust seventy-five-year-old Agriculture Committee Chairman W.R. Poage.

Born three days before the end of the nineteenth century and outranked in House seniority only by fellow Texans Wright Patman, Chairman of the House Banking Committee, and George Mahon, Chairman of the Appropriations Committee, Poage had served in Congress forty years. In representing Waco's Eleventh District, Congressman Poage had usually been re-elected without opposition since he was first elected in 1936. He replaced Harold Cooley as chairman of the Agriculture Committee in 1966. He had proven to be no innovator in farm policy, but he had a prehensile memory and a mastery of agricultural details. If he ran his committee somewhat peremptorily, he seldom sparked internal feuds. On most major policy issues, however, Poage was conservative and frequently voted with a southern Democrat-Republican bloc at a time when the Democratic Caucus was becoming increasingly liberal. More votes were cast against Chairman Poage in the 1973 Democratic Caucus than against any other chairman.[15] He was an anachronism, out of step with a newer generation of politicians. Yet on one point there was consensus: there was no "ambitious aspirant seeking the post . . . the number two Democrat, Thomas Foley of Washington, supported Poage."[16]

Foley even nominated Poage for reelection as chairman and gave a strong speech on his behalf. The chairman was so touched by the gesture that, after he was defeated, he nominated Foley for the chairmanship.

> The class of '74 summoned sitting committee chairman to come to a caucus, which they had established among their own members, to be interviewed on their fitness to serve as chairs of their committees. A number of chairmen who appeared apparently made a less than positive impression. Armed Services Committee Chairman Edward Hebert of Louisiana reportedly helped seal his fate by addressing the freshmen as "boys and girls."
>
> Mr. Poage had been singled out by a number of activists on the nutrition and food stamp issues as being insensitive and hostile. While it's true he was a critic of nutrition programs, I always thought he was fair in permitting them to be debated and voted on by the committee. While Chairman Poage's manner was somewhat autocratic, he listened to opposing views and allowed amendments to be offered. I didn't think he was guilty of the kind of abuse that I'd seen in other committees.
>
> So, [Representative] Bob Bergland [D-Minn.], who was later to be Secretary of Agriculture, and I, and a couple of other people, decided that we would try to set the record straight so that Chairman Poage didn't become the victim of exaggerated criticism. I spoke on his behalf before the freshman caucus, and Bob Bergland contacted other members of the freshmen group. We tried very hard to help because we were supporting his reelection. On the other hand, we did not believe he was going to be a principal target of those in the freshmen class who were obviously out to dethrone a couple of chairmen. It was the judgment of many of his friends that we should not encourage a major debate over his reelection. If a few of us worked behind the scenes, and he kept his head down, the wind might die out. To everyone's great surprise, he failed by three votes to win reelection.
>
> The next day my name was sent to the caucus by the Steering and Policy Committee. The principal speech on my behalf was given by Mr. Poage. It was very generous.

Foley was elected at age forty-five and became the youngest major committee chairman since the turn of the century. "[Foley] was thrust into the chairmanship over the political body of a guy he respected and worked with," recalled Representative Morris K. Udall. "It was a real test for Tom, and he handled it in a classy kind of way."[17] His first act on assuming the chairmanship was to recommend Poage as his vice chairman, and in what today would be viewed as atypical congressional practice, Foley called reporters into his office one by one to avoid having to hold a press conference. Grandstanding was not part of the Poage-Foley transition.

When Foley was elected chairman, Heather Foley, working as his adminis-trative assistant, noticed that all the women staffing the committee were listed as "clerks" while the men had fancier titles. In the first congressional staff directory printed after Foley took over the committee, everyone had become a "staff assis-tant."

As Agriculture chairman, Foley broadened the committee's traditional farm policy focus to include nutrition and consumer issues. "Agricultural legislation should be for consumers, as much as for farmers and ranchers," he said in a Janu-ary 28, 1975 interview with the *Christian Science Monitor*. He also proved to be a masterful coalition-builder, melding farm-state conservatives interested in higher price supports for farmers with urban liberals eager to expand food stamps and other nutrition programs.

> With urbanization and suburbanization, the House had fewer and fewer members who represented strictly rural districts. There had also been a breakdown in the traditional Roosevelt Democratic coalition rep-resented by urban political organizations, rural farm communities, orga-nized labor, and racial and religious minorities. Suddenly we were en-countering trouble from urban members about agricultural bills. We could no longer rely on the easy accommodation by one part of the coa-lition to another. We had to persuade urban members that the agricul-ture bills were in their constituents' best interests.
>
> We needed a link that gave a real world political interest in the urban communities for agricultural bills. The nutrition side of the committee's jurisdiction fit perfectly. I was upset, therefore, but argued unsuccessfully against it, when my predecessor as chairman agreed to the transfer of the school lunch program from Agriculture to the Committee on Education and Labor. Fortunately he didn't carry it to the extent of giving up all of the nutrition programs. We managed to keep the food stamp and WIC [Women, Infants, and Children] programs, and a few others where there was a consumer/social welfare constituency. This gave real meaning to the renaming of agriculture bills as the Food and Agriculture Act.
>
> The argument for the new strategy was obvious. In order to provide all Americans with the opportunity to enjoy the lowest food costs in the world, we had to make agriculture sustainable and profitable. That re-quired us to protect and cushion farmers against the more dramatic va-garies of price and production in a newly competitive global market. Those Americans who were unable to afford even the lowest food costs in the world, particularly children, should be assisted in receiving

adequate nutrition. It seemed to me to make a politically logical and co-herent position, and it brought a large measure of urban support to agriculture bills.

Foley was openly bipartisan in his committee leadership, usually managing to work out arrangements in advance with senior committee Republican William C. Wampler of Virginia. His handling of the 1977 farm bill was typical. Major crop support programs and food stamp legislation were up for renewal in one package, which President Jimmy Carter repeatedly threatened to veto as too costly. Foley painstakingly put together a compromise, balancing farm state pro-subsidy votes and urban bloc food stamp support.

If Foley was rewarded by the congressional reform era, surprisingly, his supporter, Phil Burton, was not. The 1976 Democratic leadership race for the 94th Congress witnessed one of the most historically intense competitions for the job of Majority Leader. As Chairman of the Democratic Caucus, Foley presided over the dramatic runoff.

The contest was a four-member race among Burton of California, Richard Bolling of Missouri, Democratic Whip John McFall of California and, a late and decisive entrant into the race, Jim Wright of Texas. On the first ballot, Burton finished first, Bolling second, and Wright third. With the lowest vote candidate dropping out, McFall was the first eliminated.

On the second ballot, Bolling was eliminated amid speculation that Burton had deflected a few votes to Wright assuming he would be easier to defeat in a final vote.

In the final ballot, many expected Burton to win. But Burton's abrasive manner had produced dedicated enemies, and Wright, although a late entry, had conducted a skilled campaign. The antipathy of both "Tip" O'Neill and Bolling hurt Burton, as did his help to unpopular House Administration Chairman Wayne Hays in retaining his chairmanship in 1974. The race came down to a difference of one vote in Wright's favor. The stakes were too high for this close of a vote, and Foley called Wright and Burton to the podium and indicated his intention to call for a recount. Burton, however, insisted that the vote be announced and Wright declared the winner. Otherwise, he told Foley, he would take the floor and concede the election.

Thus, the caucus elected Wright, whose own combative side had yet to surface. "Tip" O'Neill was unanimously elected Speaker and John Brademas of Indiana was appointed Majority Whip.

Leadership During the Carter Years

Although seen as having a fairly solid liberal voting record on most domestic issues, Foley's support for military spending projects like the anti-ballistic missile and supersonic transport programs led him to be regarded as something of a "Jackson Democrat." Indeed, Foley worked hard in the presidential campaigns of 1972 and 1976 on Jackson's behalf.

Having tested the waters in 1972, in 1976 Washington state once again had its "favorite son," Senator Henry M. "Scoop" Jackson, in the presidential race. But he failed to drain enough Carter votes in expensive campaigns in Florida, New York, and Pennsylvania primaries to garner the Democratic nomination. The underlying current of public opinion was a desire for change, a desire induced by Watergate and President Gerald Ford's pardon of Richard Nixon. People felt the country needed new leadership. Georgia's Jimmy Carter assumed the mantle of an "outsider" who would bring a new political and moral dimension to Washington, D.C. He said that he would not adhere to the Democrats' timeworn prescriptions of new government regulations and high federal spending. His brand of change was persuasive, dashing the hopes of Henry Jackson and his dedicated supporters like Tom Foley.

Even though he had been identified as a Jackson supporter and was somewhat distant from the Carter campaign, Foley's view was a traditional one in which the President initiated policy recommendations while Congress reviewed and reshaped. This was particularly so when there was a president of your own party in the White House.

In 1976, as a veteran of numerous reform battles against the seniority system, Foley defeated Shirley Chisholm of New York by a vote of 194 to 96 for the chairmanship of the Democratic Caucus. In his four years as chairman during the Carter presidency, Foley was not an activist, believing that the party's impetus and direction should more naturally come from the Democratic White House.[18]

Campaigning in "The Other Washington"

Foley's rising prominence in Washington, D.C., did not go unnoticed in eastern Washington. "Rep. Thomas S. Foley could become the most powerful man in the U.S. House of Representatives someday," reported *The Spokane Chronicle* in the summer of 1976. "House Speaker Carl Albert of Oklahoma termed Foley... 'close enough and young enough to go all the way to the speakership . . . I see nothing but a bright future for him. . . . I've encouraged him myself to start getting into the leadership.'"[19]

More than the caucus chairmanship, Foley's chairmanship of Agriculture tended to spotlight his Democratic voting record on issues not particularly popular in his essentially Republican district. In the summer of 1976 his Republican opponent, Charles Kimball, his wife, and eighteen-month-old baby were killed in a plane crash. Foley reacted by stopping his own campaign, pulling political ads, and canceling public appearances. A resourceful, well-financed, Spokane tire dealer, Duane Alton, entered the vacuum with three times as many campaign workers as Foley had. Alton campaigned against Foley as an absentee congressman. "Have you seen Tom Foley lately? He's taking you for granted." Alton challenged Foley's liberalism as symbolized by his pro-choice abortion position, held him to 56 percent of the vote, his lowest margin in years, and announced he was beginning his campaign for 1978 immediately.

The Spokesman-Review had been on the endorsement sidelines on both Senator Jackson's and Foley's reelection bids. A Jackson victory was considered a "virtual inevitability" but his voting record "gets high ratings from liberal and labor organizations; low ratings from those who adhere to conservative principles." "Rep. Foley is not the most liberal member of the state's congressional delegation," the editorial continued, "but he is perhaps third most liberal out of seven, based upon voting record ratings. This voting record causes us not to offer a positive endorsement of his candidacy, although we recognize that he has rendered good service to his district in non-ideological areas."[20]

The Spokane newspapers continued to report Foley's rising influence in Washington, D.C. Excerpting generously from a *Wall Street Journal* profile,[21] *The Spokane Chronicle* wrote in September 1977 that "a page one profile of U.S. Rep. Thomas S. Foley in the *Wall Street Journal* today extolled the heretofore largely unsung accomplishments of the 'quiet lawmaker' from Spokane." The impetus for the *Wall Street Journal* profile was Foley's deft negotiation of the 1977 agriculture bill. President Carter wanted flexibility to lower the amount of government loans to farmers. He wanted authority to withhold government subsidies on all crops from any farmer who didn't comply with a government order to "set aside" acreage planted to any one crop. Although Foley succeeded in getting Carter's support, conservatives believed the bill was too costly, and some farm-state congressmen believed it was too stingy.

"As an active reformer who has joined the ranks of committee chairmen," *The Chronicle* quoted, "he bridges the gap between Young Turks and old-timers. Younger members admire him for his leadership two years ago in making House procedures more democratic and for his patience in listening to their ideas. Yet senior members recall that during the height of the reform movement, Mr. Foley opposed efforts by House reformers to dump Agriculture Committee Chairman Bob Poage of Texas." Continuing its quotations by noting a characteristic that would become a litmus test of Foley's legislative style, *The Chronicle* stated that, "unquestionably, Tom Foley's forte is adroit legislating. Because his nature is to avoid confrontations, he rarely twists arms. Instead, he builds coalitions, but he does so by finding common interests rather than wheeling and dealing to balance opposing interests."[22]

What was excluded was as interesting as what was included in the abbreviated article. Among the *Wall Street Journal* observations which *The Chronicle* failed to include was one which noted that, "If Mr. Foley has a major flaw, congressional observers say, it is that he is too eager to build bridges between extremes in order to accomplish legislative results . . . some question whether he has the meanness to fight for the top House leadership job when Speaker O'Neill steps down one day. . . . Clearly, Tom Foley isn't an ideologue. He rarely takes the House floor to speak on any issue other than agriculture—and then only to analyze, not harangue. This approach is necessary in part because Mr. Foley, who two years ago headed the liberal House Democratic Study Group, represents the most conservative district in Washington. . . . But it also reflects Mr. Foley's own doubts that big government programs are always the answer to social problems."[23]

By the time of his reelection race in 1978, Foley's congressional prominence would prove to be a "two-edged sword." The "New Right" movement, which had proven popular in much of the Rocky Mountain area, had picked up eastern Washington supporters. A *Spokesman-Review* article noted that "no man in Congress appears to be so precariously balanced between legendary greatness and has-been obscurity." Noting that the first hint of trouble had been Foley's "surprisingly close finish in the 1976 race against Spokane tire dealer Duane Alton," the article went on to catalogue perceived vulnerabilities. He was blamed for all that troubled agriculture. Heather Foley was considered "one reason why Foley achieved success as one of the nation's most powerful congressmen," but also as a staff member who "creates tension" leading to "several months backlogged" constituent case work. Although he had been cleared of any wrongdoing by the House Ethics Committee and by Benjamin R. Civiletti, head of the U.S. Justice Department's criminal division, Foley had accepted a $500 campaign contribution from Korean rice dealer Tongsun Park and thus was potentially vulnerable to a national bribery scandal. Foley was expected to spend some $150,000 on his 1978 campaign, much of it from outside the state and an estimated 20 percent from labor unions. The Foleys drove a 1977 Cadillac convertible and preferred to vacation in Barbados. Columnist Jack Anderson had noted a proposed expenditure of $2,295.40 for Lenox china to serve guests in his role as Agriculture Committee chairman. The order was later canceled. "Analyses of Foley," noted the article, "tend to be complimentary, if not idolatrous," but the personal focus was a harbinger of campaigns to come.[24]

If the "pros" were formidable, the "cons" were enticing, and Harvey H. Hukari, regional director for the Republican National Committee (RNC) indicated that as much as $50,000 could be provided by the national party to assist in efforts to unseat Foley. The RNC representative reportedly talked to about a dozen potential Republican candidates, including State Representative A.J. Pardini, regarded by many insiders as the hands-down best candidate, who indicated that he wasn't interested. Hukari noted that "Foley is unusual because most congressional leaders come from 'safe' districts" while the Fifth District was considered marginal. Many Fifth District Republicans were fiscally conservative, and a political consulting firm's thirteen-county eastern Washington analysis indicated that "Foley actually does not line up with many Republican positions when vote comparisons are made."[25] Foley contended the Republican poll misrepresented issues involved in House votes mentioned in the survey and announced he would mail out his complete 1977 voting record to Fifth District households.[26]

Was Foley surprised at the apparent disparity of his own and his constituents' views?

> No, it didn't surprise me. I think it is probably true that on a lot of specific issues you could have taken my voting record and asked, "Do you agree with this?" and a lot of people would have said "no." But I'm not ashamed of that. I think, actually, whereas my political critics would say that this means I deceived the people, the rebuttal to that is that while a lot of people disagreed with me on specific issues, they still thought I was worthy of their support. I think that's what a good member of Congress ought to be able to do.
>
> If every time you take a position it's just reflective of the attitude of your district, that's what has to be explained, that's what has to be justified. That ought to be embarrassing because that proves you have no consequence at all as a representative, and that you're there merely as a reflection of popular opinion. Statistical polling and automatic telephone tabulations have become sophisticated enough to get a reasonable sample on every issue that comes before the Congress. You could just report national public opinion in a way that would give you a reasonable assurance that you were voting public views, and then do away with the element of human judgment.

Jack Hern, chairman of the Spokane County Republican Central Committee, announced to the press that recently disclosed lists of contributors to Foley's election campaigns proved "beyond a shadow of a doubt" that he was "a power broker for special interest forces." Hern noted that more than 80 percent of Foley's campaign contributions in 1975 and 1976 came from outside the Fifth District and from large unions and special interest groups such as Washington Bankers Political Action Committee, Washington State Labor Council, and Dairy Education Political Trust. "There can only be one conclusion reached, and that is Foley is more interested in money and power than he is in representing the people in the Fifth District," Hern said.[27]

By August Republican candidate Duane Alton had been joined by Mel Tonasket, an independent candidate, chairman of the nearby Colville Indian Tribe, and president of the National Congress of American Indians. While Foley's traditional call for a series of debates went unaccepted, the campaign issues were a continuation of the previous campaign with a sharper edge. Capitalizing on agricultural unhappiness over low wheat prices, Tonasket made much of the sources of Foley's campaign funds. The populist campaigner was reported to have become disenchanted with Foley in recent years as Foley gained power on the national scene—"power which has led him to ignore his constituents," claimed Tonasket.[28]

Alton alleged that Foley supported gun control and charged Foley and the Democratic administration with fostering a bloated and intrusive federal bureaucracy. Foley responded point-by-point with a supporting letter from the National Rifle Association. Aggressive in his own right, Foley ads focused on some of Alton's more extreme positions, including a recommended sale of Columbia River water to southwestern states and the elimination of the U.S. Department of Agriculture, Foreign Agricultural Service, and the State Department. Alton attempted to clarify his previous statements and in the late stages of the campaign asked for an investigation by the Fair Campaign Practice Committee, a private organization designed to monitor national campaigns for truth and accuracy. Alton charged that Foley had reached "a new low in Washington state politics" in misrepresenting his views. "Mr. Alton has taken some extreme and now embarrassing positions," Foley responded. "Now he wants to divert attention from his previous mistakes, charging misrepresentation. If he now wants to change his positions, he should do so directly."[29]

In the three-way race against Alton and Tonasket, Foley had spent $376,000 but was held to less than a majority in winning his eighth term in the House. He captured about 47 percent of the vote in counties outside of Spokane compared to some 45.5 percent for Alton and 7.4 percent for Tonasket. His greatest strength was in Spokane County where he had just over 48 percent compared to 42.5 for Alton and 9.2 for Tonasket. Alton won four of the district's fourteen counties but couldn't overcome Foley's Spokane stronghold. In the aftermath, Foley pledged to keep in closer touch with his district constituents.

There was an undercurrent in the 1978 election that Foley could not count on reelection being automatic and that the district's conservative voters expected to see some of that conservatism reflected in Foley's actions. He would clearly have to balance his perceived liberalism and growing national prominence with greater district attention. He could ill afford to be seen as "just another Easterner now, that he doesn't listen to his district anymore." As he explained in a *Spokesman-Review* profile interview prior to his 1980 campaign, he seemed to have heard the message.

> What I've always said is that every member of Congress has a responsibility to give the most respectful and serious attention to the views of the people they represent.
>
> On the other hand, I don't think being in Congress is a matter of taking a poll every day and deciding what the current opinion is and going like a computer robot and voting that way. . . .
>
> However, if I vote in a way that doesn't reflect 100 percent the view of my constituency on every issue, then I have the responsibility to

explain why I voted and why I think it's in their best interests and the country's best interests.[30]

The ballot boxes hadn't cooled before Foley set out on a November 10 through December 1, 1978, fence-mending, hand-shaking tour of his 20,000-square mile district. "I'm going to be more concerned and more energetic and more aggressive about explaining and clarifying positions I take in Congress," he said in an interview after the November 7 election.[31]

Chapter Four

In the Leadership:
The Reagan Years

The majority is not helpless and impotent. You can do things, and because you have the power, you have the responsibility.

—Thomas S. Foley, 1996

Dimensions of the Reagan Victory

As Thomas Mann highlighted in *Unsafe at Any Margin: Interpreting Congressional Elections* in 1978, both scholars and politicians observed that Congress had acquired a more outward focus. Congressional elections were local, not national, events. In deciding how to cast their ballots, voters were primarily influenced not by the President, the national parties, or even the state of the national economy, but by local candidates and local conditions. For the new generation of politicians, official House allowances now permitted every member travel expenses to pay for thirty-two trips home every year. The Reagan years suggested that it would be difficult to challenge a national agenda with a cohort of Democrats tied to local loyalties.

Ronald Reagan's victory in 1980 was impressive, winning 51 percent of the popular vote to Jimmy Carter's 41 percent and John Anderson's 7 percent. Republicans gained a Senate majority and, in the House, key Democratic leadership figures like Majority Whip John Brademas of Indiana and Ways and Means Chairman Al Ullman of Oregon lost. In congressional races across the country, voters reflected the Reagan message of greater control of government spending. The consequent issue of which government programs should be cut or abolished was, however, undefined.

For six years Foley's reelection victories had been shrinking, from 81 percent in 1972 to 48 percent in the three-way vote split of 1978. Since 1978 he had been making the cross-country 6,000-mile round-trip flight to Spokane an average of once every two weeks and his staff made certain that his visits were publicized so that eastern Washington residents knew he was available for public meetings and private conferences. Those constituents who didn't see him still knew he was around. At a typical three-day March 1979 Spokane visit, "Foley did everything from shine shoes at a fund-raiser to walking in a St. Patrick's Day parade with beer-drinking truck drivers. He also squeezed in time to present a U.S. Capitol flag to an Elks group, meet with an environmental alliance and attend a Jane Jefferson membership tea, among other things."[1] While he would deny ever having been out of touch with eastern Washington voters, he recognized that "in politics and public life, the perception is the reality."[2]

Although Foley ran unopposed by a Democrat in the 1980 primary, four Republicans vied for the chance to oppose him, including his 1978 independent opponent Mel Tonasket. I.F. McCray, regional representative for the Airline Employees Union, counted on mobilizing Christian voters on moral issues and fiscal conservatism. Foley was termed a big spender with the reminder that leopards don't change their spots. Spokane's George Bible, thirty-eight, had gained some notoriety after he proposed a commando force to free U.S. hostages held in Iran, criticized "pork barrel politics," and urged a "vote against programs that might bring federal money into his district if they weren't good for the nation as a whole." But Spokane physician John Sonneland, who had lost to Duane Alton in the 1978 Republican primary, emerged as Foley's opponent.[3]

The campaign resembled previous forays against Foley. "We need people in Congress who are from the mainstream. They're the ones who go through the Safeway lines. . . they're the ones who go to the high school football games. They're the ones who are working out in the fields." Such people, Sonneland suggested, understood better than Foley the inflationary impact of deficit spending by Congress. Sonneland ads charged Foley with supporting scientific experimentation on live human fetuses—although that had been legally prohibited in both 1973 and 1974 with Foley's supporting votes. Radio ads suggested Foley had "voted to let congressmen who have broken the law go free," although Representative Charles Diggs was serving prison time, the Supreme Court upheld Foley's vote that it was unconstitutional for Congress to deny Representative Adam Clayton Powell his elected seat, and Foley had supported congressional censure of Representative Charles Wilson.[4]

Whatever position Foley had taken, from an accelerated depreciation schedule for business or scrutiny of government regulations, Sonneland took it one step further. He branded Foley as "President Carter's warmest supporter in Congress" with an 81 percent support record.[5] He turned a complimentary article in the *National Journal*, which suggested Foley was "the strongest candidate" for chairman of the House Budget Committee, into a traitorous renunciation of Foley's Agriculture Committee chairmanship which was, Sonneland argued, clearly more critical to eastern Washington. Foley offered a response in a *Spokesman-Review* interview:

> The charge is kind of strange. My opponent accuses me of wanting to leave one of the most important posts in Congress. I assure everybody I'm not going to. You'd think, then, he'd be stuck with the logic that if I'm re-elected, I'm going to resume that important post he doesn't think I should leave.[6]

In actuality, however, despite protestations that he would not leave the Agriculture Committee, Foley ended up doing just that once he was offered the chance to serve as Majority Whip.

Living up to his first campaign's "I'll-debate-any opponent" promise, the two candidates traded barbs in eleven confrontations in 1980. The old "boilerplate charge" of having turned his back on his district most angered Foley. Before a Farm Bureau audience Foley underlined his local roots.

> My mother was born in Davenport and I find it continually strange to hear that I have an Eastern mentality and an Eastern frame of mind. If it's Eastern it's Eastern Washington. That's where my roots are. That's the district I represent. That's where I call home and I'll continue to call home as long as I live.[7]

The 1980 race was Foley's third against well-financed opposition. In this first Reagan landslide, Foley squeaked through with 52 percent while the president-elect carried Spokane solidly. Foley had particularly strong farm support. "There is clearly a conservative mood sweeping the country," Foley observed. The GOP tide that delivered Washington state to Ronald Reagan also unseated veteran Senator Warren Magnuson and captured the governor's office. Foley emerged to begin his ninth congressional term as the senior member of the state's House delegation.[8]

Foley had become an example of a phenomenon, particularly seen in Western congressional districts, of a member who had maintained strong popularity by attention to constituents and local problems, but who could find himself in political trouble when he became a leader of national prominence in Washington, D.C. As a Democrat who had made no effort to separate himself from his party's leadership, as was rapidly becoming the fashion with incumbents running as "outsiders," he had now suffered in two consecutive races—in 1978 and 1980—from the disenchantment of 5th District voters with the Carter administration.

While Foley had escaped defeat in the Reagan landslide, he later reflected on the importance of 1980 to Democrats nationally.

What's ironic is that the Republicans filled their war chest with sup-port from a block of Americans traditionally identified as allied with Democrats: the blue collar and middle class workers. Democrats have fallen into an image as defenders of the disadvantaged, poor and unrec-ognized masses. We seem to have been forgotten as the party that also speaks for the middle income citizens.

Because we have been identified with those groups—and we still be-lieve they are important—instead of a unified party, we have become "hyphenated Democrats." We are identified with single issues like "Democrats-for-whatever."

The task for Democrats nationwide, suggested Foley, would be to change the perceptions that Democrats are "a party incapable of fiscal discipline with only one solution to a problem. . . to spend megabucks," and that the only class of people the party is concerned with are the "millions of Americans out of the main stream of society."[9]

Foley Enters the Democratic Leadership

For Foley, the Reagan victory proved to be an example of adversity breeding op-portunity. The defeat of Brademas forced Speaker Thomas "Tip" O'Neill to choose a new Majority Whip. Chief Deputy Whip Dan Rostenkowski of Illi-nois, first in line for the promotion, faced a dilemma. He was also in line to take over defeated Oregon Democrat Al Ullman's chairmanship of the Ways and Means Committee. He could not do both. He chose Ways and Means. O'Neill had reportedly prevailed on Rostenkowski to take the chairmanship to deflect the succession of Representative Sam Gibbons of Florida, who had briefly chal-lenged O'Neill in his 1976 race for Majority Leader. If O'Neill did not com-pletely trust Rostenkowski, that was less a problem than that he did not get along with Gibbons.[10] Some Democrats urged O'Neill to select a Whip from among the 1970s Democratic generation, but O'Neill was looking for parliamentary skill in the coming arguments with House Republicans. Foley was a parliamen-tary expert and had been parliamentarian at the 1980 Democratic National Convention during which he ended up serving as a virtual referee in the conten-tious presidential nomination contest between President Carter and Senator Edward M. Kennedy of Massachusetts. Majority Leader Jim Wright called Foley in Davenport, Washington, two days after the election and asked if he would accept the Whip position. Foley had to give up chairmanship of the Agriculture Committee when he took the job.

Well, I guess that by the time the possibility of being Whip came into focus, I had pretty much decided I would take it if it were offered to me, and the opportunity came to me basically because of the defeat of two people. Al Ullman and John Brademas. I don't think there's any question that Dan Rostenkowski was in a position to accept either one of those positions, but he couldn't be both. So it was pretty much his choice what he would do. The Ways and Means Committee post was considered, perhaps, the most powerful committee chairmanship in the Congress, House or Senate, and the Whip's job, on the other hand, while obviously less imposing in an immediate sense, was historically one of the ways to the Majority Leadership and the Speakership. So, one had immediate great relevance, and the other had great possibilities that were important.

I decided I would take the Whip's job, if it were offered to me, for a number of reasons. I had enjoyed being Chairman of Agriculture. It was an important committee, but somewhat limiting. Because the focus was so closely scoped to agricultural issues, it was difficult for me to get involved in other things such as foreign affairs which had always interested me. There was a feeling on the part of other committee chairmen that their fellow chairmen shouldn't dabble much in business other than their own. And, while you might tolerate an individual member, even a new one, busying himself or herself with your particular area, a committee chairman resented other committee chairmen's involvement. It was "stick to your last, cobbler."

With Rostenkowski no longer in the running for Whip, some Democrats still had doubts as to whether the judicial and congenial Foley was hard-nosed or single-mindedly partisan enough for the job. Derived from the British term "whipper-in," the man assigned to keep the hounds from leaving the pack in a fox hunt, the term moved into the political lexicon in the eighteenth century British Parliament. With a tradition of strong party discipline, the Whip's major concern was ensuring good attendance for upcoming votes.

As it turned out, Foley was the last of the leadership-appointed Whips. As point-man for the Speaker and Majority Leader, the Whip's loyalty to and ability to work with the leadership had been considered of paramount importance. While still important, that older rationale would give way to loyalty to the full majority party membership. After Foley vacated the job, the caucus would elect their Whip as the third rung in the leadership ladder.

With its twentieth century adoption by the U.S. House of Representatives, the Whip position's role expanded beyond insuring that party members stuck to the party line. The appointment of the first Majority Whip occurred in 1897. By the end of the 1930s, the Democratic Party whip system included assistant whips chosen by and responsible for members of one geographic area or "zone." Speaker Sam Rayburn preferred a very informal leadership style and made slight use of even his chief Whip, Carl Albert, whose aide got so bored he asked for a transfer. By the 1960s, Speaker John McCormack made only marginally more use of the Whip and the White House congressional liaison staff performed most of the vote-counting functions during the Kennedy and Johnson administrations. By the 1970s, the whip system expanded, and appointive deputy whips were added to give women, African-American, Latino, and southern representatives a place at the leadership table.

> We had a whip organization which had grown rather dramatically over the years. Each successive Whip added his dimension of new members, and nobody wanted to get off. The weekly whip meetings were a very useful and informative session. Members like the access. They like to put on their stationery "Deputy Whip" or "Chief Deputy Whip," so it was worth your life to take a member off, and because people were coming on, and nobody was going off, it was like a lake with an inlet and no outlet. It just got deeper and deeper. That became an advantage. It lessened the workload. We would be able to task people with smaller numbers of members to contact. We could emphasize for everybody who was in the whip organization how important it was for them to cast a vote when asking others, and, while not conclusive, a stake in the leadership provided a little bit of extra pressure on members of the organization.

By the 103rd Congress (1993-94) the Democratic whip system consisted of the Whip, four chief deputy whips, eleven deputy whips, a floor whip, an ex officio whip, two task-force chairs, fifty-six at-large whips, and eighteen zone whips. It reflected the system's two primary functions of serving as a central conduit for information between leaders and members and playing a key role in the vote-mobilization process. The Majority Whip now ran a large poliical intelligence-gathering and dispensing operation which provided Democrats with schedules, pro-and-con arguments for pending legislation, and coordination of task forces. The whip organization by then came into play on about twenty bills a year on such major issues as the budget, debt limit, and other key legislative initiatives.[11]

The first step in the whip process is for the assistant whips to poll members of their regional zones about how they plan to vote. The question posed is always worded so the leadership position is implicit. "Yes" is always the desired answer in any whip check. After tallying the number for or against the bill, a task force contacts undecided members. The task force, an innovation most closely associated with Foley's period as Whip, typically discusses strategy and problems with the bill, and then discusses why members are undecided. Through the give-and-take, possible amendments are considered to help unify the party's support. Once a closely contested bill is ready for the floor, the whips help check attendance and "work" the floor during the debate, trying to sway members to the leadership's side. Above any other requirements, however, the Whip is expected to be a good vote counter in knowing where the support is.

> One time Tip O'Neill said, "Two people know how to count the House. Dan Rostenkowski. He's from Chicago. And Tom Foley. He's

from Spokane." He paused, and then said, "They really know how to play hard ball in Chicago." I was never quite sure how to interpret the postscript. Obviously Tip didn't think they played the same kind of ball in Spokane. It is, I think, a bit of a gift when people can intuit where the House is, or is likely to be, on an issue. Sometimes people have that ability, and sometimes they don't. There's a technical way to go about counting the House. You call members, do whip counts, check them, and re-check them, but even that has to be done with some understanding of the House's attitudes and inclinations. Some members are frank and direct. Others feel entitled to confuse if not mislead the leadership. You encourage candor with something akin to the old parental admonition, "if you tell me the truth, we won't punish you," but members seldom believe that. They believe, with some reason, that the leadership often knows how to ratchet up the pressure on them through key constituency groups. A call to an urban member from a farm organization urging support of an agricultural bill is not likely to carry much weight. A call from a consumer or labor group supporting the Food Stamp provision in the same bill will be heard. So, many members stay undecided, or simply report themselves leaning one way or another.

Two things are important. Knowing how to technically conduct a whip count, and knowing how to interpret what a member really means. It is critical to have "a sense of the House," not only where it is, but where it's going. I think you pick it up through osmosis by talking with members. Somebody told me one time that with oriental rugs, there are two kinds of experts. One can just look at the rug, and the other guy counts knots and threads. You have to be able to "feel" the House, and that you can only do when you're there. You can't do it at a distance.

The regular forum for the give-and-take is the Thursday morning whip meeting attended by fifty-plus Democrats. These take place in a sizable room on the third floor of the Capitol. In the front of the room, on an assortment of chairs sit the party leaders—the Speaker, Majority Leader, Whip, caucus chair, and vice chair. The meetings provide the leaders an opportunity to alert their members to late-breaking developments, important votes, floor strategy, and requests for support. The concerns members express and requests they make of the leadership also provide valuable information. It is also a forum for the expression of members' frustration. "The whip meetings are the single most lively expression of views and attitudes of the Democrats," said Foley. "It is a chance to sound off and say what you think the party ought to do. Members are not bashful," he added. "It's one regular place to confront the leadership," noted a leadership staff assistant. "Very often there are screaming matches. It's not a tea party."[12]

The conventional wisdom on Foley in 1981 was that while he might not have been the first choice for Whip by some people, he was a strong choice of almost all. O'Neill and Majority Leader Wright trusted him, as did Wright's chief rivals, Richard Bolling and Phil Burton. But, this diversity of support was more complicated than it appeared due to the extreme O'Neill-Wright animosities with Burton. On the one hand, Speaker O'Neill could step back and note that "the two brightest individuals I ever saw in Congress were Richard Bolling and Wilbur Mills for sheer ability. The next three were Foley, Burton, and Brademas for knowledge and depth on issues and legislation. They were masters. The most abiding Democrat, the one for whom the Democratic Party was most in his heart and in his mind, was Phil [Burton]."[13] On the other hand, O'Neill never supported Burton for a leadership post, and Wright won the Majority Leader position over Burton by a single vote in the most intensely contested Democratic leadership race in decades. For Foley to have gained the trust of these varied and powerful personalities was a tribute.

> Because of my association with Phil, I had to overcome distrust in both camps, particularly in the Wright camp. I probably didn't help myself much with Jim Wright, who went through the roof, by fulfilling a promise to appoint Phil Burton as chairman of the Democratic Caucus Committee on Organization, Study and Review. Speaker O'Neill, too, thought Phil was always plotting.

The Role of Majority Whip: A Confrontationalist or a Conciliator?

For a man selected to play the role of cheerleader and partisan point man for House Democrats, Foley's qualities seemed more those of a Speaker. When the more militant parties to a dispute had staked out positions and were emotionally involved in maintaining their positions, Foley was able to steer them to a successful compromise, as he did as Agriculture chairman. Watching him in action prompted one observer to note, "when Foley explains the politics of a legislative situation, he sounds like a curious outsider, calmly perceiving the entire situation as a human comedy he happens to have wandered into. . . this is a quality as useful as it is unusual."[14] His preference for conciliation represented to a number of colleagues his greatest weakness. He was, as Speaker O'Neill once noted, able to see three sides of every question,[15] but when an argument could be won without confrontation, he usually won. When it required confrontation, he was less effective.

> Many people thought that I was not sufficiently hard enough to be Whip. There's a theory that the Whip has to break arms, that the job requires a muscular personality. My own view is that about as much can be accomplished with a patient purchase to members, a recognition of their circumstances, and an occasional on-your-knees pleading with them, as by fingers-in-the-chest, slaps-across-the face, and knees-to-the-groin.

Most members today are not very much dependent on the leadership. They want to keep good relations, particularly in the event of some future cushy assignment on a committee or select committee. On the other hand, it's almost impossible to get a member to vote what he/she perceives might be a suicide vote.

If somebody has a tug of conscience and they have some elements of their constituency that support it and the risk can be something they can square, then you have a possibility of getting their vote. If they clearly see it as totally useful only to an opponent and guaranteed to get a well-financed one, you can sit on their chests with a knife and they're not going to say yes.

The Reagan Mandate and the Reagan Budget

The Reagan economic budget dominated congressional action in the early 1980s. As Republican Senator Warren Rudman of New Hampshire would later observe, "Reagan arrived in the White House with three passionately held beliefs: that taxes were too high, that government was too big and that the Russians might at any moment land at Cape Hatteras. Everything else stemmed from those core beliefs." Beyond his core economic beliefs, however, the President had little patience with the facts and figures that went with policy discussions about issues such as the deficit. "The man inhabited his own reality. That was both his greatness and his failure as a political leader. His greatness was his ability to make Americans share his vision of reality, be it Morning in America, supply-side economics, Star Wars or the Evil Empire. His failure was that, at least in economic affairs, his reality was a delusion."[16]

In early February 1981 I was the Majority Whip when newly-elected President Reagan came up to the Hill to speak to the combined leadership of the House and the Senate. This was a kind of a gesture he made, to put out his hand and cooperate with the Congress. The House was still under Democratic control and, after the 1980 elections, the Senate had gone to Republican control. Actually, I think most of us would have preferred to have gone down to the White House. It's got more opportunity to get on the evening news, meeting with the new President, which members of Congress like to do, if you do it from the White House lawn rather than from an inside room from the Capitol which, by tradition, can't be photographed. But, anyway, we were in the Senate "President's Room" which is a room which was used in the last century to receive the President. It's a rather small, but elaborate, room, and its most important piece of furniture is a table where, tradition says, President Lincoln signed the Emancipation Proclamation in 1862.

The table had been removed and we were sitting, about sixteen of us, I guess, in a circle, somewhat like young women at a finishing school— our backs straight, our hands in our laps, our eyes straight in front of us, our feet on the floor—listening to President Reagan talk about some of the things he thought were important to the country. And suddenly he was talking about a "welfare queen" who had been found in Chicago with allegedly seventy-two credit cards, or one-hundred-and-seventy-two, I can't remember exactly how many, and two BMWs, and a Mercedes Benz, and on and on. I was sitting next to Jack Kemp who was, at the time, Chairman of the House Republican Conference, and he leaned over and, in a rather uncomfortably loud whisper, said: "This is all campaign shit." He said, "I wish he'd get off this stuff. Nobody cares about this any more. And it's all in his imagination anyway. None of it really happened." I kind of looked the other way out of embarrassment because I was sure he was going to be overheard.

The next thing President Reagan was talking about was the discovery of some young member of the General Services Administration, or whatever it's called in California, when he was governor, who managed to reduce the size of public documents in California by some kind of electromagnetic process, or something, so that, as he said, it would reduce the number of filing cabinet purchases by California by something close to 4,000 filing cabinets a year. And Kemp leaned over and whispered in my ear. He said: "That does it. That absolutely does it." And the next thing I knew, Jack was speaking up, interrupting the President, by saying: "Mr. President, the people in my city of Buffalo, New York, don't really care very much about welfare queens in Chicago or filing cabinet procurement in California, they're interested in jobs, the economy, the future of the country, our growth, our opportunity to provide a future for our citizens and continue our economic leadership in the world."

And, without missing a beat, the President said, "That's right Jack, that's absolutely right. That's why we're going to move forward with an aggressive and dynamic policy of tax reduction and economic growth and fiscal restraint." I had to give the President some credit. He wasn't flustered or angered, as I think many might be, by the interruption. I thought, he's not only the master raconteur of telling stories, but very quick to adjust to the audience. To me, it also demonstrated another of Ronald Reagan's abilities. While his staff might visibly fume, the President seemed to rise above it all, just as he was able to assimilate such former opponents as Jim Baker and George Bush into his administration, he was also able to accept Jack's interruption with a smile. It was, in a sense, monarchical.

But the Reagan agenda was more than "welfare queens," and the Democratic leadership seemed unable to hold conservative Democratic votes in opposition to Reagan's early legislative agenda.

> President Reagan talked about cutting spending, about tax reduction, and argued that the resulting economic stimulus would not only lift all boats, but reduce the federal deficit and balance the budget in four years. The Reagan economic program had much appeal because it promised some very significant tax reductions, particularly for upper-income Americans. Nobody really wanted to get much in the way of it. In fact some of our southern colleagues were very quick to sign on and to give the President majorities in the one body he didn't control, the House of Representatives.
>
> What happened over the succeeding years was that entitlements continued to grow. Discretionary spending was reduced, but particularly the so-called middle-class entitlements, Social Security and Medicare for example, continued to rise. Defense spending as a portion of discretionary spending also went up. So the result was that the deficit rose very sharply. Then a recession hit in late 1981 and early 1982 and that combined with the defense hikes and tax cuts to set off a very sharp increase in the deficit which continued to rise during the entire Reagan period.

In 1982, President Reagan had been persuaded to support $98 billion worth of tax increases over a three-year period as a means of bringing the federal deficit down—the Tax Equity and Fiscal Responsibility Act (TEFRA). Speaker O'Neill asked Foley to make the case on national television in favor of the plan, hoping to convince wavering Democrats. In what many regarded as a masterful speech which might have influenced as many as sixty votes on the Democratic side, Foley urged members of both parties to summon up "political courage" and cast a vote in favor of "economic reality." O'Neill greeted Foley at a following press conference with the words "a star is born."

> I was asked by the Speaker to respond to the President's statement on behalf of the new tax proposal. This was an atypical Democratic response following a nationwide presidential address. I thought the President was on the right track, not on the wrong track in TEFRA, and I thought it was important that the bill be passed, and we needed bipartisanship to do it. So it was quite natural for me to start out by saying that although I disagreed in many ways with what the President was proposing to the Congress, on this issue, I thought the President was absolutely right and that I would do everything I could, and the Democrats would do everything they could, to help him achieve the result he was asking the American people to support.

I think it took the press a little bit by surprise. It's not usual for a Democratic response, or a Republican response, to agree with an opposing party's President. I tried to make the case as forcefully as I could because I knew the mind set was a little bit the other way around. The speech got perhaps more attention than it would otherwise have gotten. It was interesting to me that in Spokane, Washington, it was particularly well received.

I think a lot of people want to see the two parties work together, at least from time to time, so that they're not always at each other's throats, that they're not always jockeying, struggling to find a political advantage, an opportunity for partisan gain.

Foley's 1982 Reelection: Leadership Becomes an Issue

"He [Foley] is probably one of the best natural legislators in the House, a man who is respectful of the opinions of others even as he is forceful in the advocacy of his own," observed the *Almanac of American Politics* of the new Democratic Majority Whip.[17] As to his seemingly tenuous hold in the Fifth District, he was seen as never waffling on issues or trying to persuade constituents he was a crypto-Republican—he had that essential quality of a good leader, of being willing to risk losing when he was pretty sure he was right.

In his 1982 reelection race, Foley's opponent was again Dr. John Sonneland, who replaced the more strident personal attacks with attempts to convince voters that Foley had placed national interests above local concerns. Sonneland was buoyed by the fact that state Republicans, along with the National Conservative Political Action Committee (NCPAC) had targeted both Foley and Senator Henry Jackson. "It seems they feel it is better to carry off the head of a leader on the pike than winning other races that could influence the balance of a (legislative) body. Except for the honor of the thing," Foley said, "I'd just as soon not be targeted."[18]

Ironically, Foley's rise in the nation's capital had been accompanied by a rise in the idea that he was politically vulnerable at home. "Do voters want to push someone who is ascending the political ladder, or someone who will go to the mat?" Sonneland asked in a Fall debate. "If he [John Sonneland] thinks he can get under my skin with that one, he's right," said Foley. "My grandparents homesteaded in Davenport before Washington was a state. I was raised here and lived in the 5th District all my life. . . and I am back in the district nearly every weekend."[19]

Such charges might have resonated earlier, but by 1982 Foley had paid renewed attention to the district, including purchasing of an apartment in a tenant-owned complex on Spokane's West Sixth.

In the heat of the campaign he appeared in the second National Public Broadcasting System debate to argue House Democrats' policy on the national economy. Foley had been credited by Reagan and Secretary of Agriculture John Block as "a key element to the success" of the farm bill in the House which passed by two votes. Although explaining his key vote in the Democrats' blockage of the balanced-budget constitutional amendment was tougher, Foley argued the constitutional flaws and marshaled conservative support. "It is interesting," he observed, "that some of the most conservative economists, including those who worked for Presidents Nixon and Ford, Ford himself and [GOP Congressman] Jack Kemp were all very active in opposing that balanced-budget amendment. I have no apologies at all for having opposed that amendment."[20]

Foley's departure from the Agriculture Committee chairmanship was a keystone of Sonneland's attack. "I said I would not give up the chairmanship of the Agriculture Committee to chair the Budget Committee," Foley contended, "and I didn't." He had made no promise not to accept a leadership role that could benefit the Fifth District. Instead of being the sponsor of committee-introduced legislation and holding hearings on other bills, Foley argued, he was in a position to directly influence wheat and grain legislation and—as Whip—to schedule floor action on those items. Internationally, Foley was still recognized as a leader in the field. During a visit to Japan for an international food conference Foley had met with Japanese commodity officials. "I was able to do two things in that meeting," he said. "I was able to convince them they should not increase their cost of wheat [the resale price of wheat already bought from the U.S.]. Secondly, I was able to keep them from reducing their feed grain imports." With Japan one of Washington's big wheat buyers, both actions had a direct impact on Fifth District grain growers, Foley argued. The eastern Washington press found outside support for the argument. "*The Des Moines Register*," wrote *Spokane Daily Chronicle* journalist Dick Moody, "recognized as a leader in newspaper agriculture reporting nationally, called him [Foley] the 'single most effective agriculture vote' in Congress."[21]

Gun control had disappeared as an issue. The National Rifle Association had no doubt about the value of Foley's leadership position which they felt "made it possible for him to even more effectively stand up for the rights of gun owners." Endorsed in previous elections and presented with the organization's "Defender of Individual Rights Award" in 1978, Foley received the NRA's first endorsement during the 1982 House elections.[22]

As he had in 1980, Sonneland continued to assail the sources of Foley campaign funding, noting that almost 80 percent of the reported money came from outside the district from special interests such as farm commodity brokers, home builders, East Coast bakeries, lawyers, and other business interests. Foley campaign aides suggested that Sonneland had asked "almost all" the business-financed political action committees that eventually supported Foley to support his own Republican candidacy instead. It was a statewide Republican theme and Foley's mentor, Senator Jackson, was fending off the same attacks. A Washington, D.C., journalist who specialized in watching the impact of money on politics told *The Spokesman-Review* it was doubtful that most senators and congressmen, especially those of Jackson's stature, consulted their contribution lists before voting.[23]

Foley's entry into the House leadership proved less of a problem for *The Spokesman-Review* editorial board than for John Sonneland. "Foley, in his 18 years as a House member, has earned high marks for his intellect and political savvy," the endorsement read. "Perhaps his most difficult task has been his most recent—that of balancing between his dual roles in the House. Remarkably, he has been able to pull off—to the general satisfaction of both sides—his jobs as voice of the 5th District and House majority whip for Speaker Tip O'Neill . . . At a time when partisan bickering might have been expected, Foley substituted bipartisan cooperation." Foley's clout and his ability to "continue to be a moderating influence on the rest of his party" seemed to make the case.[24]

"Foley's stature in the Congress," echoed the *Spokane Daily Chronicle*, was "an advantage to the district so long as it doesn't interfere with his ability to represent the folks at home." What seemed most impressive to the paper's editors was the "evidence that Foley can be responsive to constituent sentiments, even when it puts him at odds with the party line." He was, the editorial pointed out, "the highest ranking House Democrat to vote for President Reagan's three-year tax-cut bill in 1981," for example. It would be up to the voters every two years, however, "to keep him honest. . . . And it will be up to the Republican Party to do something it failed to do in 1982, put up a reasonable alternative."[25]

Foley won with 64 percent and the Democrats gained two dozen seats in the U.S. House. In a dual interview with Foley and Fourth District Republican Sid Morrison, "members of the House leadership in their parties," *The Spokesman-Review* struck a regionally popular bipartisan theme. "We'll have to do a little more compromising, and get rid of some of the partisanship that has cropped up (between Reagan and the Democrats)," Morrison stated. "I don't think the American people want to see inaction as the result of political confrontation," Foley added. "If that happens, both parties will be called on to explain it."[26]

If Foley felt his days of close elections were behind him, however, the question did bother some members of the Democratic Caucus who worried about electing leaders, like Brademas, who might be defeated because they were linked with party positions that were unpopular in their districts. Some of those critical of Foley's cautious style linked it to insecurity about his conservative district. "It is a definite disadvantage for us to have . . . someone who has to look over his or her shoulder at his or her constituency. You like to have your leaders fearless."[27]

> My rationalization for it was that I thought I was in a better position
> to speak to, argue with, and successfully persuade members from

marginal districts that votes that I was taking, and I understood were dangerous and difficult votes, were not unappreciated by me when they cast them. The tendency of someone from a safe seat, an O'Neill from Boston or a Jim Wright from Texas, somebody who couldn't be defeated in his own congressional district with tanks, might have a hard time persuading a member from a marginal district to accept the risks and vulnerabilities of a vote. I could do that and look the member in the eye when I did.

Foley continued to play the role of mediator on both national and regional issues. Early in 1983 when O'Neill and Reagan again found themselves in agreement—on the need for a job-creating public works bill—the Speaker again chose Foley as spokesman and negotiator for congressional Democrats. By March, Reagan had signed a $4.6 billion jobs bill into law.

Foley's role in foreign affairs continued. In the November 1983 aftermath of the U.S. invasion of Grenada, Speaker O'Neill decided the House needed to exercise an oversight role. He knew it would be a delicate role and its success would depend on the leadership of the congressional delegation. He announced that Foley would head a bipartisan congressional fact-finding delegation to the island. "I think Congress's first reaction to the invasion was one of support because it was supposed to protect American life," Foley said. But there was "a second question" of whether the United States moved into Grenada "militarily in order to remove a potential strategic problem. That is much more controversial," he indicated. "Then the question arises about what you're going to do next. We have a serious problem with Nicaragua. So the precedent is there. This is very troubling to members of Congress." The delicacy of the policy issues were made no easier by the ideological range of the delegation—from Democratic critic Representative Ronald Dellums of California to Republican Whip and invasion defender Dick Cheney of Wyoming. The American public did not wait for the delegation's report to pronounce the invasion a resounding success—a verdict essentially endorsed by the congressional report despite some internal grumbling from the more liberal members.[28]

During the last two years of Reagan's first presidential term, Foley opposed administration proposals to reduce individual income tax rates by 25 percent over three years (adopted 238-195), and a balanced budget constitutional amendment (failed to garner the required two-thirds vote). He also opposed a Democratic-proposed capping of congressional salaries which was defeated on a 208-208 tie vote. He continued his opposition to key Reagan proposals in the 98th Congress (1983-84): raising Social Security retirement age from sixty-five to sixty-seven after the year 2000, covert action in Nicaragua, and the Reagan opposition to the Equal Rights Amendment. But Foley joined the President in supporting the 1984 Immigration Reform and Contract Act (216-211), which imposed sanctions on employers who knowingly hired illegal aliens.

Reagan's Reelection and the National Mood

A revived economy and national pride symbolized by the 1984 Olympic ceremonies in Los Angeles created an optimistic mood that swept virtually all incumbents back into office that year. President Reagan won with 59 percent of the vote. This was in sharp contrast to President Ford's 48 percent and President Carter's 41 percent as the last two incumbent presidents. In the House, all predictions of a Republican sweep came to naught. The voters returned to office 390 House members in 435 districts (just one below the all-time high reached in 1968). Pollsters had found most Americans optimistic about the direction of the nation. Their votes were a true ratification of the status quo.

In eastern Washington it was also an incumbent's election. In one debate, conservative Spokane city councilman Jack Hebner and Foley "stood on the same stage for the first time in their congressional campaign here Sunday night and called each other nice guys." The hottest sparks occurred when Hebner claimed Foley was standing beside former President Carter in 1980 when he signed the order for the grain embargo against Russia, a sore spot with eastern Washington farmers. Hebner apologized when it was made clear Foley had opposed the embargo. Even President Reagan's popularity in the Fifth District failed to be an issue. Foley pointed to his support of Reagan on such issues as the 1982 tax increase and 1983's invasion of Grenada. "As a member of the Democratic leadership, I have supported presidents of both parties when I thought they were right," Foley said. "I supported them openly and not always to the satisfaction of members of my party."[29]

"Challengers long have predicted the veteran Democrat's reign can't last in a 5th Congressional District that leans Republican," *The Spokesman-Review* reported, but "while he can preach the Democratic gospel at party functions, Foley downplays party labels on the campaign trail. . . . A cautious politician, Foley frequently discusses issues from various viewpoints without taking solid stands himself. Opponents call it double-talk; supporters say it's his judicial streak showing."[30]

> Anybody who runs for office in the Pacific Northwest, in the State of Washington in particular, on a theme of: "I'm a Republican, and I'm looking for Republican votes here. I want everybody to know I'm going to support the Republican leadership lock-stock-and-barrel. I can be counted on. I'm available, not because they order me, but because I believe it. If you don't like the Republican program in all its aspects, don't vote for me," is politically foolish.
>
> Now, turn it around and you have a Democratic agenda which is even less popular as a theology than the Republican agenda. We tend to have a lot of independents. That's taken for granted. It's an axiom in the Pacific Northwest that people, while they tend to be more conservative in

eastern Washington and more progressive in western Washington, are not fixed in their party loyalties. So it's a natural thing to talk about issues rather than party positions. "Yes, I'm a Democrat, and a proud one, but there are different ways of looking at this problem, and different approaches to it."

As to his role in the leadership, Foley argued that while "you can't pass everything you want (as a congressional leader). . . as a practical matter, I think you have a voice that's heard more clearly." *The Spokesman-Review* editorial board agreed. They noted that ranking third in the House leadership "translates into influence which Foley can bring to bear on behalf of his Eastern Washington constituents." Federal funding for a Spokane transit garage and Spokane Valley sewer system were but two examples. Of significance was Foley's generally good working relationship with Reagan and members of his administration. "Reagan has had difficulties trying to deal with either House Speaker Thomas P. O'Neill or Majority Leader James Wright," the editors wrote. But "White House sources quoted by *U.S. News and World Report* say Foley is a House Democrat the president can work with—an important consideration if Reagan's programs are to be successful. . . . Hebner insists he has the energy and tenacity to do, as a freshman, as much for the 5th District as Foley can accomplish with his seniority and leadership position. That simply isn't a realistic view of the way politics work, especially at the congressional level."[31]

Foley raised $400,000 for the race, much of it from political action committees. Hebner, with little visible support from traditional GOP power brokers, raised $32,000 in contributions and loaned his own campaign $12,000.[32] Vice President George Bush's visit to Spokane was, according to local reports at the time, a limited success. Among the GOP dignitaries on the dais, Hebner was at the end of the line and the Vice President mispronounced his name. Winning the majority of votes in each county of the district and 70 percent overall, it was Foley's second biggest win since he took 81 percent against Clarice Privette in 1972. It appeared Foley had finally become one of those national leaders of the Democratic Party with few reelection problems. He had raised his percentage from 52 percent in 1980 to 64 percent in 1982 to 70 percent in 1984.

Speaker O'Neill Announces Retirement

On March 1, 1984, Speaker O'Neill told reporters that he would step down at the end of 1986 and the 99th Congress. He would be remembered with almost universal fondness, and his legacy would include having served as midwife to the congressional reforms of the 1970s. As Speaker from 1977-87, "Tip inherited an institution that was already reformed, and he had to make it work," said Ronald M. Peters Jr., director of the Carl Albert Congressional Research and Studies Center.[33] Operating from a basic strategy of inclusion, O'Neill increased the use of leadership task forces to give junior members a voice, rejuvenated the Democratic Caucus as a policy forum, and thrust the Speakership into the public consciousness. A more troubling part of his legacy would include his contribution to increased partisanship in the House. He increased the practice of imposing strict limits on what amendments could be offered on the floor and skewed the party ratios on key committees to pad Democrats' advantage. In his defense, however, beginning in the late 1970s he had to contend with a new generation of Republicans who brought a confrontational style to the House floor. More aggressive in using delaying tactics, they forced votes on "hot button" partisan constitutional issues such as school prayer and abortion, injecting into debate a sustained criticism of Congress as an institution.

Spearheaded by the Conservative Opportunity Society (COS) under Georgia Republican Representative Newt Gingrich's leadership and including Representatives Vin Weber of Minnesota, Robert S. Walker of Pennsylvania, Dan Coats of Indiana, Judd Gregg of New Hampshire, and Connie Mack of Florida, these "self-styled Republican guerrillas" made increasing use of the gavel-to-gavel television coverage of the House initiated by the Cable Satellite Public Affairs Network (C-SPAN) in 1979. They doggedly reserved time during "special orders," the speeches given at the end of each legislative day, usually to an empty chamber. Name-calling reached a nasty level, with Republicans referring to Democrats as "dictators" and "cheaters," and Democrats retorting that the Republican agitators were "obnoxious" and "phony." The new aggressiveness put House Minority Leader Robert H. Michel of Illinois in a difficult position. "Some of the floor [Republican] tactics started without his knowledge or approval" and he felt pressure from more moderate Republicans who thought it appeared "they're running the show, not Michel." Over the course of the year, these younger Republicans increasingly set the tone of the speeches and debates, to the point that an institutionalist such as Michel found himself pushed toward a more confrontational strategy. "The most important thing we have done," said Michel to a Republican Conference at the end of 1984, "is rid ourselves of that subservient, timid mentality of the permanent minority. The Republican Party in the House is no longer content to go along. We want to go for broke."[34]

There is some question whether Michel's heart was really in confrontation for its own sake. In 1994, at former Speaker O'Neill's death, Republican Leader Michel mourned the passing of a friend—and a style of politics: "It is a kind of politics that, I am sorry to say, is fast disappearing in this country, one in which partisan fervor and personal good will can—in fact, must—coexist, and in which the heated controversies over specific policies never transcend the ultimate affection for individuals."[35]

Speaker O'Neill's final Congress proved to be far from a lame-duck performance as Congress seized the legislative initiative from the White House in 1985 and dominated the Capitol Hill agenda to an extent unmatched since President Reagan had taken office five years earlier. On issues ranging from deficit reduction to federal farm spending, South African sanctions to Middle East arms sales, Congress called the shots. "This year came as close to congressional government as we've had in a long time. The whole agenda was set by Congress. . . . The president had exhausted most of his ideas by the time he got to his second term, so he was left with a set of congressional ideas," observed political scientist Norman Ornstein of the Washington "think tank" the American Enterprise Institute.[36] Although congressional leaders enjoyed their resurgence in 1985, some, including Foley, felt the system would have been better served if President Reagan had taken more of a lead on such key issues as curbing the budget deficit: "The system functions best when there is strong, positive presidential leadership. He is an essential actor on the legislative stage."[37]

A major impulse for deficit reduction had come with the need to raise the ceiling on the federal debt, which had arisen after years of accumulated deficit spending. The federal debt had more than doubled during the preceding five years, to an unprecedented $2.079 trillion.

Addressing the Deficit: Gramm-Rudman-Hollings

The hobgoblin of deficit reduction was fresh in members' minds. Republicans remembered with pain that they had lost twenty-six House seats in 1982 after Democrats repeatedly resurrected President Reagan's 1981 call for substantial benefit cuts in Social Security to keep the program solvent. Democrats, with equal pain, recalled 1984 when Democratic presidential candidate Walter F. Mondale had said he was prepared to raise taxes and lost forty-nine states.

Congress had encountered a budget impasse compounded by President Reagan's resistance to cuts in the defense buildup and in Social Security, his adamant rejection of tax increases, and the flat rejection by many Democrats and by House Republicans of any diminution in Social Security cost-of-living increases. Avoiding those liabilities while providing a solution for the budget deficit appeared in the form of the Gramm-Rudman-Hollings plan to balance the federal budget. It was offered as an amendment to the "must pass" legislation of raising the federal debt ceiling.

Its full title was Gramm-Rudman-Hollings. Fritz Hollings' comment always was, "if you want a sure trip to anonymity, link your name after [Phil] Gramm and [Warren] Rudman. Nobody will ever hear from you again."

Described by Republican Senator Warren Rudman of New Hampshire as "a bad idea whose time has come," the plan was intended to "put into the system some institutional discipline, if you will, a backbone transplant so that Congress lives up to its responsibility." The blame for deficit spending, according to Rudman, also included the President and the American people, particularly those who routinely told Congress to limit spending, but added, "Don't cut my program."[38]

The legislation would mandate annual reductions in the federal deficit to produce a balanced budget by fiscal year 1991. If Congress and the President failed to make the mandated reductions, automatic, across-the-board spending cuts, a process called sequestration, would go into effect. Only Social Security benefits for senior and disabled citizens and interest payments on the national debt would be exempt. Senator Rudman, for one, was convinced that the automatic cuts were an unacceptable alternative and would never go into effect because the threat would force reasonable people to find a better alternative for deficit reduction.[39] Only a decade after Congress had asserted its primacy on spending decisions with the Congressional Budget and Impoundment Control Act, the institution was prepared to give up a fair degree of its discretionary authority by putting the budget on the automatic-pilot of across-the-board program cuts if Congress and the President were unable to meet the deficit-reduction targets. Gramm-Rudman-Hollings was an expression of congressional exasperation with the process of budget reconciliation in which congressional appropriation subcommittees were required to adjust the spending levels of programs under their jurisdiction in order to reconcile spending with government revenues. Those changes regularly appeared each session of Congress in the omnibus reconciliation bills.[40]

Since Congress began requiring the President to submit an annual budget in 1921 with the Budget and Accounting Act, the challenge of operating with a balanced budget had been formidable.[41] By 1985 the federal government had been spending about $24 for every $19 it raised, with the difference made up by borrowing.[42] There were several reasons why achieving a balanced budget was difficult. First, politics simply exacerbated it. Although it had received a broad bipartisan vote of 75-24 in the Senate, Gramm-Rudman-Hollings was the product of the Senate's Republican majority. Supported by President Reagan, the plan appeared to the Democratic majority in the House as a convenient way for the President to avoid responsibility for the greatly enlarged federal debt created by his tax reductions and increased defense spending. Nightly television news increasingly portrayed the Democratic House as an obstacle to a laudable objective.

Second, the plan had not been subjected to the usual committee hearings or economic and other analyses. Offered as an amendment to the must-pass legislation to increase the federal debt ceiling, it amounted to "the worst kind of . . . legislative bullying," complained Majority Whip Foley.[43] Third, the major options for balancing the budget were known by all to be cutting spending for defense and entitlement programs such as Social Security, or increasing taxes, neither of which commanded a majority of votes. It made across-the-board cuts in a wide range of favored and already strained Democratic social programs almost inevitable. And fourth, by its automatic nature, Gramm-Rudman-Hollings would potentially compromise what many members felt was their constitutional responsibility to decide on spending and taxes. As much as the House Democrats might object, from the leadership view the votes were there to pass it, and the only alternative was to try to make it more palatable.

Foley as Consensus Builder

Foley's consensus-building skills continued to be important to the House leadership's strategy for handling the Gramm-Rudman legislation after it passed the Senate. A number of House Democrats simply wanted to oppose the measure but, as Majority Whip, Foley's head count showed it could not be defeated. As chairman of a task force to devise a Democratic alternative, Foley coaxed a consensus out of liberal and conservative Democrats by including protections for certain anti-poverty programs.

Speaker O'Neill gave this assignment to Foley as House Majority Whip: chair a task force of House Democrats to monitor the legislation and to begin developing a response. Foley hosted countless meetings in an effort to find a compromise which would preserve his party's social programs without abandoning the goal of deficit reduction. The task force brought together Democrats from as far apart on the political spectrum as liberal Henry A. Waxman of California and conservative J. Marvin Leath of Texas. Finding common ground challenged Foley's consensus-building talents. "It would have been disastrous to rush out and have an up-or-down vote on the issue," Foley insisted. He became the leading proponent of the strategy ultimately followed: send the bill to conference with the Senate, thus buying time to analyze the measure, and come up with alternatives and changes to improve it. Waxman said he was persuaded by Foley's assessment. "He turned to us and said, 'We're going to get Gramm-Rudman. What kind of Gramm-Rudman is it going to be?' It was a clear statement of political reality and a convincing reason for us to work together."[44]

A larger House-Senate group of conferees was ultimately reduced to Foley, House Democratic Caucus Chairman Richard A. Gephardt of Missouri, Senate Budget Committee Chairman Pete V. Domenici of New Mexico, and Senate Finance Committee Chairman Bob Packwood of Oregon to work out the stickier compromises. Despite President Reagan's continued resistance to cuts in defense, half the automatic cuts would come from military spending and the other half from domestic discretionary funds that were not explicitly exempted. Social Security benefits, interest on the national debt, and eight programs favored by House Democrats: Supplemental Security Income, Medicaid, Aid to Families with Dependent Children, Women, Infants, and Children (WIC) program (a food program for impoverished women and children), Food Stamps, child nutrition, veterans' compensation, and veterans' pensions.[45]

> It was drafted with leaders from the Democratic House and the Republican Senate, much of it in my Whip's office. There was hardly any participation by House Republicans or by Senate Democrats. And the question I raised one time was whether we should involve them, the minorities in both houses. Senator Domenici, as I recall, suggested that Senate Democrats would, in his judgment, simply try to put political

obstacles in the path, and that the House Republicans weren't able to do anything except take orders from the White House. We were, in effect, the managing parties of the Congress. If we could work things out, that ought to be what was done, and the others would simply have to go along. Our involvement, from each party, would make it difficult for our partisan colleagues in either body to do much about it.

I thought it was a harsh comment, but the more I thought about it, the more I thought there was some element of truth in what he was saying. We both had a big stake in success. If the redrafted Gramm-Rudman program went down, there would be plenty of blame to go around. We had a big stake in seeing it succeed. Whereas the minority in each chamber, the Republicans in the House, and the Democrats in the Senate, had a bigger stake in frustrating the majority.

Majority Whip Foley helped orchestrate the agreement for which even liberal House Democrats voted. Indeed, the House alternative won the support of all but two Democrats. Some suggested the final legislation should have been called "Foley's law." But, as is the nature of compromise, what was a solution for some would continue to appear a suicide pact for others. It remained to be seen whether House Democrats' role in shaping the Gramm-Rudman-Hollings law would, in the end, be a political asset or a liability. Foley's view was that incumbents of both parties would share the praise—or blame—for Congress' performance on the budget that year. "Foley showed he could lead in a moment of crisis and pull together diverse elements of the party," said Representative Henry Waxman.[46] If President Reagan's 1981 economic policies were a "riverboat gamble," as Republican Senate Majority Leader Howard Baker of Tennessee had referred to them, the new plan "is Las Vegas and Reno put together," commented Democratic Representative Leon E. Panetta of California.[47] Although President Reagan's initial enthusiasm had been replaced by doubts when his advisers realized that the plan would now subject defense spending to potentially significant cuts, on December 12 Reagan signed into law the new, radical revision of budgeting procedures.

The status of the anti-deficit legislation was thrown into question by a July 7 Supreme Court ruling that struck down as unconstitutional the law's core provision, the role of the General Accounting Office (GAO) in triggering automatic spending cuts if Congress failed to meet the specified deficit targets. Since its creation in 1921, this congressional watchdog over how the executive branch agencies spend taxpayer dollars had become a critical auditing and investigating arm of Congress. Because Congress could remove the comptroller general of the GAO, the Court concluded the agency was too dependent on the legislative branch to play the role of reviewing and correcting the Office of Management and Budget (OMB)-Congressional Budget Office projections and then making its recommendation to the President on mandatory cuts.[48] In response to the

Court's decision, Congress passed separate legislation making the cuts according to the OMB.

While the general floor debate during the Reagan-O'Neill years had become more partisan and more democratic in the sense that even the most junior members could participate, beneath the surface the key fiscal bills that kept government operating involved much less partisanship and more oligarchic decision-making by key committees. The Appropriations Committee wrote the continuing resolution which funded all programs for which regular appropriations had not been passed. Under leadership auspices, the Budget Committee initiated the blueprint outline for spending and taxing authority. The Energy and Commerce Committee had a wide reach for much of the spending, and the Ways and Means Committee not only wrote tax bills but was key to the reconciliation process.

Another Compromise and a Change in Leadership

In another almost equally complicated final-hour compromise during the 99th Congress, Foley and Republican Senator Robert Dole of Kansas, who had replaced Tennessee's Howard Baker, who had retired as Majority Leader at the end of 1985 when the new 99th Congress was restored to a Democratic majority, managed to work out an impasse-breaking compromise on farmers' income subsidies for the 1985 farm program. The impasse had threatened to derail an omnibus, five-year farm bill dealing with commodity price supports, soil conservation, nutrition, farm exports, and farm credit. The compromise appeared to give both Democrats and Republicans a partial claim to victory.

Both Foley and Dole, each with strong ties to agriculture, feared that the farming sector's political influence was on the wane. The U.S. had been experiencing rapid declines in the farming population and in agriculture's once substantial contributions to the gross national product and the balance of trade. In addition, the ballooning cost of farm programs had been accompanied by the government's seemingly chronic failure to manage the agricultural economy. Foley's role in working out a compromise with Dole was in keeping with the open and consistent bipartisan approach. "He is trusted [by many Republicans] because he seems in his present role to be less political, until he needs to be, than the others" in the Democratic leadership, observed Republican Representative Sid Morrison of Washington.[49]

Bob Dole was elected to the House in 1960, about four years before I was. When I first was assigned to the Agriculture Committee in the House, he was already one of the ranking members on the Republican side. He was a formidable spokesman and a tough and effective legislator. He won my respect. We often had similar interests because we both came from important wheat-growing states. Bob also took a sincere and important interest in nutrition programs with which I had always been associated. I disputed the liberal skeptics who often put this down to the fact he represented an agricultural state, because like most wheat farmers, Kansas wheat farmers were not particularly enamored of the Food Stamp or WIC programs. His support was powerful and genuine.

Later on, when I became Chairman of the Agriculture Committee, and as Whip continued as Vice Chairman, I enjoyed working on agricultural bills with Bob Dole. By this time he was the ranking Republican on the Senate Agriculture Committee and an even more seasoned legislative strategist and leader. As he claimed later in the 1996 presidential race, his word given, was always good. Although he was not perhaps the best presidential campaigner, he would, in my view, have made a very good President. Naturally I was a strong supporter of Bill Clinton's, but I was proud and pleased when President Clinton awarded Bob the Medal of Freedom—as I had been with the earlier award to the former House Republican Leader Bob Michel.

As 1985 ended, Speaker O'Neill announced that he would retire in 1987 after ten consecutive years as Speaker. The announcement produced a ripple effect throughout the House Democratic leadership. Majority Leader Jim Wright had enough support to win the Speakership. But he would confront a restless generation of junior Democrats. With Richard A. Gephardt of Missouri and Tony Coelho of California at the forefront, the group focused on the need for a new leadership image. Junior Democrats had grown weary of running for reelection in the face of the Republican political ads which characterized Speaker O'Neill as "a cigar-smoking party hack."

With Wright becoming Speaker, the position of Majority Leader was open. Close congressional colleagues indicated Foley had to be "jump-started" to run for the post, but he ended up talking with every House Democrat to make clear that he wanted to become Majority Leader. By mid-1985 no other serious contenders had emerged. He was ultimately elected by acclamation. He brought with him twenty years of congressional experience, twelve in a committee chair or leadership post.

During the O'Neill Speakership, Foley had continued to emerge as a gradualist, skeptical of grand schemes and inclined at times to ask whether difficult problems could be solved legislatively at all. As he said of the farm bill he helped craft, "there is only so much that government policy can do. An agriculture bill can't turn around world economic decisions."[50] A major policy priority for Foley was to make sure that legislation didn't create more problems than it solved— "first do no harm." It was an open question as to whether this was too temperate an approach for a Majority Leader who would have to lead a younger generation of policy entrepreneurs.

CHAPTER FIVE

Majority Leader

*Nobody wants to make this place a blender of political mush. But the question is
whether or not you are going to try to find a way to approach problems of national
concern with a common effort.*

—Thomas S. Foley, 1989

Electing a Representative and a New Majority Leader

A S FOLEY SOUGHT REELECTION to his twelfth term in 1986, Fifth District voters realized they would be electing or defeating both their incumbent
member of Congress and the likely new Majority Leader of the House of Representatives. In addition to the familiar charge of Foley being the "big spender tied
to East Coast liberals," Republican opponent Floyd Wakefield loosed a volley of
more topical issues which separated the two candidates in their debates. Other
than agreeing that the communist movement and the Soviet Union were a threat
to world peace, they had little in common. Close off the border with Mexico,
break relations with Nicaragua, and buy American rather than trade abroad asserted Wakefield. Help Mexico out of its debt with trade not aid and prosecute
anyone who breaks the law by supplying covert aid to the Nicaraguan Contras,
responded Foley. To recommend abandoning foreign trade was "shocking" when
eastern Washington depended on wheat exports, he added.[1]

Wakefield suggested that with Foley's leadership influence he should have
done more to prevent the listing of the Fifth District's Hanford Nuclear Reservation as a possible nuclear waste dump. It was a delicate issue that might have
caught had not Congress passed an appropriations bill that restricted drilling at
Hanford. Although Foley was not on the House-Senate conference committee,
"he was credited with some behind the scenes lobbying" on behalf of the bill
Another local twist emerged with Wakefield's tender that, to trim the federal
budget, Congress should cut waste and fraud by rigorously following the

recommendations of the Grace Commission. Foley pointed out that the commission called for the sale of the Bonneville Power Administration, which would result in higher electric rates for many Washington customers.[2]

The Grace Commission, established by President Reagan, attempted to identify inefficiency, mismanagement, and "wasteful" spending in the federal government. Under the chairmanship of J. Peter Grace, the forty-seven volume report issued in 1984 contained 2,478 recommendations. One recommendation, not implemented, would have required the five federal power-marketing administrations, including Bonneville, to repay federal investments at market interest rates and to charge water user fees.[3]

"Ever since his election to the U.S. House as a bright young lawyer in 1964," wrote *The Spokesman-Review* editors in their endorsement, "Foley has fought the district's battles in Congress, bringing home needed federal appropriations for such things as the strengthening and survival of Fairchild Air Force Base as well as reflecting his district's fiscal conservatism by working intelligently to trim the federal budget—which does not come with a line item labeled 'waste and fraud,' as many of his unsuccessful challengers over the years seemed to think." His key role in improving provisions of the Gramm-Rudman deficit-control act, despite its shortcomings, had prodded Congress to enact a fiscal 1987 budget that actually shrunk, in real dollars, for the first time in thirty-one years.

"Granted, it is possible to dig up congressional votes for which Foley can be criticized; that is inevitable for someone who does the best he can and then supports political realities rather than holding out for impossible dreams. Indeed, it is essential to criticize Foley, and we have," the editors wrote. "His greatest challenge, now that his considerable talents are about to propel him to House majority leader . . . is to remain responsive to the needs of his district. We believe he can meet that challenge. He certainly has in the past."

". . . . Foley gives Eastern Washington a powerful voice at the highest levels of national government. When his constituents need something, he can deliver," the editorial added. As it had in its previous endorsements, *The Spokesman-Review* put a major emphasis on Foley's bipartisan efforts noting that "in the last few days, Washington's two Republican senators have reported to us that Democrat Foley not only used his clout to support their limits on Hanford nuclear repository research, but he also got House-Senate budget conferees to fortify those limits in the final budget."[4]

Foley didn't shy away from the perceived potential conflict between his role of serving as the number two person in the Democratic House leadership and his role of representing his constituents.

> I don't intend to check my personal views, or certainly my district's interests, or anything else at the door when I become majority leader . . .
> I would make it clear I am speaking from the standpoint of the Fifth

District or the Northwest or from my personal viewpoint. . . . But I intend to stay very close to the agricultural problems of our region and the country, and I think I'm going to be in an enhanced position as majority leader.[5]

While Foley was trouncing Floyd Wakefield, Washington voters were ousting senior Republican Senator Slade Gorton in favor of Democratic challenger Brock Adams. The 1986 mid-term congressional elections returned the Democrats to the majority in the Senate with a 55-45 margin thus ending the Republican six-year rule. But Foley said he didn't read the national results as a signal from American voters to be more combative with President Reagan. "I believe the public expects Congress to cooperate with the president, not to take a confrontational approach."[6]

The Legacy of Divided Congresses

The previous three divided congresses (1980-86) had failed to end the federal deficit, but there had been notable achievements under the Reagan administration, including reinforcement of the failing Social Security system and a revision of the nation's tax code and immigration laws. Divided control of Congress had generated a new set of leaders, particularly Senate Republicans. An effort at successful bipartisan public policy resulted. Senate Republicans stood in stark contrast to the increasingly irritable House Republicans, exasperated with their minority status. The past four House elections had brought in junior Republicans impatient for power and suspicious of what they viewed as an arrogant Democratic majority.

The junior Republicans had been using the C-SPAN broadcasts of the "special orders" period at the conclusion of floor business to publicize their conservative agenda. They usually spoke in front of an empty chamber. On May 8, 1984, Representative Newt Gingrich of Georgia and Robert S. Walker of Pennsylvania were criticizing foreign policy statements made by about fifty Democrats over the past fifteen years. When the camera focused on Gingrich, who paused periodically as if to give his targets a chance to respond, it gave the appearance that the Democrats had no rejoinder. On May 10, Speaker Tip O'Neill retaliated by ordering the cameras to pan the empty chamber. In defending his action, the Speaker thundered that, "it is the lowest thing I have ever seen in my thirty-two years in Congress." His use of "lowest" was ruled out of order and stricken from the record for its lack of comity. Gingrich was ecstatic over the publicity the Speaker's reaction had produced. "The minute Tip O'Neill attacked me, he and I got ninety seconds at the close of all three network news shows," Gingrich was reported to have told a group of conservative activists.[7]

Bracketed Between Partisans

Jim Wright became Speaker in 1987 with the aim of developing a Democratic Caucus consensus on a specific legislative agenda to deal with such difficult issues as trade legislation, "workfare" requiring recipients of such programs as Food Stamps to hold a job, and campaign finance reform. He gave the kind of forceful leadership that many in the Democratic Caucus had sought and, judged on the standard of an aggressive legislative program, he succeeded in leading what most considered a highly productive 100th Congress. Unlike Speaker O'Neill, who managed to keep peace with the congressional "barons," Speaker Wright didn't wait for House committee chairmen to come up with an agenda. He imposed one. The contrasting styles between the two speakers was not lost on Foley.

New Republic writer and television pundit Fred Barnes observed that, "O'Neill made himself popular as a liberal foil for Reagan, but his record was abysmal. Reagan cut taxes, slowed domestic spending, dramatically increased Pentagon spending, and funded *contra* military operations—all on O'Neill's watch. On Wright's, Reagan got nothing but liberal bills he didn't like." Spending for the homeless, plant closing legislation, the Civil Rights Restoration Act, arms control amendments, and the budget summit were examples.[8]

> Jim was very activist in terms of the Speakership. I think he viewed the Speakership as being something he remembered from the Sam Rayburn legacy. There ought to be decisions from the top, there ought to be direction from the top, there ought to be organization from the top, there ought to be follow-through and obedience. And that was expressed and demonstrated by the legislative agenda which was accomplished, not only as a pledge of that leadership, but as the product of it. And the "trophies on the hunting lodge walls" were the legislative acts.
>
> Another aspect of Jim's Speakership was his grounding in the Public Works Committee: "We do things." I remember one time, with almost a reaction of consternation, Jim told a group of us that "you know, these criticisms about taxing and spending, you know when you think about it, the whole purpose of government is to tax and to spend." Our reaction was "please Mr. Speaker, don't say that outside this room."

Jim Wright pressed to the limits his control over the Rules Committee to structure floor consideration so as to ensure that Democratic bills would not be threatened by disabling Republican amendments, particularly those emanating from the far right and intended more to embarrass Democrats than to improve legislation. The legacy of Republican resentment against Wright's majority use of the Rules Committee was not quickly forgotten and would emerge again during Foley's Speakership.

Tactically, Speaker Wright's approach was in stark contrast to the days of Speaker Rayburn and Republican Leader Joe Martin of Massachusetts, who preferred brokering agreements to find common ground. Wright negotiated very little with the Republican leadership. Intent upon laying the basis for unity within his own party, he refused to risk jeopardizing a Democratic consensus "by trucking with the Republicans."[9] More than any recent Speaker, Wright used the full powers of his office to systematically pass his own legislative agenda. Although it was a Democratic consensus agenda, the tactics were more personal and less a reflection of the combined leadership.

> The perception often, rightly or wrongly, was that you would get very little help from the Republicans. On things like budgets, for example, they would "talk a good game," but, when it came right down to it, the Budget Committee would split along party lines regardless of what [Chairman] Jim Jones or other members might want. The Republicans were enough of an entrenched and somewhat angry, if not embittered, minority to ensure that a bipartisan policy would not work unless it was very forthcoming and generous. And at that point you had the problem of creating a split in the Democratic Caucus. If you start to move so far into Republican territory that you attract the enthusiastic applause of the Conservative Democratic Forum, and the Democratic Mainstream people are cheering, and complimenting you, and saying this is the direction the party ought to go, it's almost inevitable that you're going to go from annoyance to white hot anger on the progressive, liberal side. Once you've got legislation being passed by a bare majority, or perhaps even a minority of Democrats, and a larger and larger plurality of Republicans, the more the Democratic Party is vulnerable to being seriously fractured. That outcome, on a sustained basis, would inevitably produce a challenge to the leadership, further deeply dividing the party.

Wright was an old-fashioned FDR Democrat who believed in federal spending at home and abroad, but especially at home. Constituents of his north central Texas Twelfth Congressional District, including Fort Worth and most of surrounding Tarrant County, had no doubt as to his value. During fiscal year 1986, Wright delivered more than $5.5 billion in federal funds to Tarrant County. On a per capita basis, the figure topped the nation at $5,481.[10] His record as Speaker of the 100th Congress was substantial. Early in the session the House passed a clean water bill and a highway bill over President Reagan's veto. It also passed a new trade bill, thirteen appropriations bills, legislation dealing with the homeless, catastrophic health insurance, and farm credit. And the House effectively took over foreign policy toward the Nicaraguan Contras, with U.S. support ending in 1988. But in much of this Speaker Wright was a better talker than a listener, frequently making major decisions almost alone, and occasionally impetuously.

At times, Wright pushed too hard. On October 24, 1987, five days after October 19th's "Black Monday" international stock market crash, the Budget Committee brought to the floor a reconciliation bill that included $12.8 billion in new taxes and a controversial welfare reform package. Wright and the Democratic leadership, while at the White House to discuss the stock market, learned that a coalition of Democrats and Republicans had defeated the bill and blocked further consideration. Wright reconvened the Rules Committee and brought the reconciliation bill back to the floor without the welfare provisions. However, the standing rules of the House posed an obstacle. Rules passed by the Rules Committee were required to lay over for one legislative day before being considered on the floor. Undaunted, Wright adjourned the House and reconvened it for the legislative day of October 30 on October 29. While this enabled him to win passage of the rule by 238-182, final passage appeared destined for defeat by 205-206 margin. The Speaker held the vote open long enough to persuade Democratic Representative Jim Chapman of Texas to switch his vote to insure passage. A victory, but did it cause a fissure with the Republicans unlikely to easily heal?

> Yes, that's my impression. There was a point at which Dan Lungren [Republican Representative from California] rushed up to the podium looking as if he were going to assault the Speaker. John Bryant [Democratic Representative from Texas] and a couple of others posed themselves between Lungren and the top tier of the Speaker's dais. Lungren and Bryant looked as though they were on the verge of exchanging blows. There was a physical fury that I hadn't really seen before in the House. Dick Cheney [Republican Representative from Wyoming], the Republican Whip, stalked across the floor and said, "This is just totally unacceptable. This is absolute bull shit. It's absolute bull shit," and stalked off. . . . It was pretty much the Speaker's decision. Some of us had expressed serious concerns about how it would be viewed by the Republicans, but he wasn't hearing it. The bill was going to pass, "it was going to goddamn pass." He was in that sort of mood.

In May 1988, the Republican leadership took to the floor of the House *en masse* under a special order to address what they viewed as the abusive practices of the Democratic leadership. Republican Leader Bob Michel, a man slow to anger, sputtered "in rage about Wright in Republican strategy meetings."[11] That was, however, only one side of the coin. Somewhere there was a delicate balance between being fair with the minority and protecting majority members from harassing or dilatory tactics.

> From a majority viewpoint, there is the risk that legislation, which you consider very important, will be so contorted by amendments, cleverly written to insert poison pills and other disabling provisions, that it would be, in effect, a defeat. Increasingly the argument was made that

leadership has the responsibility to produce legislation that is in accordance with the leadership's program. We have the Rules Committee and the tools of limited and restrictive rules, and we need to use them. The majority is not helpless and impotent. You can do things, and because you have the power, you have the responsibility. Maybe the Senate doesn't have the power. Maybe it can't invoke cloture and the filibuster will succeed and has to be recognized as being a successful delaying or obstructing tactic. But in the House we can overcome a minority if we have the votes. However much they may resist it, there are times when we must do that, and to voluntarily restrain ourselves in the interest of inter-party comity is to fail in our responsibility to our own members and our program.

As an interesting footnote, I noted that Representative Gingrich, as Republican Whip, constantly made the point, even while complaining about "abusive tactics," that "of course the majority must rule." "We don't expect that you will allow the ship to sink. We don't like what you're doing. We object to it. We think it's against comity and tradition in many cases. But we understand that our objections are going to be overruled if you think it's necessary in order to see that the will of the majority is achieved."

Having said that, it's important that the gain be worth the candle. In other words, the issue has to be significant and central to the majority, in this case the Democratic Party program. It should count for something as opposed to being simply a routine bill, and the tactics should, to some extent, be sensitive to the minority's reaction. When accommodations, which are not critical, can be made to the minority, they should be made. A totally bullying tactic of driving legislation through in every case, and at any cost, eventually leads to a total disruption of comity and the breakdown of all legislative process.

Surviving as Speaker did not require consistent legislative victories, but it did require the ability to be effective even when losing. Speaker O'Neill could fall back on the personal affection of members in adverse times. This was less true for Speaker Wright, but as long as things were going well, he could count on caucus support. It became more questionable when things weren't going well, as in the case of his emerging ethics problems. Foley was criticized by some in the press for misplaced loyalty to the Speaker during his ethics travails and for publicly justifying the hardball procedural tactics Wright used to pass the budget reconciliation bill. Foley had indicated the Speaker did not violate House rules, but could he have also said. . . .

That it was wise and prudent? I wasn't asked that question. But if I had been asked that question, I would probably have said it was wise and prudent. To some extent, a certain amount of public posturing is required in a political system. It isn't given to subordinates to publicly question the position of leaders. If you can't do that job, then get out of the way and let somebody else who's less scrupulous do it, or less sensitive to it. This isn't being dishonest or disingenuous. If the press says, "Do you think, Mr. Majority Leader, that it was wise for the Speaker to do this? and does he have your support?" If your response is, "the answer to both questions is no." The next question is, "are you going to resign as Majority Leader? And if not, why not?"

The number three man in the leadership, Majority Whip Tony Coelho, had emerged as the head of the Democratic Congressional Campaign Committee for the 1982 congressional campaign, appointed in 1981 after entering Congress in 1979. He would later be credited as being "the father of modern campaign financing." In 1981 the Republican Party had a huge money advantage and sought to get all the business Political Action Committees (PACs) to work together to support only Republicans and produce a Republican House. Coelho had turned the Republicans' advantage upside down. Because of "his record-breaking fund-raising efforts as chairman of the Democratic Congressional Campaign Committee," noted a *Time* magazine senior writer, "he is fairly credited by many in Congress with the Democratic lock on the House."[12]

Foley was the only leader of House Democrats who could work productively with Senate Republicans, Wright and Coelho being seen as beyond reach. "Tony Coelho is the most partisan man in either body," Wyoming's Republican Senator Alan Simpson said, "but the real Tartar is Jim Wright." "Foley has not been tagged as someone who carries with him the party of the past," noted Democratic Representative Leon E. Panetta of California. "He bridges the gap between Wright and his supporters and the younger members in the party who are looking for some change of direction."[13]

The "Budget Summit" of 1987

On October 19, 1987, "Black Monday," the world's major security exchanges took a historic plunge. On October 28th, congressional leaders met with Treasury Secretary James Baker III and White House Chief of Staff Howard Baker, Jr. The upshot was a budget summit over which Foley presided. The sessions were often acrimonious, in part reflecting the increasingly bitter relations between Speaker Wright and President Reagan. Although there were frequently more than twenty people in the room, in the end it was Foley and the "two Bakers" who pushed a compromise to cut more than $33 billion from the fiscal 1988 budget deficit and $43 billion the following year while raising taxes by $20 billion for those two years. No one had come to the table prepared initially to compromise—it was a matter of hearing all the alternatives, allowing them to be "savaged" by their opponents, and then seeking last-minute common ground.

The summit had no legal status and it was difficult for congressional leaders who attended to deliver their rank and file colleagues when it came time to vote on the package. In the House a good many Democrats thought their leaders had given too much to Reagan, while conservative Republicans were predictably bitter that the President had robbed them of their status as the party that traditionally opposed new taxes. Yet, according to Republican Senator Warren Rudman of New Hampshire, a pragmatic deficit-hawk with few peers, "this agreement was the high point of serious deficit-fighting in the 1980s . . . it proved that Congress and the president could reduce the deficit if they wanted to."[14] On December 22, 1987, President Reagan signed into law the reconciliation measure that emerged from the "budget summit."

The '87 summit was a result of a substantial market fall and a belief that if we were to avoid another perhaps catastrophic fall in the market, dramatic efforts had to be made to reduce the budget deficit. It was agreed to, rather reluctantly, by Speaker Jim Wright, who was fearful that the White House would lead us down the primrose paths of tax decreases as well as spending cuts, and that what came out of it would be philosophically unacceptable.

For a variety of reasons, I was asked to be chairman, by agreement among the White House and House and Senate leadership. I think the White House had the view that I was more acceptable than others, perhaps less partisan than others, perhaps they thought that I was more able to be manipulated than others, I don't know what their thoughts were, and I chaired the meetings day after day in the Capitol, alternatively in the House and Senate side.

There was an uncomfortable period of intense discussion, argument, and debate under a rubric which said "nothing is decided until everything is decided." It seemed to me that it was the only possible way to proceed, and there wasn't much objection to it as a principle. Nobody was willing to let one side or the other "tuck away in their knapsack" some favored concession, and then be hard-rock on the rest of the agenda. . . . So the general approach was that we'll talk about everything, we'll make some tentative decisions, but until we decide on everything, none of the tentative decisions has any final validity.

It seemed to me that in that circumstance, the easy things would be done first, the harder things would be kept selectively until the end, and the hardest things until the very end, and nothing would be finally achieved if we didn't have a sense of crisis. As long as there was some time to talk, as long as there was some ability to go on, delay in the final result was the tactic of both sides. And that was exactly the way it happened. It finally came about after many weeks.

There were several crises along the way. From the House side, the Speaker would be told by members of the Ways and Means Committee what a disaster it was and how this and that was terrible. And particularly, Jim Wright was being told by [House Ways and Means Committee chairman] Danny Rostenkowski, I don't think with intentional desire to bring down an agreement, who would explode at the idea, fundamentally irritable to him, that this summit should exist at all, and that it should deign to decide what taxes would be levied, and what Ways and Means Committee business would be interfered with. He unloaded on the Speaker on two or three occasions and Jim was, from time to time, somewhat excitable, and he would call me up, and call me in, and in Rostenkowski's presence or otherwise, announce his intention to go down and take over the summit and shut it down. I would have to plead with him not to do that, to give me a couple more days, and that nothing would be done without his being fully informed and without his acquiescence.

But he didn't like it any more than Rostenkowski. It seemed to him that the House of Representatives, in its sovereign right, was being bargained away by the administration positioning itself at the heart of the legislative process, participating with us, and so on. Meanwhile, Jim Baker would draw me aside and, in a very skilled way, I think with some truth, but also with much skill, tell me how much help he needed persuading a very reluctant President to go along with this process, chafing at the bit to close the summit down, to declare it a failure, and so forth, and urging me to give some concession here or there in order to sweeten the pot from the President's standpoint.

From all sides, the lack of enthusiasm for the endeavor was frequently palpable, but I could never see a better alternative on the horizon.

In other 100th Congress legislative action, in keeping with his own district's and Washington state's heavy dependence on exports, Foley joined Reagan in opposing Representative Richard Gephardt's amendment to the Omnibus Trade Bill. The amendment would have imposed tariffs or quotas if agreement could not be reached on lowering the trade surpluses with U.S. trading partners. It passed 218-214. But Foley opposed the President on his veto of the Civil Rights Restoration Act (passed 292-133 with 284 required to override), and opposed the Reagan-sponsored mandated death penalty for individuals convicted of drug-related murders.

The 1988 Elections: Transition to a New Republican President

By the time Democrats were gearing up to select a presidential candidate to oppose Republican Vice President George Bush, Foley had emerged as a key figure on foreign-policy and budget matters. As Majority Leader, he had served on the Permanent Select Committee on Intelligence, the Committee on the Budget, the Select Committee to Investigate Covert Arms Transactions with Iran, and chaired the Geneva Arms Talks Observer Team. His standing in Congress was such that he had been voted "the most respected member of Congress" in 1988, and would be again in 1989.

Robert S. Strauss, former Democratic National Committee chairman, had stated several years earlier that "there's no one in America, Republican or Democrat, more qualified for the Presidency than Tom Foley."[15] Foley was among those that Massachusetts Governor Michael Dukakis, the Democratic presidential candidate, considered for his running mate, but Foley withdrew his name before Dukakis made his final decision. Maybe he had been inoculated by working on two unsuccessful Scoop Jackson presidential campaigns in 1972 and 1976, or maybe he had simply observed too many campaigns. Foley lacked the "fire in the belly" for presidential politics. "To run for President, you have to have an enormous passion. You have to want it with a compelling urgency. You have to be prepared to sacrifice all kinds of things—financial security, your privacy, family well-being—on the altar of that desire, and even then the odds will usually be profoundly against you." His reservations went beyond the office to the presidential selection process itself. "I think the way we choose Presidents has terrible flaws. I know of any number of people who I think would make good Presidents, even great Presidents, who are deterred from running by the torture candidates are obliged to put themselves through."

Foley did play a role as a Dukakis adviser during the campaign and emerged outraged at the way the Republicans managed to corner the market on cultural issues such as patriotism and the flag: "It's dreadful that we let them take over the symbols of tradition." In the 1970s, Foley recalled, Representative Allard Lowenstein, a liberal New York Democrat, showed up on the House floor with a flag button in his lapel—a symbol up to that point used by conservative Republicans. Asked why he was wearing it, Congressman Lowenstein answered, "It's my flag too."[16]

To combat the effect of Republican harping on "wedge" issues such as patriotism and school prayer, Foley had unsuccessfully advised Dukakis to adopt a counter symbol by beginning every campaign event with a Pledge of Allegiance to the flag. Foley disliked cultural "wedge" issues. However, he recognized that as a politician you dismissed them at your peril. When the new Congress convened in 1989, the House opened each legislative session with the Pledge of Allegiance.

Running for reelection to his thirteenth term in 1988, Foley faced political newcomer Marlyn Derby, a nurse who had been active in local anti-abortion protests. Waging a low-key campaign and shunning debates—in contrast with a number of her predecessors—she "appeared to be faring no better than some of

Foley's recent opponents," reported *The Spokesman-Review,* "perhaps because she used some of the same tactics." She accused Foley of being a liberal in conservative's clothing and saying one thing in his eastern Washington district but doing another when he went to Washington, D.C. Foley responded that his voting record was an open book. "I think I cast votes that represent the viewpoints of my constituents," he said.[17]

"Once again, U.S. Rep. Thomas S. Foley is facing a challenger who is sounding what has become a familiar theme in Eastern Washington's 5th Congressional District: time for a change," wrote *The Spokesman-Review* editors in their endorsement. "But there's a more compelling argument: Don't mess with success." There was appreciation for the now traditional portrait of Foley as "a skilled, behind-the-scenes consensus builder who has earned the confidence and support of colleagues from both political parties" as chairman of the 1987 deficit-reduction talks and "the person in Democratic leadership" with whom Reagan White House officials could work.

But the portrait had grown. Internationally, Foley had emerged as the one Northwest leader capable of putting in a plug for agricultural products with Japanese Prime Minister Noboru Takeshita. It was also "thanks in large part to Foley" that the district had secured federal funding for a study of thyroid disease among eastern Washington residents exposed to radiation from the Hanford nuclear reservation during the Cold War, for block grants for housing in Spokane County, for construction of the Washington-Idaho Centennial Trail, and for the survival school at Fairchild Air Force Base. With the country to be under new presidential leadership, Foley's "more than two decades in the House is irreplaceable."[18] "I think the spirit of constructive cooperation is what the country expects," Foley said in what had become almost a post-election mantra. "The country expects that the election will be put behind us."[19]

After the votes were counted, the 101st Congress was Democratic with a new Republican President. Such "divided government" had prevailed for more than thirty of the preceding fifty years. But "control" was a word to use with caution in reference to Congress. Over the past few decades the 535 members of Congress had increasingly become independent political actors, with their own political bases, responsible to their own particular constituencies, possessed of their own political philosophies and instincts.

A Republican President, a Democratic Congress, and the Instinct for Bipartisanship

Many Democrats, still bitter over what they viewed as George Bush's negative 1988 presidential campaign, saw an array of problems with "Reagan's chickens coming home to roost" and asked why they should oblige his successor. Other Democrats, starting with Foley, disagreed and were ready to meet the new administration halfway, at least to "hear them out."

More than hear them out. I mean, if we're going to have the permanent campaign, the last election produces resentments that are going to carry over the years of a Congress or a presidential term, and then we have a new campaign, with new resentments, with new "pay backs," with new opportunities for political revenge, it just never ends. We don't have the natural unifying elements of a British-style parliamentary system with highly leveraged coalitions where somebody wins, and somebody loses, and, theoretically, government can function.

Although he found Bush's campaign excesses troubling, Foley liked and respected the man.

President Bush had come out of the shadow of loyalty and responsibility to others and become his own person in a political sense as well as in every other sense. He was a moderate and well-intentioned person who was creating a sense of confidence, or at least hope, that he would develop a relationship with the Democratic Congress.

In campaigns, you do whatever you can to advantage your party and the candidates of your party, within reason and within the rules of laws and ethics. But, when the election is over, I think then the task is to try to find out how to take the judgment of the public, and the decision of the public, and make it work effectively to govern the country. It's important to find opportunities for cooperation when there's a divided responsibility which the public has decided to elect and select, as they have much of the time during the period since the end of World War II.

The Fall of Speaker Wright

In December 1987, Republican Representative Newt Gingrich of Georgia announced plans to file an ethics complaint against Speaker Jim Wright. "The House has never before had to deal with allegations of unethical conduct at the Speaker's level," he said. "Since the Speaker is the most powerful member of the House, it is especially difficult to investigate him." Gingrich filed his complaint on May 26, 1988.[20]

What might have been easy to discount as partisan bomb-throwing gained more credibility when the largely liberal watchdog organization Common Cause joined Gingrich in a surprising alliance by calling for an investigation of the Speaker. By June the House Committee on Standards of Official Conduct, or Ethics Committee, unanimously voted to open a preliminary inquiry into six allegations. The charges centered around Wright's questionable investments in Texas oil and gas companies for whom the Speaker allegedly lobbied; his purported exercise of "undue influence" with officials of the Federal Home Loan Bank Board on behalf of Texas savings and loan banks; improper acceptance of gifts from a business associate; and the assertion that the sale of his book *Reflections of a Public Man* was being used as a dodge to avoid congressional limits on speaking fees.[21]

Reflections of a Public Man was 117 pages of biographic reflections and po-etry running the gamut of Wright's boyhood through his congressional career. Although the list price was a modest $5.95, the publishing agreement provided that Wright would receive $3.25 (nearly 55 percent) on all retail sales. Such "royalty" payments were unheard of in the publishing industry. Morton Janklow, literary agent for Nancy Reagan, Senator Daniel P. Moynihan, and Danielle Steele, reported to Ethics Committee counsel Richard Phelan that the standard was 10 to 15 percent and that "no rational publisher would agree to a 55 percent royalty on list price because it could not make a profit." An additional focus was on the bulk sales of *Reflections* to trade associations and other groups who had invited Wright to speak. His staff was alleged to have suggested to such groups that, rather than pay him an honorarium, they could purchase books for the same amount.[22]

Although the 100th Congress had adjourned in October 1988 with the closed-door ethics inquiry still incomplete, the issue was a scab that continued to be picked. Representative Vin Weber of Minnesota, an influential member of Gingrich's Conservative Opportunity Society, responded to a press query that "most Democrats clearly see their party would be better off with [Majority Leader] Tom Foley as Speaker. That's a powerful reality."[23] And, as House Re-publicans met in December 1988 to organize for the upcoming 101st Congress, Republican Leader Robert Michel seemed to strike an uncustomary confronta-tional tone when he suggested that he would support a Democratic challenger to Wright's reelection as Speaker.[24] Despite the goading, Democrats reelected Wright in January 1989 by the traditional party-line vote and there were still few who believed Jim Wright's hold on the Speakership was really at risk. Most Demo-crats remained confident he would be cleared of any serious ethics violation.

That confidence would soon be shaken. Early in 1989 the Quadrennial Commission, authorized in 1967 under a law designed to distance Congress from the risks of having to vote on their own salaries, had recommended, and President George Bush had endorsed, a 51 percent increase for top-level federal workers, federal judges, and members of Congress. The increase would have boosted congressional pay to $135,000 and would take effect automatically un-less Congress voted it down. There was an immediate surge in public outrage. Although the Democratic leadership closed ranks publicly in support, the press reported that Foley and Majority Whip Tony Coelho strongly disagreed with key Wright decisions on handling the issue, such as sending House members a con-fidential pay-raise survey which put them all in the position of having to indi-vidually tell their constituents where they stood on the pay raise. In the midst of the pay-raise imbroglio, "Foley for Speaker" buttons appeared on Capitol Hill distributed by a conservative youth group.[25]

Additional developments kept Wright's problems in the spotlight. Edward J. Rollins, newly hired executive director of the National Republican Congressional Committee, proclaimed in February that Wright and his ethics would be the "No. 1 target" of the 1990 congressional campaigns. "I'm going to force a lot of Democrats to stand up and defend [Wright]," he said. In response, Majority Leader Foley led a Democratic complaint that the GOP was trying to put partisan pressure on the Ethics Committee members.[26] Following President Bush's decision to nominate House Minority Whip Dick Cheney of Wyoming as Secretary of Defense, Newt Gingrich rode "on a wave of restlessness among younger [Republican] members—and on new prominence he has gained from having been the instigator of the current House ethics committee investigation of Speaker Wright"—was elected by a two-vote margin as the new Republican Whip. His campaign and election were expected to further polarize the House with its message that the existing Republican leadership had been too conciliatory with the Democrats and needed an infusion of energy and activism.[27]

By March 1989, the Speaker backed off his earlier claim of complete innocence and now suggested that he might have been guilty of bad judgment or unintentional technical violations. By spring 1989 the case had "plunged the House of Representatives into a state of disarray and malaise that veteran members say is unmatched in recent memory . . . the business of lawmaking has become uninspired at worst, distracted at best. And collegiality and respect among members continues to deteriorate."[28]

If some of this appeared largely as flak swirling around Speaker Wright, his case was dealt a substantive blow in April when two Democrats, Representatives Chester G. Atkins of Massachusetts and Bernard J. Dwyer of New Jersey, joined the six Republicans on the Ethics Committee to find Wright in violation of some House rules. After spending 10 months and $2 million on the inquiry, the committee had ended up focusing on the two areas of whether his book had been used as a vehicle to circumvent limits on outside income, and whether he and his wife had been improperly enriched by gifts from Texas developer George Mallick, a long-time friend and business associate.[29] Although the charges had not yet been proven, the Ethics Committee was now entering a trial-like phase known as a disciplinary hearing in which it would have to find "clear and convincing evidence" that rules had been violated. Only then would the committee consider what, if any, punishment it would impose upon Wright.

Foley remained an unswerving Wright supporter and on an April joint appearance with Gingrich on NBC's "Meet the Press," Foley challenged the Georgian's renewed prediction that "Mr. Foley is going to be Speaker by June." Foley said,

> I am confident he's [Wright] going to be cleared of violating any House rules and he will remain the Speaker of the House. . . . We're not

looking at a criminal charge against him. We're looking at allegations brought by Mr. Gingrich which I think are based on political efforts to vilify the leadership in the Democratic Party for a political purpose.[30]

Foley's denials aside, it was inevitable that, as embattled Speaker Wright's prospects for survival seemed to dim by the day, speculation should focus on a possible transition in the Speakership. Following press reports that Wright might step down, the National Republican Congressional Committee released a package of newspaper clippings questioning the finances of House Majority Whip Tony Coelho of California. "We may focus on him as hard as on Wright," one senior Republican said. "But Foley surely won't be a target." And even before it amounted to anything more than speculation, "some of his colleagues had slipped comfortably into talking about 'Speaker Foley.'" In the midst of the turmoil, one truth had become evident. Speaker Wright's style of "hardball pursuit of legislative victory had bred mistrust among Republicans and bruised some of his own Democrats, draining his reservoir of support in his hour of political need."[31]

While some Democrats reportedly feared that Foley's style lacked political toughness and would blur party distinctions, others were said to feel that it was just what the House needed after such a traumatic and divisive experience.

For Foley, a political navigator who was as cautious as Wright was impetuous, the circumstances could hardly have been more uncomfortable. He was a loyalist forced to witness a public weighing of his and Speaker Wright's relative merits. If Wright was a Speaker who believed that the biggest mistake was made when people thought too small, Foley conserved power like a judge and believed the biggest mistake was to act impetuously. If opportunities were sometimes lost, mistakes were avoided. Foley's political Hippocratic oath was "first, do no harm." One was a fighter, the other a healer. But Foley's preference would clearly have been to succeed a retired, not a fallen leader. That would have been the "regular order" of the House, and regular order was something in which he had always put considerable store.

CHAPTER SIX

🏛

Into the Maelstrom:
The Speakership

If all you want is a daily partisan battle, and are not interested in getting anything more than the political embarrassment of the opposition, that's not me.
—Thomas S. Foley, 1989

The Resignation of Speaker Wright

GLORIA BORGER WROTE in *U.S. News and World Report:*

> On the very day it became clear that Thomas Stephen Foley would soon be elevated to the pinnacle of his career as Speaker of the House, he was oddly preoccupied. He had planned to fly to Washington State to deliver a eulogy for former Senator Warren Magnuson, even sending his dark-blue "funeral suit" to be pressed at lunch time for the evening trip. But after a series of private, solemn sessions with other House leaders about Jim Wright's fate, the majority leader was not so sure he should leave. Magnuson was someone he had respected, the leader of a state political dynasty. To cancel would be an offense and would also be a clue to reporters that Foley's ascension as Speaker was imminent, a message he did not want to send. "It would be prudent to go," offered colleague John Dingell. "It would also be prudent to remain." Foley decided to do both. He stayed in the Capitol for the evening, then caught a flight at dawn the next day. In Foleyesque fashion, the man who will be Speaker did the respectful thing for a past mentor. And until the very day Jim Wright announces his resignation, Foley will pay his colleague similar homage.[1]

I guess all of my political life I've been a "regular order" person. Going back to Henry Jackson, the most damning thing Scoop would say about somebody was that he was disloyal. The old phrase in Washington was that somebody had every characteristic of a dog, except loyalty. The idea of advancing yourself in relation to somebody to whom you owed responsibility or loyalty has always seemed to me to be an unforgivable political sin. Also, I think there is enormous disruption that occurs when personal ambition starts to overcome the standard process of succession and responsibility in the House. Seniority has the one great redeeming factor of calming those ambitions and channeling them into constructive cooperation rather than leading to the constant turmoil of advantage and opportunity.

So I wanted in every way to be supportive of Jim Wright. We were not particularly close personally, but he was the Speaker and I was the Majority Leader, and my job was to help him and support him. I tried to give him my best advice, and I refused to cooperate in any way with efforts to advance or even discuss the possibility of my succession. I was truly sorry when I felt that his own actions sometimes damaged his case such as those occasions when he went to the floor of the House and personally responded to critical newspaper or magazine articles thereby amplifying the controversy. I agreed with him, and the vast majority of Democrats, that the Republicans had organized their attack in a cynical and totally political way.

Any transition to a new Speaker would be extremely difficult. Not only were emotions bound to be at a fever pitch, but for many on my side of the aisle, particularly those closest to Jim, it was very difficult to accept any successor, and there was a sense of a lack of legitimacy that would be bound to taint anyone who followed the Wright Speakership when it ended as it had.

On May 31, 1989, the ethics issues which had been hanging over Speaker Wright for nearly two years came to closure when he became the first Speaker of the House to resign his office. He had served as Speaker for only twenty-nine months. In a one-hour speech on the House floor, Wright asked his colleagues of the 101st Congress to, "let me give you back this job . . . as a propitiation for this season of ill-will." For most Democrats, many of the sixty-nine violations in the April 17, 1989 House Ethics Committee report seemed almost trivial next to the level of Wright's achievements. The amounts he and his wife gained from royalties on his book *Reflections of a Public Man* and from his long-time business partner and benefactor, George Mallick, were not substantial. On the other hand, his defense, that he stayed inside the limits of the rules, was not frivolous, but was at least "pushing the envelope" and seemed to lack frankness. Wright's departure would leave the House boiling with the bitterest inter-party resentments in years but, as one reporter observed, "the consensus on both sides of the aisle" was likely to be like "a quiet snowfall after the firestorm of Wright's exit."[2]

"Have I been too partisan?" Wright asked his colleagues from the well of the House. "Too insistent? Too abrasive? Too determined to have my way? Perhaps. . . . (But) when vilification becomes an accepted form of political debate, when negative campaigning becomes a full-time occupation, when members of each party become self-appointed vigilantes carrying out personal vendettas against members of the other party, in God's name that is not what this institution is supposed to be all about. . . . All of us in both parties must resolve to bring this period of mindless cannibalism to an end."[3]

There was a feeling in the House that things had gotten impossibly tense and bitter. While there were members in both parties that desperately wanted to return to a more civil and cooperative environment, the general atmosphere was poisonous. There will always be sharp philosophical disputes and emotional debates, but the level of personal tension and conflict that existed at the end of Jim Wright's Speakership was unprecedented in my experience. Some members were deeply angry. There was a feeling on the Republican side that for years they had been unfairly treated as a minority, that they had been denied either consultation or respect, and seldom given even minimum accommodation. On the Democratic side, the attack on Jim Wright was seen as a thoroughly political maneuver engineered by elements of the House Republican Party in the most cynical and calculated way. It went beyond sacking the quarterback and became killing the quarterback. In fact, they had not proven any of their charges, but had succeeded in pressuring the appointment of an independent counsel whose expanded investigation led to charges which resulted in the eventual resignation of Jim Wright. Particularly among his broad cohort of strong personal friends and supporters, there was an irreconcilably bitter feeling toward Newt Gingrich.

When I became Speaker one of the first tasks was to calm the turbulent climate in the House. I pledged in my acceptance speech that I would be unerringly fair to all members and to protect the rights of all members. Every Speaker has that responsibility, but it's important not only to do it, but to appear to do it. Appearances are often more significant than the reality. For years it had been typical for the Speaker to call voice votes not necessarily for the loudest shout but for the position of the majority party. If a question was put, and the ayes were faint, and the noes were thunderous, the Speaker would often smile and say, "The ayes appear to have it, the ayes have it," if that was the majority position. This did not impose any great damage on the minority since on almost any question it was easy for them to obtain a quick division by standing or calling for a roll call recorded vote which would absolutely determine where the House stood. . . .

I remember, just a minor incident, right after I was sworn in as Speaker, I was presiding when a Democratic motion was offered. I got a little annoyed that the Democrats didn't make any effort to speak up. So, more out of pique with the Democrats than as a gesture to the Republicans, I called the voice vote in the Republicans' favor. Thankfully there were a few energized Democrats on the floor who called for a recorded vote which, being in the majority, we won. But it was interesting to me, the reaction on the Republican side. One by one they came up and, very seriously, complimented me and thanked me for treating them fairly.

Resignation of the Majority Whip and a Call for Civility

Even while Speaker Wright had been pondering his resignation decision, California's Tony Coelho, the energetic and gifted House Majority Whip, abruptly resigned in May 1989 and press reports suggested he had made a substantial undisclosed profit in junk bonds based on a sizable loan which amounted to an alleged gift.[4] His resignation prevented the prospect of another prolonged Republican-led attack on the Democratic leadership. And finally, in early June, House Democratic Caucus Chairman and number four in the leadership hierarchy, Representative William Gray of Pennsylvania, was the target of an apparent news leak suggesting that the Justice Department had begun a preliminary investigation into alleged staff/payroll padding. Although the charge proved to be groundless and elicited an apology from Attorney General Richard Thornburgh, one press report suggested that "if a body count were the measure of success, the Republicans would already have won the war."[5] The resignation of two of the top three Democratic leaders was no proof of the Gingrich Conservative Opportunity Society charge that the Democrats were a corrupt, liberal, welfare-state majority, but it did cast the Democrats and, to the extent most voters saw no ethical differences between Republicans and Democrats, the whole House under a growing pall that would not be easily dissipated.

Into this cauldron, after receiving Jim Wright's nomination for the Speakership in the Democratic Caucus, on June 6, 1989, Thomas Stephen Foley of Washington took over the gavel as the forty-ninth Speaker of the U.S. House of Representatives. He had been following Jim Wright in the Democratic leadership since 1981, when Speaker Thomas P. O'Neill, Jr. chose him, with Wright's assent, as Majority Whip. He won on a traditional party-line vote of 251 for Foley and 164 for Minority Leader Robert Michel, the Republican candidate. A number of Republicans wore buttons that read "Reform not Revenge."[6] Michel, noting that he had lost six straight Speaker's races and looked forward "to the day when someone on the other side of the aisle learns the joys of selfless behavior," complimented Foley and quoted the poet Arthur Hugh Clough: "Look westward, the land is bright."[7]

Foley's hometown paper stated that "the people of Spokane and the rest of Eastern Washington's 5th Congressional District may be forgiven a bit of old-fashioned provincial pride." "In election after election," the editors wrote, "Democrat Foley has won the right to represent a conservative region which, in many other ballot contests, tends to vote Republican. . . . The bipartisan civility Foley has brought to his work—and that he urges upon the political process he now leads—is sorely needed in Washington, D.C. . . . As [Robert] Michel . . . noted, Congress now has 'that rare, most improbable of gifts—a second chance'. . . . If anyone can lead Congress toward a restoration of the honor and civility that public service deserves, Tom Foley can."[8]

In his first remarks to the assembled House, the new Speaker offered embattled Democrats the hope of healing. To Republicans, he noted his reputation for rising above partisanship. "We need to strengthen the House," said Foley, asking for debate "with reason and without rancor. I am a proud Democrat, but I appeal specifically to our friends on the Republican side that we should come together and put away division and hostility."

In Congress, civility or comity represents a norm of reciprocal courtesy. It presupposes that the differences between members and parties are philosophical and not personal. It also presupposes that parties to a debate are entitled to the presumption that their views are legitimate, and that those on all sides are persons of good will and integrity motivated by conviction.[9] Foley's plea for civility was not a call for any blurring of partisan differences. Strong partisanship and civility are not mutually exclusive. Rather, his was recognition that the partisan tempers in the summer of 1989 threatened the very climate which makes argument and constructive legislation possible.

Foley's election was historic in marking the first transition in which a Speaker had been driven from office. In the traditional twentieth century transition, House members knew for a year or more that a Speaker was retiring. The party caucuses picked the nominees in early December when the House was out of session, and didn't vote on the House floor until early January. Wright stayed in the Speaker's chair overseeing the roll call that marked the end of his own tenure in the leadership, and after handing the gavel to Foley, he left the rostrum. Did it cross the new Speaker's mind when he addressed the House for the first time that there were a number of Democrats who would like for him to turn to the Republicans and say, "You think you've had it tough in the past, wait until tomorrow?"

> I think there were some who had that emotional instinct, but there were two sides to this problem. One was to keep support and develop a sense of legitimacy, if you will, from those who had been most embittered by Jim's departure, and at the same time, to move away from this corrosive mood between the two parties. My immediate thought was that we had to calm the Republican side which, even after achieving the resignation of Speaker Wright, was still steaming in their resentments.

Over the previous three decades, the House Speakership had passed smoothly from Sam Rayburn to John W. McCormack to Carl Albert to Thomas P. O'Neill Jr. to Jim Wright. The Austin-Boston axis, as it was called, established the pattern of "one from the oil patch, the next from Massachusetts." Foley was the first Speaker from west of the Rocky Mountains. He also appeared to be almost an accidental Speaker.

> I have never been driven by a desire to become Speaker. I'm not a fatalist. But I am one who thinks circumstances, happenstance, accident has a lot to do with what happens in a political career.[10]

For many, this sort of political kismet made Foley an anomaly. Foley would have shared his close friend, Democratic Party benefactor and U.S. Ambassador to France, Pamela Harriman's view that much of life is luck and timing. He was not, as he described himself to *U.S. News and World Report* journalist Gloria Borger, an "A type" politician "who was boy mayor of the town, president of the student body and always planning to be governor of this great state." Instead, he described himself as "B Type," willing to step in when needed but unwilling to push others aside. "You have to be ready and willing to take the opportunities. But I have a limited belief in your ability to create all of the circumstances." Foley came across as successful, but not threatening. For a mercurial, aggressive politician like Wright, Borger concluded, "who collected chits for 10 years on his way to the Speakership," this might have sounded like a foreign political philosophy. But for Foley, "the combination of grace, good humor and obvious intellect has always been enough to propel his career."[11]

Foley exhibited little of the partisan fervor that had characterized his predecessors. "He is a superb leader and one of the best people operating at the highest level of American politics," stated Democratic Representative Barney Frank of Massachusetts. "But three Tom Foleys could be a problem. We might cross the line that divides a political body from a seminar."[12] Ways and Means Committee Chairman Dan Rostenkowski of Illinois stated that, "When you talk to Tom, you start biting your fingernails and you don't stop until you're up to your elbows. What he does is good, but sometimes getting there is frustration."[13] Foley had become known, as one colleague put it, as "the man with all reasons," and whether in Washington's Fifth District or Washington, D.C., he had the reputation of someone who took the time to ruminate about complex political matters.[14]

"Tom's great asset," observed Lynne Cheney, chairman of the National Endowment for the Humanities and a historian who, along with her husband, former Republican Whip Dick Cheney, co-authored a book on congressional leaders, "like [1920s-era Speaker] Nicholas Longworth's, is the enormous amount of affection built up on both sides of the aisle and the public at large." Dick Cheney, Secretary of Defense at the time Foley became Speaker, praised

Foley: "I consider it a great day for America that he is now the Speaker of the House. He is one of the most able members that I have served with in my political career."[15]

No recent Speaker had a comparable grasp of foreign affairs, particularly on issues surrounding U.S.-Soviet relations or U.S. ties to Japan. For some, Foley appeared as an Irish-Anglophile, with a fascination for British rule in India, who had almost fashioned himself as a figure from a nineteenth century British parliament. But, stripped of the nuances, Foley came to the Speakership as a moderate Democrat. Most of his previous legislative passions—agriculture, water, energy, and free trade—had directly affected his constituents.[16] Any uniqueness of his ascension aside, did Foley regard his experience on the traditional leadership escalator as a good proving ground for the Speakership?

> I think it's a good training ground. I can't think of anything that would be better. But, I remember when I became Speaker, I thought, this is really not the same as what it seemed while you were watching it as Majority Leader or Whip. And I remember asking some people on the Business Roundtable—in the business world you're usually President or Chief Operating Officer before you're the CEO of a company—is it very clear to you what it is going to be like when you become CEO, or are there some surprises? And almost without exception they said there were some surprises, that it was not quite what they'd thought it to be, and I think that's the nature of being Speaker.
>
> You're in the public eye more than being Majority Leader, you're subject to far more press attention, you are required to make a good many appointments, many more than people realize, to boards and commissions, you are more ceremonial, which all accompany the day-to-day legislative leadership role.

Projecting the Speaker's Role Internationally

Historically, the Senate has been regarded as the legislative body where foreign policy issues are debated. The power to ratify treaties and confirm U.S. ambassadors are two visible roles underscoring this interpretation. Among all fifty representatives who have served in the Speakership, Henry Clay's role as a major influence in the U.S. declaration of war with Great Britain and the War of 1812 would put him at the top of a list of Speakers whose foreign policy agendas had real significance.[17] Beyond constitutional provisions, however, the Speaker of the House has frequent opportunities to play an international role, from presiding over remarks by a visiting head of state at joint House-Senate meetings to presiding over a House debate on a President's deployment of U.S. troops abroad. Much of a Speaker's international role reflects that Speaker's view of the position.

Although the international role of the Speakership was a frequently over-looked aspect of the office, that was not so with the new Speaker who would be highly decorated by a number of foreign governments including the Federal Republic of Germany, France, Great Britain, and Japan.[18]

Since his mid-1960s arrival in Washington, D.C., Foley had concentrated on his agricultural district's interest in international trade. As a member and later chairman of the House Agriculture Committee, he had frequently traveled to Great Britain, West Germany, France, and Japan to promote trade. His international presence had grown with his power in Congress. He had participated almost annually in Japan Foundation of the United States-sponsored visits to Japan, headed the U.S.-Japan Parliamentary Exchange, and had become one of the most respected Americans there. He had been the only member of Congress to accompany Vice President Walter Mondale to the People's Republic of China in 1979. During the 1983 period of tense U.S.-Soviet relations, he headed the first U.S. group invited to talk to major Soviet leaders after Uri Andropov succeeded Leonid Brezhnev as premier, and he participated in the 1987 meetings with Soviet leader Mikhail Gorbachev.[19]

His political style in foreign policy was directed at fashioning bipartisan approaches, but he held strong views on a number of issues. An Anglophile, an Irish Catholic, and an early member of the congressional "Friends of Ireland," he was anti-IRA and an opponent of its U.S. fundraising operation Noraid. He emerged as one of the primary congressional opponents to the Reagan administration's efforts to provide military aid to the Contras in Nicaragua and helped forge the bipartisan agreement that limited assistance to "humanitarian" aid until the Nicaraguan government held elections.

"In a country in which separation of the three branches of government makes it vital that they work together in good spirit," toasted French Ambassador to the U.S. Jacques Andreani at a dinner honoring Foley, "the role of a parliamentary leader such as Mr. Foley is essential. Because he knows how to differ without blocking processes, how to cooperate without renouncing his own views. . . . In sum, Mr. Foley, I am proud to declare it, is a diplomat. And this ability to see the point of view of the others is important in politics. It is still more important in diplomacy, because, when diplomacy fails, it can mean war, as we know too well."[20]

It is a rarity when a visiting head-of-state, foreign minister, or parliamentary delegation does not ask to meet with the Speaker of the House. Occasionally this involves having the visitor address a joint meeting of the House and Senate in the House chamber.

> Actually there are no rules as such. A joint meeting can be addressed by anybody that Congress decides to invite. General MacArthur gave his famous "old soldiers never die, they just fade away" farewell before a joint

meeting of the House and Senate, for example, after he was fired by President Truman. But, foreign guests addressing joint meetings are almost exclusively the foreign head of state or head of government. There were exceptions. I invited Nelson Mandella to speak to a joint meeting when he was Deputy President of the African National Congress and Lech Walesa when he was Chairman of Solidarity. They both later became presidents of their respective countries, South Africa and Poland.

But I had to resist opening the flood gates. There was a widespread urging that the Dalai Lama be invited to address a joint session, and the State Department was panic-stricken that we would agree to this and create an incident with China. Instead, we organized with the Senate a joint meeting in the Rotunda of the Capitol which had the benefit of allowing the public to come in greater numbers and with less formal restrictions, but it didn't symbolize the head of state role that a joint meeting in the House chamber usually conveys.

There was wisdom in adhering to the strict tradition of heads of state or government because it prevents the awkward rejection of applications for persons of great talent, achievement, or distinction whom some group of members want to recognize. It has the advantage that all protocol rules have of being restrictive without being offensive.

For Foley, this part of the job was "second nature," as he was an "internationalist" by instinct.

It was about 1967 when a group of Japanese flour millers came to the Agriculture Committee to present a statement of appreciation to the United States and the Congress for the food aid that the U.S. had given Japan following World War II, or the Pacific War as it's called in Japan. This aid had led to a change in the Japanese dietary habit, the development of U.S. wheat exports, and the growth of the Japanese wheat-milling industry. They offered a grateful statement in Japanese in front of Bob Poage and the full Agriculture Committee. "Thank you very much," the chairman responded somewhat bluntly, "We appreciate your statement gentlemen, and now the committee must go into executive session." This meant, of course, in the language of the Congress, that all the visitors and guests had to leave. The committee was going to close the doors and sit by itself on some business. Well, the Japanese didn't understand what "executive session" meant, and they smiled, bowed, and stayed right where they were. Nobody had prodded them gently that it was time to take their leave, and so Mr. Poage repeated, in a somewhat louder voice, the same request. It produced only more smiles and bows. A third attempt also failed. At this point Mr. Poage exploded, "Will somebody please take these people out of the room!"

That message suddenly got through to our Japanese guests and, bewildered and embarrassed, they left, wondering what they had done to give offense. They were being ejected from the committee room after coming to give this statement of appreciation and, having thought that it would be well received, they seemingly had done or said something that so enraged the chairman that he had thrown them out of the room.

I was embarrassed for them, and for the committee, and I rushed out of the room myself, met them in the hallway, and thanked them all effusively for their statement. They still looked somewhat dazed and confused. Unable to think of what to do next, I impulsively invited them all to dinner. At this time I was a bachelor living in a small house in southwest Washington, D.C., and used to eating most of my meals out. Having invited them all to dinner, there were about seven or eight of them, I didn't know exactly how I was going to produce this dinner. Fortunately at the time, I had a Japanese-American intern from Whitworth College in Spokane. She suggested that she could help prepare some Japanese dishes. I asked, "Should I go out and buy some saki? "No," she said, "scotch." The dinner ultimately became an office-wide effort and success. Despite some language barriers, our guests and we wound up singing old Japanese and American university songs and had, apparently, a rousing good time.

From then on, over many years, as Foley began annual trips to Japan, his guests hosted elaborate and expensive dinners in Tokyo in his honor, keeping this relationship, that came out of that one incident, very much alive.

For some conservative Fifth District constituents, Foley's membership in the Council on Foreign Relations and the Trilateral Commission was problematical, but at innumerable town meetings, constituents sought his foreign affairs views. Wheat farmers frequently peppered him with questions about world politics, and he would routinely respond with detailed analyses of the situations in Poland, the Soviet Union, China, or Japan.

In the other Washington, at what became regular early-morning breakfasts with the Capitol's bureau chiefs and major newspaper columnists, Foley frequently defended the need for continued U.S. foreign aid. "We had something to celebrate in Europe. . . . The Cold War is won, or largely won, and it would seem to be inconceivable that after investing something . . . close to a trillion dollars . . . in those four decades, that we would suddenly say, 'Oops! We can't afford more than $100 million now to Poland, and we can't do anything for Czechoslovakia, and if they slip back into anarchy and chaos, that's too bad, we just ran out of money.'"[21] In both Washingtons, foreign affairs wasn't simply one more arrow in his political quiver, it was a deeply-rooted interest reflected in his early involvement in the congressional parliamentary-exchange effort.

Newly elected in November 1964 to represent eastern Washington's Fifth Congressional District, Thomas S. Foley poses on the steps of the U.S. Capitol. *Photo Archive, The Spokesman-Review.*

Opposite above: Washington state's longest-serving Superior Court Judge, Ralph Foley, swears son Tom into the bar in Spokane in 1957. *Opposite below:* Following his victory in the 1964 election, Tom Foley poses with his parents Helen and Ralph. *Above:* Seated in a Spokane restaurant with his wife Ellen following his November 1964 defeat after representing eastern Washington's Fifth District for twenty-two years, Walt Horan stated, "I consider Tom Foley a gentleman. I thought he conducted a fine campaign." *All courtesy Photo Archive, The Spokesman-Review.*

Opposite above: Foley discusses the 1964 campaign with his mentor, Senator Henry "Scoop" Jackson. *Washington State University Libraries. Opposite below:* Freshman Representative Foley is greeted by President Lyndon Johnson and Vice President Hubert Humphrey at a White House bill-signing ceremony in 1966. *Washington State University Libraries. Above:* Tom Foley and the former Heather Strachan clasp hands as part of a traditional marriage ceremony following their wedding on December 19, 1968 at St. Mary's Church, Colombo, Ceylon, where Heather's father represented the U.S. government's Colombo Plan assistance program. *Photo Archive, The Spokesman-Review.*

Opposite above: Gathered for a tree-planting ceremony on the Capitol grounds honoring former Speaker John McCormack in the mid-1970s are five former, then-current, or future Speakers of the House. On the right, from back to front, they are Tom Foley, Jim Wright, Thomas "Tip" O'Neill, Carl Albert, and McCormack. *Opposite below:* House Agriculture Committee Chairman Foley joins President Jimmy Carter for lunch at the White House. *Above:* As House Democratic Caucus Chair, Foley moves a resolution to accept the appointment of Democratic members to committees at the beginning of a new session of Congress in January 1978. New House members are traditionally accompanied by their families. *All courtesy Washington State University Libraries.*

President-elect Ronald Reagan suggested that members of Congress wear informal "morning attire" to his 1980 inaugural. Foley poses in his dove-gray vest, four-in-hand tie, braided collar, and striped pants. *Washington State University Libraries.*

House Majority Whip Foley confers with his two mentors, Washington's senators Henry M. Jackson and Warren G. Magnuson in May 1980. *Photo Archive, The Spokesman-Review.*

Opposite above: Getting the "Reagan touch" during an August 1982 visit to the White House are congressional leaders Speaker Tip O'Neill, Chairman of the House Rules Committee Richard Bolling, Majority Whip Foley, Chairman of the House Veterans Committee G.V. "Sonny" Montgomery, House Minority Leader Robert Michel, and Chairman of the House Ways and Means Committee Daniel Rostenkowski. *Washington State University Libraries.* *Opposite below:* Revelations that the Reagan Administration had secretly sold arms to Iran and diverted the profits to the Nicaraguan Contras burst into the news in November 1986. Majority Whip Foley questions a witness during the Iran-Contra hearings. *Washington State University Libraries. Above:* Majority Leader Foley chairs the 1987 bipartisan budget summit which aimed to reduce the federal deficit. Standing behind are Democratic House Budget Chairman William Gray, Democratic Representative Pat Williams, Foley press secretary Jeff Biggs, William Hoagland, chief of staff to ranking Senate Budget Committee member Pete Domenici, and Foley floor assistant George Kundanis. *Courtesy House Photographer/Jeffrey Biggs.*

At one of the many Shimoda Conferences he helped found, Majority Leader Foley co-hosts a May 1987 gathering in the Speaker's Capitol dining room to discuss U.S.-Japan relations. U.S. participants pictured, facing the camera are Representative David Bonior (at Foley's right hand), Foley, Ambassador to Japan Mike Mansfield, Speaker Jim Wright, Minority Whip Richard Cheney, Energy and Commerce Committee Chairman John Dingell, and Representative William Broomfield. Among the Japanese delegation is Prime Minister Nakasone, fifth from right with back to the camera. *Washington State University Libraries.*

Soviet leader Mikhail Gorbachev and members of the Soviet delegation meet with congressional leaders at the Soviet Embassy in Washington in December 1987. Members of the Soviet delegation from right to left are Alexander Yakovlev, Communist Party propaganda chief; Gorbachev; Eduard Shevardnadze, Foreign Minister; and Anatolly Dobrynin, Secretary of the Communist Party. The congressional leadership includes from left to right Democratic Senate Majority Leader Robert Byrd; Democratic Speaker of the House Jim Wright; Democratic House Majority Leader Foley; Republican House Minority Leader Robert Michel; Democratic House Majority Whip Tony Coelho; and Republican House Deputy Minority Whip Trent Lott. *Washington State University Libraries.*

Foley campaigns on the campus of Walla Walla's Whitman College in October 1988. *Washington State University Libraries.*

Tom and Heather Foley on Spokane's Centennial Trail, which runs along the banks of the Spokane River, a project for which Foley secured some federal funding. *Photo Archive, The Spokesman-Review.*

Even while campaigning in a wheatfield, Foley was legendary for dressing the way he thought voters expected a member of Congress to look. This photo was taken near Walla Walla in 1988. *Washington State University Libraries.*

In 1966, around the time that Sargent Shriver came back from a tour as U.S. Ambassador to Paris, he suggested to House members that they organize a U.S. parliamentary exchange with France. He had been concerned that, while he had been in Paris, there had been a perceptible shift of opinion, at least among certain of the French elites, to be much more critical of the United States, and much more concerned about American influence and investment in Europe. Eventually that was done and an organization of younger French and U.S. members was born.

I prepared for our first trip to France by going to the State Department's Foreign Service Institute's early morning classes to brush up on some very inadequate high school French, and was taught by the wife of a foreign service officer. Although I had private lessons, I did not progress as rapidly as I had hoped. But I did go through a number of situational French lessons which was the method that they were using at the time—registering at a hotel, renting a car, eating dinner at a restaurant, buying goods in a store, and so on. Lesson twenty-six was traveling from Paris to Rennes, stopping at a small French inn, having lunch, complimenting the proprietor and his wife, going on towards Rennes, admiring the countryside, commenting on the beautiful forests, and briefly discussing the history of the ancient city of Rennes, as we arrived.

When we went to France, my host was supposed to be a Gaullist from Paris, but he fell ill and was taken to the hospital, and the substitute was a French Lycee professor, and member of the Gaullist party in the National Assembly, from Rennes. It was decided that we should drive rather than go by train, and so, suddenly, Lesson Twenty-six was being acted out in real life. We found ourselves at a small French inn. I commented on the menu, admired the wine, congratulated the proprietor and his wife, admired the countryside, and discussed the history of Rennes. By the time we arrived, my French host expressed his surprise at how fluent I was and how easy it was for me to talk about events on the way. So, throughout my stay in Rennes I was being approached by his friends and spoken to in rapid-fire colloquial French to which I answered with a lot of shrugs and d'accords, and repeatedly told the story of our trip from Paris to Rennes. That was almost my only conversation, but it served me well for a while.

When the French returned the visit, we had a bit of an embarrassment because the American Embassy in France had prepared rather candid dossiers on the French delegation members who were arriving in the United States, describing their background and reputation. And although it was a very distinguished group of younger members, and most of the biographies were glowing in their appreciation, two or three were somewhat critical, the most critical being that of a senior member of the delegation. By some terrible mischance, instead of receiving the dossiers ourselves, they were ceremonially handed to the French as they got off the plane. So the French were reading all of their own U.S. Embassy-prepared biographies. The senior member was, of course, furious because he was described in the paper as pretending to a knowledge of French literature and history that he didn't quite have, being rather ruthless in his attitude toward fellow members, and very ambitious—a parliamentary "wolf" in French terms, and so forth.

I kept drawing individual members of the French delegation aside and apologizing profusely. But, of course, for many of them it was not only amusing but rather pleasant because they had received very positive reports. One of the French members took me aside and said "You have an expression about every cloud has a silver lining. The silver lining here is that we didn't really believe that the U.S. Embassy in Paris was capable of such acute and careful judgments about our delegation. The reputation of your political section has soared."

After Foley left Congress and the Speakership at the end of the 103rd Congress, his new affiliations gave a clear indication of how important the U.S. role internationally continued to be to him. In addition to serving as President Bill Clinton's Chairman of the President's Foreign Intelligence Advisory Board, Foley was a member of the American-Japan Society, U.S. China Council, American Council for Germany, Foreign Affairs Council of Washington, Council on Foreign Relations, Trilateral Commission, and the advisory board of the British American-Ditchley Foundation. Eventually President Clinton nominated him as Ambassador to Japan.

Foley as a Victim of Republican National Committee Attack

Concerns, including Foley's, about the chances of bipartisanship after the frequently vicious personal attacks of the 1988 presidential campaign and the Jim Wright controversy took on a personal dimension in the days just preceding Foley's transition to the Speakership. He found himself targeted by a memo prepared by a high-ranking aide to the chairman of the Republican National Committee, Lee Atwater. Dubbed "Tom Foley: Out of the Liberal Closet," the paper sought to equate Foley's voting record with that of Massachusetts Democrat and gay activist Representative Barney Frank. The memo was circulated to several hundred people within the Republican National Committee as well as state party chairmen and "surrogates" used to influence the media and public opinion. While the memo allegedly relied on ratings compiled by interest groups, the eight specific votes cited actually included several when Foley did not vote with Representative Frank, but on the side of prominent Republicans.[22] The phrase "coming out of the closet" commonly referred to homosexuals who make their sexual orientation public. In using the phrase purportedly to refer to Foley's politics, the memorandum was criticized as suggesting that the Speaker, like Mr. Frank, was gay. Appearing on the Cable News Network the morning of June 8, Foley had to make public the same denials he had made in private to other House members that, "I am, of course, not a homosexual, [having] been married for 21 years." Wanting to put the incident behind him, he went on to note that "Lee Atwater, the chairman of the Republican National Committee, called me up last night and apologized effusively for any such inference, repudiated it and totally rejected it. So I think the issue is closed."[23]

Of course, being Washington, D.C., it wasn't, and the "Foley smear" took on larger connotations as a brief partisan *cause célèbre*. President Bush rebuked Atwater, the White House seeking to blunt outrage in both parties. John H. Sununu, the White House chief of staff, said both he and Bush had reprimanded Atwater and that the President was "disgusted" at the attack on Foley. Senate Minority Leader Bob Dole condemned the memo on the floor of the Senate. However, while the aide who authored the memo resigned, the President accepted Atwater's explanation of ignorance about the memo being sent. This man, who throughout his political life had been on the scene of some of the most ferocious and cutting political campaigns, remained on the job.[24] And, although Gingrich publicly condemned the memo, the press noted that "one particularly egregious rumormonger was Karen Van Brocklin, a Gingrich aide who fed the growing press frenzy by telling more than one reporter that his or her competition was investigating Foley rumors."[25] The press consensus was summed up by *The New Republic's* Hendrik Hertzberg. "There is precisely the same amount of evidence that George Bush, Lee Atwater, and Mikhail Gorbachev are gay as that Tom Foley is—i.e., none."[26] For Foley, the frustration was that even the denunciations of the smear tended to prolong the story.

The Democrats' eagerness to be rid of Atwater was not surprising, but Republican uneasiness with the Foley memo suggested the depth of the divisions within the party over the full-scale assault against Democrats being spearheaded by House Republican Whip Newt Gingrich. Representative Jim Leach, a Republican moderate from Iowa, captured the dismay of his fellow moderate Republicans. "There is nothing in public life more unprincipled than the politics of innuendo," he said. "A kinder, gentler agenda demands an end to the poisoning of standards that assassinates, rather than holds accountable, character."[27]

For Foley, a veteran politician who had experienced almost universally good press, it was a mean christening into the center of the high-stakes game of jugular politics.

The Democratic Leadership in the House

In June 1989, House Democrats filled out the vacant leadership positions. The successful candidate for Majority Leader was Richard Gephardt of St. Louis, and for Whip, William Gray of Philadelphia.

Gephardt had risen quickly in the House since his election in 1976, aided by Missouri Representative Richard Bolling, chairman of the House Rules Committee. He emerged, after Ronald Reagan's election, as one of the recognized leaders of a generation of younger House members and was elected Chairman of the Democratic Caucus in 1984 and 1986. Following Walter Mondale's defeat to Reagan in 1984, Gephardt—a self-described "terminal centrist"—had helped found, along with Democratic Senator Sam Nunn of Georgia and governors Charles S. Robb of Virginia and Bruce Babbitt of Arizona, the Democratic Leadership Council, aimed at returning the Democratic Party to a more centrist position. Although he would emerge as more liberal and more partisan in the '90s, Gephardt resisted labels. "It may be terribly inaccurate to say that I'm a liberal or I'm a conservative or even that I'm a moderate. I don't think those terms get us very far."[28]

In 1989 the forty-eight-year-old Gephardt was widely respected throughout the House for his patience in working out legislative compromises. During his 1988 race for the Democratic presidential nomination, he emerged in some eyes as "an angry populist outsider," but appealed to younger suburban and blue-collar workers who continued to be a key electoral bloc for Democrats. The high point of his presidential bid was winning the left-leaning Iowa Democratic caucuses, but he had secured the active support of a large number of House colleagues, including Foley, who continued that support when he returned to the House.

In Gephardt's Capitol office was a photograph of himself with Foley. "In cap and shirt-sleeves is a fortysomething Richard Gephardt, the House majority leader, pitching to his beloved St. Louis Cardinals. Standing with him on the dirt mound, wearing a dark suit and the bemused look of a man lost at the ballpark, is a tall, graying figure—Speaker Thomas Foley . . . Together this pair must now produce the muscle to keep skittish Democrats in line."[29]

To serve as Majority Whip, Democrats chose Representative William Gray. Described by some as a "black version of Gephardt" because of his consensus-building skills, Gray had been chairman of both the Democratic Caucus and Budget Committee. A pastor who continued to preach two Sundays a month at his 4,000-member Philadelphia Bright Hope Baptist Church, he had drawn liberal and southern support in both of his previous leadership races.[30] Although he was an unabashed urban liberal, Gray enjoyed the trust and cooperation of southern fiscal conservative Democrats such as Representatives Marvin Leath and Charles Stenholm of Texas. Gray had a quick intelligence and a warm and diplomatic style, making him a master at getting along with turf-jealous committee chairs.[31]

This new leadership, however, could not run the House alone. In the 1980s, and even more as Speaker Wright had become distracted by his own troubles, committee and subcommittee chairs had become increasingly powerful.

Chicago Democratic Chairman of the House Ways and Means Committee Dan Rostenkowski had the reputation of treating his committee "like a big-city ward, where personal loyalty counts far more than ideology." He had "built members' allegiance the old-fashioned way, by doing favors, keeping his word, and taking down the names of those who do not go along." Detroit Democratic Chairman of the Energy and Commerce Committee John D. Dingell was considered one of the House's most skillful legislators, aggressive turf-fighters, and hard-nosed negotiators. "'Either you were with him, or you were in the doghouse," one committee member observed. Dingell reportedly sought to exclude from conference committees those members he felt had been disloyal. Texas Democratic Chairman of the Judiciary Committee Jack Brooks was a protégé of legendary Texas Speaker Sam Rayburn and reportedly nurtured an image of "an irascible, tough-talking Texan, a man of strong loyalties and fierce independence."[32]

These three powerful chairmen all had between four to twelve years more seniority in the House than did Foley. Like medieval barons, they were used to wielding power, crafting legislation, being consulted by the House leadership on the legislative agenda, and receiving loyalty from committee members and a certain deference from their colleagues, from the Speaker on down.

> I think some people felt that I was too deferential to committee chairmen, not assertive enough. The chairmen didn't think that. Most of them felt the opposite, but one has to take your committee chairmen as you get them.
>
> A number of the key chairmen I was dealing with were not only senior to me in years of service and had been committee chairmen longer than I was, but at least several of them thought that they should be Speaker. They thought that they were the right person for the job. Certainly John Dingell and Dan Rostenkowski held that opinion, and both of them publicly toyed with the idea of running for Speaker. It was only the fact that both of them probably had the good sense to realize that, over the years, they had created enough quiet abrasion among the membership that, much as they were respected and as talented and successful as they were as committee chairmen, on a personal basis there were enough of their colleagues who might like to cast a secret ballot vote against them. Indeed, Rostenkowski had once lost a critical appointment as Democratic Chairman of the Caucus when he ran against [Olin E.] "Tiger" Teague.
>
> None of this diminishes my respect for them as legislators or committee chairmen. Warts and all, chairmen like Dingell, Rostenkowski, and Brooks were brilliant chairmen and left their marks in a positive way on the legislation of the country, but they weren't always easy to deal with. John Dingell was always very deferential to the Speaker, didn't take a lot

of time, had an agenda, was constantly sensitive about the jurisdiction of his committee, as all chairmen are. Rostenkowski was, to a certain degree, civil and deferential, but had strong opinions about how his committee should be run.

What happens when you have a disagreement? Well, you have to weather through it. It doesn't help to have a lot of diversionary battles. In one case a committee chairman [David McCurdy of Oklahoma] who had openly talked about running against me for Speaker was also subject to my personal appointment as a chairman [House Permanent Select Committee on Intelligence]. Even though I felt he was a very good committee chairman, and I'd appointed him somewhat against the advice of other people, I didn't think I could ignore his active opposition so I didn't reappoint him.

But it's seldom a case where a committee chairman says, "Fie on you Mr. Speaker. I defy you. I'm not going to do it. That bill is not going to pass my committee. Do your worst." The reality is that most of them say, "Oh yes, Mr. Speaker, of course we're going to move your agenda. We're going to have some hearings. We have to look at it carefully. It's a complicated issue. I know you want us to have well-crafted legislation that we can defend on the floor and in conference with the Senate that we can get members to support and pass. But that means we have to come out of the committee with a very united Democratic side at least, if not a bipartisan majority. So, if you'll just put it in my hands and trust me to do this, I'll get it done for you, but it has to be on my time schedule. It can't be rushed or hurried." And then events come along and make it necessary to postpone the desired legislation even longer.

There are always people who say you're not tough enough, you don't knock heads enough, and so on, but in the context of a particular time you have to ask what is the best policy to get the job done, to advance the program. If diplomacy and patience are a better line of success than harsh words, then that's a better way to go.

Staff to the Speaker

Democratic Representative Charles Rangel of New York's Harlem congressional district once observed that "up here there are two classes of people, members and clerks. When the clerks start thinking they are members, that's when we have trouble."[33] His message should have been clear to the some 14,000 House and Senate congressional staffers of the 1990s. Even if the senator or representative might tell them they were indispensable, good staffers didn't believe it.

Sterling Munro had been Scoop's [Senator Henry Jackson] long-time administrative assistant. He started out working for him as an elevator operator in the Senate when he was seventeen and worked for him as administrative assistant for more than twenty years. One time [as a member of Jackson's staff] I was trying to get a letter through, drafted for the Senator's signature to a Mrs. Green, and it kept getting blocked. So I went to Sterling and said, "what's the problem?" "Well," he said, "you're telling Mrs. Green what the Senator's position on 'x' is." I said, "Well isn't that the Senator's position?" He said, "I don't think the Senator has a position quite yet." "But, doesn't Mrs. Green need to be told what it is?" "Yes, when he decides that she can be informed." "But," I said, "that could be several months." "Yes, and your job is to write a nice letter back to Mrs. Green and not presume on the Senator's good time to make his decision. He doesn't have to make it one minute before he's ready. Certainly not because of Mrs. Green, and especially because of you."

One of the rubrics in the Jackson office, not particularly from Scoop, but from Sterling, was that "first there was the Senator, then there was the staff, and not the other way around. The Senator does not exist to support the staff. The staff exists to support the Senator."

As Foley assumed the Speakership he was described by one journalist as running "perhaps the most powerful army on Capitol Hill, a platoon of about 50 employees that collects the insider knowledge he needs to stay on top of Congress." But, while Foley's image was easily recognized, "his aides remain faceless and often nameless." The staff were described as fitting Foley like his tailored suits. They were loyal and cautious and protected his power without making enemies. They generally called him Mr. Foley or Mr. Speaker. A number of his top aides had graduate or law degrees and would stay with Foley for years. Although all staff were expected to give the Fifth District their top priority, only a few of the senior aides had eastern Washington roots, and with annual salaries over $108,000, six staff earned more than Spokane's city manager.[34]

A lot of my attitudes about congressional staff were a result of my own experience in the Jackson office and in close association with, although not working for, Warren Magnuson. I think that the two senators had extraordinary people working for them.

There was a, culture is the only word I can think of, of staff relations in the Jackson office: you were supposed to do whatever had to be done. People were given some area of responsibility, and then they were not always day-to-day supervised and given instructions and told what to do and given tasks to perform and checked on. You were given a particular area of responsibility and expected to see that the necessary work was done.

In his first congressional term in 1965 Foley had a staff of seven headed by administrative assistant Dick Larsen, who went on to become editorial page editor of *The Seattle Times*. Press secretary Bill First served on the staff for some twenty years after having covered Foley's first campaign as Northwest editor of the Spokane *Spokesman-Review*. Foley's key staff in Spokane would soon be Art Hansen, who had followed his mentor's footsteps as a deputy prosecutor of Spokane County and assistant state attorney general before joining Foley's staff.

By 1989 Speaker Foley's staff were now spread across his congressional office (eighteen), the House Democratic Steering and Policy Committee (ten), his leadership office (twenty-seven), and in his district offices in Spokane and Walla Walla (eight). Foley was considered to be a "staffer's congressman," as some generals are "soldiers' generals." He tended to give his aides ready access so their information wasn't distorted by intermediaries.

> I expect them to be well-informed and to get the information to me quickly when I need it. I don't ever want people to gild over things, to accommodate what they think I want to hear. I want it very straight. Tell me if you disagree. Don't disappear on me.[35]
>
> Because everybody on a congressional staff has to deal with the public by telephone or in person, they have important representational requirements. They have to be able to talk with people, to take your place at meetings, and to exercise not only good judgment and knowledge, but to have diplomatic skills. I think we had an extraordinary staff.

Since their marriage in 1969, Heather Foley had been his unpaid chief of staff and now oversaw the three Capitol Hill offices as well as three district offices in Spokane, Walla Walla, and Spokane Valley. Legislative assistant Maxine Cooke coordinated the Speaker's official filings such as financial disclosure; Judy Crowe administered the multitude of Speaker appointments to various commissions; and Kathy Momot worked on Speaker correspondence. Heather, however, oversaw the totality of Foley's official life. Her one cardinal rule was owning up to any mistake immediately.

The "gatekeeper" to Speaker Foley's office was Mary Beth Schultheis. A Colton, Washington, native in her mid-twenties and a niece of state Court of Appeals Judge John Schultheis, she maintained Foley's fourteen-hour-plus daily schedule. The thankless part of her job was to turn away, postpone, reschedule, or delay with delicacy and diplomacy. The point was to maximize Foley's time, because most days could not accommodate all the requests upon his time. Before entering the leadership, he did not have that buffer of protection. Maxine Cooke was the legislative assistant to Heather Foley in the Speaker's office.

> Early in my career, a group participating in a program called "The Presidential Classroom" visited Washington, D.C. One of the group was a very nice senior high school student whose parents were technically from the Fifth District but actually lived, as I recall, in Hong Kong where

her father was working for an American company. She was going to school in the district. I spent about half-an-hour or forty-five minutes with her telling her what it was like to serve in the Congress and what some of the issues were. Then I took her to lunch with some of her colleagues, and then I delivered her over to the Senate side about 2 o'clock.

Later in the day I ran into her in the hallway. I said, "How has your day been?" She said, "Well, I've learned a lot of wonderful things. Interesting things. For example, I've learned that the Senate works a lot harder than the House." I said, "Oh?" She said, "Yes, you know you spent over half an hour with me this morning and took us all to lunch. When we went over to the Senate, Senator Magnuson was so busy he couldn't see me at all. He was just tied down with Senate business. His staff explained how he had all these committee meetings and requirements on the floor, and couldn't possibly get back, so he had one of his staff speak with us. Senator Jackson stepped out of a very busy meeting and spent a couple of minutes. It was wonderful of him to take all that time from his busy schedule."

Until his appointment by Foley on March 12, 1992 as House Sergeant-at-Arms, Werner Brandt served as executive assistant to the Speaker. After a decade in the Foreign Service, Brandt joined Foley's staff in 1972 after serving as an American Political Science Association (APSA) Congressional Fellow. Brandt became Foley's principal liaison to major interest groups, trade associations, organized labor, the business community, Washington state and Fifth District leaders, and was involved in foreign affairs as a legacy of his former career. Brandt was the veritable *paterfamilias* of Foley's staff. After Democratic Majority Whip Tony Coelho's resignation, Tom Nides joined Foley's staff. A political *wunderkind*, Nides had imbibed politics from an early age as a Vice President Mondale summer intern and veteran of the Democratic Congressional Campaign Committee. He was virtually unrivaled on the Foley staff for his political connections.

Another APSA Congressional Fellow from Foley's days as Chairman of the Democratic Caucus (1977-80) with a doctorate from the University of Wisconsin, George Kundanis became the Speaker's chief floor assistant and executive director of the Steering and Policy Committee. He was regarded by veteran Congress watchers as one of the best political tacticians and analysts in the House. Assisted by former Democratic Whip John Brademas staffer and deputy director of Steering and Policy, Mimi McGee-O'Hara, as well as legislative assistant Kathleen Miller, Kundanis kept tabs on House committee action, worked with the Rules Committee to structure floor presentation, apprised Foley of where members stood and helped line up Democratic votes, served as liaison to the Senate, and, in the absence of the Speaker, was the savviest point-of-contact for the 250-plus Democratic members in the caucus.

Mike O'Neil joined the staff as counsel to the Speaker in 1989, bringing the experience of twelve years as chief counsel of the House Select Committee on Intelligence and a graduate degree in tax law. In addition to serving as the primary contact point on foreign affairs, defense, and the intelligence community, O'Neil supervised a staff which followed the progress of every House committee (along with speech writer Tom LaFauci, health policy specialist Bonnie Lowrey, Jeff Swedberg, Dorothy Jackson who followed education and the Congressional Black Caucus, Nathan Marceca who scheduled meeting space, and secretary Lucia Marigan) and bookings for all Capitol space under the Speaker's purview.

Foley's congressional office was directed by Susan Moos, who had joined the staff in 1973. Her husband, Gene Moos, a former eastern Washington wheat farmer and senior Foley aide, later became a top Clinton administration official at the Department of Agriculture. Assisted by deputy administrative assistant Carolyn Scott, Moos oversaw the D.C. staff that handled district correspondence and casework on any subject of concern to eastern Washington. For example, the constant stream of environmental and timber issues went to Nick Ashmore; energy and nuclear issues related to Hanford went to Michelle Denton; agricultural concerns to Pat Ormsby; and foreign affairs matters and other casework to Andrew Valucheck, whose political credentials extended back to the days of working with ethnic communities for New York City Mayor Robert Wagner. Other staff members working in Foley's congressional office included Dana Gjelde, Temora Jones, Dwayne Malloy, Sandy Mathieson, Debbie O'Brien, Bryce Quick, Matthew Veazey, and Nancy Virtue.

With as many as fifty national, foreign, regional, and Washington state reporters' phone calls a day coming into the office, former Foreign Service officer and APSA Congressional Fellow Jeff Biggs, assisted by Spokane natives Robin Webb Mellody and Todd Woodard, staffed Foley's press office, arranged interviews, coordinated his daily and leadership press conferences, set up radio feeds to eastern Washington radio stations, and put out periodic press releases. As spokesman, Biggs had replaced veteran Foley press secretary Bill First when he retired in 1987. The press staff followed few but inviolate guidelines: be accurate, timely, authoritative in expressing the Speaker's views, and, as Foley himself would have it, don't make news unless you have to or unless it serves a real purpose, and don't criticize any member of Congress, regardless of how junior. That was Foley's job.

> There was one cardinal rule which was no staff person should ever mention the name of a member of the House, the Senate, or state or local government unless it was in a complimentary way. The last thing I wanted to hear was a story that one of the staff members had characterized another member in some way for which I had to bear the responsibility.

The assumption in Congress is that if somebody's administrative assistant says you're a fool, that's what the member thinks. It's very hard to break the assumption that the staff reflect the member. I don't want to demean staff, but it's a little like parents getting the blame for what the family says.

Wherever the Speaker went, whether it was conferring at the White House or lifting weights at the University Club, he was driven and accompanied by his security officer, former Green Beret, member of the Arlington National Cemetery honor guard, and sergeant in the Capitol Police force, Joe Powell. On those rare days when Powell wasn't available, former driver for Speaker Wright, Lionel Lawson, took his place.

All these staff were connected with Foley's key front-line staff in eastern Washington, from Pat Gregg in Walla Walla and Jeanne Zappone in the Spokane Valley to Janet Gilpatrick and Shannon Waechter in Spokane. For a Speaker representing a marginally Republican district, nothing was ever taken for granted. A veteran of the Carter presidential campaign days, Gilpatrick, a Spokane native with thirteen years on the staff, was one of Foley's closest aides, spoke for him in the Fifth District on a wide range of issues, and was the only Foley staffer to call him Thomas. The office got about 1,400 letters a week.

The secret fantasy of most House staffers was to work for the Speaker. As *Spokesman-Review* reporter Jim Lynch reported, "the right Foley aide can make rain fall." It was a heady atmosphere, but most Foley staffers recognized that whatever power and influence they exerted was derivative; it all came from "the Boss." As they were all aware, their mistakes would be his.

We had a long-tenured staff. I only had two press secretaries in the thirty years I was in Congress. I had people who commonly served ten, fifteen, twenty years. There were other offices that went through huge numbers of staff in a six months or less cycle. We had summer interns, of course, but the full-time professional staff stayed a long time and did a really great job. I relied on them absolutely.

In fact, when you leave Congress, one of the first things you realize is that the wonderful support of the staff has suddenly and abruptly come to an end. It's not that they're not willing to help you afterwards, but the day-to-day, hour-to-hour, support you've become accustomed to, particularly as one of the leadership, has ended. It's not that you've taken it for granted, but you don't understand totally and absolutely how much you're going to miss it.

Democratic Leadership in the Senate

In the opening months of the 101st Congress, the Senate came under the guiding hand of Majority Leader George J. Mitchell of Maine, the Senate

Democrats' first new leader in a dozen years. With Foley taking the Speaker's chair from Wright, and with Mitchell succeeding Robert C. Byrd of West Virginia in the Senate, George Bush would be working with a Democratic leadership that had enough in common with the President to make his "offered hand" concept more than wishful rhetoric. Foley, like Bush, had risen to the top echelon of American politics without the kind of burning ambition usually associated with such success.

Mitchell was a more partisan Democrat than Foley, but displayed impressive coalition-building skills in campaigning for the majority leadership. A former judge and top aide to Maine's Senator Edmund Muskie, his mentor, Mitchell, like Foley, had been criticized for not punishing dissident Senate Democrats. Foley and Mitchell had entered politics in the 1960s, as had Bush. Both Foley and Mitchell came from states with a centrist political tradition. Despite ideological differences, "all three are innately prudent and pragmatic figures, preferring compromise over confrontation" in contrast to the years of Reagan, Wright, and Byrd. Lynne P. Brown, a former Foley aide, described the new relationships, "It's going to be more like high tea in Britain than a shoot-out at the O.K. Corral." Juxtaposed to the potential for consensus, these same observers noted, was the momentum for excessive partisanship as a fallout of the Wright resignation. "If a tie in football is like kissing your sister, a bipartisan agreement fails to satisfy the ardent elements on both sides."[36]

Policy or Politics and the Foley Style of Governing

After more than a decade of sharing federal power with Republican administrations, divisions within the Democratic Caucus over how to work with a Republican President had intensified rather than diminished. It was a debate between seeking a governing consensus, or more aggressively playing the role of loyal opposition. Foley was comfortable working with a Republican President, a relationship he found gave him greater latitude in finding common legislative ground and softening the partisan hard edges of both parties.

> You can accomplish a lot with divided government. Properly practiced it focuses on the achievable. I don't dismiss the possibility, however, of stretches of unified government. The problem here is that, once in power, unified governments can overreach themselves without the natural check of an opposition legislation or administration. They become too enthusiastic about carrying out policies in a country which tends to be more moderate in its attitudes toward a lot of issues. I think the public often feels that divided government can facilitate that moderation and serve as a political check along with the normal checks-and-balances within government. The public doesn't seem to be distraught by division.

It is incumbent on both branches to seek common ground on national priorities if progress is to be made. That might seem commonplace, but there were many in the party who had the view that it was both sentimental and misguided. They believed in a rougher Realpolitik. In their eyes I was failing in my partisan duty if I didn't get up every morning with a fresh attack on the administration. Any kind of cooperation was suspect.

Was he indifferent to the criticism that he lacked sufficient partisanship for the job?

No, but again you can't change your stripes I guess; that's just the way I thought we ought to proceed. I always thought, too, that the best argument for the party, except for the most committed and knee-jerk Democrats, was to emphasize where we wanted to go with policy, and that we were willing to cooperate with the administration if we could find a way to do it, rather than to just embrace bombast and mindlessly blast away.

Ironically, while portions of the Democratic caucus were concerned about whether Foley would be partisan enough in pushing a Democratic agenda, many Republicans had an opposite concern. "With the expected ascendancy of Representative Tom Foley as Speaker of the House, many in the Democratic Party and the media will be portraying him as the 'darling' of the moderates. In fact," the *National Review* reported, "Mr. Foley has a long history as a liberal . . . an opponent of the death penalty for drug kingpins, of the Strategic Defense Initiative (SDI), and aid to the [Nicaraguan] contras." "Gephardt, Gray, and Foley are the most liberal House leadership in history," said Republican Whip Newt Gingrich. "They're nice people, but they're nice liberals, and they're serious about their liberal views. We have to remember that in dealing with them, because the gulf between their views and the Administration's is going to continue to cause problems."[37]

In fact, Foley's approval ratings from the liberal interest group Americans for Democratic Action had fluctuated wildly from a high of 86 percent in 1974 to a low of 30 percent in 1978. But his approval ratings from such conservative groups as Americans for Constitutional Action and the American Conservative Union had consistently been below 30 percent. A Roman Catholic from a district with a significant Roman Catholic population, throughout his career Foley had been pro-choice in the abortion controversy. He had risked alienating conservative voters by supporting the Equal Rights Amendment while opposing capital punishment, prayer in public schools, and constitutional amendments requiring a balanced federal budget and term limits. His clearest concession to Fifth District conservatism had been his consistent opposition to gun control. It was a position which inevitably prompted press questions for its seeming incongruity with his otherwise progressive politics. His responses were legion and frequently a deflection accompanied with an exaggerated western twang: "I'm from the West, where 'Drop yer guns' is fightin' words."[38]

The 101st Congress Under New Leadership

In 1986, when he was Majority Whip, Foley had observed that "[Speaker] Sam Rayburn could have walked down the streets of Spokane, Washington, without anybody noticing. Tip O'Neill couldn't do that. And it's very unlikely that any future Speaker will be anonymous to the country. The Speaker is going to join the vice president, the chief justice, and a few cabinet members in the forefront of public recognition."[39] Foley realized that public communication, in addition to agenda setting, had come to be a prominent expectation of the congressional leadership job. The message had been reinforced in the early 1980s when Reagan's media skills and a favorable political climate had allowed the President to dominate public debate, dictate the policy agenda, and convey, when it served his purposes, a negative image of Democrats as obstructionists.[40] The President's single voice frequently stood in contrast to the cacophony of 535 congressional voices.

To help level the playing field, the Democratic majority in the House needed spokespeople to counter the President. House Democrats came to expect their leaders to use their access to the media to promote the party's policy agenda and to protect and enhance the party's image. To some extent, Wright's departure had marked the end of an era when congressional leaders were selected primarily for their insider skills, their ability to work a small group of congressional power-brokers, and their willingness to enforce discipline behind the scenes. Although Foley and Mitchell were considered good at inside politics, they were also note-worthy practitioners of the outside art of video politics.[41] Appearing on television gave the Speaker and the rest of the leadership the chance to reach a broad array of audiences.

> When you went on a television program you were trying to reach the public, the press beyond the program itself, and your own congressional colleagues. It depended on the issue, but part of the way you influence your colleagues is by having some impact on public opinion and creating a mood or attitude toward legislation, or explaining what might otherwise be difficult for the public to understand. You don't do that all alone, but it's part of the task of being Speaker to try to explain the Congress, to justify what might be unpopular legislation, to defend the institution during periods when it comes under fire or attack. I think members appreciate that. They want someone to speak up and defend them, particularly if all they see on television are critics, both from within and without Congress: commentators, editorialists, and activists of various persuasions.

When members find themselves caught in that kind of crossfire, they want a strong defender. It has become too easy to attack or even malign the institution of Congress. For example, all somebody has to say is, "We all know what an arrogant, unbridled, self-serving Congress we have. It's focused largely on its own perquisites and career interests, bloated with. . . ." Heads tend to nod to such verbal assaults, but they're seldom personalized down to the level of the individual member. If somebody says, "Congressman Jones is an arrogant so-and-so," somebody else can say, "No, I don't think that's true." But when the charge is against the institution it's easier.

The proliferation of professional punditry is much greater today than it was twenty-five years ago. But the problem with Congress is that it really doesn't have an institutional voice. The members themselves are so often posing as "outsiders" or exceptions to the rule, criticizing everything except their own service, that it's become difficult for the public to get a balanced view.

The telegenic demands on the leadership led to an epiphany of sorts for Foley, a man whose weight had so widely fluctuated that his closet held three sets of different-sized suits. At the point of his transition to the Speakership, he was concentrating on the larger sizes to accommodate the 287 pounds on his 6-foot-4 frame, almost 100 pounds more than when we was sworn in as a freshman. After consulting a New York physician specializing in weight-loss, Foley and wife Heather went on an extended eight-month Optifast program during which he lost eighty pounds while Heather lost fifty. The physician also recommended that an exercise regimen be combined with his low-fat diet, and thereafter, six days a week, Foley would frequently ride his mountain bike or drive the three-and-a-half miles from home, arriving at around 6 a.m. at the University Club on 16th Street where he would don sweat pants and a sleeveless tank top for his workout.

The bike routine was interrupted for one day in 1991 when President Bush had a minor heart problem possibly requiring an operation. The White House had planned to briefly transfer presidential powers to Vice President Dan Quayle. As third in the line of presidential succession, the Secret Service balked at the Speaker, as acting Vice President, riding his bike, and he was escorted to his workout in a limo with a large group of agents and several follow cars.[42]

There is a certain "keeping the world at bay" quality about the University Club, to which nine presidents have been members since its founding in 1904 and to which all nine Supreme Court justices belong. Women were admitted to membership in 1984. Warming up on a Gravitron, Foley moved to a floor mat for abdominal crunches, shoulder presses, leg extensions, leg curls, leg presses, pullovers, lat pulldowns, and the vertical pec deck. All this was preliminary to the free-weights. As one reporter who watched a workout observed, "he took a teenager's joy in bench pressing over 200 pounds." Gone were the days when Foley would pull into a Burger King and order a Whopper with cheese and fries and several fast-food pies. He would have to grow to love broccoli.[43]

When Foley succeeded Wright, he inherited an agenda which he had helped formulate as Majority Leader. The legislative priorities focused on raising the minimum wage, child care, clean air, ethics reform, and campaign-finance reform. But, under Foley, the process of setting an agenda was to become less single-minded and more evolutionary and participatory than under Wright. What had become critical about the legislative agenda was the greater recognition that it could not take place in a vacuum; the substance was crucial but would be ineffective without an outside media strategy.

In the 100th Congress the Democratic leadership had made an effort to coordinate the one-minute member speeches which preceded each legislative session and were carried live on C-SPAN's gavel-to-gavel television cable coverage. Over the course of that Congress some one hundred Democrats, 38 percent of the membership, had participated with one-minute speeches supporting such issues as the trade bill, welfare reform, and plant-closing notification.[44] The Democrats began an even more ambitious effort in July 1989. A daily message group chaired by Majority Leader Gephardt represented a conscious attempt to coordinate the majority message. Every morning before the House was in session, a group of about eighteen members—leaders and mid-level activists who understood the media—met to harmonize and orchestrate the themes and points of view being expressed by the leadership and by Democratic members into a coherent message. In addition to Gephardt, Majority Whip Bill Gray, who would be succeeded by David Bonior, Caucus Chair Steny Hoyer, and Vic Fazio, the caucus vice chair and chair of the Democratic Congressional Campaign Committee (DCCC), other media-astute members such as David Obey, Charles Shumer, David Skaggs, Rosa Delauro, Nancy Pelosi, Sam Gejdenson, Dan Glickman, Bob Wise, Bill Richardson, Martin Frost, and George Miller, met to work out media strategy.

While Foley didn't attend the message meetings, he remained the point man for the themes they developed and emphasized them in his own frequent media events including the Speaker's daily press conference. Dating back to at least the O'Neill Speakership, this encounter with the congressional press corps before each legislative day became more formalized with Foley. In the past reporters had simply taken their own notes with no official record. Now an unedited transcript of the question-and-answer session was made available each day, providing the press with access to the thinking of the majority leadership. It also provided rank-and-file members with a benchmark on where the leadership stood on topical issues from one day to the next.

There was also a lighter side to the press conferences as Foley developed a working relationship with reporters. Conferences frequently ended with an almost comic routine with the Speaker's page having an uncanny ability to announce the Speaker's next appointment when a controversial question had been asked, an ability much praised by Foley.

Symbolic of Speaker Foley's relationship with the congressional press was the press conference day when members of the press presented him with a T-shirt that many of them had shown up wearing. A cartoon from the *Baltimore Sun* portrayed the Speaker as a bonneted and exasperated nanny surrounded by a pack of childlike adults dressed in knickers in the midst of a food fight. The text quoted Foley from his June 10, 1993 press conference when he was asked whether there was a lack of leadership being marshaled on behalf of the President's agenda. Foley's response: *Everybody is exercising sufficient leadership. It is the followership we are having trouble with.*

The interaction between leadership and followership has always been a delicate balance in the House, but seldom challenged more than in the unprecedented circumstances Foley faced as he took over the Speakership in the 101st Congress. He saw clearly his new role in striking the balance:

> The Constitution of the United States of America puts the legislative branch of the government in first place. It is the Congress and especially the House of Representatives that must perform the truly representative function under our system of government. It is the Speaker's obligation to make the representative process work, to ensure that the House is a productive place to do the people's business[45]

It would prove to be a challenge.

President George Bush and Speaker Foley confer in Foley's U.S. Capitol office in 1989. *Washington State University Libraries.*

CHAPTER SEVEN

A New Democratic Speaker with an Established Republican President

My power is to bring legislation to the floor, to set the agenda, to influence the nature of the bill.

—Thomas S. Foley, 1996

Party Discipline, Flag Burning, and Other Issues

I T WAS PROBABLY FITTING THAT, as the son of a judge, one of Speaker Foley's earliest challenges was to prevent a ground swell for a constitutional amendment. At the 1984 Republican National Convention in Dallas, Gregory Lee Johnson burned a U.S. flag to protest government policies. Lee violated a Texas flag-desecration law. In 1989, by a 5-4 vote, the U.S. Supreme Court threw out the Texas law, ruling that Lee was exercising his First Amendment right to free expression. In 1969 and twice in 1974 the Supreme Court had similarly reversed convictions of defendants accused of burning, defacing, or otherwise misusing the flag in violation of state laws.[1]

On June 27, 1989, President Bush put congressional Democrats on the defensive when he announced he wanted a constitutional amendment to reverse the Supreme Court's ruling. "I think respect for the flag transcends political party," the President said. "It isn't Republican or Democrat. It isn't liberal or conservative." Congressional Republicans, however, suggested failure to support an anti-flag-burning constitutional amendment amounted to a question of patriotism. It would be "hard to explain" a vote against a constitutional amendment suggested Republican Whip Newt Gingrich. By June 28, a total of 172 House members and 43 senators had signed onto 39 separate resolutions for a constitutional amendment outlawing desecration of the U.S. flag.[2]

Despite the public uproar which had greeted the Court's ruling, Speaker Foley had stated his public opposition to amending the Constitution, and, responding to the President and congressional Republicans in his own June 27 daily news conference, Foley said that "anybody who suggests that there is a party difference in respect for the American flag is using this deep affection of Americans, twisting it, manipulating it, using it for the most base and crass political purposes."[3] Although legal opinion was divided as to whether protection of the flag could be achieved by statute rather than constitutional amendment, Foley saw this course as the only alternative.

> I think it is . . . a position of the Democratic leadership . . . [that] partisanship is not a part of protecting the flag. . . . we Democrats in the vast majority want to take action to protect the flag. . . . most of us believe that can be done by the statute and we [can] avoid unnecessary . . . and unneeded amendments to the Constitution.[4]

On September 12, the House passed House Resolution 2978 prohibiting physical desecration of the U.S. flag.

Even when the courts eventually threw out the statute as unconstitutional in 1990, Foley continued to oppose a constitutional amendment in both his press conferences and from the floor of the House, and the House eventually rejected the amendment.

> In the event that a constitutional amendment comes to the floor, I will vote against. . . . I do not favor an amendment to the First Amendment of the Constitution of the United States which provides the basis of the elemental freedoms of the country in terms of speech and press and religion. . . . If it is not conservative to protect the Bill of Rights, then I don't know what conservatism is today.[5]

"The impression that he's cautious or unwilling to engage in battle—that's dead wrong," noted Majority Leader Richard Gephardt of Missouri. "On the flag . . . he was standing in front of a stampede saying 'Slow down, take another look,' and won. He fights, and goes after things he thinks are important and does it very well."[6] Having begun the fight virtually alone, Foley had persevered and won. "House Speaker Tom Foley," wrote *The New Republic* editors, "is to be applauded for his early, frankly stated reservations about an anti-flag burning amendment."[7]

The issue of flag burning was akin to the 1960s issue of draft card burning when Foley felt he had made a mistake in joining the emotional crowd.

> I had voted, along with every other member of the House save one, to make it a crime to burn a draft card. There had been a kind of revulsion against organized resistance to the draft, although I thought the draft law was patently unfair and unequal in its application and voted against the extension of the draft from time to time on those grounds. Despite those reservations, I joined the congressional mob that voted to make it an offense to burn a draft card. The only opposing vote was that of Henry P. Smith, II of New York, a Republican, not particularly known for defending liberal causes, to put it mildly, but he thought, quite correctly, that, among other things, it was going to be more provocative than effective. He thought it was silly, and voted against it. In retrospect, he was clearly right and every other member of the House of Representatives, including me, was wrong.

Foley had little hesitation in bucking an emotional current such as flag burning when the proposed solution trampled a deeply held sense of principle such as amending the Bill of Rights. His frustration grew when the issues were less clear cut. In the fall of 1989 Republicans were joined by sixty-four Democrats who rejected the Democratic House leadership in passing a Bush administration-sponsored capital gains cut. Foley's opposition was clear.

> I don't see that there is any budget, economic, growth or other strategy that justifies a reduction in capital gains. . . . I think it's foolish to do, and I am disappointed that the Administration is supporting it. . . . I think it is damaging to the budget. It is inequitable. It can't be justified in terms of any value that we, the two parties, share in terms of economic growth or investment, and it's simply a tax break primarily for people in the highest income brackets who need it least.[8]

Democratic defeat on the capital gains reduction disappointed hard-line Democrats but also reflected Foley's sense that fairness to both political sides of the aisle meant clear House majorities should have their way. Foley's moderate, understated style had changed little over the years, but this leadership style as Speaker did not satisfy a strong desire among those Democrats looking for imposed discipline. This contrast arose during Foley's daily press conference whenever there were close votes and journalists asked about leadership "arm-twisting" to maintain discipline among Democratic members. Foley never failed to minimize the degree to which such tactics were effective.

> The arm-twisting days were largely over among the Democrats by the time I became Speaker. It is extraordinarily difficult to persuade a member to cast a vote that violates his or her conscience or dramatically

conflicts with constituent opinion. You don't go to a member of Congress who's spoken out time and again against the death penalty and say, "We need your vote on this death penalty bill because if we don't get it we'll lose the bill." The response to that is "good, I hope it goes down, it should." So, you don't approach people to get votes on issues which are a basic part of their conscience. Even to ask that can be offensive.

The next question is asking somebody to do something which is egregiously against their best political judgment. You don't ask somebody from a very conservative district to vote for a fifty cent gasoline tax. Sometimes people will vote for that, not because you arm-twist them but because they think it's the right thing to do. People have to have a very strong conviction about something for them to be willing to undertake what would be a real political risk.

Members often display extraordinary political courage and sometimes go to the extent of risking their political lives. But, like courage on a battlefield, extraordinary valor is exceptional, not commonplace. You don't ask for it casually.

Although in many ways Speakers O'Neill, Wright, and Foley arguably had more authority in House rules than most Speakers since the days of Speaker Joe Cannon (1903-1911), the political culture had altered significantly. The American political system was now marked by weaker national political parties and more autonomous members of Congress who were more independent of the power structure in the House. But the Speaker's primary obligation was no different than in the past. He still had to do all in his power to enable the House to function as a legislative institution. While in previous eras Speakers would fulfill this obligation by commanding discipline, or brokering agreements, the modern House required a different kind of leadership. The Speakership had become an office more reactive to the demands of its members. A Speaker who attempted to control events that he could not command faced a higher risk of failure.[9]

While President Reagan had needed only twenty-six conservative southern House Democratic, or "Boll Weevil," votes to join the Republicans in order to deliver a winning floor vote, President Bush needed forty-two votes for such a majority. Political survival of these Southern Democrats against Republican opposition at home frequently required that they become fiscal and defense conservatives. If the Democratic leadership lost their support on some votes, they could be counted on to vote with the leaders on other issues. Foley attempted to keep them inside the tent. He appointed Texan Charles Stenholm, head of the Conservative Democratic Forum, a deputy whip, giving him access to weekly whip meetings. Southern Democrats were "more satisfied" with the new Speaker. "I believe we can count on him to be fair. I think we can count on him to give us a shot to get our legislation on the floor, not bottle it up in the Rules Committee," said Georgia Democratic Congressman Richard Ray. "Foley and the other national Democrats are smart enough to realize that they benefit from having these people as part of the party," observed American Enterprise Institute congressional scholar Norman Ornstein. "The last thing they want to do—the worst thing you could do—would be to try to be heavy-handed with them."[10]

I've never seen any great benefit in trying to sanction members for not supporting the leadership. You can sometimes ask them to mute their opposition, but attempting to punish them is almost always fruitless. It usually requires the "offending" subcommittee chairman or committee chairman to become the "offended" subcommittee or committee chairman and, in effect, go "public" with the fact that he's being punished by the leadership for his independence and honesty.

Foley believed the House needed a sense of comity, a respect for procedure, and a spirit of mutual forbearance. A legislative body was, after all, a venue of representative government, a place where disagreement, debate, and deliberation about the public good was possible. Power without judgment was worse than judgment without power. A good Speaker had to have both and use both.[11] But, when the majority couldn't count on Republican support, and couldn't muster a majority among its own, Foley's unwillingness to exert a heavy-hand was not without criticism by some party members who wanted discipline meted out as an object lesson. He was not oblivious to the dissension.

You have to be careful. You can't win totally because there will be people who are disappointed in your lack of firmness, your lack of guts, your lack of courage, whatever, to go after committee chairmen x, y, or z. But it's so obvious that what they want is that their opponents, or their philosophical adversaries, or their not-too-friendly committee or subcommittee chairmen be sanctioned, punished, or criticized. They don't want it for themselves, they don't want it for their friends, or their associates.

A Democratic Majority

The fragile nature of the Democratic majority was illustrated most poignantly—not in clearly partisan projects which favored a distinct Democratic constituency—but in generally popular legislation which appealed to bipartisan congressional majorities. One example was failure on issues with a popular majority of support, but which lacked sufficient bipartisan support to provide the two-thirds requirement to override a presidential veto. The first came with Bush's veto of a Democratic effort to raise the minimum wage from $3.35 to $4.55 over three years. The 247 to 178 support did not meet the 284 two-thirds threshold. The second veto override failure dealt with the Family and Medical Leave Act which would have required businesses to provide up to twelve weeks of unpaid leave for the birth or adoption of a child, or for the serious illness of the worker or an immediate family member. While the bill enjoyed broad bipartisan support in both the House and Senate, President Bush accepted business objections that the bill created a new mandate for employee benefits and Congress could not muster the supermajority needed to override his veto.

A more striking example was when the House was stampeded into repealing the catastrophic health care law one year after it had passed with both presidential and broad bipartisan support. The law had been intended to protect moderate-to-low-income senior citizens from the potentially devastating costs of a major health problem and to provide prescription-drug assistance. Although the legislation addressed a clear health care need, neither the provisions nor funding had been comprehensively explained to the public. After its passage in 1988, the better-organized, more vocal, and wealthier senior citizen lobbies, whose members would have paid a progressively greater share of the expenses, rebelled. The panic in Congress began with a flood of five million post cards, letters, petitions, and telegrams engineered by the National Committee to Preserve Social Security and Medicare headed by FDR's son James Roosevelt and the Conservative Caucus run by Howard Phillips. The less organized voice of the original moderate-to-low-income beneficiaries was drowned out. Although the mass mailings implied that taxes on all seniors would increase by $1,600 to fund the program, only the wealthiest 5 percent, those with annual incomes over $50,000, would owe up to a maximum $800 under the bill.

The repeal stood as an example of congressional inability to thoroughly explain groundbreaking legislation. It was also an example of the potency of small, but well-organized and financed, lobbying efforts.[12] These legislative failures also suggest that a bill's strongest supporters are sometimes overly optimistic about the chances of passage and may want a vote even if the prospects of victory are slim. This pressure for a vote to promote or attract attention to an issue frequently runs at cross purposes to the leadership's instincts to never bring a bill to the floor unless it is sure of passage.[13]

The Ethics Reform in Government Act and other Successes

Foley was handicapped within the Democratic Caucus because of the unprecedented transition of assuming the Speakership through the forced resignation of his predecessor. But he gained much immediate support with his successful orchestration of the congressional salary increase in 1989. He accomplished what his predecessor Jim Wright could not, and the exercise represented a rare expression of genuine bipartisanship in what could have generated a thoroughly partisan political climate.[14]

Voting for an increase in their own salaries has never made members of Congress popular with their constituents. As a result, they've seldom done it and the disparity between their salaries and private sector equivalents, steadily widened.

The salaries of many judicial and senior executive branch officials were tied to congressional salaries, and the discrepancy grew so serious that the National Institutes of Health, for example, could no longer offer competitive salaries to senior research staff. For more than two decades an independent commission had made salary adjustment recommendations for senior officials in all three branches of government which would go automatically into effect unless turned down by a congressional vote. This method was intended to correct public and private sector salary imbalances without requiring active congressional concurrence.

In early 1989 this group of government officials was destined to receive a 51 percent increase of pay. This would have given members of Congress, judges, and senior executive branch employees an annual salary of $135,000 and would have gone into effect unless Congress voted against it before February 9, 1989. Speaker of the House Wright attempted to attract reformist support by banning traditional congressional salary supplements—honoraria—earned through speaking fees after the pay raise took effect. Despite the support of both Presidents Reagan and Bush and a last-minute attempt to cut the increase to 30 percent, public outcry forced the House to vote against the measure on February 7. As a leading supporter of the measure, Wright's reputation was hurt for having tried and failed at a time he could least afford it.

> The press had bated breath on this issue. It's easy to understand and to calculate negative public reaction. There's nothing the public hates more, not even foreign aid, than a congressional pay raise, and there's no way the issue can be handled in a benign way. We have tried appointing independent commissions to make recommendations. That often became ludicrous because the commissions, usually drawn from Republican-leaning CEOs of major corporations, would come back with outrageously high salary recommendations. It demonstrated the vast difference between private and public sector pay today. The public thinks that officials are tremendously overpaid, but the President hasn't had a salary increase in twenty-five years.

> It's hard to understand how you're suppose to handle the question of any kind of government pay raise. Sooner or later, at least theoretically, Congress would have to review its pay. Do they take the responsibility of doing it themselves, and run into the charge that "you raised your own pay?" Do you pass if off, as was attempted, to an automatic pay raise if recommended by a national commission? "Ducking the responsibility" is the charge there.

> So there's no way to do it except do it. I think Jim Wright's concern about it was understandable, but he infuriated many members who felt hard-pressed and felt they needed a pay raise, but expected the leadership to be unblinking and unequivocal in support of it. When 1989 came

around, it seemed to me that we had to do this in some bipartisan way or it wasn't going to be done. Democratic members were not willing to bear the responsibility for a pay raise if Republican members in great numbers voted against the bill. There used to be a catch-all phrase that was used by Republican whips at the Republican doors as their members entered the chamber whenever issues of pay or allowances came before the House: "Vote no and take the dough." It was the duty of the Democratic majority, many Republicans felt, to take all the abuse, including the abuse that they might initiate. As part of the privilege of being in the majority, it was the Democrats' duty to supply appropriate benefits to all the members. It did not include any minority Republican responsibility to support those issues or to forebear in attacking majority Democrats who did supply the votes.

That wouldn't wash any longer. I think the Republican leadership understood this and we made what many people considered a "devil's bargain" in 1989. We agreed that we would not officially support a campaign against a sitting member if the challenger made the pay raise the principal issue. None of us could control what the Republican or Democratic challenger did because we don't have party-directed campaigns. But, to the extent that we could in the way of appearing with the candidate, supporting the campaign, or providing funds to candidates, if a Republican challenged a Democratic incumbent largely on the basis of the pay raise, they would not support that candidate, and vice versa. The Democratic leadership went before the Republican Conference and the Republican leadership before the Democratic Caucus. It passed on a record vote with every supporter's name out there to be seen and attacked. The vote was taken in broad daylight thirteen months before the next general election and it did not become effective until after that next general election.

Most of the big legislative battles in the 1980s pitted Democrats against Republicans. The 1989 ethics reform/pay raise issue was an exception in that it was thoroughly bipartisan. The House version would increase members' salaries by 25 percent to approximately $125,000. Tying the pay raise to ethics reform was the key element in Foley's strategy as it allowed proponents to argue that voting against the legislation was tantamount to voting against ethics reform. It was no sham. The bill abolished honoraria paid to members of Congress who spoke before businesses which clearly had an interest in legislation affecting them. Honoraria had long raised the specter of conflict of interest. Would accepting a speaking fee influence a member's future votes? Few serious congressional observers would have argued that a member would "sell" their vote for $2,000, but the appearance of a conflict was more important than any reality. The abolition of honoraria helped win the support of the public interest group Common Cause which carried real weight with the public on ethics reform.

Foley and Republican Leader Michel appointed a task force headed by Democratic Whip Bill Gray and Republican Whip Newt Gingrich. Both leaderships briefed each other's caucuses. In a joint letter, the chairs of the Republican and Democratic National Committees and the two congressional campaign committees promised to oppose the use of a supportive vote as an election issue. There was an informal agreement between the two leaderships specifying that a majority of each party's members would vote for the package, which provided bipartisan cover for the other.

In what would ultimately appear to be a stroke of genius, it was a pay raise that required an intervening House election before it went into effect. House members were not voting for their own salary increase but that of the members of the next Congress. The vote would be on the record. If voters were irritated, it was available as a campaign issue for opponents.[15]

Foley and Michel had put the full weight and prestige of their offices behind the pay raise package. The House passed the bill 252-174, with 84 Republicans joining 168 Democrats to approve it. Republicans split 84 to 89 and Democrats 156 to 85. Vulnerable members, those who won election in 1988 by 55 percent of the vote or less, were allowed to oppose the pay raise. "It was a show of bipartisanship and leadership force missing in the first pay-raise drive," but it was also a matter of fine-tuning the first effort.[16]

What Foley regarded as his greatest accomplishment in the early months of his Speakership was the restoration of comity and cooperation between House Democrats and Republicans. "The relation between the two parties, and the relation between the two leaders, has not been better in years," he indicated in an interview. Even the notoriously acid-tongued California Republican Robert K. Dornan observed that "Speaker Tom Foley is as liked today on both sides of the aisle as he was the day he was sworn in as speaker, and that's a big compliment." "I think Tom Foley is likely to be viewed as a real statesman," observed the American Enterprise Institute's Norman Ornstein, "[someone] not cheap-shotting it, not second-guessing the president, not fanning ideological flames."[17]

The 1990 Budget Summit

The White House announced on May 9, 1990 that, following a meeting between President Bush and the leadership of Congress, it would pursue bipartisan deficit-reduction summit negotiations with "no preconditions." It would be the fifth such negotiation in nine years, and the process would continue into the late 1990s—although then between a Republican majority congressional leadership and a Democratic President. Inevitably it would be the congressional minority which found it difficult getting a seat at the table.

We don't call it a summit any more because it's so distasteful to people . . . but it's a summit by another name. There is grumbling and there are unhappy dissidents, and there will be votes against it, but both sides see that it brings something to budget issues. . . . The committee process doesn't lend itself to this kind of thing. If you take the Ways and Means Committee, for example, its function today is to cut taxes. If the Republicans in the majority on the committee see no reason to increase taxes, even though the budget agreement calls for the resumption of certain taxes, that is not naturally agreeable to the Republican majority in the House. Democrats, on the other hand, don't think that any taxes ought to be cut while the deficit is still a problem, including conservative Democrats who could certainly not be called tax-and-spend Democrats. They just simply don't think it's fiscally responsible to do that.

You get all these different attitudes in the House and the Senate between the parties and the administration, and you have divided government, and unless you get some kind of mechanism where people with responsible power can sit around the table and try to do something, the process grinds to a halt.

Recall that during the Gramm-Rudman summit the question came up, "well, what about the minority. Should we engage the minority" where the Democrats were the minority in the Senate and the Republicans in the House? When I raised the issue whether we shouldn't have some greater participation of the minorities in both chambers, [Senator] Pete Domenici said to me, "Don't do it. They have nothing to offer. We are the managing parties of the Congress. Democrats control the House. We control the Senate. We're responsible for outcomes that are productive and effective. The minority doesn't care about that. All they thrive on are failure and defeat, obstruction and objection."

The prospect of an October 1 onset of more than a hundred billion dollars in Gramm-Rudman automatic across-the-board budget cuts, euphemistically called a sequester, proved added incentive to holding a summit. In broad terms this could have reduced spending in some domestic programs by as much as 38.4 percent and military spending either 25.1 or 41.3 percent, depending on whether the President used his discretionary authority to exempt military personnel accounts. The projected cuts were particularly high because social security, most domestic "safety net" programs, and previously committed spending was exempt. The largest sequester ever left in effect under Gramm-Rudman had been $11.7 billion in fiscal year 1986. Highlighting the adverse impact of the projected cuts, Office of Management and Budget Director Richard G. Darman noted it would deny Head Start preschool enrollment to 208,400 eligible four-year-olds, eliminate 106 million subsidized meals for the elderly, and eliminate enough air traffic controllers to increase flight delays by 400 to 600 percent.[18]

Yet there was already public posturing on issues like taxes and the debt ceiling. During periods of deficit spending, the debt limit had to be raised periodically to avoid a default on federal obligations. It dealt with past, not future, spending and, because it was essential legislation, became a potential vehicle for unrelated amendments dealing with other programs. To argue that supporting a debt limit extension was optional amounted to suggesting that paying the national debt was unnecessary because the government decided it had changed its mind about some of its previous purchases. By wrangling over issues such as the debt ceiling, members of Congress were backing into a corner before they had even begun negotiations. A veteran of previous summits, Foley had a certain impatience with too much public posturing. As to a legislative strategy to tie various budget reform measures to the debt limit, he had no patience:

> I think I [have] made my position known many times . . . [messing around with] what I consider specific approval to meet debt obligations, is foolish, unnecessary, redundant and mischief-making . . . that isn't any more responsible than not paying your personal bills. It is fully your responsibility. I could use the example of American Express. You say: "Thank you very much for your latest bill, but my wife and I have reached our personal debt ceiling, and I'm not able to pay this bill," or put in another way, "I'm not able to pay this bill because it violates my personal debt ceiling. I am sending the gold card back. Please send me the platinum card."
>
> . . . If we're going to have an agreement, it has to be a sort of seamless whole. It has to reflect a . . . consensus on a number of issues . . . and we shouldn't underestimate the difficulty of reaching an agreement or underestimate the difficulty of getting Members of Congress and both parties in both Houses to support it. It's something that has to be considered as a serious challenge, and it's not helpful, I think, for us to sort of individually lay out agendas outside the meeting. . . . I would hope . . . all members of the delegation . . . will try to focus on the problem and not engage in public rhetorical debate or blame assessment. [19]

Democrats, fearful they would be lured into a trap, insisted that any initiatives first come from Republicans. Republicans worried about how far President Bush might stray from his pledge made during the 1988 campaign not to raise any new taxes. A senior White House official, later identified as Chief of Staff John Sununu, indicated in the May 10 *Washington Post* that Democrats could propose tax increases at the summit, but the administration was likely to oppose them. President Bush quickly distanced himself from the remarks, assuring Foley in a phone call the same day that he stood by his pledge not to impose preconditions on the talks. [20]

It was characteristic of Foley throughout his political career, but particularly during his Speakership, that he placed a high premium on the confidentiality of private conversations. In a political era where press releases were occasionally distributed before conversations even took place, Foley's discretion could prove frustrating to the press. Foley's conversations with President Bush on the budget summit were an example:

> If I have suggestions to the President, I would like to make them first to him, and not—with the greatest respect—through you [the press] to him. . . . my view is, if you were going to give advice to the President and consult with him, you should do him the courtesy of telling him personally rather than issuing a press release.[21]

The ambiguity about pre-conditions, however, continued and stymied the negotiations until a June 26 White House breakfast meeting where the bipartisan congressional leadership, Treasury Secretary James Brady, Office of Management and Budget Director Richard Darman, and Chief of Staff John Sununu drafted a presidential statement to clear the air.

> At the White House breakfast, we finally focused on a statement that would touch the delicate question of tax increases. Darman produced a text which was read to us. We [Senate Majority Leader George Mitchell, House Majority Leader Richard Gephardt, and Foley] then requested an opportunity to discuss the construction of the language alone. We were taken into an adjoining room where the three of us went over the statement line-by-line, word-by-word.
>
> All three of us, but particularly George, were determined that there not be any later ambiguity or obfuscation about the meaning of the statement. The fact that Darman had produced it added a bit to our suspicion. Dick Darman was an extraordinarily bright and competent OMB Director, but he also had the reputation of being devious, if not duplicitous. Our mood was to put ourselves in the position of a Republican arguing that this statement really didn't mean what it appeared to mean. How would the words lend themselves to any such deception?
>
> The original text included something like "including the consideration of tax revenues." Well, that might theoretically include reduction of taxes rather than increases. So, we redrafted it to say "tax revenue increases" as a way of hedging this possibility.

The White House released the presidential statement on June 26 stating that "tax revenue increases" would be part of any deficit-reduction plan.

> I was not unmindful of the political risks, frankly the almost certain political damage, that President Bush would suffer by agreeing to this statement. His [1988 campaign pledge] "read my lips, no new taxes" had become the watchword of the Republican Party. Resistance to communism, tax reduction, and the social agenda had been the three prongs of

Republican political ideology. The communist threat had declined. To now throw away the tax issue would be a serious blow to Republican political opportunity and, in many cases, put Republicans on the defensive.

I thought it was an example of President Bush acting presidential by putting the country ahead of politics. Far from condemning him, I thought Democrats should be respectful of a President rising above party. But, the partisan instinct is hard to quell, and Democrats, in many cases, rushed in to exploit one of the braver acts of the Bush presidency.

In the interest of a long-term bipartisan consensus, the leadership strove in vain to downplay any political damage to the President. "I would hope that this would not be the subject of anybody's effort to create political advantage," stated Foley. "The statement speaks for itself," noted Senate Majority Leader George J. Mitchell. But more than 100 House Republicans signed a letter to the President saying they were "stunned" by the announcement and would not vote for a budget package with a tax increase. "Bush and his GOP congressional candidates can no longer . . . try to deceive the American people," said Arkansas Representative Beryl Anthony, Jr., chairman of the Democratic Congressional Campaign Committee. Bush's turnabout had an immediate impact on the 1990 campaign trail as Republican candidates tried to control the damage and Democrats to exploit the opening. "I knew I'd catch some flak on this decision," said President Bush, "but I've got to do what I think is right."[22]

In the budget summit of 1990 Foley, though adamantly opposed to a balanced budget constitutional amendment which he felt, among other results, might be unenforceable and threaten to improperly draw the judicial branch into budget issues, was also determined to whittle down the deficit. He was ready to raise taxes and sharply reduce expenditures to accomplish the objective. Foley had urged that Majority Leader Richard Gephardt be named to chair the congressional/administration talks because Gephardt had a long demonstrated history of Job-like patience in negotiations, in addition to great legislative and political skills. The White House for its part had an almost allergic reaction to anything associated with Gephardt, and although the administration later conceded that Gephardt had conducted the negotiations with skill and fairness, the initial reaction was such that Foley had to press hard with the President himself to get his reluctant consent.

Meeting at Andrews Air Force Base, Gephardt kept the negotiators gathered periodically at the table for a marathon five months. With no agreement in sight among the two-dozen negotiators, by September 17 congressional unrest had become widespread. A group of conservative House Republicans, not part of the negotiations, began wearing "Junk the Summit" buttons. A counterpart group of liberal Democrats was reportedly working on its own package. The meetings at Andrews were eventually disbanded and a core of eight congressional leaders and White House officials picked up the negotiations in Speaker Foley's Capitol office.[23] While many questions divided Democratic and Republican negotiators, it was the dispute over President Bush's proposal to cut capital gains taxes that had brought those differences to a head. Bush's bargaining position appeared to suffer a blow when both Senator Robert Dole and House Minority Leader Robert Michel appeared to be backing off an insistence on a capital gains tax reduction. "Since Michel was regarded as the president's most loyal soldier on the Hill, his comments were considered devastating to Bush's chances for a capital gains cut."[24] As negotiators got closer to a deal inside the room, comity was shredding outside among rank-and-file Democrats and Republicans who had remained largely in the dark.

Outside the negotiating room it had become a rhetorical war driven by a growing Republican anxiety that Democrats were winning the public relations fight with charges that the GOP was stalling an agreement over its insistence on a capital gains tax break for the rich. Trying to shore up his own troops, President Bush began speaking as though his key advisers were not a part of the negotiations. "The hang-up is not capital gains; the hang-up is with Democrats on Capitol Hill. . . . I've gone the extra mile, and I believe the Republicans in Congress have gone the extra mile. . . . And if and when the ax falls, the Democratic Congress knows that it will be held accountable, and I will take that message to every state in the Union. It is their fault." Foley and Mitchell quickly protested and Bush later had to "apologize for misspeaking" and acknowledge that the Democrats had indeed come forward with offers in the talks.[25]

When the core negotiators finally came out with a summit package, too much time had passed for rank-and-file members on either side of the aisle to accept a take-it-or-leave-it proposition. The negotiators thought they might have avoided a major partisan debate over tax philosophy when they decided to take the two most divisive revenue proposals off the table—raising income tax rates and lowering the capital gains rate. They were wrong. Deep differences between and even within the parties quickly rose to the surface. For Democrats, increasing taxes progressively by levying higher rates on wealthier taxpayers had become the linchpin of many members' campaign themes and the apparent failure of the budget deal to shift the tax burden to the rich was insupportable. Republicans complained that the deal would impede economic growth by calling for too many new taxes and too few breaks for investors.

Bipartisan success for a package filled with taxing and budget-cutting pain required 50-percent-plus-one support from both parties to insulate them from partisan campaign attacks. For all their consensus-building talents Foley and Gephardt could sell the package to only fourteen of the House's twenty-seven Democratic committee chairmen. The Speaker "was appealing to reason," said Energy and Commerce Committee Chairman John Dingell of Michigan. "He's a gentleman—perhaps too much so for the circumstances he finds himself in."[26] Even Gephardt seemed to distance himself from the compromise package before it reached the floor. "I must tell you that I was personally deeply disappointed with the results that we achieved."[27]

On the Republican side, President Bush put his personal prestige and White House lobbying machinery behind the effort to pass the summit package. Minority Leader Michel, who had faced increasing difficulty in holding his party's right-wing in check, saw his top deputy, Minority Whip Gingrich, defect along with most of the party's whip organization, leading a successful revolt. Gingrich's defection meant that Michel and the rest of the GOP leaders had to sell the pact without their chief institutional tool—their whip organization. "Gingrich, a skilled guerrilla fighter not known for his ability to put together coalitions beyond his fiercely loyal conservative adherents, suddenly looked as if he might have been elevated to an uneasy new level of leadership."[28] He remained firmly opposed to any new taxes and was unwilling to relinquish such a central GOP theme. This represented the most serious, but not the last, schism within the House GOP leadership between Michel and Gingrich.

> Our instinct was always to work with Bob Michel, but Newt Gingrich could be very beguiling when he wanted to be. He would come over early and sit down. Maybe Bob Michel was due to come to the meeting, but hadn't arrived yet, and so we were just sitting and chatting, Dick Gephardt, Dave Bonior, Vic Fazio. There would be some staff there. All of a sudden Newt would say, "you know, we could work this deal out. We could do this and we could do that, and if you did this, and we did that, we would be glad to support that." Well, before you knew it, you were negotiating with the Minority Whip outside the presence of the Minority Leader, and you'd have to stop yourself and say, "whoa, you can't start making commitments here, it's Bob Michel's job to decide what the Republican line is going to be. If we can reach an agreement, we're going to have to reach it with Michel."
>
> Gingrich was not all oppositional and contrary. Every once in a while he would put his negotiating hat on and he would want to do business. At that time, you had to be careful that you always were insuring that Bob Michel was in the room.

Even with the pressure of November off-year elections only weeks away and a congressional membership which wanted the arguing to end so they could go home and campaign, by early October it proved impossible to put together a package that would satisfy House Democrats without antagonizing House Republicans. The five-year budget plan, which fell only slightly short of the $500 billion aim of the summit negotiators, contained dozens of increases in taxes and user fees (charges for using federal facilities or services), along with $184 billion savings in programs, including defense, Medicare, farm price supports, and student loans. With none of the regular thirteen appropriations bills enacted, and running out of time on the third stop-gap continuing resolution which kept the government running, the summit plan was rejected by the full House 179-254 with both Democrats and Republicans some thirty votes shy of meeting their target support. The defeat led to a federal government shutdown over the Columbus Day weekend and Congress stayed in session to put together a fallback budget resolution.

Foley was sorely disappointed that a majority of neither Democrats nor Republicans were prepared to unite behind a bipartisan summit package. A degree of common ground on some of the vexing economic issues facing the country might have depoliticized these highly charged policies. Instead, partisan budget politics would continue to haunt upcoming Congresses.

The budget process eventually returned to the traditional process and a House-Senate conference to resolve the differences, aided by the fourth stopgap spending bill signed by President Bush, kept the government operating through midnight October 27. While the final bill satisfied the Gramm-Rudman requirements, it did not end the ideological struggle, with Republicans vowing to resume the struggle over sharp cuts in capital gains in the upcoming 102nd Congress and the Democrats clamoring to reopen the fight to put a surtax on millionaires.

For Foley, Republican Leader Bob Michel, the rest of the bipartisan congressional leadership, and President Bush, failure of the budget summit budget package also appeared to underscore "the limits of leadership power at a time when even the newest members of Congress feared the wrath of their home-state constituents more than the ire of their political leaders."[29]

The Bush Mid-Term 1990 Congressional Elections

In his first two years as Speaker, Foley neither disappointed his admirers nor confounded his critics. He brought the judicious sort of presence to the job that had been expected, presiding over the House as a kind of *paterfamilias*. While capable of being intensely political, he just as often defined his politics in terms of the institution as he did in terms of its two parties. At times he was seen as leader of the House first, the leading figure among Democrats second. In his mind the former also served the latter. "Above everything else, I am concerned about protecting the reputation and position of the House as an institution," Foley told *The Wall Street Journal* in May 1991. "It happens to be one of the foundations of democratic party influence in the country. That is not lost on me."[30]

More than nearly any of his predecessors, Foley was a student of the House, having studied its history going back to its British parliamentary roots. But he would concede that while the office of Speaker was shaped by its history, it was also subject to more contemporary American political forces. Since he first served as a freshman member under Speaker John McCormack in the 1960s, the

U.S. political system had become more diffuse, depended more upon electronic communication, and was more ideological while being more democratic. As reflected in the House, the diffusion of power since the reforms of the 1970s had reinforced the need for more centralization in the Speaker's role. While Speaker O'Neill would have responded to this need by waiting for a legislative consensus among Democrats to develop, Speaker Wright had been more insistent and frequently sought to impose an agenda from above. Foley appeared to reflect both characteristics by striving to fulfill the symbolic character of a post-reform Democratic Speakership, while recognizing the inability of the Democratic Caucus to develop policy cohesion and party discipline in the absence of a strong Speaker.

Seen narrowly, the powers of the Speaker are a combination of what's in the Rules of the House and what the British call conventions or traditions. The need in the House for a strong central coordinating role in the office of the Speaker goes beyond that. Every member, junior or senior, is subject to a variety of influences within the institution. Less understood are the almost daily pressures on these same members from outside the House. A torrent of phone calls, letters, e-mail, and faxes from constituents, interest groups, businesses, and the press amount to a sizable countervailing force to any leadership effort in formulating and passing a legislative agenda. If the office of the Speaker doesn't operate as a centrally important institution it is very hard to move legislative programs or keep a focus on the House's business. It cannot be the equivalent of simply one more letter or one more fax with an opinion on legislation. In my experience the problem was less the House as a whole or the Republican minority. It was in the Democratic Caucus, the inability of Democratic members to coalesce around a single position on key issues.

Those who had predicted defeats for the House Democrats based on the flag issue, the salary increase, economics, or on Bush's popularity, turned out to be wrong when the Democrats gained nine seats in the 1990 elections. In congressional races since 1980 the Democrats had won most contests in open seats and done a better job of holding onto the seats they held. The Republicans had yet to present themselves convincingly as a party of reform.

By mid-summer in his own race for a fourteenth term Foley seemed close to being handed reelection by default. There were no Republican candidate filings by the July 27 closing date and the state Republican Party declined to file its own candidate. "Tom Foley already has $700,000 in his campaign war chest and we didn't feel we had the resources to make a challenge," said party spokesman Lance Henderson.[31] "Good for Foley maybe, but bad for his constituents," observed a *Spokesman-Review* editorial. "Even if a public figure such as Foley is performing well and deserves to be re-elected, as Foley does, a formal test forces elected officials to defend their actions, and affords the voters a chance to grade them on it."[32]

By mid-September, however, Foley's 1988 opponent, registered nurse and anti-abortion activist Marlyn Derby, had secured the 1 percent of total primary votes, some 700 write-in ballots, to appear on the general election ballot.[33] One of the longest Congresses in recent history had kept Foley out of eastern Washington for most of the campaign, and although Derby had again declined any debates, the two did make a joint appearance at Spokane's downtown Rotary. Her main theme was that the nation was facing a recession with a huge deficit, an overgrown bureaucracy, and entrenched politicians who received money from special interest groups. "Maybe we should fire the coach." "Foley's speech six days before the election was no different in tone than it would be six months before or six days after," reported *The Spokesman-Review*'s Jim Camden. "Instead of campaign rhetoric, he provided an update on 'the other Washington' from his vantage point as top Democrat in the House." He praised President Bush's handling of the Middle East crisis. Asked why Congress had failed to pass campaign finance reform . . . Foley pled guilty "to disappointment on that. . . . It was not because I bottled it up." The House and Senate couldn't agree on key provisions and Republicans and Democrats had different ideas on whether to limit contributions or spending.[34]

"Speaker of the House Tom Foley has set the tone for a new way of conducting business in Congress," wrote *The Spokesman-Review* editors. "His style of politics—quiet consensus building—has been a letdown to people more attuned to mud slinging and knock-down, drag-out battles in Congress. But it has helped to repair divisions, has restored some measure of public confidence, and has generally served the nation well." Praising his voice of reason against tampering with the First Amendment on flag burning and applauding his stance in favor of reauthorizing the National Endowment for the Arts, the endorsement still reminded readers that Foley's most important job was, first and foremost, representing the Fifth Congressional District, but "with 26 years seniority, Foley has experience the nation and his district need."[35]

Foley beat the significantly under-financed Marlyn A. Derby a second time with 76 percent of the vote. Expectations as to what being represented by the Speaker meant were also far more modest in eastern Washington than in Washington, D.C., where political pundits frequently equated power with "pork." Few eastern Washington voters appeared to expect Foley to bring them much more than good representation. "Political and business leaders here in the Fifth Congressional District," wrote *The New York Times* regional correspondent, "say Federal pork in this timber and agricultural hub has been as thin as sliced bacon during Mr. Foley's 24 years in Congress."[36] The most obvious examples of his influence were a biking and hiking trail along the Spokane River, a high technology library at Gonzaga University named for Ralph and Helen Foley, and the continued presence of the forty-five-year-old Fairchild Air Force Base west of Spokane whose updated tanker transport missions and survival school training had helped keep it off the base closure list.

During the campaign, Foley frequently pointed out that his first honor was representing the Fifth District regardless of his new responsibilities in the other Washington. While Foley felt he got "a certain sense of support" for his district from his national duties as Speaker, he added that "it's not something you can rely on to carry you through an election." There were a good many Republicans who were hoping Foley would become such a national figure that he would lose touch with eastern Washington voters. "We're concerned he'll be playing up to the more liberal wing of his party, rather than representing his conservative district," said Robert Yates, a Republican precinct committeeman.[37]

No member of a Washington state congressional delegation was ever likely to forget that Senator Warren Magnuson was chairman of the Appropriations Committee and "about as high as you can get in influence in the Senate" when the voters turned him out in 1980. The message was clear. Tending one's district was important for the loftiest of leaders. The conventional wisdom suggested that Foley's strength at home was very strong and, unlike 1976, 1978, and 1980, his strong points had become so deeply appreciated that he was no longer seriously opposed.

Still, not all believed in that "conventional wisdom." It was a small dark cloud representing only sixty-nine votes, but "let the record reflect that if and when U.S. Rep. Tom Foley is voted out of office," wrote *The Spokesman-Review*'s Eric Sorensen from Dusty, "his ouster began in this struggling farm town on the western edge of the Palouse." Lying outside the higher rainfall area to the east and producing thirty bushels an acre rather than eighty to a hundred, farmers around Dusty were frustrated with low wheat prices and budget negotiations that had slashed billions of dollars from the farm bill. Rather than the 63 and 62 percent majorities Dusty voters gave Foley in 1986 and 1988, in 1990 they gave him 22 percent. The vote was clearly not for Derby, but against Foley for his inability to help farmers when they believed they needed help badly. "They figure as Speaker of the House, he should be able to do something," one observer said. Noted Steve Appel, "We have an opportunity to set a precedent and be the first district to vote the Speaker of the House out of office."[38]

> My view was that obviously the fact that I had become Speaker was not overwhelming the district with a sense of absolute urgency about sending me back to Congress. That was a bit of a concern. Being Speaker appeared to be adding stresses without advantages.

At President Bush's request, the bipartisan congressional leadership accompanied him to Saudi Arabia on a November 1990 visit as events in the Persian Gulf became increasingly delicate. Spending Thanksgiving Day with the troops at a Saudi airfield are, from left to right, Republican Minority Leader Robert Michel, Speaker Foley, President Bush, Democratic Senate Majority Leader George Mitchell, and Republican Senate Minority Leader Robert Dole. *Washington State University Libraries.*

🏛

CHAPTER EIGHT

War Without
and Within

The public expects to see congressional governance, not partisan finger-pointing and bickering when a problem emerges.

—Thomas S. Foley, 1991

Prelude to War

IN THE EARLY HOURS of August 2, 1990, Kuwait's ruling emir fled to Saudi Arabia as Saddam Hussein's Iraqi troops invaded Kuwait. On August 8, President George Bush spoke to the nation from the Oval Office about his decision to send U.S. air and ground forces to Saudi Arabia. He spoke of the four principles which would guide the administration's policy including the immediate, unconditional, and complete withdrawal of all Iraqi forces from Kuwait; the restoration of Kuwait's legitimate government; the national commitment since the time of Franklin D. Roosevelt to security and stability in the Persian Gulf; and his determination to protect the lives of American citizens in the area. He went on to explain that Iraq, with over a million men under arms, was the world's fourth-largest military. This was not an American, European, or Middle East problem. It was the world's problem. "The stakes are high," he said. "Mr. President, are we in a war?" he was asked at a press conference following his address to the nation. "We're not in a war," President Bush responded.[1]

It was a question that would be raised frequently in the following months. Throughout U.S. history, the undeclared war has been more the rule than the exception. Since World War II the nation's military involvement has included two convulsive land wars, in Korea in the 1950s and Vietnam in the 1960s and 70s, two Marine landings in Lebanon, air strikes against Libya, the overthrow of the Noriega government in Panama, and an invasion of Grenada—none of which has been accompanied by a declaration of war. Since Congress was granted the Constitutional power to declare war in 1789, the power has been exercised only five times: against Great Britain in 1812, Mexico in 1846, Spain in 1898, the Central Powers in 1917, and the Axis Powers in 1941. In the years after 1941, Americans grew used to "police actions," "limited incursions," and "surgical strikes" as a modern military phenomenon.[2]

From the early days of August 1990 through the end of the year, events in the Persian Gulf outgrew those minimalist terms. In August alone, the Arab League condemned the invasion, the European Community imposed an oil boycott on Iraq and Kuwait, President Bush called up more than 40,000 reserves, the price of a barrel of oil rose to its highest price in five years, and the United Nations Security Council voted to authorize a multilateral naval force to uphold the anti-Iraq embargo. The pace of events accelerated through the fall and into the winter with the Security Council adopting Resolution 679 which authorized "all means necessary" to remove Iraq from Kuwait if it had not withdrawn by January 15, 1991. By October 17, U.S. forces in the Persian Gulf had reached 200,000, a level President Bush nearly doubled on November 8 stating that the U.S. required an "adequate offensive option." By November 19 Iraq had added 250,000 troops to its 430,000 already in or near Kuwait.[3]

The military buildup was accompanied by a comparable buildup in institutional tensions between the White House and Congress. In his October 17 testimony before the Senate Foreign Relations Committee, Secretary of State James Baker "had refused to promise that the administration would seek congressional approval before any attack on Iraq." In reaction, fifty-four Democratic members of Congress filed suit to force the President to seek congressional approval before launching an attack against Iraq.[4]

The 102nd Congress opened January 3, 1991. Memories were fresh of the October 1990 divisive budget battles. The economy had slipped into a recession. And the nation had come face to face with the prospect of war in the Gulf. On a traditional party-line vote of 262 Democrats to 165 Republican votes for Republican Leader Robert Michel, Thomas S. Foley was reelected Speaker of the House. In his opening remarks he voiced what was on every member's mind:

> We convene the 102nd Congress in trying times, confronted by difficult—perhaps critical—choices in both domestic and foreign affairs.[5]

The first order of business for the new Congress was the January 12, 1991 House Joint Resolution 77, to authorize the use of military force if Iraq had not withdrawn from Kuwait and complied with U.N. Security Council resolutions by January 15. For several months, Foley and other Democratic leaders had urged President Bush to stay the course with the economic sanctions imposed on Iraq after its invasion of Kuwait on August 2, 1990. Two letters from President

Bush set the stage and helped shape the debate. One letter, from Bush to Iraqi President Saddam Hussein which largely reiterated the U.S. demand that Iraqi troops be withdrawn, was delivered to Iraqi Foreign Minister Tariq Aziz by Secretary of State James Baker. Aziz refused to pass the letter on to Hussein. Bush's letter to leaders of Congress on January 8 marked the first time the President had openly requested congressional action on the gulf crisis, and the first such request by a President since the 1964 Gulf of Tonkin resolution that authorized force in Vietnam. Bush wrote, "I therefore request that the House of Representatives and the Senate adopt a Resolution stating that Congress supports the use of all necessary means to implement U.N. Security Council Resolution 678."

Most legal scholars agree that a vote by Congress authorizing the use of force qualifies as an exercise of its constitutional authority to "declare war." Scholars continued to be divided on the issue of the 1973 War Powers Resolution. Did President Bush, in requesting congressional backing, effectively acknowledge that he lacked the authority to wage war against Iraq without such legislative action?[6] The administration appeared to have delayed introducing a resolution supporting force until the second day of the Senate debate, January 11, when it felt it would prevail. Asking for support and being denied was a more unacceptable political risk than acting without asking at all.

> It was my judgment that when the vote was taken, the resolution was going to pass. I think that was the judgment of the President too. I commend President Bush for sending the resolution to the Hill, but I'm not at all sure that if it had been rejected that he would have forsworn or delayed military action. That's really what the resolution was about, the timing of such action. We had 500,000 troops in Saudi Arabia, and I think the consensus of an overwhelming number of members in the House was that if there wasn't some backing-down by Saddam Hussein at some point, in the not too distant future, that military force would be authorized. The President wanted to bring that time table into focus. He sent the resolution up to the Hill and I think he and his advisers felt that the votes existed to support him. I agreed with that. So, when I was speaking out against acting immediately, I was really expressing my concerns about a momentous decision rather than so much believing that I and others were going to persuade a critical number of others to vote against the resolution.

Key committee chairmen such as Wisconsin's Les Aspin of Armed Services, Florida's Dante Fascell of Foreign Affairs, incoming chairman of Select Intelligence Committee David McCurdy of Oklahoma, and Foreign Affairs subcommittee chairman Stephen Solarz of New York supported President Bush's request for authorized use of force. Did this constitute defection from the House leadership's opposition? Did it cause Foley concern?

Not to me, but I think it did for some of the liberal members of the [Democratic] party. But this was an issue that I felt very strongly was an issue of conscience, and there should be no hint of party pressure or party discipline over a vote like this.

Foley and the House leadership, along with Senate Majority Leader Mitchell and Senate Armed Services Committee Chairman Sam Nunn of Georgia, united against the administration's request. Still, the Senate voted 52-47 to authorize the use of military force, the narrowest margin backing military action since the War of 1812.[7] Minutes later, the House approved identical legislation by a vote of 250-183 (D 86-179) following more than twenty hours of deliberation. It was one of the longest debates in the history of the House.

The leadership had determined that the resolution was to be "a conscience vote" so there would be no recriminations against those who voted with the administration. Passage of the resolution, however, left most Democrats on the losing side. Quite apart from the substance of the issue, much of the leadership emphasized the historic nature of the debate itself. "In 26 years in the House of Representatives," Foley said from the well, "I have never seen this House more serious nor more determined to speak its heart and mind on a question than they are at this time on this day." House Majority Leader Gephardt said before the final vote, "Whatever our decision, we will leave this room one again and whole again." And, after the vote, Republican Leader Michel observed that "normally, after a bipartisan victory, for me there's jubilation. This is different."[8]

I'll never forget Bob Michel coming up to the [Speaker's] podium and just chatting for a minute during the course of the debate. Bob was a very proud holder of the Combat Infantryman's Badge during World War II. He wore a miniature version of it on his jacket most of the time. He's a very strong, husky, man, but he had tears in his eyes and was on the point of openly weeping. He told me that this was the hardest thing he thought a member ever had to do, casting a vote which would mean the death of young men and women, and deciding when the country required that risk and sacrifice, and being responsible for calling for it.

The occasion was historic: the first time since World War II that Congress had directly authorized sending large numbers of U.S. troops into combat. At issue in the debate was whether the United States should go to war. Although he remained silent throughout most of the debate, Foley "emerged in the closing hours as his chamber's most eloquent opponent of a resolution authorizing force."[9] As a Henry Jackson protégé, Foley brought to the issue an instinctive support for Presidents on foreign policy issues. But Foley also brought his own earlier experience with military decisions on Vietnam and Lebanon. In the case of Lebanon, a civil war had broken out in 1975 between Christians and the Muslim-PLO alliance, and although full-scale fighting had ended in late 1976, intermittent skirmishes continued and reached a critical stage in June 1982 when a large Israeli force invaded Lebanon. The Lebanese government had requested that a foreign presence be stationed in the country to help keep order. In addition to a UN peacekeeping force, Israeli, and Syrian troops already in the country, the United States, France, Italy, and Britain sent troops. In late 1983, these foreign troops became victims of deadly terrorist bombings. On October 23, a suicide terrorist crashed a truck loaded with explosives into U.S. Marine headquarters at the Beirut airport. The consequent explosion resulted in 241 casualties. At about the same time, a similar attack killed 54 French troops in a nearby building.[10]

Going back to the Vietnam War, I had largely gone along with support with the Vietnam War for a fairly long time. I was never an enthusiast about Vietnam, but I was terribly worried about how we extricated ourselves from Vietnam, and I was troubled by the notion that an abrupt congressional/presidential confrontation on Vietnam, a constitutional crisis perhaps, or the abrupt pull-out of American forces similar to the French decision in Algeria, could create an embittering, corrosive, and divisive issue in American politics for decades. I didn't know whether it was possible or not, but was always hoping that there might be some peace with honor exit. That was not to be.

In any event, my experience during that period, including one visit to Vietnam, convinced me that winning the war was a political, if not military, impossibility, and that the longer it persisted the more lives would be lost and more tragedy imposed on both sides of the conflict. Anyway, eventually I voted to cut off funds. During that period I had consistently voted against authorizing the draft because I felt that if we were in the position of sending a lot of young men and women, mostly working class, that there was something inherently unfair about the process. I myself had a graduate deferment during the Korean War, and looking back on it in the context of Vietnam, it seemed to me that one of the responsibilities we had was to at least make the sacrifices across our population as general as possible.

When President Reagan asked Speaker Tip O'Neill to give support for a resolution authorizing the sending of American troops to Lebanon, I voted for it with great misgivings and, in private, told Speaker O'Neill that I thought that this was a dangerous, and perhaps disastrous, course. All the intelligence reports I had seen indicated a very questionable future for such a decision. The danger being it would create a flash-point for a variety of terrorist actions which eventually happened. One of the things about Speaker O'Neill for which he has too seldom been given credit, or blame I guess, is that, with the exception of Nicaragua, he was a very strong believer in congressional support for the President on foreign policy issues. Time and time again I saw him take actions at the request of the President which the President told him were in the interests of the country—taking bills off the calendar, changing the schedule, modifying positions based on the assurances by Presidents Reagan or Carter that this was a crucial foreign policy problem for the country. I was influenced by the Lebanon decision because instead of the troops being cheered in the streets by thousands waving little American flags as President Reagan had told Speaker O'Neill would be the case, there was the terrible bloody incident costing the loss of 241 American lives.

Foley felt that the administration's primary claim—that it was seeking authorization to threaten war in order to avoid it—was flawed. In a relatively rare speech from the floor for a Speaker, he argued: "Do not do it under the notion that you merely hand him [President Bush] another diplomatic tool, another arrow in the quiver of economic leverage or international leverage. The president has signaled no doubt about this. He has said again and again that, if given the power, he may well use it, perhaps sooner than we realize."

There had been a number of discussions at the White House about the possible use of force in dealing with Saddam Hussein. I became increasingly convinced that the President was determined to move in the direction of the use of actual military force rather than to continue the presence of American troops in the region as a lever for diplomacy and a negotiated withdrawal. I remember at one point in a White House meeting, rather atypical for me, I burst out with a plea, "Mr. President, don't lead this country into war." But, notwithstanding my concern, I think the administration wanted to have the blessing of the Congress for the use of military power, a sharing of the political responsibility so to speak. It would also have eliminated a complicated constitutional question about the congressional willingness to support the effort.

On the other hand, they didn't want the Congress to be asked and to say no. The proposal of marriage had to be accepted. Subsequently, of course, it was. I've been asked many times what, in my judgment, would have happened if the House or the Senate, most likely the House, had decided on a narrow vote to adopt the Hamilton Amendment and to reject the immediate use of force. What would the President have done?

I have no authority to say this, I've never discussed it with President Bush, and it's pure speculation, but I believe the President would have gone ahead anyway on some construction that there was division between the House and the Senate, there was a confusion of legislative response, and in that circumstance it was important for him not to allow a constitutional ambiguity or constitutional uncertainty to inhibit the essential foreign and military and defense requirements of the United

States. So, it was going to happen. If it happened with congressional assent, so much the better, but I think it would have happened one way or the other.

On January 16, President Bush ordered the aerial bombardment of Iraq. The bombers had been in the air some thirty minutes before "heads up" calls were made to members of the congressional leadership or the chairmen and ranking Republicans of national security-oriented committees. At the top of the list was a group known informally as the "Big Five"—Speaker Foley, Senate Majority Leader Mitchell, Senate Minority Leader Dole, House Majority Leader Gephardt, and House Republican Leader Michel. The calls were merely protocol designed to notify, not consult. Not everyone on the list was waiting beside a phone, and the White House call from President Bush located Foley at 5:30 p.m., buying shirts at Brooks Brothers in downtown Washington. He was asked to return the call to Bush from a secured telephone. The Speaker hastened back to the Capitol and did so.[11] At 6:30 p.m. Foley and Gephardt received a thirty-minute briefing from Robert M. Gates, Bush's deputy national security adviser. At 6:35 p.m., in compliance with the congressional authorization of force against Iraq, President Bush's letter to the Speaker and Senate president pro tempore, Democratic Senator Robert C. Byrd of West Virginia, indicating that efforts to secure Iraq's peaceful compliance with the U.N. Security Council resolutions had failed, arrived at Foley's office in the Capitol. At 6:34 p.m. ABC broadcast its first report of the airstrikes. A minute later, Cable News Network (CNN) correspondents began broadcasting eyewitness reports of damage from the Al-Rashid Hotel in downtown Baghdad.

Following the beginning of the aerial bombardment, in what was widely interpreted as an effort to protect dissident Democrats from later electoral retribution, Foley and the leadership offered a resolution (S. Con. Res. 2) of support for U.S. troops which received overwhelming bipartisan support. The major aim was to signal the unity of the country during a time of crisis. "I think it's not inappropriate at this time to demonstrate that, regardless of the debate last week, that the Congress stands behind the armed services," said Foley.[12]

> It is certainly true that we organized a vote following the decision on the resolution which gave members an opportunity to express their support for the President, as commander-in-chief, and for the troops. We didn't want the American military engagement of this tremendous size to proceed with an apparent divided Congress, sitting back, unwilling to give its whole-hearted commitment of loyalty and support to the men and women who would fight the battles.
>
> Beyond that, however, there was the suggestion from many that we were simply attempting to cover the political vulnerability of Democrats who might have voted against the original resolution. But one has to

remember that, at this time, it was uncertain what might occur in the up-coming Gulf War. We now know that it was remarkable in its low level of American casualties. But that's the benefit of hindsight. Facing a cruel and dangerous foe, well-armed and equipped, and perfectly willing to sacrifice thousands, perhaps hundreds of thousands, of his [Saddam Hussein's] troops as was done in the earlier Iran-Iraq war, one couldn't know at the time that this might not have been an extraordinarily high-casualty exercise for Americans. In this situation, leaving on the record the last vote as a vote against the engagement might have seemed to some a political advantage as much as a political risk. To put aside all those considerations and to stand together behind the country and its forces was the object of this particular resolution.

With the rapid success of American forces, public opinion switched from evenly divided to overwhelmingly in favor of intercession. Less that two months after the Gulf War began, a triumphant President Bush ascended the dais in the House of Representatives to tell a joint session of Congress and the nation that, "Aggression is defeated; the war is over." On February 27, 1991, following six weeks of devastating air strikes and a brief but bloody ground campaign, President Bush felt confident in announcing, "Our objectives are met." Kuwait was liberated and Iraq had been defeated, Bush said.[13]

Foley would later call the 102nd "the most constitutionally important Congress since World War II . . . because of the action on the gulf resolution. This is the first time since World War II that Congress and the President have carried out their constitutional responsibilities on the war-making powers, to the great credit of both. Now it's sort of ho-hum that it happened. But it didn't happen in Vietnam. It didn't happen in Korea. And it didn't happen in any of the other military engagements that have taken place since the end of World War II. It restored Congress to its constitutional primacy and responsibility in the war-making powers."[14] "What he didn't say," wrote a *Roll Call* editorialist, "was that the wise and modulated tone of the debate was set by the Speaker himself. It is hard to imagine, for example, Mr. Foley's predecessor setting such a tone. Tom Foley is a *mensch* of the first order—a man of integrity, courage, and humanity. He is the right person to be leading the House in this dangerous hour."[15]

The Democratic Agenda

When Congress was finally free to return to domestic issues, it focused on controversial items on the Democrats' agenda, which managed to generate more division than cohesion, including gun control, a civil rights measure intended to overturn a series of Supreme Court decisions which had limited the use of affirmative action judgments to prevent employment discrimination, and a concession to strong labor union pressure aimed at guaranteeing the jobs of striking workers. "Where we often find dissension in the Democratic Party," observed Oklahoma Representative David McCurdy, "is on issues that are important to many constituency groups but are not so important to the public as a whole."[16] President Bush successfully vetoed the civil rights bill—on which the Republican rhetorical assault on "quotas" seemed to hit home with the public—striker replacement, and the Family and Medical Leave Act (a second time). Family Leave represented eight years of effort and compromise by women's groups, labor, and business. Proponents argued that the United States was almost alone among industrialized democracies in forcing workers to choose between the birth or adoption of a child or serious family illness and the retention of their jobs. Opponents repeatedly defined the bill as yet another Democratic effort to regulate industry, increase the bureaucracy, and encourage costly litigation.[17]

As with the flag-burning amendment, these were not issues likely to be large Democratic vote-getters. But Foley and the leadership felt they were philosophically, even morally, right. As the *Almanac of American Politics* for 1991 observed, "Foley, insisting on taking the unpopular side . . . seems to be treating issues like the judge his father was, deciding issues on moral principles without regard for public opinion. No one in electoral politics can do this more elegantly than Foley . . . to watch him argue his positions is one of the rich pleasures of American politics."

Throughout the divided government periods of O'Neill's, Wright's, and now Foley's Speakership, the task of coalition building had become more difficult. Comity among members was strained; bipartisan coalitions in support of legislation were unusual. Increasingly, the majority Democrats had to seek consensus and votes among themselves for passage. The Class of 1974 had criticized Speaker Carl Albert for inadequate communication with the whole caucus. Albert's aloofness was not repeated. In an ever-escalating crescendo, the leadership employed various techniques to create common ground among Democrats through a greatly expanded use of task forces, caucus meetings, multi-member press conferences, and retreats away from the Capitol. It has been estimated that House Democrats held more formal and ad hoc meetings from 1977 through 1990 than during the entire congressional history prior to 1977.[18]

While Foley might question how many Democratic votes were changed in the process, he did recognize the desire among some caucus members for what was loosely termed "party effectiveness," to have the party treated as a party. "I think without some effort in that direction," Foley conceded, "you would have had the natural differences and attitudes within the caucus deepened." The efforts went beyond talking, and on major bills, and politically sensitive amendments, the Democratic leadership used its control over the Rules Committee to limit debate and minimize the damage that Republican amendments could create in the highly-charged partisan atmosphere. Although Republicans disliked the tactic, utilizing powers of the Rules Committee responded to one of the critical expectations of the Speaker, to protect his Democratic members.

At times on major legislation, we had to seek the votes for passage entirely from within our own ranks. It led to some of the claims of abuse of the Rules Committee to which the Republicans objected. When you're held to your own numbers some amendments can become very dangerous. Without bipartisan support for a bill, the minority can construct superficially appealing amendments whose aim is destruction, not improvement, of the bill. These "poison pill" amendments might be irresistible to enough Democratic members that, once adopted, would create enough disaffection among the rest of the Democratic Caucus to doom the legislation. The answer to that was not to let the poison be swallowed.

The Democrats' most significant legislative successes came when the leadership managed to reach agreement with a veto-wielding President: the Americans With Disabilities Act, the Clean Air Act, child care, the extension of unemployment benefits, and the minimum wage. President Bush, whose popularity ratings had plummeted because of the economy, was blaming a "gridlocked" Congress for the nation's problems. Foley pushed for approval of a hotly disputed crime bill, which passed the House on a 205-203 vote, and campaign finance reform, which passed both chambers, all in an effort to indicate that any lassitude in Washington was not the fault of Congress.

Following the Persian Gulf War, the major legislative focus of the 102nd Congress became a Democratic leadership-forced transition from foreign to domestic affairs, but the spending cap constraints of the 1990 budget agreement, combined with the increasing partisan atmosphere in 1991, made significant progress on a domestic agenda difficult. Foley recognized the frustration of his Democratic colleagues. Their most immediate concerns, he said, were less with possible electoral setbacks, and more that the Bush administration was either offering little or no domestic agenda of its own and, at the same time, employing a liberal use of the veto against a Democratic congressional agenda.[19]

On November 9, 1990, Bush chief of staff John Sununu had made the administration's case for doing nothing on the domestic front beyond passing the appropriations bills. "Frankly," said Sununu, "this president doesn't need another single piece of legislation, unless it's absolutely right. There's not a single piece of legislation that need be passed in the [next] two years for this president. In fact, if Congress wants to come together, adjourn, and leave, it's all right with us." As *The New Republic* observed, "there is apparently no problem in the country—not the abjection and isolation of the underclass, not the failure of the education system to perform the job of education, not the grotesquely distorted, inequitous, and inefficient health care system—that is worthy of the president's concentrated attention."[20]

Savings and Loan Bailout

What became one of the largest financial debacles in the nation's history had its genesis in the ebb and flow of political attitudes toward the regulatory function of the federal government. Although the New Deal's response to the 1930s Depression had resulted in a surge of administrative regulation (e.g. Federal Home Loan Bank Board, Federal Deposit Insurance Corporation, Securities and Exchange Commission), there was a general tapering off until President Lyndon B. Johnson's Great Society programs of the 1960s—which gave birth to such regulatory agencies as the Equal Employment Opportunity Commission—and the next decade's growth of environmental and consumer-concerned agencies. By the late 1970s the regulatory impulse faced widespread attack, and President Ronald Reagan emerged in the 1980s "in zealous pursuit of what he considered unnecessary and meddlesome government regulations." Telephone and airline services were deregulated, as were financial institutions as Congress eased federal controls on banks and savings and loan associations or so-called "thrifts" or S&Ls. Most far-reaching proved to be the decision to allow the thrifts to make consumer and business loans, where S&Ls had formerly been limited to mortgage lending. Saddled by low-interest mortgages when interest rates rose rapidly in the late 1970s, many S&Ls compounded their problems with risky loans in real estate and oil enterprises, causing havoc when oil prices collapsed in 1986-87. The result was "the biggest federally financed bailout in U.S. history." By May 1990 Treasury Secretary Nicholas F. Brady testified before Congress that more than 1,000 savings and loan associations, 40 percent of the nation's total, might require government intervention. Although he said the cost might rise to as high as $130 billion, Comptroller General Charles A. Bowsher gave Congress a higher cumulative figure of between $325 and $500 billion over the following three decades. Ironically, the move to deregulate financial institutions resulted in the creation of five new regulatory entities in the late 1980s, including the Resolution Trust Corporation (RTC), whose task was to close or merge bankrupt thrifts and pay off depositors.[21]

For the school of thought which felt that the primary role of a Democratic Congress dealing with a Republican President was "a concerted effort by Congress to foster conflict, to test the president on issue after issue, to show that he is not really the strong leader he has appeared to be,"[22] the high cost of the savings and loan bailout—with a Republican in the White House—would have been ideal. But, at the height of public anger about the S&L scandal, Foley urged that members not raise it as a partisan issue. It was an extremely complex issue and the Republicans arguably would have been equally adept at exposing Democratic vulnerabilities in the scandal as Democrats would have been at hurting Republicans.[23]

The public, which has placed its trust in the "full faith and credit of the U.S. government" backing their deposits, expects to see congressional governance not congressional partisan finger-pointing and bickering when a problem emerges which appears to challenge their trust.

The Resolution Trust Corporation was funded with $50 billion to cover some 370 insolvent savings and loan banks when it was created in August of 1989, a sum the Bush administration insisted would be sufficient. Yet by the summer of 1990 administration officials estimated the cost would range from $89 to $132 billion. At the beginning of the 102nd Congress an administration request of $30 billion was at issue, simply to last through 1991. This would cover losses in about 125 additional failed thrifts. It would not complete the task. By March of 1991 the House had voted on, and defeated, four legislative variations, Democratic and Republican. Members believed the bailout costs were completely out of hand. The Banking Committee's troubles were seen by friends and foes alike as a defeat for Chairman Henry B. Gonzalez of Texas. For most members, Ohio Democratic Representative Dennis Eckart's reaction was typical: "I'm voting no. I don't want my fingerprints at the scene of this crime." "There are 100 guys who will vote against anything," said Democratic Representative Barney Frank of Massachusetts, a key member of the Banking Committee.[24]

On the morning of March 13, President Bush called Speaker Foley, urging him to find a way to give more money to the RTC. The compromise (S. 419 as amended by the House) that finally gained a majority of the House, albeit not a majority of Democrats, was hammered out early that afternoon in Foley's office by the Speaker, Republican Leader Michel, Treasury Secretary Nicholas Brady, Banking Chairman Gonzalez, and ranking Banking Committee Republican Chalmers Wylie of Ohio, along with officials of the RTC. Passage of the compromise was not without drama when, as the running electronic vote tally board showed 144 in favor and 145 against, the Speaker stepped down from the Speaker's rostrum, picked up a green card, signifying a "yes" vote, and handed it to the clerk. The gesture appeared to turn the momentum and the final vote was 192-181. Unfortunately, the story was not over and by the summer the administration was asking for additional funding. In the final hours of the 1991 session Congress cleared a bill (HR 3435) providing another $25 billion for the RTC and restructuring the agency.

Foley wanted the RTC refunded, but wanted it done quickly and quietly. He had indicated to the committee his support for the Senate's "clean" bill as opposed to other alternatives which contained additional provisions and had failed to gain a majority of the House. The eventual compromise was devoid of some controversial minority and women's contracting rights amendments and added a few low-income housing provisions to pick up enough Democratic votes to supplement Republican support. While Foley's relative silence did not indicate much about his views on banking, it spoke volumes about his leadership style and his preference to let the House work its will. A former committee chairman himself, Foley's tendency, even when he didn't necessarily support the proposal, was to give chairs a wide berth. The costs, which he understood and reluctantly accepted, were that some chairmen, in running their own bastions, tended to be unresponsive to party needs unless pressured. In that respect, chairs were similar to rank-and-file members who might support a more aggressive partisan posture and voice concern about the party's image, but were also willing to act independently to protect their own constituent interests when it came to the crunch.[25]

Publicly, Foley appeared to stand above the fray, appearing content to watch things bubble up. Privately, he led by consulting, laying down markers, and prodding. He resisted giving orders, and almost never gave rebukes. It was the "hidden-hand leadership" said New York University political scientist Lynne Brown. In what one observer called Foley's "Taoist approach" to power, the Speaker got personally involved only when the job wasn't getting done, and his involvement managed to "save face" for the other principals involved.[26]

In a city like Washington where most people devote considerable effort to building the illusion that they have more power than they do, what accounted for Foley's seeming habit of making it appear that he had less?

> It's deliberate, I suppose, to some extent, because I think it reflects the reality. Sometimes people believe you can pick up the telephone and write a rule or instruct members. That is simply not true. I don't discount the fact that Speakers have influence, and I have some that is real, not just deference to the office. On the other hand, I think it is also important to recognize that other people have responsibilities here, committee chairmen and others, and that my style of approaching the legislative process is to try to get cooperation rather than presume to give orders. Simply giving orders is not an effective way to operate. It's unrealistic.[27]

Gun Control and the Brady Bill

In what had become a recurrent conflict on controlling crime, the Bush administration had indicated that in 1991 it would push for an expanded death penalty and other anti-crime initiatives. The Democrats planned more moderate alternative proposals including a handgun control bill (HR 6) named for James Brady, the former White House press secretary who was seriously injured in the 1981 assassination attempt on President Ronald Reagan. Americans had long been divided over how to balance their right to bear firearms and the need to keep guns out of the hands of criminals.

Historically, it had taken crimes of national significance, such as the assassinations of the Kennedys and Martin Luther King, Jr., to push gun control to the forefront. Now, under the direction of Sarah Brady, the lobbying organization Handgun Control had become a prominent advocate, but according to 1990 Federal Elections Commission reports, it was still substantially behind the National Rifle Association (NRA) in campaign spending, $178,882 versus $916,135. Among members of Congress, the NRA's successful history in derailing previous gun control legislation, the intensity of its membership, its money, and its ability to quickly mobilize members continued to cause trepidation when it came to bills advocating some type of gun control.

Foley's eastern Washington constituents had always been vigilant in their defense of what they saw as a Second Amendment guarantee of an individual's right to keep and bear arms. Frequent bumper stickers read: "This family is insured by Smith & Wesson," "You'll take my gun from my cold dead hand," or, in the 1970s and 1980s, in recognition of Foley's opposition to gun control, "Another Sportsman for Foley." In describing his own campaign experience with the issue, Foley noted that:

> The question at a plant gate, if there is one, will nine times out of ten be about gun control. It is hardly ever a question about unemployment compensation or parental leave.

It was the intensity, almost religious fervor, more than the number of National Rifle Association members that made the issue so volatile. Foley wasn't defensive about his opposition to gun control. His experience as a prosecutor had convinced him that "laws verging on national registration would have substantial noncompliance and that it would be unhealthy to have otherwise good citizens breaking the law."[28] He had been faithful to the creed and the argument for twenty-six years of his political life. In reporting on its annual banquet in 1987 where he was among the first members of Congress to receive the NRA's "Defender of Individual Rights Award," *The American Rifleman*, NRA's official journal, had praised his efforts.[29]

Washington's eastern slope of the Cascade Mountains has more in common with the conservative Republicanism of Idaho, Montana, and Wyoming, than with the more liberal, urban regions of western Washington. Walfred Peterson, professor of political science at Washington State University, described the comfortable familiarity with guns that was etched into the terrain and culture. "This is a place where the pickup trucks have a fly rod in the back in the summer and a gun the rest of the year," he noted. "You can't, in this district, be for any kind of gun control." As with other liberal Democrats of the region such as Representatives Pat Williams of Montana and Byron L. Dorgan of North Dakota and Senator Frank Church of Idaho, opposition to gun control was one issue where Foley stayed in step with his conservative constituents. This one issue almost seemed to excuse more liberal positions in other areas with which his voters might disagree.[30] As the representative of his district, Foley was on record opposing the

Brady bill. As the leading Democrat in the House, he was leading a party with a majority favoring the bill. As Speaker, he saw his principal responsibility as ensuring that both sides were treated fairly.

Toward the end of the 101st Congress the issue of gun control reached a watershed when the House Judiciary Committee, in a vote of 27-9 with both Democratic and Republican majorities, reported out a handgun control bill. Three years before, the whole House had defeated a comparable measure by forty-six votes. The recent success prompted one dissident member to say, "There's been a kinder and gentler NRA that has led to this wash of anti-gun hysteria across the nation. . . . We need to have a meat-eating NRA that won't be kind to any legislator who votes against the citizens' right to keep and bear arms." As adjournment neared, Foley became the center of controversy, not so much because of his personal views on gun control, but because of allegations that he was using control over the floor schedule to block consideration of the Brady bill. Handgun Control sent out fundraising letters criticizing Foley. A *New York Times* editorial published his office telephone number, and the resulting calls jammed his switchboard for days at a time.

The Speaker resisted the pressure and did not bring the bill to the floor because Senate Majority Leader Mitchell, himself a traditional opponent of gun control, had indicated that the Senate could not schedule the legislation in the remaining days of the session. Because the Senate would not take up the issue that session, Foley did not want to force House members to cast a difficult and meaningless vote on the emotional gun-control issue on the eve of the 1990 midterm elections. He promised at the time to schedule a floor vote in early 1991.

In January, 1991 he had told reporters,

> I think the problem that the Brady bill will face, if it faces any, is not that it won't be scheduled . . . but whether the people who support it have the support in the House to pass it. That's where they ought to direct their attention—not to the false and fraudulent argument that it can't be brought up because I'm somehow going to be a barrier to it.[31]

Under the House bill and its Senate counterpart (S. 257), firearms dealers would not be able to sell a handgun until they had sent the local police a form completed by the would-be buyer and had waited seven days. Although the bill would not require local law officials to do a background check, they would at least be alerted.

With the floor debate approaching, Foley tried to keep his distance, but he became the focus of intense lobbying because of his influence over the Rules Committee, which would decide what amendments would be allowed on the floor and in what order they would be considered. As Speaker, Foley placed a higher premium on the fairness of the process than he did on his own opposition to gun control. House Democratic Rules Committee Chairman Joe Moakley of

Massachusetts said Foley wanted the process to be as fair as possible. Moakley, who supported the handgun control bill, said, "I had a meeting with the Speaker and he said, 'I just want a fair bill. I don't want any parliamentary chicanery so that one side can say that it lost because of the rule.' He said, 'I've been accused of a lot of things and I just want to get this bill behind us.'"[32]

The Bush administration opposed the Brady Bill's waiting period and supported an alternative bill offered by Democratic Representative Harley O. Staggers, Jr. of West Virginia which would have required states to set up an instant check system under which a gun dealer could find out by telephone whether a buyer had a criminal record. Estimates ranged from one to ten years for such a national checking system to be implemented. On May 8, the House passed the handgun waiting period 239-186 after defeating the Staggers amendment by forty-one votes. The impressive House passage put pressure on the Senate to develop a similar measure, and a bipartisan compromise was endorsed by the Bradys and adopted in that chamber on June 28 by an impressive 67-32 vote as part of a Senate crime bill (S 1241).

Democratic Representative Edward F. Feighan of Ohio, leading sponsor of the Brady bill, saw Foley's pursuit of "fairness" as a reflection of his personal preference. "Clearly, if the Speaker were totally committed to passage of the Brady bill, he would not have been as concerned about balancing the tensions between opponents and proponents," he said.[33] In the years before he became Speaker, Foley would not have had to choose between fairness in the procedures and advocacy for a position supported by an important segment of his eastern Washington constituents.

Among other key legislative initiatives in the first session was HR 1, the "Civil Rights and Women's Equity in Employment Act of 1991." The bill attempted to counter recent Supreme Court rulings which had narrowed the reach of anti-bias laws by limiting money damages for victims of harassment and other intentional discrimination based on sex, religion, or disability. The bill would incorporate protections similar to those afforded victims of racial discrimination. As they had with similar legislation the year before which was vetoed, President Bush and congressional Republicans pounded away anew asserting that the measure would force employers to use quotas to avoid costly lawsuits. After a number of floor defeats and vitriolic debate, concessions were eventually brokered with the administration, of which the most controversial was a flexible $150,000 limit on new money damages for women, religious minorities, and disabled people who were victims of intentional job bias. Women objected that the cap placed them on a less equal footing with racial minorities, who had no money limit.[34] Some questioned why the leadership made a priority of a difficult bill when the GOP had threatened to use the emotional quota issue in the 1992 election.

We undertook it because we thought it was important. We are sometimes accused on the Democratic side of doing things for political reasons. This is clearly not one because anyone with eyes to see knows this is not a political plus.[35]

A two-year extension of the fast-track trade procedures for negotiations on the General Agreement on Tariffs and Trade (GATT) was passed; the extension of unemployment benefits ran a tortuous course but was finally successful. Direct public subsidies of congressional campaigns was added to the 1990 version of campaign finance reform legislation. The House passed a modest federal highway bill. The funding had been significantly reduced after Foley tried to take Democrats where they didn't want to go—which was to raise the gasoline tax a nickel a gallon to underwrite the rebuilding of the nation's decaying transportation system.[36] But the one issue that rivaled the Persian Gulf for media and public attention during the first session dealt more with the image of the Congress, and particularly the House of Representatives. That issue featured an institution created at the time of President Abraham Lincoln—the "House Bank."

Flanked by Majority Whip David Bonior and Majority Leader Richard Gephardt, Speaker Foley answers journalists' questions in the House Radio and Television gallery—an event which followed every major legislative initiative. Observing below the podium, second from left, is Foley's press secretary, Jeff Biggs. *Washington State University Libraries.*

CHAPTER NINE

Congress on the Defensive:
The "House Bank" and Other "Scandals"

The House Bank issue touched a public raw nerve about what they considered the excessive privileges and perquisites members of Congress received which distanced them from ordinary citizens.

—Thomas S. Foley, 1996

WHILE MOST OBSERVERS would have judged the Persian Gulf debate as Congress's finest hour in 1991, there was more competition as to a congressional low point. One candidate was the "Keating Five" scandal, which became symbolic of the costly near collapse of the nation's savings and loan industry. Charles H. Keating, Jr. ran Lincoln Savings and Loan Association, a California-based thrift, whose failure in 1989 cost taxpayers an estimated $2 billion. In 1989 Keating reportedly boasted to the press of the influence his political contributions had provided him in Congress: "One question among the many raised in recent weeks had to do with whether my financial support in any way influenced several political figures to take up my cause. . . . I want to say in the most forceful way I can, I certainly hope so."

Although he later said his response had been misinterpreted, it was a major factor in Senate Ethics Committee hearings from November 15, 1990 to January 16, 1991, which provided the public with a view of possible senatorial wrongdoing. The senators, who rapidly became known as the "Keating Five," were Democrats Alan Cranston of California, Dennis DeConcini of Arizona, John Glenn of Ohio, and Donald W. Riegle, Jr., of Michigan, and Republican John McCain of Arizona. Although all five denied wrongdoing, the hearings raised a delicate question for all members of Congress: How far can a politician go to aid a constituent or supporter? Establishing the facts turned out to be much easier than deciding at what point a senator's conduct crossed ethical boundaries. When it announced its findings on February 17, 1991, the Ethics Committee decided to proceed against Senator Cranston because it felt there was evidence that some of his official actions were "substantially linked" with his campaign fundraising. The other four senators were criticized for poor judgment, with DeConcini and Riegle also rebuked for giving the appearance of acting improperly.[1]

Another contender for a congressional low point was the second round of Senate confirmation hearings of Clarence Thomas to the Supreme Court, which followed disclosure of the lurid details of Anita F. Hill's public allegation that Thomas had sexually harassed her. The public testimony did not prevent confirmation, but the Senate's handling of the issues left women outraged and led to a public call for the repair of a flawed confirmation process.

Adding fuel to the increasingly tarnished congressional reputation was a September 19, 1991 article published in the bi-weekly congressionally focused newspaper *Roll Call*. The article followed up on its own and a *Washington Post* story of seven months earlier on the extent of House members' overdrafts at the House Bank.[2] While the earlier stories had attracted little attention, the new story fell on fertile Congress-bashing ground. The paper noted the results of an annual General Accounting Office (GAO) audit of the House Sergeant at Arms, which revealed that "bank officials have not taken action to suspend, terminate, or otherwise penalize any account holder, even though many of these account holders have continued to cash checks when there are insufficient funds in their accounts to cover the checks." *Roll Call's* somewhat clinical description unearthed a story which would gather force and extend well into the next year.

The cumulative effect of these stories had an almost immediate impact on the public's perception of government in general, and Congress in specific. In an October 10-13 Gallup Poll on "public mistrust," respondents rated those institutions in which they had "a great deal" or "quite a lot" of confidence. At the top was the military (69 percent), followed by organized religion (56 percent), the presidency (50 percent), and the Supreme Court (39 percent). Separating the two co-equal branches of government from the third were public schools (35 percent), newspapers (32 percent), banks (29 percent), television (24 percent), organized labor (22 percent), big business (22 percent), and finally the Congress (18 percent).[3]

In itself, a low public esteem for the Congress was not new. For decades, the Gallup Poll had periodically asked citizens whether they "approve or disapprove of the way the U.S. Congress is handling its job." Following the 1974 Watergate scandal, 48 percent said they approved, but that level fell steadily for the rest of the '70s to a low of 19 percent. During the 1980s, public approval ranged between 32 percent in 1980 and 56 percent in 1987. The Persian Gulf War congressional debate attracted a congressional approval rating of 49 percent in January 1991, but approval quickly dropped back to the 20 percent range and reached an all-time low of 17 percent with the House Bank scandal.[4]

Congressional Republicans hoped to turn the anti-Congress sentiment to their tactical advantage in 1992, and President Bush gave the theme national prominence in an October 24 speech the White House had billed as presenting the President's suggestions for improving the Senate confirmation process. But it was his broadside against lawmakers which captured the newspaper headlines and television evening news, and built on the "image of the Capitol as a perk palace run amok." "When Congress exempts itself from the very laws that it writes for others, it strikes at its own reputation and shatters public confidence in government," Bush said. "These exemptions encourage special interest groups to press them for reckless regulations, knowing that Congress might adopt such laws if it won't feel the sting of these laws. This practice creates the appearance and reality of a privileged class of rulers who stand above the law." President Bush listed the Equal Pay Act of 1963, the Civil Rights Act of 1964, the Americans with Disabilities Act of 1990, and the Age Discrimination in Employment Act as among those from which Congress had exempted itself.[5]

Within hours, Senate Majority Leader George Mitchell and Speaker Foley fired back, accusing the President of seeking to divert attention from the nation's economic woes. They also noted that some of the same laws in question also exempted the President's staff. The congressional leaders insisted that Congress already had applied major civil rights protections to its staff, through internal enforcement. While Foley called it the "beginning of a kind of Congress-bashing presidential campaign rhetoric that I think is not helpful," President Bush had hit a hot button that would cool but slowly.[6]

The institutional substance of President Bush's charges had a long history rooted in the constitutional concept of separation-of-powers. Congress had frequently exempted itself from coverage when the laws included remedies that involved policing by the executive branch and adjudication by the courts. Despite the specter of executive branch oversight, Congress had long before decided it had to tolerate executive branch enforcement of criminal laws that relate to its official functions, such as bribery statutes. "What we want to do is be treated like the rest of the folks in the country and make sure our people are protected, but within the bounds of what our forefathers have set out," observed House Majority Whip David Bonior of Michigan.[7]

But, as the congressional leadership recognized, it was not separation-of-powers arguments that attracted media or public attention, but the more easily understood, almost commonplace, issues that fed cynicism about the Congress. Foley, Mitchell, and the rest of the leadership went on a "perk war." The price of a haircut at the subsidized barbershop was doubled, the first increase in a decade. The Sergeant at Arms staff would no longer "fix" members' District of Columbia parking tickets whether the business was official or not. The "Members' Gym" began charging an annual membership fee. Free prescriptions provided by the pharmacy in the Office of the Attending Physician, dating back to an accommodation for Congress and the Supreme Court by President Franklin D. Roosevelt in the 1930s, were eliminated and members required to carry their own health and pharmaceutical insurance. Virtually nothing which might be viewed as a congressional "perk" escaped media scrutiny, including an estimated $20,000 to replace worn-out rugs in Capitol elevators with marble to match the floors. At this point Foley drew the line. Noting that during a recent interview he'd noticed that the Cable News Network's headquarters had eight marble-floor elevators, the Speaker stated that in his opinion:

> We should continue a responsible renovation of the Capitol. . . . These are not Members' elevators, but they are public elevators that handle the traffic of the public visiting the galleries and so forth, and they are designed to match the floors of the Capitol and to be there probably as long as the elevators will last and the Capitol stands, so I think it's an investment that I'm neither ashamed of nor apologetic for. It's an investment in what is the great monument of this building.[8]

A Media Appetite for Scandal and the "House Bank"

A certain level of public antipathy toward politicians and their institutions has been part of the American character since nationhood. But a number of factors had intensified this public antipathy. The highly publicized issues facing Congress (e.g. health care, the deficit, welfare, or crime) were complex and defied easy solution. The general public's unhappiness with the economy, lack of job security, anxiety about their children's futures, and distrust of authority all exacerbated anti-Congress sentiments. In their fundraising efforts, interest groups often focused on creating a sense of anger and outrage at Congress. Members of Congress tried to distance themselves from the institution in their reelection campaigns. And, in a fundamentally partisan sense, Newt Gingrich, eventually to become Speaker, and his Conservative Opportunity Society (COS) spent the 1980s and early 1990s undermining the legitimacy of Congress in an effort to so repulse the public that it would throw the longtime Democratic majority out and allow the Republicans to govern. In metronomic cadence, Congress was presented as a tyranny of Democratic incumbency, in debt to special interests, and victimized by personal scandal.[9]

While all of these factors contributed to public disenchantment, one could not look at the public's attitude toward Congress without looking at the central source and filter of its knowledge, the press. Those issues the media chose to cover, and whatever "slant" they brought, inevitably influenced the public's views. During this period, media scholars observed a change in press focus on Congress, particularly on television. The media's self-styled adversarial role acquired a more hostile tone. A traditional policy focus gave way to a new emphasis on scandal, and, when the story seemed "hot," a pack quality took over.[10]

The House Bank, more than a century old, was not a full-service "bank." Since the days when Abraham Lincoln was a member of the House, the Sergeant at Arms had supervised a disbursing service of salaries and allowances for members. As the Speaker repeated endlessly in his daily press conferences over the course of months during the scandal, there was no loss of any taxpayer funds. The only funds on deposit belonged to members. These were not interest-bearing accounts, and arrearages in one member's account were made up from another member's. Most members routinely drew on the accounts, into which their salary checks were regularly deposited. The Sergeant at Arms received no special management training for his financial management position and was elected by the members of the House at the beginning of each congressional session. The Speaker was ultimately accountable for the performance of the House officers, but he was not responsible for their appointment and had no authority to fire them. As run by the Sergeant at Arms, the "Bank" was an archaic legacy of the mid-1800s, and whatever similarities it bore to a typical community bank were more misleading than instructive—a point lost in most of the press treatment.

One of the important reforms of the 103rd Congress (1993-94) to strengthen the Speakership was to give the Speaker the power to appoint the officers of the House. Since the mid-1970s, the Sergeant at Arms, Clerk, Postmaster, and Doorkeeper had been nominated, and thereafter almost routinely renominated, by the Steering and Policy Committee. The nominated officers were in turn elected by the caucus and, in a more perfunctory way, by the whole House. Together, these officers shared responsibility for the basic day-do-day administrative operations of the House of Representatives.

Many of the officers had come to think of themselves as almost independent candidates with their supporters, friends, and associates in the caucus. Their constituency was the Democratic membership of the House. But in that context, the Speaker had ceased being of any unique significance to their retaining their positions. In effect, they all saw themselves as running for sheriff every two years and saw their reelection as the result of their own efforts and popularity—their own successful campaigning.

What transpired in the 103rd Congress was that we were able to develop the same kind of relationship to the officers of the House that the Speaker had with the Democratic members of the Rules Committee. They could only be nominated by the Speaker. They could be rejected by the caucus or the House, but they could not appeal the Speaker's failure to nominate them. They could only become a candidate with the Speaker's nomination and serve, in effect, at his pleasure, from Congress to Congress.

The Speaker had always been ultimately responsible for the performance of the officers of the House. Now he could realistically be accountable as their selection would be based on the Speaker's assessment of fitness for the job.

This was not, of course, the relationship of the Speaker to the House Sergeant at Arms during the "House Bank" scandal.

Following the GAO audit, the Sergeant at Arms failed to implement the new guidelines formulated by the Speaker and GAO with advice from Washington, D.C., banking consultants. Member overdrafts continued. On September 25, 1991, Speaker Foley announced that overdrafts would no longer be tolerated, and that "members will have the same rights, no more, no less, than another member of the public."[11] By this time, however, the media coverage had shifted from highlighting a House management problem to an issue of potential scandal involving the entire House membership. In any political organization, the transition from an internal management issue to a political issue is stark and, in consultation with the Republican leadership, the Speaker concluded that simply reforming Bank procedures was now an inadequate solution. He recommended that the Bank be abolished and the members take advantage of the services of the federal credit union. On October 3, 1991, the House voted 390 to 8 to cease all bank and check-cashing operations as soon as practicable, but no later than December 31, 1991. The Bank formally ceased operations on December 30, 1991. The story might have ended there.

However, in addition to closing the Bank, the House instructed the Committee on Standards of Official Conduct (traditionally referred to as the Ethics Committee, and the only committee to have an equal number of Democratic and Republican members) to review the audit records and determine whether any applicable standards of conduct had been violated. On March 10, 1992, lacking any clear legal definition of what constituted abuse of members' banking privileges, the Ethics Committee outlined what it considered a sustained and systematic abuse of overdrafts and recommended, with the support of the Democratic and Republican leadership, on a bipartisan 10-4 vote, to publicly disclose the names and pertinent information for nineteen current and five former members who represented "significant abusers."

The recommendation did not stand. The 1990 congressional elections had brought to the House a new crop of Republican freshmen "drawn to the slash-and-burn tactics" of Gingrich's Conservative Opportunity Society, seven of whom organized an informal "Gang of Seven" (Jim Nussle of Iowa, Rick Santorum of Pennsylvania, John Boehner of Ohio, Scott Klug of Wisconsin, Charles Taylor of North Carolina, and Frank Riggs and John Doolittle of California). *Roll Call* editorialized that although the congressmen were ostensibly concerned with congressional reform, "often, the attitude seems to be that the Seven feel they have to destroy Congress in order to save it."[12] They now took to the House floor to demand that the name of every member with even a single Bank overdraft be released. Congressman Nussle, standing in the House chamber wearing a paper bag over his head, announced to the television cameras that "it is time to take the mask off this institution. . . . Mr. Speaker, announce the list of names."[13]

But the Speaker stuck to a rationale based on the integrity of the Ethics Committee and the bipartisan instructions its members had been given.

> The committee conducted this inquiry without knowledge of the accounts they were examining. They were examined under coded account numbers, which prevented any Member from having the identity of any account that they were reviewing. I think that was an appropriate and proper procedure, and it is one that I fully support and approve of. . . .
>
> The bipartisan resolution of the House, which directed the committee to bring this report, charged them with the responsibility of reviewing the management of the Bank and identifying any Members that they thought might have abused the banking privilege. That is the instruction. Now, in my judgment, that is what the committee did, and that is what we should support. . . . The committee made this determination and recommended it to the full committee with 3 Republicans and 3 Democratic members making the recommendation unanimously. . . .
> I always trust the voters, and they ultimately make the decision of who sits here. But I believe that the committee was charged with a responsibility, which they carried out, and I am going to support the recommendation.[14]

Although the Ethics Committee had tried to strike a balance in differentiating abuse from inadvertence, two days later, on March 12, the Republican leadership withdrew its support of the committee's recommendation, and the House voted to release the names of all members and former members who had written any overdrafts. The same day, the Sergeant at Arms resigned, and eight days later, March 20, 1992, President Bush's U.S. Attorney General William P. Barr announced the appointment of a "special counsel," retired federal judge Malcolm R. Wilkey. Wilkey, seventy-three, was a former federal prosecutor who sat on the U.S. Court of Appeals for the District of Columbia from 1970 to 1985, after which he served as ambassador to Uruguay until 1990. "My direction to Judge Wilkey," Barr said in his statement, "is to conduct a fair, thorough and expeditious review of this matter, and to report to me as promptly as possible on whether there is any individual wrongdoing which requires further action." Wilkey's preliminary inquiry would consume eight-and-a-half months, involve investigation of some 325 current and former members, and conclude that "actual criminal conduct by some members appears to have taken place, but it is quite limited." "The credo of the House bank was to serve the House of Representatives and never embarrass a member," Wilkey would conclude. "This credo, which underlay the bank's policies, indeed its very existence, ultimately led to its downfall."[15]

Fallout from the release of the names was widespread public demand for congressional reform, without any translation into specific proposals. The congressional response came on two separate fronts. The pressure prompted a desire in both the House and Senate to demonstrate publicly that members strongly supported institutional reorganization. The two chambers created a bipartisan, bicameral committee, the Joint Committee on the Organization of Congress, to evaluate the internal operations of the Congress and to provide long-term recommendations.[16] The resolution specified that the joint committee look into the committee system, the relationship between the House and Senate, and the responsibilities and powers of the congressional leadership. This was not a mandate for a "quick fix," but authorized a review of some of the most basic organizational relationships of the Congress. The twenty-eight member panel would include equal numbers of Republicans and Democrats from both the House and the Senate.[17]

On a more immediate level, Foley wanted to minimize any future House Bank scandals and partisan controversies over the kind of essential internal managerial issues that President Bush, in the campaign rhetoric of the season, termed "a two-bit post office or a lousy little bank."[18] He had contemplated bringing a Democratic leadership-drafted resolution to the floor but, with the prospect of Republican opposition, convened a bipartisan task force to discuss reforms rather than simply assign the task to the committee with jurisdiction, the House Administration Committee. Democratic members included Foley, Majority Leader Richard Gephardt, Chairmen Joe Moakley and Charlie Rose of the Rules and House Administration Committees, Representatives Steny Hoyer and Vic Fazio as chair and vice chair of the Democratic Caucus, Representative Louise Slaughter as chair of Organization, Study and Review, and Representative David Obey. Robert Michel's appointees also included top party officials, "but not Whip Newt Gingrich, who had tried to turn the bank scandal to partisan advantage."[19]

The reforms needed to be significant and quick. Republicans, seeing the task force as an opportunity to redress long-standing complaints, sought broad changes beyond House administration. In the task force's closed-door meetings, Foley initially expressed some willingness to include certain proposals from the Republican list, but the differences in agenda essentially doomed the effort's bipartisan prospects.[20] In the end, a bipartisan agreement proved unattainable, but Foley and the Democrats largely achieved their aims. A solid package of reforms that did not undermine majority control passed in the House. As one veteran Congress watcher concluded, "while enactment of management reforms did not repair the damage done by the bank scandal, it began that process. It enabled Democrats to say they had taken the problems seriously and responded in a responsible fashion."[21]

> I have said publicly I think the age of patronage was over. . . . The process of this institution as far as I am concerned will be that people will have jobs only if they are qualified to conduct them and will have them only as long as they continue to perform properly.
> . . . We are going to go ahead and do what we think is right, to place this nonlegislative support service area of the House activities on a nonpartisan business administrative basis that is above reproach and get the best person we can recruit for that position.
> In 1977 I supported [Rep.] Dave Obey's effort to establish an administrator and then to create an appropriate system of internal audits of the administrative aspects of the House of Representatives. Unfortunately, at that time we did not get a majority for it. One of the reasons was that 133 Republicans voted against taking the bill up . . . and I think almost everybody would agree that if we had installed that system in 1977, that the situation would have been one of improvement.[22]

Although the overhaul failed to go as far as Republicans wanted, the proposal changed a patronage system that had been in place for years. It eliminated the postmaster, vastly shrunk the other officers' purview, and placed all financial and non-legislative functions such as payroll, office supplies, and printing under an administrative director to be chosen jointly by the Speaker and the majority and minority leaders. The arrangement, in effect, gave the Republican leader an effective veto over the selection of the House Administrator. Final passage by the House of the Administrative Reform Resolution on April 9 took place with a debate interrupted by partisan shouting matches and was largely along party lines. "House-keeping" would now be the responsibility of a nonpartisan management professional.[23]

By the time of the November 1992 elections, the multi-month investigation by the special counsel had led to no prosecution of a sitting member of Congress based upon that member's Bank activities. However, opinion polls, fed in large part by the unremitting media coverage, had already rendered their verdict with 63 percent of those polled believing that members who had overdrawn House accounts had acted illegally.[24]

Led initially by the national media, the story spread to the smallest of local media outlets across the country. News organizations found that "the high degree of public hostility toward Congress makes it a particularly easy target, one that doesn't require any of the usual or customary checks and balances. If you bash Congress, even in a patently unfair fashion, who will protest?"[25] Even when defending Congress the press was harsh. A *Washington Post* analysis piece suggested that "there's no shortage of buffoons, charlatans, blowhards, and intellectually dishonest people on Capitol Hill." But with all the criticism of the national legislature, "perhaps a little Congress-defending is in order. Not much, mind you, but if [mass murderer] Jeffrey Dahmer deserves a defense, then Congress does too."[26]

Legal specialists of the Library of Congress's Law Library and Congressional Research Service reviewed the legislative ethics restrictions in twenty-four parliamentary democracies across a range of ethical issues such as outside income, financial disclosure, acceptance of gifts or gratuities, and accountability of campaign contributions. The study concluded that "the overall scheme of regulation of legislative ethics within United States law and congressional rules is substantially more restrictive than the other countries surveyed."[27] One cannot dismiss the instances of real abuse in the House Bank case, but as the story continued to dominate media attention into the spring of 1992, it created what *Washington Post* reporter/columnist David Broder had called the "trivialization of substance."[28]

Whatever Foley and the Democrats achieved in the 102nd Congress came dangerously close to being eclipsed by the media and public focus on the House Bank. While the traditional daily Speaker's press conference served to influence the perceptions of opinion leaders in Congress and the congressional media, it proved to be a very limited vehicle for reaching the American people.

> On some days I regarded the daily press conference as simply a chore to get through and a task to see if we could avoid making any news. Obviously on other days we were trying to convey a message. If I had it to do over again, I would have experimented occasionally with radio and television coverage. The electronic media were represented at the press conferences, but without tape recorders or cameras. It was, perhaps, an anachronism for a Speaker to be carrying on his principal communication with the press through the print media at the same time that the entire proceedings of the House were being carried live on cable television's C-SPAN. However, I think television cameras, in particular, would have changed the character of the daily press conferences. It's almost inevitable that you would have had the broadcast media trying to press issues that were more contentious than just informational "thank you very much Mr. Speaker" kind of thing. And maybe that's what I had

in mind when we were so cautious. It's fine in the periods of relative calm, but if you get a blow up of an issue like the House Bank, then you would have created an opportunity for even more of a fire storm.

The House Bank crisis proved to be a storm that went beyond the Speaker. For twenty years Heather Foley's work went largely unnoticed outside the Capitol. Now she was coming under a more intense, intrusive, scrutiny. "Congress is hyper-male dominated, and the staff is supposed to be seen but not heard. The fact that she's the chief of staff, a woman and a spouse is almost more than they can take," said a senior Democratic staff member. "I've never been a public figure and I don't intend to become one," Heather said, but a higher profile had ceased to be an exclusively voluntary decision. In 1990 Heather Foley was chosen in a *Business Week* poll as the congressional staff member with the greatest influence in shaping legislation. Now, in April 1992, *Washingtonian Magazine* included her in its snide roster of "Women Who Scare Men" in Washington, D.C. Heather's "greatest moment" was described as having "stunned a roomful of meeker men by telling [Speaker] Tip O'Neill to put out his smelly cigar." Her "worst moment" was described "when Tip continued to puff."[29]

In March 1992, she testified before a federal grand jury investigating alleged criminal activity at the House post office. The *Washington Times* alleged she had been involved in a cover-up of the investigation of the post office when, in reality, a one-month hiatus had occurred when the probe was officially transferred from the Capitol Police to U.S. Postal Service inspectors. The paper also said Heather was a grand jury target. The U.S. attorney heading up the investigation was finally forced to release a letter indicating that she was neither a target nor a subject of the grand jury. "I'm somewhat bewildered by the attention I'm getting, but I assume it's an effort to get at my husband," she said in a rare interview with the hometown Spokane newspaper. "I'm not considering resigning. I love public service, and I still believe in it. Right now, I'm just taking it one day at a time." The intense anger that seemed to be sweeping the Capitol, she felt, reflected distress over the Bank disclosures. "There are private tragedies being played out here. It's very painful," she said.[30]

"Other wives on the Hill may be powerful because of their ability to put together receptions or their social skills," observed Democratic Representative Pat Williams of Montana after Foley's ascension to the Speakership. "But Heather's power is the raw power of the House. . . . She assigns office space, among other things. She determines winners and losers, and therefore she's a bit of a target." The Speaker tried to clear the air on a March 27, 1992 ABC "Nightline" program.[31]

She's capable. She's hard-working. She's honest. She has my full confidence.

He rejected anonymous calls that he and Heather resign, and went on to say,

I think that's one thing that would be really very unjustified . . . to somehow make my wife a scapegoat. . . . She's my chief of staff, and she'll remain my chief of staff.

Assuming responsibility as the man at the helm, Foley appeared on innumerable media programs defending the House. He had reassured Democratic members on the debate over the use of force in the Persian Gulf and the flag-burning amendment that their "no" votes would not come back to haunt them in any future election, but the furor over the House Bank was of a different order of magnitude.

First of all, the issue of the Gulf War was one of being on the losing side of a majority, bipartisan, decision. I was really quite confident that people who opposed giving authority to the President to invade Kuwait at that time could very successfully say that "I supported the troops when they were committed, and I supported the President after the Congress voted, and maybe I was wrong, but I thought it was better to wait." There aren't too many people who will stand up and respond by saying "you cowardly, pusillanimous, traitor."

The Bank issue, however, touched a public raw nerve about several things. One, the public's cynical view of the low ethical standards of Congress, and resentment about what they considered the excessive privileges and perquisites members of Congress received which distanced them from ordinary citizens. It was as if somebody alleged that members of Congress didn't have to pay gasoline tax when they went to a gas station. As a matter of fact, there was, for example, a totally false report at one point during the gasoline crisis of President Carter's administration that members of Congress were getting free gas. Even though easily disproved, it caused an enormous stir for a while. I remember we actually did a news spot with one of the television networks where I drove up to a station, waited in line, and, when we arrived at the pump, the reporter who was riding with me got out and asked, "Does Mr. Foley have to pay for gas?" The gas attendant's eyes rolled and he said, "Of course he does. He doesn't get it free." Then, after a pause, he said, "If you don't believe me, you can tap my tanks."

But, with the House Bank, people knew that if they had an overdraft at their bank they'd have to pay for it. It made them angry.

In the twentieth century the Democratic Caucus had witnessed very few challenges to an incumbent leader: Morris Udall mounted a symbolic candidacy against John McCormack in 1969, and John Conyers of Michigan won about twenty votes in two quixotic runs against Carl Albert in the 1970s. By contrast, two Republican leaders had been unseated since World War II. If the Republicans were a party of leader factions, the Democrats were primarily a party of regional and ideological factions. Traditionally, House Democrats had always recoiled at the prospect of divisive leadership fights.[32]

"The Speaker is at one and the same time the leader and the servant of the House," noted Ronald M. Peters, Jr., author of *The American Speakership*. Shortly after becoming Speaker, Foley had orchestrated the ethics reform which led to House members getting a 40 percent pay raise and shielded them from attacks when Ralph Nader and other critics howled. Two years later he was fighting term limits. But when he appeared to have failed to adequately anticipate the public's backlash to the Bank scandal, his colleagues felt exposed and their own political futures threatened. The Bank had become a sufficiently hot button that several Democratic members called for Foley's resignation. Since the days of Speaker Cannon early in the century, no Speaker of the House had become a national campaign issue, but the Republicans had broken that tradition in the 1980s with attacks on Speaker O'Neill. There was now speculation that attacks from within the Democratic Party might target Foley. If his leadership reached a nadir, it was probably on April 2 when Texas Democrat John Bryant stood on the floor of the House and called for Foley to resign. "For Tom Foley," Bryant ventured, "political combat, even when absolutely necessary in order to present the nation with a Democratic alternative, is to be avoided if at all possible."[33]

For Democrats such as Congressmen George Miller of California or David McCurdy of Oklahoma, the criticism went beyond the Bank. Those qualities of bipartisanship, lack of an aggressive political agenda, and deliberative legislative style that had once made him so appealing, now seemed exasperating. For them, the period of healing had passed, and with President Bush sneering at "the Democrat Congress" as a place of "perks, PACs, and privilege," these House Democrats wanted a fighter.[34] Congressman McCurdy had accused the Speaker of inadequate leadership in forestalling the Bank crisis and of responding weakly to Republican efforts to capitalize on it. "He also suggested to Democratic colleagues that Mr. Foley should be replaced as Speaker and that he might be available as a replacement."[35]

Foley had given his answer to that challenge nearly a week earlier on a March 27 ABC "Nightline" interview with Ted Koppel in which he made it clear he wasn't contemplating offering himself as a sacrifice.

> Oh, if I thought the institution would be improved and the public attitude would be restored and the members of Congress would all be able to go forward and move on the public issues if I were to leave, I would leave. No question about that. But that's not in my judgment what's needed. In my judgment, what is needed today is that we get back to . . . doing the country's business. . . . I want us to put in place reforms in management and operations of the House, and then I want to go forward.[36]

A visiting *Spokesman-Review* journalist observed that Foley hadn't collared Rep. Bryant and threatened retaliation after his April speech. After almost three serene decades in public office, he set out to overcome "a year of guerrilla politics" in which his wife was castigated, his courage questioned, and his career threatened. "He did it the Tom Foley way. He politely persuaded people—in private—that keeping him in power was the smart thing to do."[37]

As reluctant a campaigner on his own behalf as he might be, Foley had to measure his level of caucus support and embarked on a series of dinners to which he would invite four or five members and listen to their concerns. To test his support, Foley explained in a press interview, his staff rated all 268 Democrats on a scale ranging from "hopelessly opposed" to "strongly supportive." By mid-summer Foley was fairly sure there would be no challengers. "I was getting very confident," he admitted, "but until the last day of an election, I'm very careful about getting overconfident."[38] As former Speaker O'Neill press secretary Chris Mathews was quoted, "He's speaker and he could never be beat. I'll make that prediction. That is a 1 million dollar bet you can make. If anyone ever challenges him, he will sit down with all the enemies and competitors of that person and they will back him."[39]

How seriously did he take the challenges to his leadership?

> I took them at about ten cents on the dollar, I guess. A remote possibility, but unlikely in my judgment. In the first place you have to gauge how much disaffection really exists. There is always an undercurrent of unhappiness with whomever is leader. I've never known anyone who's been Speaker where there wasn't a fairly significant sort of grousing within the caucus. There was talk about the inadequacies of John McCormack, the failures of Carl Albert, the good-hearted but ineffectiveness of Tip O'Neill, the heavy-handedness of Jim Wright, and complaints against me that I wasn't focused enough or partisan or effective enough. But you have to be able to see that level of unhappiness appearing to a potential opponent as being a winning strategy.
>
> Mark Shields says that running for election is the brave act of a great ego. It's a good line because people who are in politics, by the very nature of it, have healthy egos. But it is dangerous to your own self esteem, as well as your reputation, to put yourself on the line and face the possibility of humiliating rejection. Most people don't do it lightly. They calculate the odds pretty well and, if they're any good at it, they only make a move when the time is ripe. Otherwise they fall into the category of being too cautious or too brazen. If they're brazen and bold, they often embarrass themselves.

"My opinion was that Foley was very vulnerable," said Democratic fiscal conservative Charles W. Stenholm of Texas. By August after the Democratic

Convention nominated Governor William J. Clinton of Arkansas as its presidential candidate, Stenholm amended his predictions on Foley's Speakership. "I was wrong. Based on my soundings, I'd say he is a shoo-in."[40] Foley had engaged in a reform campaign, eliminated a number of long-cherished perks for members, established the new position of House Administrator responsible for "housekeeping functions," and endorsed a proposal for a Joint Committee on the Organization of Congress. But it also helped that the situation for Democrats looked far different when Clinton emerged from the July Democratic National Convention with a commanding lead over President Bush. They had little to gain and much to lose by engaging in an intra-party conflict over their leadership and, with the prospect of a Democratic President, it would be less important to have a hard-charging, partisan leader with the kind of agenda-setting skill his critics said Foley lacked.

Ironically, it was not personal challenges but President Bush's campaign attacks on the Democratic Congress that brought out a harder edge in Foley. "An angry House Speaker Thomas S. Foley labeled as a 'big lie' Republican accusations against the 'spend-thrift' Democratic Congress," wrote David Broder, "and said President Bush has only himself to blame for what Bush has called 'the gridlock' in Congress. Responding to the President's anti-Congress campaigning, the normally even-tempered Foley pounded the table at a breakfast with reporters and said, 'It is the biggest lie, in the institutional sense, that any political party tells when Republicans go around talking about the spendthrift Congress. We have appropriated less money consistently than the presidents requested in both the Reagan administration and this one—$20 billion below since 1980, $12.5 billion below this year.'"

Broder went on to note that figures supplied by the Republican staff of the House Appropriations Committee substantiated Foley's claim for the most recent year.[41]

> I had responded to the question with a genuine sense of anger. I got along quite well with the Bush administration and with the President personally. But every White House puts out press releases, unlike the House which had many individual member press secretaries, but has never had an institutional press office to speak on behalf of the House of Representatives. This was a case which called for an institutional response by the House.
>
> One of the frustrating realities over a long period of divided government were the assumptions that many people have grown to make too easily. My old boss Scoop Jackson used to quote Will Rogers to the effect that, "it ain't what people don't know that's the problem, it's what they know for sure that ain't so." People know for sure that the House of Representatives and the Senate spend more money than the administration

requests. It ain't so. For most administrations, particularly those of presidents Reagan and Bush, it was usual that the House appropriated less money, fewer dollars, than the administrations requested. What went over the budget sometimes, and led to deficit increases, were the entitlement programs which, written into the law, automatically increased spending without an annual appropriation, for example, during a recession.

But if you told people that a Democratic Congress almost always spent less money than was requested by a Republican administration, they'd look at you as though aliens from outer space had just seized your mind.

Still, Foley wasn't prepared to take caucus support for granted. "Most of the time, sitting Speakers wouldn't have to go and campaign," Foley admitted in an interview. "But there were real questions here whether some people would or would not be able to support [me]."[42]

"People wanted to be wanted," noted California Democrat and Foley ally Vic Fazio, head of the Democratic Congressional Campaign Committee. "You need to make a message that if they make a commitment to stick with the Speaker, there will be a benefit from that." From his leadership PAC, Foley provided $230,056 to some 134 Democratic candidates, and visited the districts of a number of the same candidates during their campaigns. By mid-summer, Foley felt fairly sure that there would be no challengers for the Speakership.[43]

Reform and Preparations for the 103rd Congress

The legacy of the House Bank and other congressional scandals was a heightened reform sentiment among the public and particularly among candidates running for elected office. Incumbent members of Congress, particularly the leadership, expected there would be a large class of reform-minded freshman legislators elected in the fall who might arrive in Washington demanding a reorganization of Congress. The leadership felt that a credible reform package from the Democratic Caucus might soak up some of the reform instincts of the new class of '92. Throughout 1992, groups inside and outside the House had been working on a reform agenda. Two Washington, D.C., think tanks, for example, the American Enterprise Institute (AEI) and the Brookings Institution, had established the "Renewing Congress" project with the objective of providing an independent assessment. Two veteran scholars of Congress, Thomas Mann of Brookings and Norman Ornstein of AEI, drew on legislative analysts across the country and had discussed their ideas a number of times with Foley and other congressional leaders.[44]

After the election, the Democratic leadership, including Foley and Majority Leader Richard Gephardt, held regional meetings in Los Angeles, Chicago, and Atlanta with the newly elected Democrats.[45] As explained by vice chair of the

Democratic Caucus, Representative Vic Fazio of California, "We want to know what this class is thinking, particularly as they get together and compare notes for the first time. What is it that they are expecting from their leaders? What is it that they hope to accomplish in terms of . . . rules changes?"[46]

Was Foley the reformer of the '70s now turning his back on the reforming ideas of a new generation of legislators?

> There was a difference. Originally, in the late '50s and very early '60s, before I arrived in Congress, the Democratic Study Group [DSG] did try to bring about a kind of catechism of reform. They assaulted the establishment with a top to bottom variation of Luther's Ninety-five Theses tacked onto the cathedral door. And it didn't work. It created a resentment and a reaction and a rejection.
>
> The danger of large new classes of members, my own class of 1964, or 1974, or 1992, coming in with a great sudden agenda is that they don't have any experience in the institution. By their nature they're new, but that doesn't stop the young and the new from thinking they have drawn from the well of public wisdom, that they've been elected in ways others have not, they are blessed with a reformist vision and redemption, that the scales have fallen from their eyes, that they've had the epiphany. The risk is that they will gum it up because every change in the structure of the institution of Congress creates other changes and usually unintended consequences.
>
> There's what amounts to a conservation of power rule in the congressional universe. When someone is curbed here, someone else inherits the power there. At its best, congressional reform requires the kind of careful review and analysis that the Democratic Study Group did in the 1970s.

Inside the House, Democratic Representative Bob Wise of West Virginia, chairman of the Democratic Study Group, was working with the Committee on Organization, Study and Review (OSR) under Representative Louise Slaughter of New York to develop a reform package, but had run into predictable opposition from committee chairs. In its final draft, the OSR reforms, while not insignificant, were less than many had hoped.[47]

The reasons were many. The entering freshman members had the zeal, but lacked the coherence of a well-developed reform program. House Democrats were divided over such key policy issues as health care, crime, and the deficit, and many resisted centralizing power in the leadership in the absence of policy consensus. In the absence of an overriding consensus for any major redistribution of power, Foley and the leadership did not want a divisive internal battle on their hands at a time when a Democrat had just been elected President. Not all Democrats embraced internal reform. During the summer of 1992, House standing committee chairs, worried that reforms might encroach upon their powers, began meeting to discuss how they could influence any reorganization process. "We're the ones who have to work under the effects of what these proposals are going to be," was a typical reaction by a senior chair, "and we ought to be able to give the reformers the benefit of our experience." Reading between the lines, savvier members saw an unwanted gauntlet thrown to the floor. Pressure from these House "barons" contributed to taking a good deal of the edge off the Democratic Study Group recommendations and the final Committee on Organization, Study, and Review reform package offered to the Democratic Caucus.

The lack of cohesion around a clear reform agenda prompted Foley to discourage suggestions that the formal prerogatives of his office be significantly expanded, including proposals that he be allowed to appoint and remove committee chairs.[48] This, ironically, would stand in contrast to the Republican-led 104th Congress two years later. After gaining the majority in 1995, Republicans would, albeit more informally than through formal changes in the House rules, grant their new Speaker and leadership much of the recommended authority the Democrats would not give their own leadership in 1992.

Regardless of the reasons, the picture of the leadership reaching out to freshmen represented how far the House had come over the past thirty years, from the time when Foley had sat docilely as a freshman while instructed to follow the leadership rather than think for himself. At one meeting, Foley did find the occasion to hearken back to remarks made decades earlier by Texas Speaker Sam Rayburn when he warned the incoming freshmen, "It takes a skilled carpenter to build a barn. Any jackass can kick it down." In December the leadership gave the freshmen a ninety-day extension during which they could propose additional reforms for consideration by the Democratic Caucus. In general, however, when the new class spoke out more clearly, it became evident that most of its members were moderate rather than extreme in their reformist agenda. They lacked the cohesion, knowledge of congressional procedures, time, and staff support to craft a comprehensive reform alternative to the OSR package. Their principal interest was legislative cooperation with the new administration on such issues as deficit reduction and health care reform.[49]

CHAPTER TEN

The End of "Gridlock"

When a Democratic Congress gets a President of its own party, then the expectation levels go way up on both sides. Mutual disappointment is inevitable.
—Thomas S. Foley, 1997

The 1992 Presidential Campaign

WITHOUT CREDITING SOME RESPONSIBILITY to a post-Cold War, post-Gulf War instability it would be hard to account for the wide oscillations in public opinion polls in the early 1990s: how George Bush went from a 91 percent approval rating in March 1991 to 25 percent in July 1992; how Ross Perot went from nowhere to first in the presidential race from March to July 1992; or how Bill Clinton climbed from 25 percent in June 1992 to 57 percent in July 1992, then fell to 43 percent of the final vote. Ross Perot was a real catalyst. Democratic strategist Paul Tully credited him with having "departisanized the critique of Bush." Perot was running even or ahead in the three-way presidential polling in June 1992 when he withdrew during the Democratic convention and saluted a revitalized Democratic Party. He would later re-enter the race, but only after he had lost his previous momentum.

In his own district, Foley became a Clinton loyalist. A traditionalist—although the political costs with his relatively conservative constituents were predictable—there was never any question that Foley would conclude that his role as Speaker was to support the new President's agenda.

> It's the old story of if you take the king's shilling, you're the king's man. The responsibility of being Speaker is a responsibility to the House as an institution. But, when there's a President of your own party, it's a responsibility to him as well. If you were to duck a tough decision, whether it's a budget, health care reform, or an assault weapons ban, on

the excuse that it was personally too dangerous, then you ought to get out of the way and let a braver person lead. If you're going to seek the role of leader then you must accept a leader's risks.

Perhaps I failed to prepare my own constituents for this aspect of my role as Speaker. I may have taken it too much for granted that they understood.

Heading into the 1992 campaign cycle there was a public sense that the American political system had lost its capacity for renewal. Even though significant "new blood" had entered Congress in the 1980s, the public still had a negative perception of Congress. The legislative branch was seen as a perpetual incumbency club, one whose privileged members could gorge themselves on special interest cash, and wage lavishly funded campaigns that frequently drove away or ran over any challengers. It was an atmosphere that prompted talk of career politicians and fed the appetite for partisans of term limits.

Those who stay a long time, as I did, are relatively rare in the congressional environment today. There are only a handful of people still serving in Congress who were elected when I was in 1964. Some two-thirds of the new Republican majority has been elected in the last four years. So, the picture of members, left to their own devices, wanting to stay forever in the Congress, and never wanting to leave or engage in another career, is just wrong.

You don't sit back and say, "I think I'm going to stay here fifteen or twenty years." In the House you're on a two-year lease. What used to be considered safe Republican districts in New England or the Midwest, or the South for Democrats, don't really exist any more. Marginal districts, like my own in eastern Washington, are more common where incumbents can expect a challenger with every election.

Admittedly, there are things that pull you toward staying engaged congressionally. There are things you want to do, programs or policies you still want to accomplish in whatever your area of interest or expertise. But, it's not like making the decision to be a lawyer or doctor where you expect to practice until your abilities or physical condition lead you to retirement.

I also think one has to ask the question what would be the case if you had a six or twelve-year term limit for members of the House? I think the tendency might well be for members to try to serve the full limit, and with that decision would come a different kind of risk. With the certainty that members were going to have to leave office, in the last couple of terms they might be focused inappropriately on what they were going to do when they reached their congressional term limit. Would the country be better served with these members' attention divided between their onward career planning and the legislative job at hand?

In May *The Spokesman-Review* ran the results of a poll of 202 residents which indicated that, in the face of continuing problems in Congress, support for Foley's performance as congressman and House Speaker appeared to be eroding in Spokane County. In his traditional stronghold representing some 60 percent of the Fifth District vote, Foley registered a 54 percent approval rating as congressman and 56 percent as Speaker.[1] The poll appeared to offer a margin of encouragement to the four GOP candidates vying to oppose the incumbent. In addition to Cheney engineer William Johns and perennial Foley challenger Marlyn Derby, prospective challengers included Spokane State Representative Duane Sommers, the first legislator to run against Foley, and veteran opponent Dr. John Sonneland, who had unleashed billboards with his new battle cry, "Fed up with Congress? Fire the Speaker!" Speaking of the latter pair, Spokane County Republican chairman George Nethercutt said, "I think we've got two real strong candidates there."[2]

Sonneland emerged from the primary as the Republican candidate, having drawn on his personal wealth from the sale of his cellular phone business to fund a campaign which would dump the nation's troubles on Foley's doorstep. "The doctor's campaign doesn't dwell on what he can do in Washington or deliver to Eastern Washington," reported Spokane journalist Jim Lynch in his campaign series. "His campaign manager didn't even know Sonneland was interested in spending federal dollars on 5th District roads until he mentioned it at a Pullman gathering. Instead, Sonneland's ads and speeches focus on the House bank and post office scandals, the deficit and the need for campaign, health and fiscal reforms."[3]

"Sonneland admits Foley tends to the district's material needs," reported Lynch, "but he is gambling at least $100,000 of his own cash that Foley has lost constituents who think something stinks in Washington, D.C." But "the same man who meets with the president and foreign leaders still resembles the eager new politician when he returns to the state, milling around after speeches, listening to every voter, shaking every hand."[4]

"As the third most powerful person in Washington," wrote *New York Times* regional correspondent Timothy Egan, "Mr. Foley is as much a symbol of all that is perceived to be wrong with Government as is President Bush." The other side of the coin was "perhaps the hardest obstacle for Mr. Sonneland to overcome . . . the self-interest vote, people who favor Mr. Foley because of his power and influence as Speaker. . . . Ever courteous, Mr. Foley has debated his opponent, allowed him to speak at a rally in which he was not invited, all the while working the same political circuit he has worked for the last third of a century." There was an enormous outpouring of television advertising, at least by eastern Washington standards.[5]

The Spokesman-Review editors wrote that "as the representative Eastern Washingtonians turn [to] for help dealing with the federal government, Foley has been dedicated and effective ever since he was sworn into the House in 1965." They dismissed any possibility of Sonneland being as effective. "Whether the White House is in Democratic or Republican hands, Foley has shown himself to be the kind of statesman the nation needs to forge thoughtful, broad-based solutions." With an eye on polls indicating a Democratic victory by Bill Clinton, the editorial endorsement seemed to underscore how "much better if the House is in Foley's hands, rather than those of liberals who would jockey to succeed him as speaker were he to be defeated."[6]

As Speaker, Foley's stature meant that he was frequently accompanied on his swings through the district by state and national press. But he held town meetings the way he had for years before the events became news stories. "A visit home by Foley," wrote *Seattle Post-Intelligencer* national correspondent Joel Connelly from Walla Walla, "is a journey back to small-town America. Crowds of 250 to 350 people show up. . . .They remain rapt even when Foley has held forth and taken questions for nearly two hours." Connelly noted that on this trip home Foley was accompanied by a reporter-photographer team from *The Washington Times*, the conservative capital newspaper owned by followers of the Rev. Sun Myung Moon. "The paper," wrote Connelly, "has trumpeted allegations of House scandals and targeted Heather, who serves as her husband's chief of staff. After Foley's meeting in Walla Walla, the *Times* reporter walked out and said, 'They aren't asking questions on any of the things we write about.'. . . Constituents bring Eagle Scouts and other achieving young people to meet the Spokane judge's son who went on to great deeds in Washington, D.C. The Speaker doesn't play busy big shot. . . . *'People drive a long way to these meetings. They want to talk to you for a while. I have an obligation to see people who want to see me,'* the Speaker was quoted as saying."[7]

Foley carried Spokane solidly but lost four rural counties. The conventional wisdom was that he would not necessarily be in political jeopardy even if a victorious Clinton became unpopular, because Foley had many political assets beyond his association with Clinton.

For years, with important Republican voter support, Foley had run ahead of the Democratic ticket in the Fifth District, winning in 1988 and 1990 with 76 percent and 69 percent. But in 1992, against the free-spending Sonneland, who had run before and held Foley to 52 percent in 1980 and 64 percent in 1982, Foley won with just 55 percent. When reminded by Dr. Sonneland of a question Foley had asked of his first opponent "isn't 22 years enough?" Foley, a veteran of 28 years in Congress, said his 1964 remark was a "youthful indiscretion."[8]

The Public Message in the Aftermath of the 1992 Election

Public agitation translated into 110 candidates winning their first House terms in 1992, an influx of newcomers exceeding anything Washington, D.C., had seen in more than forty years. Although Clinton won with only a 43 percent plurality, the 1992 election returned unified government to the Congress and the White House. It appeared to be a momentous opportunity for the Democratic Party. Yet the public verdict was indecisive. More than 100 House districts (24 percent of the total) registered a split decision in House and presidential voting. Fifty-three districts elected a Democrat to the House but voted for Bush. In fifty other districts, Clinton prevailed in the presidential vote, but a Republican won the House seat.

This kind of mixed-mind behavior at the polls translated directly into the sort of legislative activity in the capital that voters purport to abhor: time-consuming horse-trading aimed at luring members who are torn between loyalty to party, loyalty to constituency, and loyalty to their own best judgment. "Gridlock" or "politics as usual" frequently comes down to the normal functioning of a system that is compelled to resolve on an almost daily basis these seemingly irreconcilable differences.

As this would be the first Democratic Congress working with a Democratic President in twelve years, the orientation program for the new freshmen took on a more important cast than previously for Speaker Foley. But even for this media-conscious group of new members who were determined to treat their legislative role as something other than "business as usual," some of the more nuts-and-bolts advice they got from the leadership during the orientation sessions would have been better if received "behind closed doors."

> The 103rd class went through several days of orientation with information about hiring staff, office management, and legislative strategy. By the time I spoke, thinking we were free of any press presence, I said, "let me give you a few last words of personal advice that you can take or leave." I said, "I would strongly urge that at the earliest opportunity, you miss a vote. Not an important vote, not one that affects your district or would be embarrassing to you substantively, but a procedural vote. Just something. Sit through it. Let the time run out. Stare it in the face and ruin forever a 100 percent voting record so that nothing you can do in God's world can ever get it back again. Try as you will, you can only have a 99.99 percent voting record but never have 100 percent. Because if you don't do that, sometime down the road, you're going to have to decide whether to break that 100 percent record or miss your sister's funeral. This is crazy. Two members did this for a long time. One of them missed a vote and wept on the House floor. The second was wheeled on to the floor on a gantry with life-support systems, taking oxygen, Congressman Bill Natcher. His physician told me he thought it was life-threatening, but that his condition was terminal anyway and didn't know that it did us any good to argue with him about coming to the floor. It was the way he wanted to end his life and I felt his wishes should be respected."

The other thing I said was that one of the hardest things in Congress was to get to know members on the other side of the aisle. "You'll know some of them on your committee, but it is hard to really get to know them. The tendency of the place is that the cloakrooms are separate, you sit together with friends in the dining room, but one way to get to know somebody pretty well is to take a trip where you'll find that you are thrown with people from both parties, from different parts of the country, people from different political persuasions and committee jurisdictions, and very often those trips give you an acquaintance that lasts for years. Even though you don't see each other much between times, but once in a while, when it doesn't make a difference to one or the other of you, it may make a big difference in getting some support on a bill that would otherwise never have come to you."

The next day, the *Roll Call* story appeared indicating that I had personally advised the freshman members of the 103rd Congress that "they should promptly miss a vote and take a junket." Fox Morning News, the day after that, did a "Casablanca" number on me. They were "shocked, shocked to hear that the Speaker of the House had told the freshman members of the 103rd Congress that they should take as many junkets as possible and miss as many votes as they could."

The 103rd Congress and the President's Agenda

In my experience there's sometimes an awkward expectation level between the White House and the Congress. When the President is Republican and the Congress is Democratic, it unquestionably affects everybody's expectations. The Republican administration is skeptical that the Democrats in Congress will give it even minimum support, and the Democrats don't expect the administration will consult them in a serious way on most issues. But when a Democratic Congress gets a President of its own party, then the expectation levels go way up on both sides. Congress thinks that it ought to get a much higher degree of consultation than it hoped for with Republicans, and the Democratic administration thinks that the Democratic Congress should be loyal, supportive, and follow their lead almost reflexively. Mutual disappointment is inevitable.

The relationship between the Speakership and the Presidency is more complex than simply supporting a President of the same party or advancing a competing legislative agenda when the opposing party has the White House. Speakers are torn between their own policy preferences (usually reflecting those of their congressional districts), the dominant sentiments within their party caucus, and the President's program. When the President is of the same party as the Speaker the relationship is smooth only if the two are in general accord on policy and the administration is effective in the art of congressional relations.[9]

When this is not the case, as in the relationship between Speaker O'Neill and President Carter, the Speaker's job will be difficult. When the President is of the opposite party, as had been the case with Democratic Speakers and Republican Presidents since 1980, the Speaker is freer to resist and chart a more independent course. The nature of a Speaker's opposition clearly depends upon two main factors—the President's popularity and the degree of policy consensus within the Speaker's own party. It had been clear that Tip O'Neill had a much more difficult time in dealing with Ronald Reagan from 1981 to 1982 than Jim Wright did in 1987 and 1988 because Reagan was weakened politically during the 100th Congress and Wright aggressively pushed his own competitive legislative agenda.

For the first time in more than a decade Foley now had the opportunity to test the advantages of unified government. President-elect Clinton wasted little time in getting together with the Democratic congressional leadership. At a December 15 dinner in Little Rock with Foley, Mitchell, Gephardt and Hillary Rodham Clinton which had originally been expected to touch only lightly on substance, the group spent some three hours on the issues Bill Clinton expected to ask Congress to address, from the economy to health care to campaign finance reform.[10] Clinton was focusing on the congressional leaders of the Democratic Party, people he considered to be his prime constituency if he wanted to "get things done" in Washington, D.C.

As Foley recalled the dinner, "at one point, he asked me how often we met with Jimmy Carter when he was President. I told him, 'Every other Tuesday.' He expressed surprise and said, 'We'll have to do better than that. I met with the leaders of the Arkansas legislature every day.'" The new President's two key advisers on congressional affairs, former Democratic congressman from California Leon Panetta and former Gephardt key staff aide George Stephanopoulos, tended to reinforce the Democratic unity theme. They were products of what had been the poisonous legislative atmosphere following Congressman Gingrich's attacks and Speaker Wright's resignation.

> We left the dinner in Little Rock less with an attitude of demanding that we sit down with the President and have a hand in drafting the particulars or talking over what we felt was realistic, and more with an attitude of "yes, Mr. President, send us your program and we'll try to pass it." In retrospect, we all could probably have used a little bit of the former. Perhaps more the case in the House than the Senate, and with almost the singular but enormous exception of health care, the House swallowed hard and took up and passed virtually every Clinton initiative.

During the first two years, the House did more than the White House might admit in subordinating ourselves to the President's agenda. It was on the theory that we'd been out of office for twelve years, and with a Democratic President we had a duty to do whatever we could to advance those programs that his administration wanted.

At a euphoric Democratic Caucus, with only a stark minority of members ever having served with a Democratic President, Foley won nomination to another term as Speaker without opposition. He noted that "nobody's going to have divided government to blame any more. We will have the first opportunity we've had in a long time to prove that Democratic Party government can work—and the people will be watching." Foley's politics of inclusion, illustrated by the sizable whip organization he had put together in the early 1980s, would be crucial to holding the diverse Democratic factions together. There was also the suspicion that unified government might reveal more of an iron fist in his traditional silk glove. "There's a tough side to him that people overlook because he's so soft-spoken," noted Democrat Representative Brian Donnelly of Massachusetts. Foley admitted as much himself. "People make mistakes about me based upon manner. I hope I never forget favors and there's a point at which I'm not going to fail to remember opposition, particularly if I think it is not justified by either principle or circumstance."[11]

Somebody in the caucus had made a passing comment that "Well, now we've got a new Democratic administration, all of our problems are going to be over." And I said, "No, simply a different set. All of you remember some of our problems in the early days of the Carter administration." It was as though I was talking about [Franklin] Pierce or [James] Buchanan or, at the latest, [Woodrow] Wilson. I mean there were just absolute blind looks. And I asked, "How many of you served with the Carter administration?" Out of seventy people, maybe seven raised their hands. It was a sobering example of congressional turnover and its impact on the historic memory of Congress.

If Congress felt its attitude was cooperative and almost subordinate, a new administration coming into office seemed inevitably to be filled with hubris. They had proven the naysayers wrong. They had confounded the odds and won. The force was with them. They knew what was right and what needed to be done. The seeking of congressional advice always seemed to be perfunctory and not particularly real. Perhaps on a mere tactical question of congressional procedure, an administration might listen. But they seldom sought or took to heart serious policy advice. They knew better.

Why should the Clinton administration be any different than its predecessors? They had come to victory from further behind than any recent administration. At a gala event before the inauguration a huge television screen had reviewed the recent history of political pundits' predictions to the jeers and cheers of assembled thousands. One after another, from "This Week with David Brinkley," "Meet the Press," "Face the Nation," "The McLaughlin Group," or "Washington Week in Review," at one point the professional pundits had written the Clinton campaign off.

If I account for a personal failure it's that I didn't say enough of what I thought was the real situation during those first two years. For example, I thought the health care bill was getting much too complicated. It was the big initiative, along with deficit reduction, and we all too casually signed on to try to do our best to produce it.

Between the leadership and the rank-and-file membership of the Democratic Caucus were the Democratic committee and subcommittee chairs who would now have to play the role of expediting a Democratic President's agenda after years of playing defense with Republican Presidents. Heading into the 1992 elections, the House had 166 committee and subcommittee chairmanships for 267 Democrats.[12] Many members had become used to exercising their clout vis-à-vis a Republican President. Only two permanent House committee chairmen, Ronald V. Dellums of California and Jack Brooks of Texas, had ever chaired a committee under a Democratic President. With a Democratic administration, policy direction would shift from a committee chair to a Cabinet secretary or a White House aide. It would be a task calling for different skills. Historically, the exercise of negative power through blocking legislation has tended to be stronger than the positive power of advancing a bill.[13]

Although committees had lost some of their unquestioned authority over the years, the anatomy of the committees remained basically unchanged. In recent decades, in order to move legislation around committees' blockades or to expedite action, congressional leaders had resorted to summits, task forces, budget process requirements, and regulating floor amendments. These developments had weakened committee power, as had the federal deficit, which discouraged new initiatives. But these forces did not diminish the central fact of legislative life that most legislation still came from individual committees. The committees would continue to be the incubator for Clinton's legislative agenda. Running parallel to the 103rd Congress's focus on the new administration's legislative agenda was the effort of the Joint Committee on the Organization of Congress to reorganize the internal operations of Congress. While committee chairs were tenacious in asserting authority over the legislative goals, they were generally equally tenacious in resisting reform.[14]

> The committee chairmen are the most institutionally conservative group in the Congress. They have the most to conserve. They think almost any reform package aims at them, their procedures, or policies.

Committee chairmen hate the idea of abolishing proxies in committees. It means you have to beg and wheedle every day to keep a majority of members of your party present, and majorities, by their very nature, are less disciplined than minorities. The Democratic majority was much less disciplined than the Republican minority. It was much easier for them to give the message of attendance to their members than the somewhat relaxed members of the majority.

Change in committee jurisdiction absolutely goes to the heart of congressional influence and position. If you say, cut the committees by a third and give the Republicans more, it means you have to eliminate two Democrats in order to add one Republican. Try that on in a Democratic Caucus.

The way of reform is difficult at best, and the way of the reformer is hard indeed. Dan Rostenkowski once participated in a humorous skit before the Alfalfa Club: "The law of politics is give and take. As I practice it, it's take and take."

By the time members had risen to become committee chairs, they had a vested interest in maintaining the *status quo* and were likely to oppose much reform which diluted committee influence. When Representative Lee Hamilton of Indiana, the Democratic co-chair of the Joint Committee created in the wake of the House Bank scandal, asked a senior chairman why he opposed the proposed reforms, the cryptic response was that previous reforms "were s___ then, and they're s___ now. . . . I like the concentration of power if I'm part of the organization. The concentration of power warms my heart."[15]

> Committee chairmen were jealous, obviously, of the prerogatives of their own committees, and while they paid lip service to leadership programs, they wanted to do it on their terms and in their time. They would often come forward and say "we'll be glad to do this and that." Some were pretty much as good as their word, in terms of achieving at least the broad outlines of the leadership objectives. Others were more difficult. In a couple of cases, for example, I had difficulty getting Chairman [Henry] Gonzalez of the Banking Committee even to return phone calls. Any time there was a problem or he sensed pressure, he was just difficult to reach. I resented this because on several occasions I was openly instrumental in heading off efforts to replace him as chairman. Henry could be a wonderful populist figure in Congress or very difficult, depending on how you saw him at the moment.
>
> Rostenkowski and [John] Dingell prided themselves on their influence over their committees. . . . Both of them had for many years wanted to be Speaker. Sometimes it was just a matter of trying to move them forward. They were both superior legislators and prided themselves on

controlling their committees and producing well-crafted legislation. But like good military generals, they were wary of committing themselves to battle unless they were confident of victory. This could be frustrating when the administration was pressing for early action.

Both Rostenkowski and Dingell used delay as a means of control. In the last weeks of the session, for example, Dingell used delay as a means of either manipulating people on his committee or people he resented. Sometimes he'd get a conference report and you'd wonder whether we were going to get it done by the end of that year's session. . . .

In 1995 with the new Speaker Newt Gingrich there were rumors that he was moving in and pressuring committee chairmen and taking over more, at least ostensibly, of a role for the leadership in directing legislation. I thought it made good sense. He didn't have to face stiff-necked senior committee chairmen with strong personalities. The Republicans had been out of the majority for forty years, and consequently, no serving Republican had ever served as a committee chairman. Speaker Gingrich had the luxury of being King John without the barons.

The public thinks political battles are always fought between Democrats and Republicans, and the press loves to use sports analogies in describing those wars. But in the congressional context, there are often many adversaries as well as multiple agendas. In one case the House enemy might be the U.S. Senate. In another context, as when the White House renegotiated the energy tax in the House-passed Clinton stimulus package, the administration and the Senate. Or, one House committee versus another. Little of this means much outside Washington, D.C., but the reality exists nonetheless.

During the leadership eras of Rayburn, McCormack, Martin, and Halleck, the House represented a highly structured politics with committees combining congressional legislation and politics. The substance of politics was frequently the result of close negotiations between the Speaker and committee chairs with active involvement of rank-and-file members circumscribed by such restrictive norms of apprenticeship and deference to chairmen. The formal leadership, particularly senior chairs, was thoroughly capable of exercising internal sanctions to keep junior members in line. Through the post-1970s reforms of Congress the stability of the old order was shaken. The new breed of member was more individualistic and expected to exercise a "policy entrepreneur" role almost immediately. The changes in House politics were reflected in a transformation of leadership styles. Democratic Party Speakers of the House acquired more leverage at the expense of senior committee chairmen. The formal transfer of authority included appointment of majority members to the Rules Committee and chairmanship of the Steering and Policy Committee which made committee assignments and nominated chairmen. Speakers adopted a more inclusive and extensive leadership that reflected the new member aggressiveness.[16]

The power of the Speaker and leadership was evident when Congress was addressing issues of political consequence on which there was a policy consensus. When individual members had a significant stake in the legislation and were unwilling to rely solely on committee leaders, only the leadership, the elected agent of the members, possessed the legitimacy to speak and make decisions for the members. This would come to play during Clinton's budget issues when there was concerted Republican opposition.[17]

The Speaker's leverage was more limited in conflicts between chairs, and Foley's instinct, occasionally a kind of "time heals all wounds theory," was frequently to let them sort things out rather than leap immediately into the fray as peacemaker.

> Those jurisdictional fights between chairmen can become very unpleasant particularly when their staffs get heavily involved. Key committee staff tend to operate as sort of collective Shakespearean Iagos whispering in their principal's ear, "They're stealing your purse; they're stealing your reputation; they're stealing your authority, my lord. This is unjust." They keep it going even when there are some easier ways to settle the dispute.
>
> One of the benefits of occasional good fortune is when you have two disputing committee chairmen who also like each other such as Chairmen Jack Brooks of Judiciary and John Dingell of Energy and Commerce. But, occasionally, you have chairmen who aren't particularly friendly. Their confrontations are often very bitter and they insult each other even in your presence: Grown children fighting over the toys of their committees.

On January 5, 1993, the House, in an atmosphere of rejuvenation and change, symbolized by the record numbers of women and minorities (women members of the 103rd Congress had increased from twenty-nine to forty-eight, blacks from twenty-six to thirty-nine, and Hispanics from thirteen to nineteen), had met, with its first order of business the election of the Speaker. As is customary for the majority party candidate, Democrat Foley defeated Republican Leader Robert Michel on a party-line vote 259 to 176.

Foley's speech to the House after his election to his second full term as Speaker fully described Democratic legislative hopes:

> There is an impatience that we have not moved fast enough or effectively enough to deal with the national deficit, to deal with our economic system and its advancement and growth, to deal with the problems of our health system that denies still to millions of Americans adequate and affordable health care, to provide educational opportunity for all of our

citizens, to reduce crime and to attack the problems of drugs and other social ills.[18]

Partisan strife over a first day rules change that would broaden the voting franchise of delegates from Guam, American Samoa, the Virgin Islands, the District of Colombia, and Puerto Rico appeared, in press reports, to overwhelm Foley's and Michel's efforts to downplay partisan tempers and restore public confidence in Congress.[19] "We have an opportunity," the Speaker emphasized to his colleagues, "We have a challenge, and we are under the close scrutiny of the American people." Republican Leader Michel said of the rules fight: "In every instance, ceremonial or political, mutual respect and good will should be at the heart of our endeavors."[20]

Within ten months, Michel would announce his intention to resign at the end of the 103rd Congress. His retirement, after fourteen years as Republican leader, would clear the way for the party hierarchy to be dominated by the confrontational brand of Republicanism that was in the ascendance and would make Michel's tough but civil style an anachronism. Without naming names, Michel had decried members bent on "trashing the institution [of Congress]" as well as "those who choose confrontation before compromise." As Thomas E. Mann, director of governmental studies at the Brookings Institution, noted, "his job, as he saw it, was to work constructively with his presidents, to keep government legitimacy intact." Michel had increasingly found himself surrounded by a growing cadre of more confrontational conservatives which included Republican Minority Whip Newt Gingrich of Georgia, who was already leaving the clear impression among his Republican colleagues that he would run for the Republican Leader position in the next Congress whether or not Michel retired. Michel was reported to have said that forty of the forty-seven new Republicans were hardliners, creating a GOP conference that was "the most conservative and antagonistic to the other side" that he had seen in his forty years in Congress.[21] Was it obvious that the Whip was ever undercutting his Republican Leader?

> It was and it wasn't. He would never be embarrassingly obvious. There were never any words exchanged. He didn't contradict Bob and he had the normal deference to him in our presence, but the word was all around that there was a lot of frustration on the Michel side with the Whip, Newt Gingrich, going around and making arrangements inside the Republican Conference on one thing or another. It was an open secret that he had threatened Michel that, if he ran for Leader again, that he would oppose him. Now, as it happened, Bob Michel retired, and Newt Gingrich, instead of becoming Republican Leader, as he was destined to be at that point, became Speaker.

It was not lost on most congressional observers that Gingrich lacked the affection for Congress as an institution that Foley and Michel shared and, in light of Gingrich's bitter history with Democrats, some questioned how much more difficult it might be to build bipartisan coalitions on legislation.

By 1992 the Democrats had maintained a majority in the House for thirty-eight years and the power structure was well in place. Debates over key legislation and proposal for reform more frequently took place within the diversity of the Democratic Caucus than in the more traditional Democrat-Republican partisan context. Republican dissatisfaction with simply influencing Democratic legislative proposals was growing. For the House GOP, many of whom believed that the Democratic majority had become arrogantly indifferent to the Republican minority, confrontation was becoming more attractive than bipartisan cooperation.

During a majority of these years, governance had required a congressional Democratic majority to work with a Republican White House. Divided government was a smorgasbord allowing Democrats to pick and choose what they would support and what they would oppose from a Republican President's legislative agenda. In 1992, the presidential victory of Bill Clinton eliminated that flexibility. It was an electoral victory greeted by euphoria in the House Democratic Caucus, where most members had never experienced the mixed blessings of governance with a Democratic Congress and a Democratic President. Expectations of unified government were inflated. Pitfalls were overlooked. When the gloss passed, however, unified government would prove a challenge for the House, particularly Speaker Foley.

CHAPTER ELEVEN

Unified Government:
Looking for a Majority

As compared to the 1960s, there was far less consensus on how to achieve these goals, a much smaller congressional majority, and relatively fewer fiscal resources to address the priorities.

—Thomas S. Foley, 1997

PASSAGE OF THE FAMILY AND MEDICAL LEAVE ACT in February 1993 came close to fulfilling the expectation of a unified government under a Democratic President and Congress. "With the passage of this bill," said subcommittee chairman Representative Pat Williams of Montana, "we hear the sounds of cracking ice as the iceberg breaks away."[1] Former President George Bush had vetoed the measure in 1990 and 1992, arguing that it was another federal mandate imposed on business. Reflecting that concern, the final bill provided an exemption for businesses employing fewer than fifty people and an exemption of key employees whose leave would result in "substantial and grievous economic injury to the business." The measure, however, finally placed the U.S. in the company of most industrial democracies by allowing workers to take up to twelve weeks of unpaid leave during any twelve-month period because of the birth or adoption of a child, the need to care for a child, spouse or parent with a serious health condition, or the worker's own serious illness. Family and medical leave had been one of President Clinton's top campaign issues, and on February 5, 1993 it became the first bill he signed in his presidency. Three-and-a-half years later, at the Democratic National Convention in Chicago which renominated Clinton for a second term, the family leave law would be praised as one of the most significant acts of the first term, benefiting some twelve million American families. In response, Republican presidential candidate Robert Dole criticized the law as one more example of "the long arm of the federal government" interfering with rights of business owners.[2]

Passage of family and medical leave, however, built upon a consensus among Democrats and moderate Republicans which had been growing since the idea took root in 1985. Family leave, along with "motor-voter" legislation that made it possible to register to vote while renewing a driver's license, and the renewal of the National Institutes of Health, which had been stalled by abortion-related controversies, represented success for a consensus that would have been unlikely if George Bush had been reelected. The same could not be said of other major portions of the Clinton agenda. After surveying the caucus, a *New York Times* congressional correspondent found that influential conservative Democrats complained that President Clinton's budget package was too heavy on taxes and too light on budget cuts; liberals and conservatives were split over health care; and senior members grumbled about proposed changes in campaign finance reform which they felt threatened Democratic control of the House. "Many Democrats wonder whether their leadership has the muscle and calluses to drive the deals and resist the armies of lobbyists. With near unanimous opposition developing among House Republicans, the leaders will need to persuade the vast majority of House Democrats to cast tough votes for tax increases and cuts in programs that benefit their districts."[3]

Campaign Finance Reform

From the time of his involvement in the Democratic Study Group's congressional reforms of the 1970s, few issues followed Thomas Foley more tenaciously than campaign finance reform.

The United States, with its seemingly endless political campaigns, has an estimated half million jobs filled by elections. With the country's relatively weak party system, most elections are personalized. Candidates run less as standard-bearers furthering the principles of a political party and more as entrepreneurs depending on their own rather than the party's ability to raise campaign funds. At the federal level, the U.S. House of Representatives is rare among world democratic legislatures in the brevity of its terms. In most other countries, reasonably conscientious parliamentarians worry far less about their renomination, primary opponents, or campaign finances. Although the relatively high rate of congressional incumbent reelections would seem to contradict these vulnerabilities, "Congressmen and senators go to inordinate lengths to secure re-election because, although they may objectively be safe, they do not know they are safe and, even if they think they are, the price of being wrong is enormous."[4]

It is not surprising that within the U.S. electoral system, members of Congress as a whole regard themselves as more expert on campaign finance than any other subject. They alone carry the major burden of their own electoral success, and it is difficult for them to view as reform anything that would complicate their own reelection.

Unfortunately, as presented to the public through editorials and news reports, the press has tended to over-simplify the issue of campaign finance reform by implying that the only barrier to passage is the self-indulgence and self-interest of legislators or their leaders. The truth is that there is a strenuous and healthy debate among academics and other experts as to what constitutes reform. The high cost of campaigns, the inordinate amount of a senator or representative's time spent fundraising, and the sources of those funds, has given rise to a public perception that Congress is compromised. The reality is that a legislator's support for an interest group's agenda, for example, is frequently determined by the fact that the group represents views akin to the member's long-standing political ideology, an important economic interest within the member's district or state, or strong grassroots support within the constituency.

At a September 29, 1994 press conference, with Foley conceding that a Senate Republican filibuster had effectively killed campaign finance reform, Senate Majority Leader George Mitchell of Maine stated his belief that "the public has come to believe that members of Congress are not responsive to their constituents, but rather are responsive to those who contribute the funds that help the members of Congress get elected. . . . I think it obviously creates the appearance of conflict and casts doubt on the independence of judgment. Even though there may not be any reality of undue influence, there is the perception of it. Most people come here [to the Senate] with fixed views. Many of them have long records in the House of Representatives or as governors or other public office. . . . For the most part, [campaign] contributions tend to result from those views, rather than the views resulting from the contributions. That's why I think the view of the public is inaccurate and over-stated—but nonetheless real." Although Senator Mitchell argued that most contributors give to members of Congress whose views are consistent with their own, he also recognized the chicken-and-egg aspect of the position. Foley agreed.

> It certainly gives the appearance of compromising [Congress], I think, and that's one thing that is a problem. As far as the attitude of the members is concerned, I think there is a tendency to seek contributions from people or groups where it might . . . create some favorable response. But that doesn't mean people are in favor of building highways because there's a way of getting contributions from various highway contracting groups or suppliers. . . .
>
> I never felt there was a very direct connection between solicitation and how the Congress works. I think that contributions tend to follow actions, not produce them. There are those who suggest that the financing system that relies heavily on private contributions produces a kind of

marketplace Congress . . . where special interests are being sought for campaign purposes. Well, there may be some occasion or circumstance of that kind—one cannot say it doesn't happen ever—[but] I don't think it characterizes the way the Congress works or the campaign financing system works.

. . . I remember once being accused by Ralph Nader . . . of having sold out to the used-car lobby for having voted against a provision that would have required the posting of defects of a used car, exactly as they post the options on a new car. . . . Al Swift [Democratic Representative of Washington] was on the [Energy and] Commerce Committee and told me he thought it was a very bad idea. . . . He thought used-car buyers could be in effect denied claims by just having that posting of defects; they'd say the buyer knew it. So I voted against, along with Swift.

They claimed I did it because I got a contribution from the used-car association. As a matter of fact, I did get a $150 contribution from the new- and used-car people—I didn't even know about it. But my opponents had year after year had a prominent automobile dealer on the Republican finance committee, and most every year . . . they had given $10,000 to my opponent. So the point is, . . . you'd think I should have been trying to punish the car dealers if contributions were behind my vote, not help them.

It's hard to say so because people usually won't accept it. They say there's got to be something more manipulative about this.[5]

The Watergate scandal surrounding the presidential election of 1972 had spawned efforts to limit spending on congressional campaigns, building on a 1971 law providing partial public funding for presidential campaigns. Legislation enacted in 1974 limited, for the first time, what congressional candidates could spend on their campaigns, but within two years, in *Buckley v. Valeo*, the Supreme Court declared mandatory limits unconstitutional as a violation of the free speech guarantee of the First Amendment. The result has been to give wealthy candidates a distinct advantage. They can spend their own funds without restriction. The hurdle for candidates having to raise their own campaign funds is that Americans reportedly want campaigns to be conducted with less money spent and less potential conflict of interest from campaign contributors with a special interest in legislation.[6] Since the court decision, congressional action on campaign reform had been a struggle over whether and how to hold down spending.[7]

I think *Buckley v. Valeo* was wrongly decided and we should reconsider it. . . . I'd want to put some restrictions on individuals loaning themselves money . . . the [Rep. Michael] Huffington example [the California Republican who set a record in 1994 by spending more than $28 million of his own money on his unsuccessful Senate campaign] presents a really serious problem, because it more and more allows people of great wealth to move away from any restrictions. And the public likes that. All the arguments that it will produce a gilded Congress of rich people don't affect people very much. They sort of like it when [Ross] Perot says, "I'm buying the election for you."[8]

The preference of the purists in the reform movement was the constitutionally questionable abolition of Political Action Committees (PACs). A distant fallback was a severe curtailment of the more than $112 million spent in the 1992 election cycle, and public financing, estimated to cost taxpayers as much as $300 million per cycle, to entice candidates to voluntarily comply with candidate spending caps.[9] Foley's support of public financing of campaigns (while understanding the futility of the effort) was long-standing.

I still believe in it, in principle, [but] I despair of getting it enacted because the public attitudes are so hostile to it.[10]

The royal road to fairness is public financing, and the fact that it is unpopular does not change its essential merit, [but] the notion that political action committees are some kind of essential evil is flat-out wrong.[11]

Without public financing, the spending limits that had always been the cornerstone of Democratic proposals would likely be ruled unconstitutional. This was but one of many constitutional issues bedeviling reform: Would bans on PAC contributions, and bundling of contributions such as EMILY's list which was critical for many women candidates, take away individual rights of association? Would a prohibition on lobbyists' contacting members within a year of making political contributions force them to choose between their right to petition government for redress of grievances and their right of free speech? Would providing federal funds to counter an independent campaign by a wealthy candidate encroach on the constitutionally protected right to run such a campaign?[12]

For years, House Democrats had battled against a widespread public perception that equated PACs with those special interests inimical to the public good. It had been a position made more uncomfortable by the widespread condemnation of Republicans who felt Democrats had the greater dependency on PACs. Originally enacted in 1972 as part of a political reform bill, political action committees, except those associated with labor and some environmental groups, were originally thought by Republicans to favor their candidates. To their dismay, many trade and business PACs began to make significant contributions to Democratic incumbents.

Soon Republicans were almost universal in their condemnation of PACs and were calling for their abolition. House Democratic women and black members, in particular, felt that PACs were essential to the financing of their campaigns. Senate Democrats, for their part, had statewide and national fundraising sources and were less willing to defend PACs than their House colleagues. Within the House, an analysis of the percentage of campaign funds in 1992 that were provided by PACs indicated that returning Democrats and Republicans received 52 percent and 40 percent respectively. Among freshman members the figures were: Democrats overall 32 percent, Republicans 17 percent, blacks 36 percent, Hispanics 33 percent, women 31 percent. Foley's defense of PACs found a responsive chord within the class of 1992 with its increased number of black, women, and Hispanic members.

"We don't need to go back to a time when rich white men in blue suits controlled the House," said Democratic Representative Corrine Brown of Florida who headed a new Black Caucus task force on campaign finance. "The whole rationale for having PACs was to enable small contributors to have an influence. What is wrong with that?" asked North Carolina Democratic Representative Melvin Watt. "PACs came into being as part of the last reform," said Democratic Representative John Lewis of Georgia. "They allow working people to pool their dollars so the millionaires and the big-money interests won't be in the game alone." Although a longtime advocate of public financing, Foley was not prepared to scuttle PACs, even though groups such as Common Cause and the Center for Responsive Politics continued to lobby for "clean" public financing. "I don't think it's reform . . . to cut off the opportunity of women and African-Americans and Hispanics and other minorities to seek office and be elected," said Foley in March as he was defending PAC money against Senate and White House efforts to craft a party plan that would slash PAC participation."[13]

In February meetings at the White House with congressional leaders, the President had indicated he would support, if not strengthen, the 1992 reform bill which President Bush had vetoed. Common Cause suggested it had more than 260 commitments to vote for such legislation in the House. The U.S. legislative process imposes two hurdles for congressional majorities. In divided government where the other party controls the White House there is the presidential veto which President Bush used in 1992 to stop a Democratic campaign finance reform plan. Even in the unified government of President Clinton and a Democratic-controlled Congress, without some Republican support, the fifty-seven seat Democratic majority in the Senate was not sufficient to prevent a filibuster, which needed sixty votes to bring cloture. On campaign finance, "the Republicans in the Senate are the only ones who have any say in this process," said Vermont Republican Senator James M. Jeffords.[14]

Senate Republicans may have been the ultimate arbiter, but congressional differences of fundraising abilities between Democrats and Republicans, differences between the House and Senate reelection campaigns, and how much of campaign costs the public was prepared to accept were substantial obstacles in themselves. By May of 1993, after sustained consultation with the congressional Democratic leadership, President Clinton's campaign finance proposal emerged with much the same basics as the 1992 bill. Speaker Foley had "despair[ed]" of passing a campaign finance bill that included significant public funding, but he recognized that without it any campaign spending limits would be unconstitutional.[15]

In an effort to force a reluctant consensus, toward the end of the first session Foley began to violate his long-standing policy against setting self-imposed deadlines and designated October as "reform month." The price, when the schedule slipped, was that he became the lightening rod for outside criticism. *The New York Times* began running editorials criticizing Foley in harsh, personal terms for not doing more to pass a major overhaul of campaign finance. *The Times* labeled Foley "a grand artificer" in a blistering September 26 editorial. *Mother Jones* magazine ran a summer article portraying Foley as a major obstacle to reform.

From the vantage point of Foley and Majority Leader Richard Gephardt, who was spending countless hours in discussions with caucus members, the Democrats faced a no-win dilemma on campaign finance reform. They could bring to the floor a bill that included substantial public financing of House campaigns and face certain defeat, or they could try to find a compromise that might pass but get hammered in editorials. Common Cause argued that the Democrats had overwhelmingly approved public funding in 1992 when a veto by President Bush was guaranteed. Unless that earlier support was hypocritical, why not offer the same for a signature by Democratic President Clinton? The Democratic Caucus responded that the public would hardly applaud their taxes being raised in August to help publicly fund congressional campaigns in October. Second, the revenues from a new tax on lobbying expenses that Clinton and congressional Democrats had hoped would pay for campaign finance were usurped for deficit reduction in the August reconciliation bill. And third, if less than 20 percent of taxpayers currently checked the box that allowed $1 of their taxes to go to presidential campaign funds, would not far fewer check a box for Congress?[16]

On the last day of the first session, November 22, the House passed its own sweeping overhaul of the congressional campaign finance system. It would provide partial public funding of House campaigns for candidates who agreed to comply with federal spending caps. It also limited the aggregate amounts candidates could receive from PACs and from those individual contributors who gave more than $200.

To ensure the troops held, Foley made a final appeal from the well of the House. "We have promised to deal with this issue this year," Foley exhorted. "Let us do it." The GOP alternative, which was rejected 173-263, would have banned PACs. Throughout the debate, Republicans chastised Democrats for retaining their "special interest money." The leadership bill, which finally passed 255-175 with twenty-two Republican votes, would face an even more difficult conference with the Senate to resolve the major differences between the House and Senate versions, including the Senate's steep new tax on candidates who rejected spending limits and a constitutionally questionable PAC ban. As with many compromises, the House effort failed to satisfy all its critics. The *Washington Post* called the House bill "the best of the lemons on the lot."[17] Others were more generous. "The House of Representatives has taken a very important step forward," said Fred Wertheimer, president of Common Cause. "I have a firm conviction that very important, significant, meaningful campaign finance reform legislation will be enacted," said Speaker Foley, who expressed confidence that a compromise could be reached in a Senate-House conference committee the next year.[18]

Proceeding in the Absence of a Consensus: The Clinton Budget

At the outset of the new administration, Foley and Senate Majority Leader Mitchell responded to the spirit of Clinton's White House staff cuts with a pledge to cut 1,400 congressional staff by 1995 and moved quickly to address the cornerstone of the Clinton legislative program, its budget proposals.[19]

The first session's experiment in Democratic one-party government came down to the mid-summer's budget reconciliation bill, which traditionally reconciles revenues and spending for the federal government. Negotiations are difficult, make for poor television visuals, are difficult to understand, and get little press coverage, but are at the heart of contemporary legislative policy.

Presidential candidate Clinton had campaigned on the idea of tax cuts for the middle class. As the president-elect he had indicated he wanted to cut two dollars in spending for every dollar in tax increases. Neither of these turned out to be firm commitments as the plan emerged. When President Clinton outlined his economic proposals to a joint session of Congress on February 17, 1993 he emphasized the need for deficit reduction. He unveiled a proposal for deep spending cuts but also a substantial reliance on tax increases to bring the budget closer to balance. There were sharp new taxes on the wealthy, but rather than a tax cut, middle-income taxpayers would be asked to carry part of the load. Wealthier Social Security beneficiaries were also asked to help by having a somewhat higher portion of their benefits taxed.

Pegged as the largest budget-cutting plan in history, projections went as high as savings of $704 billion over five years, or some $200 billion more than the 1990 budget summit agreement. Of that amount, however, only two-thirds was destined to reduce the deficit with the other third to be used to pay for increased job creation and long-term investment spending in what was called a "stimulus package"—which ultimately failed to pass the Senate. In the final conference bill representing the House and Senate versions, the five-year, $496 billion deficit-reduction package represented deep cutbacks to Medicare providers but few or no new burdens on Medicare beneficiaries, sharp cuts in defense spending, some new social spending including an increase in the earned-income tax credit for the working poor, and funds for childhood immunization and food stamps. A strict new spending policy would freeze congressional appropriations almost until the next century.[20]

The plan represented a legislative compromise on the administration's mixed message of the critical need for massive deficit reduction on one hand and job-creating stimulus and social investment spending on the other. As such, the plan marked an abrupt change from the low-tax policies of Republican Presidents Reagan and Bush.

The potential for significantly cutting the deficit could be found in relatively few places: entitlement programs, defense and domestic appropriations, and taxes on individuals and businesses. Defense appropriations represented about one-sixth of the federal budget, while entitlement programs, such as Social Security, Medicare, food stamps, and veterans' benefits, made up roughly half of the budget. Among the constants were that negotiators had found it politically easier to slash doctors and hospitals that provide services to Medicare beneficiaries than the beneficiaries themselves. While tax increases represented about a third of the 1990 deficit reduction package, in 1993 they were about half. In both instances, however, negotiators decided to protect the middle class, which got better treatment in 1993. Roughly ninety cents of every dollar would come from families earning more than $100,000 a year. The only direct hit on middle-class working families would come from a 4.3-cent per gallon increase in the federal gasoline tax.[21]

Unlike the budget summits of 1987 and 1990 when junior members had complained about being shut out of the discussions, during the House-Senate conference negotiations of 1993 nearly every Democratic member was consulted, cajoled, and in many cases accommodated. More than 200 House and Senate budget negotiators gathered on July 15 to begin the conference committee negotiations. It was, however, a distinct departure from textbook descriptions of the legislative process. For example, Republican members were all but irrelevant to the talks. The GOP had been unanimous in its opposition to the plan from the outset, so Democrats wasted no time wooing Republican votes for the final bill. The conference became a family feud among Democrats. Liberals sought such things as tax credits for inner cities, the creation of enterprise zones to help improve blighted urban areas, expanded eligibility for food stamps, and mandatory immunizations for poor and uninsured children. The Conservative Democratic Forum, led by Democratic Representative Charles W. Stenholm of Texas, wanted greater cuts in spending.[22]

Democratic fiscal conservatives such as Stenholm came from rural districts, similar to Foley's, where voters tended to split their tickets between Republican presidential candidates and Democratic members of Congress. "None of us come from safe Democratic districts, and we have to explain every vote we cast," noted Minnesota's Democratic Representative Timothy J. Penny. "Twelve years ago we were having a lot more fun," said Stenholm with reference to the Reagan administration's tax-cutting fervor. "When you're cutting spending, that's tougher because every dime of spending benefits somebody."[23] Further complicating the picture was the fact that the Clinton legislative agenda had not emerged from the presidential campaign as a broad public or congressional Democratic consensus.

> We had to try to construct a consensus. I guess this is one of the differences I see between the so-called Great Society programs of the early 1960s and the period of the first two years of the Clinton administration. In the '60s most of us who were elected had campaigned for ideas that became part of President Johnson's program—Medicare, aid to education, a "war" on poverty. These legislative proposals had an important core of pre-existing support among Democrats.
>
> In contrast, although there was a general consensus that Democratic legislative priorities in President Clinton's new administration would include health care reform, the reduction of crime, restructuring of the welfare system, and campaign finance, there was also a pressing need for deficit reduction. As compared to the 1960s, there was far less consensus on how to achieve these goals, a much smaller congressional majority, and relatively fewer fiscal resources to address the priorities.

Foley had to call on a gambler's instinct when he pushed for a final vote on the conference bill even though it was far from clear that he had a majority. The watershed took place during a meeting with a leading fiscal Democratic conservative, Representative Timothy J. Penny of Minnesota, whom the Speaker had always found to be "very straight" in advocating spending cuts. "I felt that they either would wrestle me to the ground or ask for my help," noted Penny. The leadership got Penny's support by striking an agreement which called on President Clinton to propose a package of additional spending cuts for House consideration later in the year. "The leadership was heavily invested in passing this bill . . . as a test of whether the Democratic Party could govern," Foley observed. "Having passed that bill, there is a sense of satisfaction. There would have been disillusionment and disappointment in the House if we had failed."[24]

"Tonight is the time for courage," Speaker Foley said in a final appeal to Democrats who had been bludgeoned by GOP attacks and pressured by constituent phone calls that were generally running against the plan. Republicans had decided months before that they wanted no fingerprints on a plan including taxes which they asserted would hobble the economy and kill jobs. "Tonight is the time to put away the old, easy ways," said Foley. "Tonight is the time for responsibility. Tonight is the night to vote." If the deficit-reduction gamble worked, Democrats would get sole credit because the package passed without a single Republican vote (218-216) in the House and, twenty-four hours later in the Senate, it took Vice President Al Gore to break a tie and make the final tally 51-50. It was the first time in post-war congressional history that the majority party had passed major legislation with absolutely no support from the opposition.[25]

On the stimulus package, however, the White House had taken a hard line with both Republicans and Democrats in the House. Its own calculation suggested the House had the votes to pass the administration's version. This hard-nosed approach might work in the House with its strict rules, but not in the Senate where there were no time limits on debate. After four failed attempts to end Republican filibusters, Majority Leader Mitchell had to concede defeat for Clinton's stimulus package. Ironically, it was in the Senate, not the House, where moderate Republicans had sought a passable compromise. Republican Senator Arlen Specter of Pennsylvania was anything but jubilant about the defeat of the stimulus package. "The most important factor . . . is that the American people should not think that we are at loggerheads." "There are a lot of people out there hurting," Republican Senator Mark Hatfield of Oregon said. "They thought they saw hope in this package."[26]

Foley had publicly defended the $16.3 billion economic stimulus package despite his unstated reservations. Part of the package consisted of funding for public works projects that were easily and effectively criticized by Republican opponents. Foley was skeptical of both the economic and rhetorical rationale behind the program. He questioned whether these shot-in-the-arm projects would effectively meliorate the economic impact of sharp deficit reduction. In its reduced final form, however, the deficit-reduction bill did include social initiatives of the sort that had languished in the Reagan-Bush years: an expansion of food stamps, new aid for vaccinating children, a broadened earned-income tax credit aimed primarily at lower income citizens, and an overhaul of the government's student loan program.

For some, the House victory on the Clinton budget marked the premier success to date of Foley's four-year Speakership. "Without his help," Richard Cohen in the *National Journal* wrote, "Congress might not have shifted gears to reverse 12 years of Republican fiscal policy. And in the highly charged atmosphere that is likely to continue on Capitol Hill, his solid and calm demeanor provides a safe port for Clinton and the Democrats."[27] As described by *Washington Post* political columnist David Broder, the budget votes were "a display of legislative muscle that would have done credit to Texas titans Lyndon B. Johnson and Sam Rayburn when they were running the Senate and House almost four decades ago." As Democratic conservative Charles Stenholm noted, however, the darker side of the success was that the Republicans had gone into an opposition mode that effectively ended any prospect of cross-party coalitions.[28]

Even a few minority party votes can be helpful. When you do it all within the Democratic Caucus you have a lot of potential vetoes. Every group thinks, "Hell, they don't have a majority without us. They can't pass this without our support. Therefore, we ought to accept nothing less than this, that, or the other thing." It tends to put everyone at war with each other within the majority trying to maximize their leverage. It tends to sharpen differences within the party and make issues more parochial. It encourages party factions with a particular position on an issue to heighten their demands.

On bills where there wasn't a single Republican vote, and where it's politically risky for a number of Democrats, the solutions almost have to be pieced together. It's a matter of cut and paste, adjust here and adjust there, in order to get a clear majority. When it's very close, as it was in this case, the slightest bad weather can upset the vessel.

Passage was very difficult, there was no question. The votes showed that. We passed it by one vote. We had a relatively solid majority in the House, so we were not getting the votes of some Democrats in addition to losing the votes of every single Republican. Another vote or two and we would have lost the budget act and that would have been not only a mistake for the country but an early and critical blow for the administration.

Although it may not be surprising, securing party discipline has become more difficult. Individual members today depend more on themselves, their own resources, and their own positioning on issues than they do on identification with the party. The test always seems to me to be will it hurt a member of Congress if it is reported in their local newspaper that they have been severely chastised by the party leadership and by the general Republican Conference or Democratic Caucus? For most members that would be worn as a badge of honor. "I'm a Democrat, and a proud Democrat, but I don't work for the Democratic majority. I work for you, my constituents, and if I am guilty of pushing your interests, your concerns, and your values ahead of any Democratic platform position or majority, so be it, I'm guilty." That's a winning speech in many parts of the country.

It's the same thing the other way around, but it's my bias, maybe it's nothing but a bias, but I think the Republicans have a naturally stronger disciplinary strain than it is on the Democratic side. This is symbolized by Tip O'Neill's observation that if the Democratic Party were a European party, it would be five political parties. The Republican Party is not monolithic, but I think it's a more serious matter in many Republican districts for a member to be accused of disloyalty to the party and insufficiently supportive of the party leadership. That's likely to cause more strain, tension, and heartburn for a Republican member than a Democratic one. But there was another dynamic at work during the budget act beyond party discipline.

When I first came to Congress and was assigned to the Agriculture Committee, a senior member from one of the southern states had taken an avuncular interest in my new membership. He told me he had a simple piece of advice for me. "When it comes to the big agriculture bills," he said, "always vote for the ones that fail and against the ones that pass." I said, "Why should I do that sir?" "Oh," he said, "listen, it's so obvious. If you vote against a bill that passes and becomes the law, the farmers are going to be happy with it for a while. But sooner or later, the Secretary of Agriculture will do some damn fool thing and his excuse will be that the law required him to do it and didn't give him any discretion. There it was, it was Section 14(c) that required him to do it. But you can say, when the farmers complain to you about it, 'well you know, I voted against the bill because of that. I knew it was going to be trouble.' On the other hand, if the bill goes down and fails, run right down to the well and change your vote if you voted against it, and get a positive vote up there."

Unfortunately, you could probably not find anyone on the Democratic side who voted against the budget of 1993 and found it to be a political embarrassment. If anything, they probably boasted about it.

Looking back on it, if I had it to do over again, there were several things on which I would have been more outspoken. The stimulus package would have been one. We were trying to go along with the new administration. There was less questioning and less criticism than there should have been.

Most administrations follow the same pattern. They really think that the job of the congressional majority, when it's their majority, is to take unquestioningly what they send up, and execute.

In the early months of 1993 Foley and the House Democrats largely delivered for the administration, and largely with Democratic votes against Republican opposition. Along with the Clinton budget and the stimulus package, the House passed legislation on family and medical leave and the motor voter bill. The close votes on these issues, and the near total reliance on Democrats led some observers to question, in hindsight, why there wasn't more of a bipartisan effort. White House political adviser Richard Morris later advanced the argument that President Clinton had been "captured" by a congressional Democratic leadership that wanted to go it alone without seeking Republican support.

Morris would rise to prominence as the principal author of Clinton's "Reaganesque" 1995 State of the Union speech and as the 1996 presidential re-election strategist who moved the President into a more moderate position on issues such as a balanced budget and welfare reform.

In *Showdown*, political writer Elizabeth Drew described Morris's interpretation of Clinton's reaction to the Democratic congressional leadership. When President-elect Clinton first met with the Democratic leaders in Little Rock after the 1992 election, "his worry at that point was that he'd be marginalized by the Congress. When he found that Foley and Mitchell were willing to block for him, help him, he was delighted and relieved. They were loyal to him, but this scrambler, this intuitive, imaginative player became dependent on them, and he was in the pocket, throwing balls. In this process, he didn't realize at the time that the majority on which he depended would be more and more tenuous as various groups in the Democratic caucus had to be appeased. Because the Republicans gave him total opposition, he had to govern with only Democratic votes, and as he tried to get every last vote on the Democratic side he was pulled to the left. . . .When a candidate becomes dependent on a congressional base he becomes their hostage." Morris and the President reportedly shared the view that a large part of what had gone wrong in Clinton's first two years "was the result of taking too much heed of the liberal Democratic Congress."[29]

> I don't recall that we told the President-elect that only Democratic votes should be sought. I think we did tell him that, realistically, on much of the agenda Republican support would be very thin indeed. Our view was that on most sensitive issues we didn't often get many votes from Republicans in a Republican presidency. Even when Ronald Reagan or George Bush was supporting the tax bill of 1982 or the budget summit of 1990, getting Republican support had been hard going. In particular, most Republican House members, long experienced in the subtle practice of almost permanent opposition, were unlikely to see the benefit of helping a new Democratic President achieve his goals.
>
> I guess the attitude is, a little bit, that when you have a new President, you want to be supportive. I always thought that even when we had a Republican President we should try to find ways of working together even though we were a Democratic Congress. But especially when you have a President of your own party, you want to be supportive, and the tendency is, I think, not to be too critical, not to be too negative, to try to see the most optimistic view of the situation, even to the point of maybe working a little bit against your own best judgment. But, there was no indication that the new President wanted to dramatically compromise his objectives to find the common ground to attract significant Republican support. I am talking about the President Clinton of 1993 and 1994, not the President Clinton of 1995 and 1996

Although lacking the public focus of bills such as the Family and Medical Leave Act, budget reconciliation represents the national checkbook. It is the blueprint which balances the federal government's power to tax and to spend—

its revenues and expenditures. With Republicans largely on the sidelines, the budget bill, in which President Clinton laid out his February 17 $500 billion deficit-reduction plan to Congress, was the fulcrum on which the Democrats' six-month experiment in one-party government balanced. The Democrats had been badly divided, as suggested by the Senate's one-vote passage of the original version which, under pressure from conservative and Western senators, had reduced the House's tax on virtually all forms of energy to a 4.3-cents-per-gallon gas tax and thereby reduced proposed revenues from $72 to $23 billion. With the difference between passage and defeat measured by the votes of one hand, President Clinton had been forced to personally meet with a staggering array of House organizations and factions including the House Democratic Caucus, the Congressional Black Caucus, the Hispanic Caucus, women, and freshmen, the Conservative Democratic Forum, the liberal Democratic Study Group, and the Mainstream Forum. And whatever compromises were made had to be calculated in terms of a Senate where every senator represented a veto. Congressional Democratic leaders had little more ammunition than moral suasion—failure to pass the package would provoke an adverse reaction on stock markets and mean disaster for the Democrats' efforts at unified government. But divisions abounded.

The Congressional Black Caucus, for example, strongly supported a broad array of social spending including increases in the earned-income tax credit for poor working families and expansion of the food stamp program. Conservative House Democrats, represented by Representative Timothy J. Penny of Minnesota, had a different complaint with the Senate bill. They had fought hard to set targets for entitlement spending and enforceable requirements that the President and Congress act if spending went higher. Efforts to satisfy congressional factions had emboldened individual members of Congress to demand their own concessions. In response, the White House produced a state-by-state analysis of projected job growth under the Clinton plan and had engaged in one-on-one discussions between the President and individual members of Congress in an environment where negotiations "had as much room to maneuver as an elephant in a phone booth."[30]

If the House took up the legislation first and passed it, it would dissolve the House-Senate conference and leave the Senate with few procedural motions to delay a vote. With time for added negotiations no longer an advantage, Foley, master of the legislative timing and agenda in the House, announced the vote in the House for August 5. Having passed by one vote in the House, budget reconciliation passed the Senate on August 5 with Vice President Gore's deciding vote. It represented a $496 billion deficit reduction over five years. Budget reconciliation passed both the House and the Senate without a single Republican vote, a fact which would resonate in the 1994 mid-term elections.[31]

When Leadership Disagrees:
The North American Free Trade Agreement

The 2,000-page North American Free Trade Agreement (NAFTA), which would lower trade and investment barriers between the United States, Mexico, and Canada, forced the debates between proponents and opponents to rely more on predictions of indirect consequences than verifiable facts. Several outside factors impacted the debates: under the "fast-track" rules adopted by the Congress, NAFTA had to pass or be defeated within ninety days of its submission by the President, and it could not be amended; it was also a late fall 1993 "free trade" debate influenced by the sluggish U.S. economy when many Americans were concerned about their own economic futures. NAFTA's basic outline provided the following: over the course of ten years, it would eliminate all tariffs on goods produced and sold in North America; it would guarantee investors from the three countries treatment as favorable as each country's own investors received; countries outside the pact could not use a NAFTA country as a so-called export platform from which products would be assembled and sold in North America; it would obligate the three countries to work toward common standards to protect the food supply and environment; as a last resort, a provision was included to temporarily reimpose tariffs if imports of a particular product flooded the market; and there was a Mexican commitment to open up its market for services such as banking, telecommunications, transportation, and government procurement.[32]

Up to this point, President Clinton's biggest legislative victories in the House had been purely Democratic events. No Republicans, for example, had voted for the budget reconciliation legislation. NAFTA represented part of a broader phenomenon described by George Washington University's professor Chris Deering in which congressional coalitions had become fluid and tied to a particular set of issues at play, and Clinton emerged as more of the centrist "new Democrat" he had claimed to be during his presidential campaign. Only 73 of the 208 Democrats who had supported the President on his big economic votes backed him on NAFTA. Those Democrats who had relied most on union support, cast a lopsided vote against the agreement.[33]

Although NAFTA passed, in the House the November 17 vote of 234-200 included a 102-156 vote among Democrats. Foley's support had been complicated not only because he had long been a friend of unions, but also because the legislation prompted a split in the House Democratic leadership with Michigan's Majority Whip David Bonior and Missouri's Majority Leader Richard Gephardt in the opposition. Of the two, Bonior's was the more highly visible personal crusade. He represented a blue-collar district near Detroit "where NAFTA was viewed as the economic death knell for the region." Although a majority of House Democrats agreed with Bonior's position, one-third of the caucus did not. This split reflected the regional and philosophical divisions within the party.[34]

I think we handled this rare split in our leadership pretty well. There are obviously cases where members of the leadership are more enthusiastic and less enthusiastic about something. There have been a few examples other than NAFTA. When he was Chairman of the Democratic Caucus, Steny Hoyer supported the idea of a balanced budget amendment. Except for Steny, the leadership was all against it to the last person. Steny not only didn't apologize for it, he didn't retreat from it. He made it clear he was going to go out and speak for it, he felt strongly about it. Dave Bonior, although he interpreted his responsibility on the Rules Committee as one where he was an agent for the leadership, had a pro-life position which was different than the pro-choice position of most of the members of the leadership.

NAFTA presented the most dramatic case where Dick Gephardt and Dave Bonior were on the other side; a real split in the leadership. Because it was unusual and reflected a big split within the Democratic Caucus as well, we simply had to live with this division.

For some observers this major leadership schism on such a far-reaching issue of U.S. policy was not handled "pretty well." These critics would point, in particular, to the extraordinary situation of the Majority Whip using the machinery of a Democratic whip organization to publicly oppose both a President and a Speaker of the same party. For some in the administration this was an unacceptable breakdown in party discipline. Some called for the Democratic Caucus to rein-in their fellow dissidents.

What I mean when I say it was handled pretty well was that, under the circumstances, members kept their cool in the midst of a very hot issue without resorting to any personal attacks.

Realistically, I had to expect that the majority of the whip organization, which was opposed to NAFTA, would function as a group.

If I'd pushed the issue by taking it to the Democratic Caucus, they'd probably have tried to instruct me to oppose it. It only takes fifty members to call a caucus, and no one did. You have to start out with the fact that the President was supporting NAFTA, I think, as a very correct and courageous thing. Why courageous? Because he was taking on the visceral opinion of the majority of Democrats in the House of Representatives and some of the most powerful constituent groups in the Democratic Party, organized labor most especially. He was confronting them on an issue about which they were emotional and cared deeply. You can make the argument, perhaps, that more than anything else, certainly along with the gun control issue and the failure of health care, the demise of the 1994 Democratic majority was based on the unrequited disaffection of many rank-and-file Democrats out in the country over NAFTA, including the Fifth District.

This was an example of issues which cost elections. You can say it was the President's mistake, or mine, or whatever, but when you face the reality of that and still stand by your guns, I think that's courageous. It may be a mistake, it may be wrong, but it's an act of courage. That's where you have to judge courage in Congress. It's not courageous for someone from New York City to stand up for civil rights or to be supportive of organized labor, but if you get a Democrat who represents Oklahoma like Synar [Congressman Mike Synar defeated for reelection in his 1994 Democratic primary] and he takes on tobacco growers, miners, ranchers, and gun owners, that guy's a hero in political terms.

It was actually suggested to me several times by both Democrats and members of the administration that, since the President was for NAFTA, we ought to go to the caucus, demand a vote, and bring this dissident group to heel. I said, "It's a majority, it's not a minority. If we go to the caucus, what we'll get is a resolution that the President should cease and desist from supporting NAFTA, and asking all House Democrats to vote against it if he doesn't." There were enough people who knew the folly of the suggestion. We had to worry the other way around, and it was a sign of some forbearance on Dick Gephardt and Dave Bonior's part that they didn't demand a caucus.

By the end of the first session of the 103rd Congress, President Clinton had prevailed on 88.6 percent of the roll call votes in Congress on which he had taken a position. He emerged with the highest success rate in Congress of any first-year President since Dwight D. Eisenhower. Much of the record was highlighted by the year's two most controversial measures, the deficit-reduction bill passed in August and NAFTA. Both were triumphs for Clinton, but were passed with enormous difficulty and were hardly universally popular among voters, as indicated by the President's continuing weak approval ratings at or below 50 percent.

The legislative productivity also did not translate into greater public confidence in the Congress. Just 36 percent of respondents in a December 2 *Time/CNN* poll thought the bills Congress passed would have a positive effect and 48 percent felt "gridlock" in government had increased or stayed the same. "The fact that this was a productive Congress is one of the best kept secrets in the country," said Democratic Senator John B. Breaux of Louisiana.[35]

ﬁ

Legislating a Presidential Agenda

To some degree it's almost easier to construct legislation in an environment of divided government because each side has to accept limitations on what can be done. In unified governments, one part of the party always wants to go forward farther and faster and harder and stronger than the other.

—Thomas S. Foley, 1997

The Second Session 103rd Congress: Crime, Reforms, Trade, and Health Care

A S PRODUCTIVE AS THE FIRST SESSION had been on budget, trade, and social policy, the sense was that Congress would face even bigger issues in 1994. When Congress convened on January 25, 1994 for President Clinton's second State of the Union address, an annual event which traditionally provides important clues to a President's priorities for the year, it had long been obvious that his health care overhaul would get top billing. The political dynamics had already changed, however, from the earlier bipartisan consensus on health care reform. Now Republicans questioned whether there really was a crisis in health care. Senate Minority Leader Bob Dole had joined House Democratic leaders in urging Clinton not to push simultaneously for welfare reform, a task almost as ambitious as health care. Even without a new second session presidential agenda, the unfinished business from the first session was daunting with significant issues still pending, such as House-Senate differences on campaign finance and lobbying reform, acting on congressional reform recommendations made by the Joint Committee on the Organization of Congress, revamping of telecommunications policy, streamlining the complex system for regulating banks, updating a 122-year-old mining law, voting on a balanced budget constitutional amendment, reauthorizing clean water legislation, converting more than seven million acres of the California desert into national parks and wilderness, elevating the Environmental Protection Agency to cabinet status, acting on the cleanup of toxic wastes, and addressing major new highway legislation.[1]

While it touched virtually all these issues, President Clinton's State of the Union address welcomed the new session of Congress with a mandate to tackle health care, welfare, and crime. With the economy improving, polls had found that fighting crime had now emerged as the public's top priority. The polls also indicated a new wariness about a "big fix" for health. For some there was a Reaganesque strain in the President's rhetoric and priorities. House GOP Whip Newt Gingrich said Clinton's talk about the decline of the family, the failings of the welfare system, and the need to get tough on crime sounded like a speech he could have given. But Senate Minority Leader Bob Dole took a tougher partisan line in the official Republican response to the address: "Far more often than not, the president and his Democratic majority have taken what we believe is the wrong fork in the road, not just on one or two matters of policy, but on their entire approach to government."[2]

One index of the increasingly partisan and hostile anti-Washington political atmosphere during the 1994 election cycle was that, as of mid-February, twenty-one members had announced their retirements, and an additional seventeen were running for another office. The rate of projected departures at this point in the session exceeded the fifty-two retirements and thirteen candidacies for other office in 1992, which had set the postwar record for voluntary departures. Anti-Congress sentiment had been institutionalized in a way unheard of a decade before, finding voice in a presidential candidate (Ross Perot), a radio personality (Rush Limbaugh), and a political agenda (term limits). In the process, critics of Congress were transformed from a largely silent mass of apathetic citizens into an organized force that turned up at lawmakers' town hall meetings, jammed telephone switchboards, and tended to vote in large numbers. Media treatment of Congress had also taken on an adversarial tone that many politicians and analysts suggested was palpably more strident than in the past. "There are more people now making it their stock in trade to deprecate their government," observed Democratic Senator Paul S. Sarbanes of Maryland. "I will admit to some frustration when I find myself frequently put in the position of defending my character simply for being a member of Congress," said Democratic Representative Matthew F. McHugh of New York when he announced his retirement in 1992. "It's not healthy for the most fundamental institution in a democracy to lose the confidence of the country," added Speaker Foley.[3]

Two of Foley's particularly close Democratic colleagues in the House decided not to seek reelection, Philip Sharp of Indiana and Matt McHugh of New York. For many Republicans, smarting under the constraints of their minority status,

Congress-bashing had practically become party dogma.[4] Did Foley share the disillusionment of those who were leaving and those who were bashing Congress?

> I can trace the differences in the congresses of the '60s and early '70s, and later on in the '80s and '90s. Part of it was a general decline in public confidence in political institutions. Not just Congress, but city government, state government, the presidency, and beyond that, national institutions in general. Over the last decade hardly any institution has escaped a certain degree of public dissatisfaction and disdain, whether it's the church, business, labor, civil institutions of nearly every kind. I don't think you can lay the blame alone on the media, in its broadest sense—including the entertainment industry, talk shows, political pundits—because they too have come in for criticism.

> But the media have simply gone along with the flow and tended to stroke public dissatisfaction and encourage doubt. I guess it's the old story of good news is not news, but the steady diet day-after-day of scandal, revelation, and shock. The presentation creates an environment where people have difficulty seeing anything good about the future. I think it's sad, but I don't know exactly how to correct it.

In addition to House Republican Leader Robert Michel, most significant among those newly announced as departing from Congress was Senate Majority Leader George J. Mitchell of Maine, who had assumed his leadership role the same year Foley became Speaker in 1989. "He was getting worn down," said Democratic Senator Christopher Dodd of Connecticut. "The prospect of six more years of doing that is a long commitment."[5]

Anti-incumbency and Term Limits

The virtual assurance of continued and significant congressional turnover might have tempered the ardor for congressional terms limits, but U.S. Term Limits and other citizen groups vowed to press on despite a February 10 federal court ruling against a 1992 Washington state ballot initiative that would have imposed limits on state and federal elected officials. "A state may not diminish its voters' constitutional freedom of choice by making would-be candidates for Congress ineligible on the basis of incumbency," wrote Seattle's U.S. District Judge William L. Dwyer. Speaker Foley, a plaintiff in the case, hailed the Dwyer ruling as a vindication of his own position.[6] But others saw it as a new political vulnerability for him in eastern Washington.

> I think some publication during my reelection campaign, maybe *Time* magazine, called the decision "Foley's Folly." I felt profoundly that this was an unconstitutional act. It was, by the way, never one in which I could be properly accused of standing in the way of my constituents

because in both 1990, when it was defeated in the state, and 1991 when it passed, the majority of the Fifth Congressional District voted against it. You don't very often have a demonstration of where your constituents stand except to elect or not to elect you. In this case they voted for me, and against term limits.

Just as I voted on issues in the House when I thought members shouldn't be asked to do it if I didn't do it, I didn't think I could be an opponent of term limits and then be shy about joining the suit.

Well, if I'd known everything in advance, all the misunderstanding and confusion and so forth, I can't say I wouldn't have reconsidered, but at the time it didn't seem right for me to pass the duty on to somebody else. I was also the senior member of the [state] delegation. At the time, the law firm felt there was an issue of standing that could only be protected if there was a sitting member as a party to the suit. Now, as it happened, when the case went to argument, the standing issue was brushed aside. The presence of a member of Congress on the suit was totally unnecessary. In the meeting, the staff were concerned, and the lawyers' reaction was, "well, we understand if you can't do this, but it would be very helpful."

Throughout my career one of my own unspoken standards was that if I didn't take at least one vote a term that jeopardized my job, then I was maybe going down a slippery slide. If I went through a term never having felt that there was an issue of importance where my opinion was such that I hadn't taken an unpopular or dangerous vote then I ought to start a really serious debate with myself about whether I was becoming addicted to the office to the extent that I was compromising my views. The test was not my opinion. The test was the risk. In a conservative district there were generally a variety of risks and perils.

That Foley's decision to join the suit was a political vulnerability was subsequently borne out by his weak showing in the September 20 Washington state primary. While many incumbents in both parties had misgivings about term limits, most members, other than Foley and Republican Representative Henry J. Hyde of Illinois, who characterized term limits backers as "a lot of sore losers at the ballot box," were reluctant to take a high-profile stand against a cause with such grassroots appeal.[7] More than 300 Republican House incumbents and challengers who signed the highly publicized "Contract With America" carefully pledged themselves to bring a term limits constitutional amendment to the floor, even though they did not obligate themselves to vote for it.

"By knocking out powerful, long-serving Democrats, term limits are seen by many Republicans as the best chance to gain control of the House of Representatives, where Democrats have long been the majority party," wrote *The New*

York Times regional correspondent covering the Northwest.[8] In Washington state the term limits advocates tended to personalize their arguments, using Foley as their "poster boy." "It would be wrenching for him to give up the high salary, chauffeured limos, private accommodations paid for by the taxpayers, dinners with the President, Hollywood stars and return to the regular life of a taxpaying citizen in Spokane," wrote Washington term limits advocate Sherry Bockwinkel in a statewide mailing.[9]

Foley's windfall profits from initial public offerings (IPOs) would soon be added to that list of "perks" Foley would face. For a number of years former high school debate partner Peter de Roeth, now a Boston investment adviser, had managed the Foleys' savings. de Roeth was a first-class specialist in stock of new companies that, when it first hit the market, frequently shot up in price in the first few days of trading. If sold quickly, an IPO could create impressive profits. The offerings were generally reserved for preferred customers with large accounts, a category the Foleys' small investment did not match. "I'm not what you'd call a big investor," Foley stated. "I couldn't tell you today without going and looking it up what stocks I own or don't own." de Roeth managed the account on a discretionary basis, meaning he was empowered to decide which stocks to buy and sell, and when to do so. He described his efforts on Foley's behalf as "almost like a public service. I think a guy like Tom deserves to be supported."[10]

A 1998 *Spokesman-Review* story about the de Roeth/Foley investment relationship caused little stir until it reappeared in Capitol Hill's newspaper *Roll Call* in the highly partisan summer of 1993.[11] The paper documented more than $100,000 in profits over four years by analyzing Foley's annual financial disclosure statements. Because the account was small by preferred customer standards, didn't involve a management fee, wasn't held in a "blind trust," and because de Roeth had been unusually successful for an old friend who was now Speaker, it became a bigger story. Foley eventually had to respond to accusatory questions from Republicans suggesting the appearance of "unauthorized gifts." Republican Minority Whip Newt Gingrich said if Foley couldn't explain the deals he should face an ethics investigation. In his three-page response to his critics, Foley denied any gift was given. He indicated that, even though House rules don't consider a return on a private investment, no matter how successful, to be a gift, he was closing the account and asked for a bill for the usual 1 percent handling fee so as "to avoid even the appearance of a gift." "Mr. de Roeth has never sought from me or anyone associated with me as a member of Congress or as Speaker any advice or assistance on any legislative interest or concern." The letter satisfied his questioners, but the episode remained a painful lesson in the power of the perception of impropriety.[12]

Following a June 20, 1994 Supreme Court decision to review the legal status of state-imposed term limits, the issue came to a head on May 22, 1995 when, in a 5-4 decision, the Court left a constitutional amendment as the only legitimate route for imposing such restrictions. As to Washington state and the other twenty-two states that had imposed their own term limits, Justice John Paul Stevens, writing for the majority, noted that the framers of the 1787 Constitutional Convention had considered term limits, then deleted them. Specifically addressing an Arkansas-imposed term limits law in *U.S. Term Limits Inc. v. Thornton* and *Bryant v. Hill*, the majority ruled that the founding fathers had wanted to give voters a wide choice for their representatives in Congress and had fixed three specific qualifications in the Constitution—age, residency, and citizenship—and meant that list to be exclusive. "Allowing individual states to adopt their own qualifications for congressional service would be inconsistent with the Framers' vision of a uniform national legislature representing the people of the United States," wrote Justice Stevens.[13] This was essentially the argument Alexander Hamilton had made in the Federalist Papers: "The qualifications of the persons who may . . . be chosen are defined and fixed in the Constitution, and are unalterable by the legislature."[14]

Vaunted Expectations and the Second Session of the 103rd Congress

An institutionalist, Foley continued to be a strong believer in the legislative axiom that "the President proposes and Congress disposes," and it carried extra meaning when the President was of your own party.

Following the successful first session, there was a shift in GOP tactics. Instead of merely voting against administration-backed bills, Republicans grew increasingly bolder about using parliamentary maneuvers to block action entirely. The strategy helped assure a fractious session. Crime, health care, and welfare reform were highly charged issues with little or no public or congressional consensus.

Overall, Clinton's "wish list" proved to be too ambitious an agenda for the increasingly politicized 103rd Congress, especially in an election year. With no Republican stake in legislative success, the debate to secure a majority of votes for passage of the agenda again took place solely within the Democratic Party.

> You can almost make the case that, to a degree, as much is accomplished from divided government arrangements as from unified government. It's very hard, sometimes, to hold back the expectations of organizations, and groups, and supporters of a party if they think that this now is our time, our day, our moment. It's interesting in political terms that President Clinton, after the 1994 congressional elections, enjoyed stronger support within the Democratic Party, certainly less opposition. Part of the reason for this was the existence of the new Republican congressional

majority that presented a vision of what might happen if the Republican majority were joined by a Republican President.

With a Democratic administration the environmental community, for example, pushes harder than Congress can provide or the public support. The same is true of campaign reform or a host of Democratic constituencies. There are huge, cautionary, restrictive, real world, restraints on what people should expect and demand. You wind up not only getting opposition from the other side which has no particular stake in the success of an administration or congressional majority of which they're not a part. But you also face obstacles on your own side, dissatisfaction that it isn't better and bigger. Between the carping of your own party and opposition of your opponents, it's not a very happy situation.

Health Care

Yale political scientist David R. Mayhew couldn't think of "something a president has put so much into and gotten so little out of since [Woodrow] Wilson and the Versailles treaty in 1919." Timing was certainly a factor. When Clinton first raised the health care issue during the 1992 campaign, the country was in a recession that caused middle-class people to fear losing their jobs and their health insurance. Compounding that fear was the precipitous rise in health insurance costs in the late 1980s and early 1990s—nearly three times the rate of inflation. By 1994, however, insurance premiums and health care costs had moderated and the sense of urgency about the need for health care reform was beginning to fade.[15]

But there was no lessening of urgency in President Clinton's January 25 State of the Union address to Congress when he referred to the millions of Americans without health insurance and said, "If any of you believe there's no crisis, you tell it to those people, because I can't." In a final flourish, Clinton underscored his bottom line while holding up a pen: "If you send me legislation that does not guarantee every American private health insurance that can never be taken away, you will force me to take this pen, veto the legislation, and we'll come right back here and start all over again."[16]

Not having participated in First Lady Hillary Rodham Clinton's task forces which developed the health care legislative package, congressional committees of jurisdiction, such as the House Energy and Commerce and Ways and Means committees, found themselves confronted by coalitions which had less stake in the President's proposal and more in their own. The alternatives proposed by various members of Congress included a broad government-financed single-payer insurance program under Medicare advocated by Democratic Representative Pete Stark of California; a Canadian-style, government-run, single-payer health care package fashioned by Washington's Democratic Representative Jim

McDermott; and a moderate bipartisan set of proposals offered by Democratic Representative Jim Cooper of Tennessee and Republican Representative Fred Grandy of Iowa. The list would ultimately include other efforts to piece together majorities in the House and Senate by Majority Leader Gephardt, Republican Senator John Chafee of Rhode Island, and Senate Majority Leader Mitchell. For all of these plans, Foley and Mitchell had asked the Congressional Budget Office (CBO) to analyze the costs involved. Even on a priority basis, it took the CBO three months to complete work on the Clinton plan alone.[17]

At its core, the legislative process involves exchanges among various coalitions coming together through bargains, concessions, and compromise. It is a process that is costly in terms of time, effort, and resources—even when the debate and disagreement is among reasonably unified partisan blocs. These same negotiations, reduced to a committee level, take place on an issue-by-issue basis with a smaller group of members frequently getting "locked in," making subsequent negotiations between or among committees infinitely more difficult because of jurisdictional feuds, calculated delays, and cross-cutting priorities from one chairman's turf to another's. This was, in part, the fate of health care reform.[18]

Nine months after the President had announced that he would propose a comprehensive reform of the nation's health care system, the introduction of his 1,342-page plan faced a storm of negative advertising by the insurance industry, which created confusion more than it clarified issues. Competing health industry voices added to the turbulence with a deluge of direct mail, radio spots, and print advertising that picked out pieces of the plan and argued for keeping or deleting them. The Health Insurance Association of America spent $14 million to make "Harry and Louise"—the anti-Clinton plan characters in its TV spots— famous. (The actors, it would much later come out, were themselves uncovered by any health plans.) While Washington was debating alliances, employer mandates, state regulatory power, and cost controls, constituents at town hall meetings were asking questions about far more incremental reform, including changes in insurance laws to prohibit companies from dropping people who get sick and the portability of insurance coverage between jobs. By mid-summer 1994 some polls suggested that a majority of the public preferred to delay major reform of health care.

By late July, after weeks of almost constant House consultations, negotiations, and meetings coordinated by Majority Leader Gephardt and Majority Whip David Bonior, Gephardt was prepared to offer a leadership health plan to the Democratic Caucus, an alternative to the President's, based on combining provisions from most of the proposals being debated. Phased in over several years, the plan would ultimately require all employers to pay for as much as 80 percent of the cost of their workers' insurance. Low-wage companies with fifty or fewer employees could have their costs reduced through a tax credit, and small businesses of up to a hundred workers could cover their employees through a new Medicare-like government insurance alternative to private carriers. With the President's concurrence, the leadership had been forced to backtrack somewhat on universal coverage, and the new proposal was weighed down by an unpopular requirement that employers pay the majority of the costs of their workers' health insurance. While most Democrats recognized the importance of passing some version of health care reform, it was difficult to find an enthusiastic consensus.

In the midst of this search for common ground on health care reform, Republican strategist and former Bush Aide William Kristol wrote a July 28 memo to members of the Republican Party, "Opposition without Apology." Chairman of the Project for the Republican Future, Kristol urged Republican members of Congress to defeat any Democratic health care bill. "If our analysis is correct that no principled, conservative reform bill is likely to prevail this year," wrote Kristol, "then the appropriate Republican response is to take the noble road of opposing any alternative that Democrats offer and insist on starting over in '95."[19]

"That they would be so obvious about their obstruction and about their desire to see any bill . . . defeated," commented Foley, "is a remarkable confession of their putting politics above the interests of the people."[20]

The House leadership health care bill failed to attract either conservative Democrats or moderate Republicans who were continuing to push their own proposals. By August 19 the leadership backed away, indefinitely postponing bringing the matter to the floor. The publicly stated reason was factual, that the Congressional Budget Office had yet to complete cost estimates, but this could not disguise another reality suggested by Ways and Means Committee Chairman and veteran nose-counter Dan Rostenkowski of Illinois. "It's whispered by the lower echelons of the leadership," he observed, "that we don't have the votes, and we don't know what we can [do] . . . to get the 218 votes."[21]

In what amounted to a last-ditch effort in early September, Foley suggested that House Democratic and Republican leaders meet to see whether there was any incremental health insurance legislation they could agree on, but Republican leaders could not agree on their response. "The House Republican leader [Robert H. Michel] is receptive to the idea," a spokesman said. But Republican Whip Newt Gingrich of Georgia, all but certain to succeed Michel after his retirement at the end of the 103rd Congress, signaled the tone that Republicans were increasingly taking in the House: "I don't want to be suckered," he said. "I do not trust them."[22]

The House leadership was further unprepared to take a plan to the floor until it became clear what the other chamber could support. In the Senate, Republican intransigence, through the power of the filibuster, thwarted any action and on September 26 Senate Majority Leader George Mitchell publicly acknowledged what had become almost conventional wisdom. Health care reform, the center-piece legislation of the session, was officially dead.

Overall damage was even greater. Health care had soaked up enormous quantities of energy and time in a futile effort and robbed attention from other priorities. Any effort at finding bipartisan common ground appeared to have vanished. Democrats were forced to go before the television cameras to announce the demise of new campaign finance legislation and to state that they had failed to rewrite the 122-year old mining law, revise low-income housing programs, revamp the superfund hazardous waste cleanup law, or accomplish any reorganization of Congress.[23]

> I think, in the first place, there's often a problem of letting rhetoric dictate substance rather than deciding what you're going to do, and then designing the most attractive rhetoric to sell it. Once you get the rhetoric out there, then it has to be all-encompassing, not selectively applied. First of all, health care started out being universal. Then that raised some flags with the pollsters about whether illegal immigrants were going to get medical care, so it became every American. And once you had this kind of commitment that every single American was going to get the same basic, fundamental, comprehensive coverage that was never going to be taken away from them, you had a matrix that couldn't be broken. Everybody wants to be on the committee with the action and you had endless fights and resentments.
>
> If I had it to do over again, I think I would have earnestly tried to persuade, first George Mitchell and the members on both sides of the aisle in the House and Senate, at least Democrats in both chambers, that we ought to first of all scale down the health care bill dramatically, and take something like the Kennedy and Kassebaum bill which passed to great applause in the Senate in the 104th Congress. Do it incrementally. Do it fast. And do it with at least an overture to the Republicans. I think they would have been compelled to accept. They would have rejected it at their peril. And if they wouldn't go along with it, we could have probably pushed it through. Then we could have gone on to welfare reform, campaign reform, and other priorities. I think we should have advised the administration that we couldn't simultaneously accomplish all three or four of these objectives without overloading the Congress. But the size, complexity, and ambition of the health care program was simply indigestible and, as it turned out, unpassable.

The lesson, according to Tom Mann of the Brookings Institution, was that a president elected with only 43 percent of the vote cannot attempt far-reaching social legislation without bipartisanship, without involving members of the other party, particularly when the public is dubious and the interest group community in Washington is largely opposed.

The Crime Bill

The President's $30 billion omnibus crime bill was intended to showcase congressional response to a major public concern, with the funding provided through a trust fund with savings realized from an equally popular issue, the elimination of 270,000 federal jobs. Omnibus was not misplaced in the title as the legislation ranged over a wide philosophical array of crime prevention measures including hiring 100,000 new police officers, $7.9 billion for building new state and local prisons, banning nineteen specific assault weapons, expanding the death penalty to dozens of new federal crimes, mandating life imprisonment without parole for three-time violent felons, providing community notification of violent sex offenders, and allowing prior sex offenses to be admitted in federal trials. Although the House had passed the package piecemeal, both chambers had previously endorsed the legislation by comfortable margins when the House-Senate bill came before the House for a rule-governing floor debate. House Democrats knew better than to expect Republican support on rules which represented Democratic control over the minority and are almost always party-line votes, but the leadership was confident the bill would pass if they won the vote on the rule.[24]

From the beginning, the assault weapons ban galvanized the greatest opposition. With an estimated 3.4 million members, the National Rifle Association (NRA), with its deep pockets, was legendary for striking terror into lawmakers from regions of the country with substantial pro-gun sentiment. The NRA's twenty-four-hour hotline message, "Please remember that with this being an election year, it is critical that gun owners across the nation register to vote and then go to the polls on Election Day," managed to hold their anti-assault weapons ban members in line.

White House chief of staff Leon E. Panetta and other administration lobbyists worked members in the Capitol corridors, attempting to persuade them to support a ban on the sale of assault weapons. House Democratic leadership whips coordinated a command post off the floor with an open line for President Clinton to speak to wavering members. The assault weapons vote became a partisan showdown between Democrats set on producing a win for a major Clinton initiative and Republicans wanting to deny that victory or at least force changes in the legislation.

"The society that cannot protect the physical security of its citizens is a pretty useless society whatever else it can accomplish," Speaker Foley said in a rare closing speech for a Speaker.[25] Having concluded that the support wasn't there for the scheduled August 1 vote, Speaker Foley had delayed consideration until August 11 to give the House whip organization more time. The first target of that effort was the forty-eight anti-gun control Democratic members who had voted against the May assault weapons ban and were now threatening to vote against the crime bill after the Senate version had included assault weapons. A second group was the ten Black Caucus members who were opposed to the increased death penalties.

The Democratic leadership had only marginal persuasive abilities with Republican members, but was banking upon the votes of thirty-eight Republican moderates who had voted earlier for the assault weapons ban before it had become part of the comprehensive crime bill. On August 9 the Republican National Committee hand-delivered copies of a proposed resolution condemning Republicans who backed the assault weapons ban and threatening to deny them future campaign funding.

Before the vote on the merits of legislation is a vote on the rules determining what amendments can be offered, in what order, and the amount of debate time allocated between opponents and proponents of the measure. These procedural rule votes can be either routine or controversial party-line votes. For the majority, procedural votes represent the spirit and muscle of majority control over the minority. For the minority they can symbolize a test of identification. The Democratic leadership realized they needed support by assault weapons ban advocates from both parties. Only that bipartisan support could make up for defections among anti-gun control Democratic members and Black Caucus death penalty opponents. If the vote on the rule failed, the crime bill would never reach the floor.

> We were anxious to pass the crime bill, and worked hard to do so, but we were faced with a very tough issue in the assault weapons ban. Many members were persuaded by their own judgment, or the clear expression of their constituents, and felt it was a big mistake to put the assault weapons ban in the crime bill. They were quite angry about being put in the position of having to vote against the rule and appearing to be "soft on crime." For others, of course, the inclusion of the assault weapons ban was simply an excuse to be able to vote against the crime bill.

The leadership gambled and lost 210-225. The rule got eleven of the thirty-eight Republican votes and lost almost all of the anti-gun control Democrats. Why had the Democratic leadership allowed the rule to go to the floor only to lose?

> It is a long explanation which really requires you to go back to the beginnings of the crime bill.
>
> The problem was that the conference report had included the ban on assault weapons. This issue had dogged the crime bill for many months. The Senate had adopted the Feinstein Amendment, offered by Diane Feinstein, Democratic Senator from California, to include the assault weapons ban in the Senate version of the crime bill. When the House took up the crime bill, Jack Brooks, the chairman of the Judiciary Committee, resolutely opposed the idea of including any such amendment in

the House version of the crime bill, but agreed to a separate vote on the ban in a separate bill which he hoped, and expected, would be defeated in the House. When the House and Senate went to conference, Brooks hoped he could say to the Senate, "we voted on that issue in the House and the House said no. Therefore, I am not at liberty to do anything but reject a crime bill which includes the assault weapons ban." That was Brooks' plan.

We finally settled on the policy, and I stuck with it, of having a separate vote. I knew the vote was going to be close, and I had privately told the House sponsor of the weapons ban bill, Congressman [Charles] Shumer of New York, that if it came to my having to break a tie, I would not see the legislation defeated.

Most observers expected that the bill would lose narrowly in the House. When the vote was actually taken, it see-sawed back and forth dramatically in the final minutes. In those final moments, the bill was one vote up, and [Democratic] Congressman [Douglas] Applegate of Ohio had not yet voted. He was sitting on the Republican side of the aisle and widely expected to vote against the assault weapons ban, having voted in the past against gun control. He was being urged by Republican friends to go to the well and cast his vote. I was later accused of keeping the vote open for an artificially long period of time. We were waiting for Applegate to vote. It's my duty as Speaker to allow every member to vote, and here was a member in the chamber who hadn't voted. He finally slowly rose and made his way to the well of the House to take a card which is the late method of voting after the automatic electronic system has been closed. The green card is an "aye" vote and the red card a "nay" vote. Instead of going to the red card deck which would have tied the vote and led me to have to break the tie, he went to the green card stack. His Republican friends, and others opposed to the bill on the Democratic side, were shouting, "no, no, the red card." He shrugged them off and voted for the assault weapons ban. At that point my vote would have had no consequence as the bill was two votes ahead.

The story I heard later was that Applegate was furious with the NRA. Announcing his retirement, he had expected them to support his choice for successor, his administrative assistant, but instead they had thrown their support for some other candidate in the primary. Perhaps this was "pay back" time.

The House having voted for it, there was no way for Jack Brooks to withstand the demand that it be included in the conference.

At this point I was under a good deal of pressure to get the conference report on the bill up and we were trying desperately to get the votes to pass it. We were burdened with two huge millstones. One was the death penalty provisions in the crime bill. I think the bill created sixty new death penalty offenses. Most of them were inconsequential in terms of actual prosecution because they were highly specified federal crimes that weren't likely to lead to very many death sentences. But philosophically, the Black Caucus was vehemently opposed, almost to a person, to the death penalty because of their view that the death penalty was imposed along racial and class lines and that African-Americans, Latinos, and poor people in general were likely to be executed more frequently than those who could afford top-flight legal counsel. So, on that side, we had the Black Caucus and others opposed to the death penalty who view it as an issue of conscience. No way were we going to get their votes despite efforts to put language in the bill that would ameliorate their opposition by requiring some special reviews of death sentences by the Attorney General.

On the other side there were dozens of Democrats who felt that the assault weapons ban was another legislative "third rail" which would kill them if they touched it. For many years these members had stoutly opposed gun control and they weren't about to reverse course now, even at the price of voting against the crime bill. But because they didn't want to publicly admit that they were voting no on the crime bill because of the weapons ban, they seized upon the specious objections of the NRA and others that the basis of their opposition was because the bill was too soft and was too coddling in its application. That was a charade. The real straight-out problem was the inclusion of the weapons ban.

If we had been able somehow to take the death penalty provisions or weapons ban out of the bill and offer those in separate free-standing legislation, the bill would have sailed through the House. But, fixed by the deadly stare of these two issues, we were trapped into having to demonstrate what the consequences were, and the only way to do that was to go forward with the vote on the rule for the conference committee report. The situation wasn't improving with the passage of time; we were losing votes rather than gaining them.

After losing the rule vote, Foley held a series of strategy meetings with White House chief of staff Leon Panetta and the Democratic leadership. The White House indicated a new willingness to compromise, as long as key provisions remained in tact: 100,000 new police, strong crime prevention measures, the "three strikes and you're out" life imprisonment for violent felons, and the assault weapons ban. The continued insistence that the assault weapons ban not be separated from the crime bill pushed House leaders toward arriving at a compromise, not with the harder-line Republican leadership which was most concerned with denying Clinton a legislative victory, but with moderate Republicans including Representatives Michael Castle of Delaware, Susan Molinari of New York, and Scott Klug of Wisconsin.

The revised omnibus anti-crime bill was reduced by $3.3 billion. Changes to the bill required reopening the House-Senate conference and subjecting the report to additional changes in the Senate. Throughout the renegotiations of the crime bill there were questions as to whether the moderate Republicans were sincere or merely pawns of their leadership to further sabotage a Clinton victory. The renegotiation also threatened Democratic support at every step.

I think it was a very legitimate group that we negotiated with, and I had great respect for Congressman Castle and the others who participated. They didn't want to simply stand by as the crime bill went down and take the political benefit, if there was one, from its defeat. In fact, I think many of them felt it would not simply be a political liability for the Democrats, but for the entire Congress, Republicans included. But they felt they needed a significantly toughened and tightened crime bill before they could conscientiously cast their votes for it. They told me that their [Republican] leadership had given them permission, quote unquote, to discuss with us, and reach a conclusion. I think that was a fairly objective reality.

Now from our [Democratic] side, it was hard enough to keep the support without further toughening the legislation with additional punitive provisions. For example, at one point we made an effort, led by [Massachusetts Democrat] Barney Frank, to have some exceptions to the mandatory sentencing rules that had plagued federal courts and won almost the unanimous opposition of federal judges. Today we incarcerate more than a million people, many of them non-violent first-time minor drug offenders. Under the sentencing guidelines, there's little the courts can do if prosecutors bring cases even though there's been no violence, the defendant has cooperated, and it's a first-time offense. We ended up being shocked when we couldn't win any exceptions to the mandatory sentencing rules even when we offered to make it a condition that the United States attorney prosecuting the case agreed with the exception. "Nope," said the particularly conservative members of Congress. They simply would not tolerate anything other than mandatory sentences.

On August 25 the revised crime bill passed the Senate in an atmosphere of partisan rancor which poisoned the waters for any subsequent legislation.

The Price of Leadership on Gun Control

As it turned out, Foley's support of the Brady Bill and the assault weapons ban were key problems for him in his own congressional district. He was the target of a major media campaign by the National Rifle Association. Many of his more conservative supporters of the past, who had excused his liberal positions on other issues on the basis of his long-standing opposition to gun control legislation, were no longer as tolerant. Did Foley know it would be a problem of these dimensions?

> Years ago, when I was a staff member working for Senator Jackson, I was asked to go to the floor and talk to Senator [Barry] Goldwater about an upcoming amendment. I thought that was big stuff. I had just come from Spokane, Washington, and I was suddenly on the floor of the Senate having a serious legislative conversation with Barry Goldwater.
>
> The next day Father [Jack] Leary, who was president of Gonzaga University in Spokane and an old debate coach of mine, came to visit. Scoop saw him and Father Leary said, "You know, I'm an old friend of Mike Mansfield, and I'd like to go by and see him." The office called up and, indeed, Senator Mansfield, then the Majority Leader of the Senate, invited Father Leary over for coffee. I was the accompanying person, and so here I was, with Senator Goldwater one day and the Senate Majority Leader the next. "Mike, how do you like being Majority Leader?" Father Leary asked. "Well, it's not always an easy job, Jack," Senator Mansfield replied. "You know I've got to be loyal to the Senate, to represent the Senate Democrats in particular. I also have to be loyal to the administration. The President expects me to be his legislative point man in the Senate. And sometimes," the Majority Leader added, "you're between two fires."
>
> By the time I became Speaker of the House, I had felt the fire.

One month after passage of the crime bill, Speaker Foley's shaky hold on his Fifth District, represented by only 35 percent of the vote in Washington's open primary September 20, 1994, and subsequent polls showing him trailing his Republican opponent George Nethercutt, was not lost on Washington, D.C. Despite some grumbling about the shortcomings of the current Congress, House Democrats indicated that, barring a disaster in the November elections, "Foley can hang on to his gavel if he hangs on to his seat."[26] But even as "unthinkable" as a Foley defeat might be, it did not prevent speculative scenarios which suggested that Gephardt would move into the Speaker's seat with David Bonior as Majority Leader and Representative Vic Fazio of California the likely Majority Whip.

Campaign Finance, Lobbying and Gift Reforms

"After promising to change Washington in the 1992 election, the failure of President Clinton and the 103rd Congress to clean up the system will only deepen the cynicism citizens now feel about elected officials," commented Fred Wertheimer, president of Common Cause, a major citizens' group long supportive of public financing of campaigns.[27] Beginning in the first session and continuing for some ten months into the second, leadership negotiations had led to agreement on many aspects of campaign finance reform that would have applied in the 1996 election cycle, including spending limits ranging from $1.2 to $5.5. million in the Senate and $675,000 in the House; restrictions on in-kind "soft money," inducements for candidates to stay within the spending limits which would have provided Senate candidates with a 50 percent discount for television broadcast time and House candidates with vouchers for advertising and postage costs up to one-third of the spending limit, restrictions on contributions from political action committees, stricter limits on the amounts an individual could contribute to candidates, political parties, and PACs, and prohibitions on incumbent Senators and House members' use of the franking privilege on mail during an election year.

For the media and many outside observers, the negotiations over campaign finance reform seemed to drag on endlessly without producing a passable package. Common Cause, for example, had been pressuring Foley through his Fifth District press to act more quickly on a bill. There had been majorities for a similar bill which President Bush had vetoed in 1992, so why not simply pass the same bill for a Democratic President to sign?

> There's a natural difference between what the media want to see happen and what members of Congress want to see happen. The media want to see members put on the spot and forced to take a position that involves risk to their office. The instinct is to put every member in jeopardy every day, to hear the screams, to hear the flesh sizzle. On the other hand, the member's reaction, even members who are able, upright, and well-intended, is to demand some virtue of their legislative sacrifice. There aren't too many members, short of legislative masochists, who don't want to see their courage and their political life-risking activity rewarded with a result. This is particularly true of campaign finance reform when the goal is to level the playing field between incumbents and opponents through some version of public financing.
>
> The average incumbent feels, "Hey, I'm helping my opponent by leveling the playing field. I'm taking the advantage away from myself and restoring some of that advantage to my opponent. I'm doing this gratuitously, against my own self-interest, in the furtherance of reform. I should receive some kind of positive recognition." What he would like to read is a local editorial which reads: "We've disagreed with Congressman Fogbound on a number of issues, but we are compelled to salute him this week for supporting public financing for congressional elections. While he will receive public financing funds himself, the more important fact is that public financing will enable a challenger to have a better opportunity to undertake a campaign against him. In this instance, Congressman

Fogbound has acted with dignity, intelligence, and self-effacing interest in reform and, on this occasion, this newspaper compliments him."

Instead, much public and editorial reaction is negative, focusing on the fact that the member, along with the challenger, is going to get public financing. In the average incumbent's mind, the editorial would more likely read: "After shoving millions of dollars down a hundred rat roles, Congressman Fogbound now has the audacity to support a bill that asks the hard-pressed taxpayers to pay for his campaign costs. It's outrageous. Is there no end to his avarice?"

So, the natural instinct is to save the courage for another day. Take the risk in the next battle, not this one. Members expect the leadership to act as wise generals in battle and to control the casualties.

The final inning of House-Senate leadership negotiations on campaign finance reform had taken place simultaneously with on-going efforts on the health care and crime bills. Now, in the session's final days, Foley relented on the last outstanding issue of a limit on PAC contributions, and a compromise bill awaited only a formal endorsement from the House-Senate conference committee to reach the floor. Death came from an unexpected quarter when Senate Democrats failed to muster the sixty votes required to prevent a Republican filibuster. That defeat prevented any further discussion on the merits of campaign reform.

Of the unprecedented twenty-eight Republican filibusters in the 103rd Congress, eighteen had taken place in the election year of 1994. During the 1960s the average was two per year. "The Republicans applied the *coup de grace*," noted a *New York Times* editorial. "With disregard for both the nation's needs and the truth, a G.O.P. squad led by Newt Gingrich in the House and Bob Dole in the Senate gleefully killed off a decent campaign finance measure, and a strong lobbyist disclosure and Congressional gift ban bill."[28]

While campaign financing garnered much of the attention, the Congress grappled with other reform ideas. "For hypocrisy," noted *Washington Post* columnist David Broder, "the GOP's last-minute defeat of the lobbying and gift measure was unmatched. Republicans had previously cast their votes for the same provisions." On most of the bills that died at the end of the session, Broder wrote, "the Republicans were the executioners."

In late September, all had looked well for lobbying and gift reform. "It's a major achievement in the fight to end the practice of special interests paying for the life styles of members of Congress," commented Fred Wertheimer, president of the public interest lobbying group Common Cause. The new rules would have prohibited lobbyists from giving members and staff just about any "gifts" except campaign contributions, tickets to fundraisers and other political events, and minimal food items such as coffee and doughnuts. The legislation would have required nearly anyone spending money or being paid to contact Congress or the executive branch to register and report regularly on their activities. The lobbyist registration portion of the bill represented decades of effort. Previous attempts to revamp the loophole-ridden lobbyist registration laws had been killed by one faction or another of the lobbying industry.[29]

The bill would have spelled the end of "Boca Raton eighteen-hole congressional travel" which investigative television programs such as *Prime Time Live* had featured with great fanfare. All travel would now have to be related to official duties. Largely recreational trips, paid for by outside groups, would be banned. Yet by October 7, the Senate Democrats twice failed to break a Republican filibuster and the House-passed conference report on lobby and gift reform died in the Senate.

A characterization of the corrosive state in which Congress operated in the final month of the session was summed up by *The New Republic* as "the October massacre."[30] In the Senate there were five separate Republican filibusters to deny votes on five separate issues. Once a serious, last-ditch, measure reserved for deeply held philosophical issues such as desegregation, the filibuster had become a favored legislative gear-jammer for almost any occasion. Under Senate Rule 22, any senator can block a measure through extended debate, or filibuster, unless sixty senators vote to cut off further discussion and bring the issue to a vote by invoking cloture. Democratic Senate Majority Leader George Mitchell summed up the frustration of Democrats in both the Senate and the House. "In the House, a common complaint is that the majority tramples on or ignores the minority. In the Senate the complaint is often the opposite; that archaic rules permit a small minority to thwart the will of the majority. . . . The threat of a filibuster is now a regular event in the Senate, weekly at least, sometimes daily. It is invoked by minorities of as few as one or two senators and for reasons as trivial as a senator's travel schedule."[31]

The lobbying legislation had previously passed overwhelmingly in the House, and in the Senate by a 95 to 4 margin. But the conference report, which had ironed out the differences between the Senate and House versions of the legislation, became the target of a Senate Republican filibuster after House Republican Whip Newt Gingrich and talk show hosts raised the issue of the bill's possible effect on grassroots lobbying. Gingrich denied that he had waited until the last moment to kill the bill, saying that he had made his objections to the provision known during the conference on the bill. He conceded, however, that he had not called attention to the provisions when the House passed the bill "because he said he was not paying attention." As a result, lobbying reform became another victim of partisan obstruction and filibuster.[32]

It was ironic that, in the final days of the 103rd Congress, amidst the mixed reviews of congressional action on health care, crime, and campaign finance reform, the House passed the little-noticed Resolution 4822 which would have applied congressional statutes to Congress itself. It would become the highly publicized key item of the 1995 Republican majority's "Contract with America." Failing to secure Senate action which would have made it law, Speaker Foley had to content himself with the pale substitute of a House Rule which limited its application to members of the House. The new House rule applied to the House the same laws which it passed for everyone else. It required congressional compliance with such key federal labor and civil rights laws as the Americans With Disabilities Act of 1990, the Occupational Safety and Health Act of 1970, the Fair Labor Standards Act of 1938, and the Civil Rights Act of 1964. The irony lay in the fact that this unpublicized gesture addressed a growing public cynicism about Congress becoming an elite class which held itself immune to the laws it imposed on the rest of the public. Speaker Foley would have been reluctant to accept responsibility of much of future Speaker Gingrich's "Contract with America," but on applying congressional laws to the Congress, he shared major authorship.[33]

In a final case of key legislation, the outcome was delay rather than defeat. Faced with an erosion of previous strong bipartisan support, the 103rd Congress delayed action on strengthening the General Agreement on Tariffs and Trade (GATT) until after the election. With Foley's strong support, the Clinton administration had touted the new worldwide trade agreement—which would lower tariffs and extend trading rules to previously uncovered aspects of world commerce, such as intellectual property and agricultural commodities—as a substantial economic boon to the United States. Put simply, GATT represented a comprehensive international agreement on the rules of world trade. It was before the Congress on a "fast-track" procedure which barred amendments to the final bill and allowed a simple yes-or-no vote.[34] In the view of Yale government professor David R. Mayhew, GATT authorization ranked along with the crime bill and interstate branch banking as among the top three legislative achievements for 1994.[35]

Opposition to the GATT revision was similar to that against the North American Free Trade Agreement—labor unions, Ross Perot supporters, and political populists all spoke out against the measure. For many opponents, approval of GATT became synonymous with approval of our trade relations with Japan. If a strengthened relationship with Japan was anathema to free trade opponents, support from Foley had been second nature for decades. The momentum for passage during the regular session had been broken by an unforeseen flap over an obscure provision setting license fees for the use of the broadcast spectrum by three telecommunications companies. The issue was seized on and fanned by GATT opponents and talk show hosts. House Republicans denied any complicity in an effort to make the Democrats look bad just prior to the election.

Where was the Bipartisanship?

"Most troubling to those who care about our political process," wrote the *Christian Science Monitor* in October 1994, "should be the way in which this Congress conducted its business. Bipartisanship seemed to reach a new low; even basic civility was often absent." The prevailing view among lawmakers was that, at least on major issues, the partisan brawling that marked the last session of the 103rd Congress would be the rule for the future. "There seems to be a further hardening of sentiments around here every year," said moderate Republican Senator William S. Cohen of Maine. "That's not very good for the institution and not very good for the country."

Speaker Foley and Republican Leader Michel had both been inheritors of an inherent respect for civility in Congress, but such notions increasingly went out of fashion in the House in the 1980s as more and more Republicans came to regard old-fashioned comity as synonymous with the shackles of minority status. "I think Republicans tend to be more partisan when there is not a Republican president in office," Foley had observed. "When there is a Republican president . . . there's a kind of forced cooperation on issue after issue between the Democratic leadership and the Republican president."

Foley might have argued that Congress would benefit from occasional changes in the majority. However, he would not have picked 1994 as the best time for such a change!

> The trouble is you always have difficulty determining what year you think you should have lost, and who were going to be the losers. Theoretically one can argue, without knowing what the exact time cycle should be, that there should be periodic changes of power. From the standpoint of each party, having been in the minority should sharpen responsibility when it eventually takes over majority direction of the House. It also gives the majority an opportunity to feel the limitations and the sufferings of being in the minority. Each party tends to have sacred cows that the other can slaughter, and if one looks at the benefit to the country, every once in a while you need to change herdsmen so that you can have a slaughtering of the sacred cows. There aren't too many of these, but each side could afford to sacrifice a few.

In 1994, when the Republicans stormed into the majority, victory seemed to vindicate their recent fealty to confrontational tactics. History may attribute the fall of the House Democrats to a combination of factors such as weakness in their traditional political base, unpopular policies, the unfulfilled rhetorical promises of a new President, the House leadership's undue reliance on Democratic votes to pass legislation, a Democratic congressional membership which had ceased to give much premium to party discipline, or apathy of Democratic Party voters who took electoral victory for granted. The new Republican majority clearly believed its aggressiveness helped and, when the 104th Congress convened in 1995, they remained on the attack.

Newly elected as the forty-ninth Speaker of the U.S. House of Representatives, Thomas S. Foley is viewed from outside his Capitol office in June 1989. *Photo Archive, The Spokesman-Review.*

Opposite above: Speaker of the House Jim Wright conducts his last daily Speaker's press conference in May 1989. Foley, seated at his right, would be elected Speaker on June 6 and would continue the tradition of daily meetings with the press before every session of Congress. *Opposite below:* On June 6, 1989 Minority Leader Robert Michel passed the gavel at the Speaker's podium in the House. Foley had just defeated Michel in a traditional straight party-line vote. *Above:* Foley speaks on the Capitol steps at a "Housing Now" march on Washington in October 1989. *All courtesy Washington State University Libraries.*

Opposite above: President George Bush and Speaker Foley meet in 1991. To the right are Craig Hanna, executive floor assistant to House Majority Leader Richard Gephardt, and Foley press secretary Jeff Biggs. *Courtesy House Photographer/Jeffrey Biggs. Opposite below:* The bipartisan congressional leadership shares some humor in Foley's office. From left to right, Foley, Senate Minority Leader Robert Dole, Senate Majority Leader George Mitchell, and House Minority Leader Robert Michel. *Washington State University Libraries. Above:* Following the January 1993 inauguration of President Bill Clinton and Vice President Albert Gore, Speaker Foley accompanies the two down the Capitol steps where the new commander-in-chief will take "the first salute" initiating the Inaugural Parade down Pennsylvania Avenue. *Washington State University Libraries.*

Opposite above: Vice President Gore and Speaker Foley applaud presentations before a joint meeting of the Congress by King Hussein of Jordan and Prime Minister Rabin of Israel. *Opposite below:* Foley introduces Palestinian leader Yasser Arafat to members of the House. Pictured at right is Foley security officer Joseph Powell. *Above:* Soviet leader Mikhail Gorbachev and Foley share some political humor during remarks preceding a Statuary Hall dinner for the visiting Soviet delegation at the Capitol. *All courtesy Washington State University Libraries.*

Above: A Fifth Congressional District high school class visits "the other Washington" during spring break 1990. *Washington State University Libraries. Opposite above:* Some of Foley's staff gather for a 1991 Christmas party in his Capitol office. From left to right: Mimi McGee O'Hara, George Kundanis, Robin Webb Melody, Paul Mays, Mary Beth Schultheis, Mike O'Neil, Heather Foley, Elisabeth Brown, Speaker Foley, Melinda Lucke, Joe Powell, Judy Crowe, Mindy Snook, Kathryn Momot, Lambert van der Walde. *Washington State University Libraries. Opposite below:* Left to right: Foley, press secretary Jeff Biggs, House Parliamentarian Charles W. Johnson, and House Sergeant-at-Arms Werner Brandt. *Courtesy House Photographer/Jeffrey Biggs.*

Opposite above: On virtually every visit back to eastern Washington Foley answered questions on call-in radio programs. Here he is with Alex Wood of KXLY News Radio. *Photo Archive, The Spokesman-Review. Above and opposite below:* In the fall of 1992 Foley visits the Whitman County farm of longtime friend and wheat grower Mac Crowe. *Washington State University Libraries.*

Above: In the 1990s Foley joined a number of House colleagues in the House Karate Club. *Washington State University Libraries. Left:* After beginning an ascetic diet-and-exercise regimen in 1990 Foley lost eighty pounds. Nearly every morning at 5:30 a.m. he worked out, here under the super-vision of trainer Gregg Raleigh and Foley's security guard Joseph Powell. *Washington State University Libraries.*

Foley is honored in an Oakesdale, Washington, Memorial Day Parade in 1989. *Photo Archive, The Spokesman-Review.*

Opposite: The Foleys pose for their annual holiday card. *Washington State University Libraries. Above:* Heather and Tom Foley, along with Alice, get used to their new quarters in the U.S. Capitol's Speaker's Office in July 1989. *Photo Archive, The Spokesman-Review. Below:* The Foleys at halftime of a Washington State University football game. *Washington State University Libraries.*

Spokesman-Review political cartoonist Milt Priggee's June 1992 view of the Speaker of the House. *Courtesy Milt Priggee and The Spokesman-Review.*

CHAPTER THIRTEEN

Unseating a Speaker:
The 1994 Reelection Race

Throughout my career one of my own unspoken standards was that if I didn't take at least one vote a term that jeopardized my job, then I was maybe going down a slippery slide. The test was not my opinion. The test was the risk.
                                                        —Thomas F. Foley, 1997

The 1994 Congressional Races

HOUSE DEMOCRATS WENT INTO the 1994 elections with 256 members, 78 more than the Republicans, with Representative Bernie Sanders the lone independent from Vermont. The anti-incumbent, anti-Congress public sentiment measured by CBS News/*New York Times* polls in September showed that 63 percent of voters disapproved of the way Congress was handling its job. In 1992 there were similarly low numbers, but that election cycle had been dominated by a public focus on President George Bush.[1] This year, with the White House and both chambers of Congress in Democratic hands, unless the public vented its anxiety on Republican obstructionism, there was only one party to blame, the Democrats. The last Republican House majority occurred in the 83rd Congress (1953-55). To reach the 218 seats required for a majority in 1995, Republicans needed a net gain of 40 seats.[2] From the outset of the Democratic presidential and congressional victories of November 1992, Speaker Foley had a good appreciation of the "downside" of unified Democratic government.

I think it was clear in our mind that we were in difficulty. I made a speech to a Democratic Caucus retreat in January 1993 in which I underscored our heavy responsibility with a new administration and that, if we didn't perform well, the repercussions could be very serious for the party. More specifically, Vic Fazio [chairman of the Democratic Congressional Campaign Committee] kept reporting in late spring and early summer 1994 on the tracking polls that were indicating that we had 60 or 70 seats that were in pretty serious jeopardy. We Democrats had financial problems to cover so many races and we had retirements that were also damaging to us.

I think it was a shock to some when the curtain actually fell and the reality appeared that, after forty years, the majority had switched. In a couple of periods we had been in risk of losing the House when events such as Watergate intervened. The Watergate scandal, for example, led to a dramatic falloff in Republican support in 1974. But the presence of Republican presidents during much of this period created the balanced insurance argument on our side. It may not have been as blunt as "don't also give the Republicans a Republican Congress," but it was similar to the Republican theme in late 1996 of "don't give Clinton a Democratic Congress." A significant percent of the public seemed to acquiesce in the idea of divided government.

My own view, and it's not intended to be critical of President Clinton, is that a number of Democratic members, including my own case, despite all my other problems, would have been reelected with President George Bush still in the White House.

President Bill Clinton, after his victory in 1992, saw his party lose control of both the Senate and the House in 1994, the most disastrous first-term loss for a President since Herbert Hoover during the Great Depression of 1930. The average loss for the party-in-power's first-term election has been thirteen seats in the House since World War II. In 1994, during a period of peace and a growing economy, the Democratic Party lost eight seats in the Senate and fifty-two in the House. It appeared to represent more of a repudiation of the Democrats than it did a mandate for the Republicans. So why did the Democrats lose the House?

Some may regard it as heresy for a Democrat to admit, but the 1994 election was bound to happen some time. We had a very long run from 1954 to 1994, a forty year period, which almost no parliament in the world has shared. And, one can argue, to some degree, the reality, or at least the threat of turnover, is a useful discipline on a parliamentary party. Otherwise, it's very hard to convince members that decisions have to be made, not only to accommodate differences, but that they involve real adjustments, real rethinking, real restructuring, and not just depending upon the weaknesses of the opposition. The threat of the ax isn't necessarily sufficient, you have to actually feel the blade.

The verdict of the *Almanac of American Politics 1994* was that "the two [national] issues which the president himself made number one"—the taxes in the first session's 1993 budget reconciliation bill and the second session's 1994 health care finance reform package—were the catalysts of the defeat. In a similar vein, the authors of *How the Republicans Captured the House*[3] argued that those members in districts with low Clinton support in 1992 were severely hurt by casting votes in support of the 1993 Clinton budget.

The historic relationship between presidential and House politics over the previous four decades had tended to be mutually reinforcing. Credit for good times tended to be shared, so incumbent congressional Democrats generally had not been threatened by successful Republican administrations. The most serious threat to congressional Democrats had come from failed Democratic administrations, and the party had won its fewest House seats when losing the presidency (1952, 1968, 1980), and second fewest at midterm elections with a Democrat in the White House (1946, 1950, 1962, 1966, 1978).[4] The 1994 mid-term election represented the best hope of Republicans making substantial congressional gains.

Foley's 1994 Reelection Campaign: A More Moderate Opponent?

"A tough re-election race can persuade even House Speaker Tom Foley to drop his dignity, for a couple of seconds," wrote a veteran reporter of Foley campaigns. "After speaking to students at Touchet High School yesterday, Congress' most powerful Democrat was given a red baseball cap decorated with the black letter 'T.' He put it on backwards, in a momentary bow to fashion preferences of the American teen-ager."[5]

The scholarship of congressional elections suggests that the conjunction of three circumstances are required to defeat congressional incumbents: a good opposition candidate, a good reason for voters to desert the incumbent, and enough money to acquaint voters with the challenge.[6] David Ammons, veteran Associated Press correspondent in Washington state, offered a localized variation. "Washington traditionally treats its incumbents kindly. Defeat of a sitting member of Congress is a rarity. But this year, it's a political sin to be an insider and even worse to be a known Democrat."[7] Added to that was the constant which had dogged Foley throughout his recent elections. "Republicans have spent years building a case against Foley," wrote *Seattle Post-Intelligencer* national correspondent Joel Connelly, "and longing for the day they can recapture his conservative district. They argue he has served too long. They say he can't serve three masters at once—his district, the Democratic Party and President Clinton."[8]

In April 1994 George R. Nethercutt, Jr. announced his candidacy for the Fifth District congressional seat. Nethercutt had been approached by a number of local Republican party activists about challenging the Speaker. In December

1993, he had approached Ed Rollins, his friend of more than twenty years, about the advisability of running against Foley. Despite Rollins's initial reaction that "nobody beats a Speaker," Nethercutt suggested that Foley had hurt himself seriously by supporting the lawsuit to overturn the term limits Washington state voters had approved in 1993. Nethercutt argued that the action had "smacked of arrogance and proved Foley was out of touch with his constituents."[9] Nethercutt pledged to be a "citizen-lawmaker," promising to serve only three terms.[10]

Nethercutt's own February 1994 poll results appeared to suggest that Foley was vulnerable to a conservative challenge as long as the opponent wasn't a "right-wing extremist, as Foley's last two challengers had been."[11] Nethercutt appeared to be such a candidate. "He was intelligent, pleasant, thoughtful. He wasn't a screamer. . . . The 50-year-old Nethercutt [was] a successful attorney, had been active in community affairs for years. He had headed the local Diabetes Foundation and helped start a nursery for abused children. He was the former chairman of the Spokane County Republican Party. He knew Washington and had served as chief of staff for Alaska senator Ted Stevens in the 1970s."[12]

Rollins reflected that a Foley defeat "would be far more than a crushing blow to the Democratic Party. It would be the final nail in the liberal agenda he'd faithfully supported since he was elected in the Johnson landslide of 1964. It would also be a huge embarrassment to Bill Clinton. . . . It would be the showcase congressional race in the country."[13] Rollins, the one-time Robert Kennedy Democrat turned Reagan revolutionary, was, along with colleagues such as Lee Atwater and Lyn Nofziger, one of the Republicans' quintessential hard-nosed professionals, having managed President Reagan's 1984 reelection campaign, headed the House Republican Congressional Campaign Committee, and temporarily served as co-chair of Ross Perot's 1992 presidential race. In the process he had earned the distrust of former-President George Bush who recounted: "You know, Ed Rollins sent me a beautiful letter of total support in 1992. A couple of weeks later, he was with Ross Perot."[14]

Rollins's approach to political campaigning would bring something totally new to the eastern Washington political experience. Rollins was the emblematic "political consultant." That title had not existed in the 1960s; by the 1990s an estimated 30,000 political consultants influenced elections on every level.[15]

James A. Thurber, Director of American University's Center for Congressional and Presidential Studies, summarizing the results of interviews with 200 top level campaign professionals, noted that "critics argue that consultants have encouraged negative campaigning, suppressed voter turnout, escalated campaign costs, reduced debates to sound bites, corrupted survey research, and reduced participation by once-eager campaign volunteers." Some 68 percent of campaign consultants rated journalists unfavorably and 98 percent said the media paid more attention to negatives in campaigns than positives. Not surprisingly, they admitted they were committed to negative campaign tactics as an option of proven effectiveness. More than 75 percent of both Democratic and Republican consultants conceded it was they, not the candidates, who tended to recommend taking a campaign negative. Most campaign consultants also believed that campaigning on behalf of a candidate by issue-advocacy groups helped a campaign because it represented "free, unregulated advertising for the candidates."[16]

Rollins signed on with the Nethercutt campaign and had his first planning session in Spokane with Rich Kueling, a prominent lawyer active in local Republican politics who had been George Bush's state chairman in 1992. Among the early decisions were to minimize Rollins's high visibility as a professional campaign operator, to keep him "out of the headlines and behind the scenes," and to make Foley "the local poster boy for everything American voters didn't like about their government." "Our strategy," wrote Rollins, "was to treat the Speaker with respect, thank him for his thirty years of splendid service, and give him his gold watch. The Nethercutt slogan made the point succinctly: 'What this district needs is a listener, not a Speaker.'"[17]

The phrase "a listener not a Speaker" suggested the central conundrum of Speaker Foley's reelection campaign. "For Thomas S. Foley," wrote *New York Times* Northwest regional correspondent Tim Egan, "who clearly loves Congress . . . this may be the most painful month of a distinguished political life. . . .Defending Congress gets him nowhere at a time when, national surveys find, only one person in five has any faith in it to do the right thing, and yet he must defend the legislative system that has made him its leader, or at least explain how his Speakership works to his constituents' benefit."[18]

> There was some confusion about my being Speaker. There's no tradition for it. Nobody from the western United States had ever been Speaker before, and I think there was uncertainty about what the Speaker's job was and whether there was any benefit in having the local representative as Speaker.
>
> It was possible to argue that an inexperienced new member of Congress, devoting himself exclusively to issues of direct concern to the district, without the power, privileges, and position of the Speaker, would be a better representative. It was arguable with people that focus and intensity could make up for the influence of the Speakership.

It was a debate that would not have occurred in the safe Democratic seats of Tip O'Neill's Massachusetts or Jim Wright's Texas, but as a Democrat in eastern Washington, Foley had long relied on crossover votes to win majorities in his Republican-leaning district. "For at least a decade, Republicans trying to knock off Foley tried to paint him as out of touch with his district, playing their perceptions of eastern Washington against 'that other Washington,'" *Spokesman Review* journalist Jim Camden noted. "Every two years, like clockwork, Foley would dispatch them [his reelection opposition] with a series of debates or joint appearances, campaign swings through wheat country and timber towns, and rallies in Spokane. His campaign was such a well-oiled machine that observers argued Foley's coattails helped Michael Dukakis and Clinton win Washington in 1988 and 1992, not the other way around. In the summer of 1994, the machine was sputtering."[19]

In the state's all-party September primary, Nethercutt won 29 percent against two previous Foley opponents. "There ought to be term limits on Foley. And there ought to be term limits on the number of times people can run against him," first-time opponent Nethercutt had quipped in an interview in Walla Walla with reference to his Republican primary opponents. Spokane tire salesman Duane Alton had lost two previous times to Foley and Spokane physician John Sonneland had lost three times.[20]

The greater surprise was that Foley won only 35 percent of the vote during the primary, equaling his worst showing. Nethercutt had outpolled Foley in four of the five legislative districts that were completely or partially in Spokane County, a traditional Foley stronghold. Two years before, when anger over congressional perquisites was at a peak, Foley had collected more votes than all of the other candidates combined and more than twice as many as his nearest GOP rival—he won 53 percent of the primary vote against four Republicans.[21] In a poll released by Spokane's KHQ-TV shortly after the primary, Nethercutt emerged with a 58-39 percent lead over the Speaker, with 3 percent undecided. A Foley spokesman had stated that the poll came "after six weeks of unrelenting attacks all focused on Foley. . . . You don't emerge from that kind of battering unscathed."[22]

Beyond the attractiveness of the opposition, a major difference from 1992 was that in 1994 national issues played a key role. Foley's involvement in challenging the state referendum on term limits and his support for the Brady handgun bill and the assault weapons ban coalesced opposition to his reelection bid. In Ferry County, the Republican Party held a raffle. In front of a large American flag was the prize available for a $1 chance: a Chinese-made, SKS semi-automatic assault rifle, complete with folding bayonet.[23]

In contrast to Nethercutt's opposition to the assault weapons ban, Foley, after a nearly thirty-year record of opposing gun control, had come out publicly in support. The National Rifle Association (NRA), which had previously supported him, launched an all-out assault on the Speaker and gave its support to Nethercutt.[24] With polls showing eastern Washington citizens favoring the assault weapons ban by 2 to 1,[25] Foley ran advertisements reminding voters of the tragedy in Spokane earlier in June when Dean Melberg, a former psychiatric patient armed with an assault rifle, killed four people and wounded more than twenty-six at nearby Fairchild Air Force Base. But the intensity of the gun lobby in rural Washington, as Foley well knew, was deep, active, and abiding.

"If Tom Foley had set out to provoke a showdown with all the self-styled, populist movements of the decade," wrote *The Wall Street Journal's* David Rogers, "he couldn't have done a better job. From term-limit advocates and the National Rifle Association to radio talk show hosts and Ross Perot, the speaker of the House is under a conservative assault. . . . Republican challenger George Nethercutt runs as 'Everyman' vs. that 'aristocratic' Washington on the other side of the nation."[26]

Immediately after the primary, both campaigns received reinforcements. While Foley maintained a financial advantage, Nethercutt was aided by a number of outside groups. The NRA, for example, reacted by featuring actor Charlton Heston in ads opposing Foley.[27] Did Foley ever entertain an alternative to supporting the President's crime bill and its gun control provisions?

> At first it wasn't clear what they would do, or at least it wasn't clear to me. The NRA had taken that year, and has subsequently taken, very hard positions. The Washington, D.C., conventional wisdom has always argued that when you draw your sword against the prince, throw away the scabbard. It didn't turn out badly for them, I guess, in the sense that I was defeated, but generally you have to be careful when you take on a Speaker, Majority or Minority Leader, or someone in a powerful position such as a committee chairman, who might remember, after the race is over, that you were not neutral, you were trying to defeat them.
>
> I suppose, in a way, you can say it's almost a matter of giving them credit for being brave and courageous in putting their money, support, endorsement, and voting members where their principles are. But it also had an aspect of an increasingly hard-edged policy that you were either with them on everything, or against them, that there was no middle ground. Sometimes I think the internal politics of big organizations very often tends to move toward the most activist philosophical or ideological group in the organization. In this sense, I think that the NRA has inevitably moved toward the right.
>
> There is a special and important constituency that follows these gun issues. Hunters, sportsmen, and gun supporters include many people who may have a different position on other political issues, but are intensely motivated by the so-called gun issue. If they think you're "right" on guns, it excuses positions on a lot of other issues.

There was an unforgiving quality about the new NRA leadership that discounted support over previous decades. In Spokane, NRA chief executive Wayne LaPierre said Foley had lost touch with the people of his district, was not the same person the NRA had supported in the past.[28] Foley's congressional career had long been punctuated with contact between his constituents and their guns.

For many years the State Department hosted visits by foreign visitors under the U.S. Information Agency's "leader grant" program. Among those brought to the United States in 1968 was a leading member of the French diplomatic service, Jean Francois Ponce, who had wanted to see U.S. election activity. He came to Spokane to spend a couple of days with me. We picked him up at the airport and took him up to Pend Oreille County. After arriving late and not getting to bed until one or two in the morning, we got him up at five to visit a mine, a lumber mill, a cement plant at Ione, and finally, about seven o'clock in the morning we were in the warm-up shed at a huge dam project that was being built for Seattle City Light called Boundary Dam which was near the border between the United States and Canada.

As the shift workers began arriving, I started shaking hands and talking to them, and our French guest was sitting over in the corner taking notes. At that point an enormous guy arrived. He must have been seven feet two or three inches tall and weighed in excess of three hundred pounds, and he had a double bandoleer of 30-30 ammunition strapped across his chest. In a voice that sounded like a barge fog horn, he said, "Where's Foley?" Others in the group eagerly pointed me out. He stripped off one of these bandoleers and twirled it around over his head until it made a singing noise. He strode across the room and threw it down on a desk beside me. I stood up and faced about the third button above his belt. He looked about six feet across. He said, "These are my shells, goddamnit Foley, and the guns that go with them, and neither you nor any other sonofabitch in Congress is going to take them away from me."

Speaking as firmly as I could I said, "You're absolutely right. Nobody's going to take away your guns," or something to that effect. I walked him to the door, clapped him on the shoulder, and assured him his guns were safe.

As he left he said, "they'd better be Foley, because I know who you are and where I can find you."

Although Fifth District voters had twice opposed the state referendum on term limits, Foley's court challenge to the state-passed term limits initiative drew the charge in a Nethercutt ad that Foley was suing his constituents to save his job. The issue prompted a $300,000 anti-Foley advertising campaign by Americans for Limited Terms. Other outside groups and individuals also participated in the campaign. Florida Republican Representative Bill McCollum, a candidate for House Republican Whip, ran radio and television ads telling voters that "Bill Clinton and Tom Foley want to destroy the best health care system in the world." A conservative Virginia political action group opposing statehood for the District of Columbia injected a racial tone with radio spots suggesting that Foley would put the Rev. Jesse Jackson in the Senate. An Internet user collected more than $10,000 from other computer users nationwide with the Spokane "de-Foley-ate" the Fifth District project.[29]

Former presidential candidate Ross Perot and Reagan Education Secretary William Bennett were featured at Nethercutt campaign events and helped raise the stakes of campaign costs for both sides. By defeating Foley, Bennett suggested, eastern Washington voters could shift power away from Washington, D.C. "We'll be able to govern our own lives and make our own decisions."[30]

With Nethercutt at his side at Spokane's Ag Center, Ross Perot asked the audience, "Are you for sale? Can you be bought for pork?" He suggested Foley was a puppet of the White House. "President Clinton says paint the Washington Monument pink, Speaker Foley salutes and it's painted." Along with most of the Democrats in the congressional delegation, Foley had received a failing grade from Perot's "United We Stand America" organization.[31]

While Spokane voters appeared to hunger for undefined change, those concerned about the government's role in regional economics looked on nervously. An independent, bipartisan pro-Foley business group, including top executives from Microsoft, Kaiser, Weyerhaeuser, and Boeing, weighed-in, speaking at a Spokane news conference. Boeing Senior Vice President Larry Clarkson cited a 500-person office the aircraft company opened in Spokane and noted that "he [Foley] was the one who really pushed for this . . . [he] has been there for this district." Perot tried to rebut the notion, reinforcing Nethercutt's claim that ending big government and deficit spending was vital and that sending that message by ousting the Speaker was more important than the "pork" he could deliver.[32]

Half-a-dozen radio talk show hosts carried sustained Rush Limbaugh-modeled anti-Foley themes. "The radio talk-show hosts in this area have really been bashing Foley," noted Spokane Mayor Jack Geraghty. "And that is really a new phenomenon."[33]

Foley "suffered indignities that were unheard of in his campaigns of yesteryear," wrote *New York Times* regional correspondent Timothy Egan. "For one thing, there are fewer and fewer people around who know that he is the son of Ralph and Helen Foley . . . who were so revered that their names are chiseled into the biggest new building at Gonzaga University, near the statue of Bing Crosby, who was a student there. Today talk radio hosts here call Mr. Foley things that are unprintable. Mr. Foley, in fact, seems perplexed at the degree of change he sees on the American political landscape." In an October by-lined column, *Spokesman-Review* Managing Editor Chris Peck provided a flavor of Spokane talk shows. "It's not really about politics as Todd Herman, the foulest mouth on Spokane talk radio, honestly said just the other day. 'When you are in talk radio you sit there and look at empty phone lines,' he said. 'I've gotta do what it takes to light up those phone lines.' Hence, the 27-year-old former Spokane Falls Community College student has tried to boost the ratings of KSBN AM 1230 by referring to Tom Foley as 'The Sphincter of the House.'"[34]

To the degree that the coarseness of talk radio was discordant for Foley, even the high cost, high-tech style of the modern campaign seemed to prompt a nostalgic note.

> At one point in the campaign we were filming a spot in the middle of a wheat field in Walla Walla County. My extremely experienced political consultant Bob Shrum had contracted a competent film crew equipped with the usual cameras and sound mixers, but also with portable generators producing great quantities of lighting balanced with reflectors. I remember thinking to myself, "do we really need lights out here at high noon on a sunny day?" Of course, from the technicians' standpoint, the natural sunlight, with its glaring, produces a bad image and you needed the special lighting. It did seem strange though that, instead of talking to audiences in Grange halls, you were talking to farmers by television. It's the way of the world today, and you're not just standing in a wheat field, but you're standing surrounded by a production company.

Foley's concerns about politics in the 1990s went beyond the new glitz or cost of campaigns, as he had earlier explained to *New York Times* congressional correspondent Adam Clymer who had accompanied the Speaker on an August 1993 visit to eastern Washington. Foley conveyed "a sense that the problems of the 90s are harder and more complicated than those of the 60s when he came to Congress, and that the tone of politics is nastier, more simplistic, more extreme." In speeches, town meetings with constituents, and interviews, Foley dwelt on the institution of Congress and its membership, calling it a "tremendous distortion of reality" to say that Congress was more corrupt today. Congress was, in fact, more honest than it used to be and some "advocacy" talk radio programs and sensation-seeking television news magazines were largely responsible for the false image.

In order to raise money, many interest groups flog the fears and anxieties of their members with the most extremist language. Whatever the issue—the environment, civil liberties, abortion, or trade—fundraising letters suggest the most dire consequences are at hand. Often Congress, one way or the other, is part of the threat, and thus organizations on both the right and the left contribute to the feeling of anger and insecurity about congressional action on policy. "For the people who have served in Congress a long time," Foley reflected, "most look back on the greater certitude of the 60s and 70s as a much more rewarding time."[35]

A Speaker or a Listener?

The Spokesman-Review gave Foley a strong endorsement, saying he was "the sort of man most Americans would love to have as their Congressman, a prodigious intellect, a man of unusual integrity." But for the first time in his political career, Foley routinely ran into hecklers at speeches. He was criticized as too erudite, too intellectual. "I don't intend to change my style or my manner," was his brief response.[36]

Under the tutelage of Rollins, Nethercutt ran what he characterized as a "Foley-like" campaign. As one veteran Northwest political observer wrote, Nethercutt began with "the same respectful style deployed in 1964 when Foley, a 35-year-old Spokane lawyer, upset 22-year GOP incumbent Walt Horan.[37] "I'm not going to run negatively against Tom Foley because I respect him," Nethercutt said. "He's a gentleman . . . and some people think he's done some good things for the district . . . [but] he's got too many constituents to represent. He's got the Democrats in Congress, President Clinton, and our district."[38]

At a Chamber of Commerce debate before some 850 Spokane residents, Nethercutt suggested that Foley did not understand the concerns of families. "Four times the challenger spoke the words, 'I'm a dad,'" wrote Tim Egan, "leaving unsaid that Mr. Foley is not. The strategy, said . . . Mr. Nethercutt's spokesman, is to show that 'Tom Foley is not like the rest of us.'"[39]

Asked what he would do if he defeated Foley and House Republicans offered to make him Speaker, Nethercutt said he would decline because it was more important to have a vote on the Agriculture Committee than to be the leader of the House. Some district polls even suggested that as many as a quarter of Foley's eastern Washington electorate thought that Nethercutt would somehow inherit the Speakership if he defeated Foley.[40] Foley attempted to make the point that he was still listening to his constituents and that, as Speaker, he had the power to amplify the response. He highlighted improvements to Fairchild Air Force Base, twenty-five heavily traveled miles of U.S. 395 in eastern Washington made less dangerous by being widened to four lanes, his support for wheat farmers, funding in the crime bill for new police officers, and a $15 million research and technology grant directed to the district. Nethercutt used those same cases as examples of how Congress serves members' reelection needs, arguing that it would be better to have never collected the tax money to pay for them in the first place.[41]

Nethercutt's message resonated across the countryside in many traditionally Republican farm communities that were willing to think less in terms of their livelihood and more in terms of sending an anti-government message. "Green as a gourd," was how Reardan farmer Fred Fleming described Nethercutt on agriculture, but he still counted himself among the former Foley supporters now in favor of Nethercutt. "I'm shooting my foot off my body to say I'm willing to get rid of Tom Foley," he said. "A rational, intelligent person would not get rid of Tom Foley." Yet Fleming associated Foley with the Clinton presidency and a broad range of social problems, from the decline in individual responsibility to "dummied down schools." For the sake of change, he said, "I'm willing to take a hit."[42]

The Foley campaign suggested that Nethercutt's support of Newt Gingrich's "Contract with America" would lead to cuts in support for education and Medicare for the elderly. Foley contrasted Nethercutt's "outsider" campaign portrayal with his years as Alaska Republican Senator Stevens's chief of staff. He criticized Nethercutt for his opposition to the assault weapon ban. If that nettled the Nethercutt campaign, Rollins's television ads dealt in kind with their portrayal of Foley's House-provided Lincoln Town car. "The Speaker has a limo the size of the president's," Rollins observed. "One of our first spots was about the Speaker and his big, black limo."[43]

To counter Nethercutt's "a listener not a Speaker" mantra, Foley brought up the issue of Representative Newt Gingrich. He told audiences that if Nethercutt won the congressional seat in a Republican tide, the Speaker's post would move from Spokane to Marietta, Georgia, and Nethercutt would have minimal influence in helping the home district in eastern Washington.[44]

Elsewhere the argument might have had more impact. In O'Neill's Massachusetts, Wright's Texas, or even Gingrich's Georgia, there appeared to have been more appreciation for one's representative being at the top of the ladder than in Foley's eastern Washington. Polls indicated that 60 percent of Gingrich's heavily Republican Georgia constituents did not mind his national role. It would have been harder to say the same for Foley's Fifth Congressional District constituents and his own national role.[45]

A Culmination of Earlier Vulnerability?

The election of 1994 ended up as an extension of 1992, when Foley failed to carry a number of the rural counties he had traditionally won in the past. Nethercutt's approximately 4,000 vote margin of victory came primarily from the nine timber- and agriculture-dominated counties. Although Foley had given considerable attention to these rural constituents over the years, in 1994 national issues offered greater appeal to the voters' more parochial conservative instincts. "Much of the criticism of Foley is as a result of the public's frustration with government," the *Walla Walla Union-Bulletin* had stated in its editorial endorsement. "But it took decades to get to this point, and the public can't realistically expect it to change quickly."[46]

> In many ways I think 1994 was a referendum on the first two years of the Clinton administration, and the failure of the Democratic Congress and the Clinton administration to produce legislation that made sense to the country. I think the health care bill, in particular, was too big and too complicated. It was easy to attack. Most people had only a blurred idea of what was involved. And then, after all that, it failed. At the end of the day, it wasn't passed, so you got the worst of both worlds.

From a public perception standpoint, some of the early actions of the administration created problems. I think the President was right on the issue of gays in the military, but when the press put it at the forefront of the administration's agenda, it tended to become too prominent. In retrospect, it might have been wise to start out with a commission to decide how the policy would be implemented. Not backing away from the commitment, but delaying, for a few months, the argument.

You also have the sort of challenges the opponents of congressional incumbents pose to constituents of "you're not going to be bought" in your vote and opinion by the fact "Congressman Incumbent here has put in the street lights, or rehabilitated the court house, or provided funds for the local college, or paved the streets? You're not that kind of person are you?" And then the variation on that argument. "Now that we have the benefits, shouldn't we question whether it wouldn't have been better if we hadn't had them at all? Would it have been more virtuous to have offered them up in support of smaller government or lower taxes? Now we can't tear up the streets or dismantle the courthouse, but one has to wonder whether this sort of thing is really good for the country. . . ." At times, one suspects, it's exciting to have the benefits of the projects and to reject the provider.

In the last three weeks of the campaign, the Foley campaign's own tracking surveys never had the Speaker reaching 50 percent of the vote while Clinton's popularity hovered at 27 percent. In early October former Democratic Congressional Campaign Committee chairman, House Majority Whip, and Foley confidant Tony Coelho had criticized the failure of "the low-key congressional veteran" to go on the attack. "I have never attacked people in any of my campaigns, and I'm not going to do that in this campaign" Foley responded when asked by the press for a reaction. Negative campaign advertising may be distasteful, Coelho said, but "the professionals will tell you, and every poll that you look at tells you, it works."[47]

Having watched Foley's Fifth District races for twenty-three years, Gonzaga University political science professor Blaine M. Garvin observed that there were more negative ads from both sides than he'd seen in the past. "But compared to what goes on in other parts of the country, these ads are awfully tame," he concluded. "In some campaigns, they just come out and say, 'This guy's a crook.' Foley insiders say Nethercutt is trying to claim the high road because outside groups are willing [to] take the cheap shots for him."[48]

Reporters who had sensed an upset in the making questioned Foley's seeming calm demeanor in the final weeks.

First of all, I had seriously thought about retiring in early 1994. I'd spent thirty years in the Congress and perhaps it was time to move on.

But exit strategies are difficult when you're in the leadership. In the first place, you make the decision not just for yourself and your spouse, you make it for your staff and their spouses. It's a decision not just for eighteen staff, but as many as forty-five. It's a heavy burden. The House gets consumed with leadership races when major vacancies occur. Even though the Speaker would inevitably have been Dick Gephardt in an orderly transition of continued Democratic control, the question of the Majority Leader might well have been contested between Dave Bonior and Vic Fazio, and the question of the Whip's job down through caucus chair and vice chair would be open to other challengers. So you could have three races with all the candidates talking to all the members about hopes and ambitions in the midst of a final last-ditch effort to pass the administration's major undertakings, including the health care bill. George Mitchell had announced his intention to retire so we would have had leadership struggles going on in the House and the Senate, and I think by their very nature they're more disruptive in the House.

So, by the time I'd thought about it and weighed all the alternatives and difficulties, it was then very late in the game, and the election became one bridge too far.

Second, we were overwhelmed by a whole series of problems fighting off attacks by the term limits people, the National Rifle Association, and other groups such as anti-D.C. statehood. There was the unpopularity of the President in eastern Washington. Between 1994 and 1996 when he was reelected, the President's numbers doubled. The nadir was 1994. I've never, and don't, blame my loss on the President, but it was not a good climate for Democrats.

Third, the Speakership, which in other circumstances and geographies would be considered an impregnable advantage, was ironically a disadvantage in 1994 in eastern Washington. The approach of the opposition was: If there is any problem in the district, why hasn't it been corrected if the Speaker is so powerful? Why does the rain not fall on our crops, why do children rebel against their parents, why is there trouble in the land? And, if he does good things, are you really comfortable with this long self-indulgence by Congress? Isn't it time for some new Puritanism and self restraint? There was also the wonderful argument that you here in the Fifth District are empowered more than any other people in the country. If you're sick and tired of what's going on in the federal government and Washington, D.C., you have a voice amplified beyond imagination in other parts of the country. They can only fire a member of Congress. You can fire the Speaker. It was a rather clever approach.

I think another factor in my alleged calmness was that we pretty much knew where we were all the time. We had very expensive but excellent polling. We reached the end of the race about a point behind. It was a question of whether it was going to come or not, and it didn't.

In the aftermath of Foley's defeat, *The Spokesman Review* ran an editorial reflecting on the Foley legacy to the Spokane community: "While George Nethercutt's backers crowed and talk radio gibbered in glee that Tom Foley had become 'road kill,' Foley turned that familiar, St. Bernard visage toward the clicking cameras and spoke in the accents of another time: He offered Nethercutt sincere congratulations, as another congressman once did for a younger Foley 30 years ago . . . He thanked colleagues . . . He thanked staff: 'You made me better than I am.'"[49]

The Aftermath

The two hundred-plus years that have passed since Edmund Burke spoke to the Electors of Bristol on November 3, 1774, have not dulled his wisdom. "Your representative owes you," he said, "not his industry only, but his judgment; and he betrays instead of serving you if he sacrifices it to your opinion." A modern variation suggests that whether perceived or real, the vulnerability of American politicians has made it more difficult for them to take tough decisions, court unpopularity, ask for sacrifices, fly in the face of conventional wisdom, or act in what their judgment tells them is in their constituents' or the nation's best interest rather than their own.[50]

In 1964 Foley had won his seat to become one of only two members to represent the district since 1942. Over the next decade he concentrated on district interests. Wheat growers benefited from his work as chairman of the Agriculture Committee and he was able to look after Spokane's Fairchild Air Force Base and the quasi-government agencies that provided the cheapest electric power in the country. In the process, he became a legislator of national scope and, as he rose in the House leadership, his identification with national policies became more visibly at odds with the political leanings of his conservative district.

> I suspect that many people on the west side of the state and from other parts of the country, who knew something about the generally conservative bent of the Fifth District, were surprised that I hadn't lost in previous years.
>
> In 1968 there was a primary challenge in the Republican Party and an old high school debating colleague of mine, from another school, ran as a Republican in the primary and had a very energetic campaign. His name was Ray Tanksley. Ray put out one simple campaign pamphlet that I thought was very effective. It resembled a Christmas card. It said on the outside: "Suppose, for a moment, that you were a congressman." And you opened it up and, on the left-hand side, it said: "Would you vote to

keep students who riot in college on federal scholarships?" And in smaller print under that: "Tom Foley did." "Would you vote to take the sacred gold backing away from our American dollar?" "Tom Foley did." "Would you vote to abolish the House Un-American Activities Committee that keeps our country safe from communists?" "Tom Foley did." "Would you vote against prayer in the public schools?" "Tom Foley did." Would you vote, et cetera, et cetera, through about ten, obviously inflammatory, challenges to my voting record.

And the right hand side of the piece said: "If you're thinking about this time that you'd be a better congressman than Foley, we agree with you—almost anybody would—but in case you're not running this year, Ray Tanksley is. He's a red-blooded American, just like you, who believes in keeping the crooks in jail, throwing the left-wing students out of college, and winning the war in Vietnam with a military victory."

I thought this was a devastating piece. When I was up in Okanogan County I ran into a rancher friend, the kind of guy who was still trying to squeeze into the trousers that he wore when he was twenty-five and that were held up, in part, by a huge silver-and-turquoise belt-buckle. I went up to him and took the occasion to ask if he'd seen this piece of Tanksley's. He said "It's all over town, Tom. They got them everywhere. Every bar and barbershop and used-car lot and grocery store has got 'em." And I said "Well, pretty effective, I suppose?" He said "Nooo, it's not effective." "It's not?" I asked, and then blurted out, "Why not?"

"Well," he said, "Tom, folks around here don't believe those lies about you. They know those are all cheap-shot falsehoods that Tanksley's spreading about your voting record. My God, you'd have to be some crazy socialist to vote the way he's got you down, and people know you, and know you're not that kind of guy. And the next time Tanksley comes to town, believe me, he's going to get a lot of heat for spreading lies about Tom Foley."

I didn't correct the record too much. In the worst context, the votes were technically correct. I shook my friend's hand and warmly said "George, I appreciate your support."

I suppose every member has his or her own way of sorting out the balance between personal judgment and constituent opinion. I'm not sure it's even something that some members can carefully parse out. Most people think their own judgment has got to be the bottom line on what is in the national and district interest. If you just follow popularity polls on issues with constituents, then really nobody's very important in the representative sense. You could do it all by electronic polling.

On the other hand, it would be naive to believe that every member just routinely stands up against popular pressures. I mean, obviously, if the district has a strong opinion on some question or other that's so fundamental to their belief that a member might face defeat if he or she took an opposite opinion, the capacity to adjust to the district's view is pretty great with most members. And they obviously rationalize this, in part, on the grounds that it becomes either their view or it's their duty to represent the district's viewpoint.

But there are other examples, I think, in almost every member's career where he or she takes some pretty serious political risks because they believe very strongly about an issue that doesn't comport with the popular opinion of the time. And the job then is to convince your constituents to accept your judgment.

I've taken positions that I think were damaging in a political sense, but I don't have any regrets taking them. I used to say that the most important thing about votes on the floor and positions you take in Congress is that when you consider them at election time you're able to say with some satisfaction that you can still vote for yourself.

Foley's exit from the local scene the day after the election was as gracious in defeat as it had been in victory thirty years earlier: "I know the thrill of election as well as the honor of service. We understand the thrill George Nethercutt and his family are feeling." He went on, however, to comment less as the defeated incumbent from the Fifth District and more as a departing Speaker. "It is finally my hope that we will have with this new Congress an opportunity to see a new spirit of bipartisanship. . . . Despite what some might think, the overwhelming membership of Congress, Republicans and Democrats, are wonderful, upstanding, talented people."[51]

Following Foley around on his last day in the House, *Washington Post* congressional correspondent Kevin Merida was taken aback when Foley seemed concerned that a photograph had been taken during his regular workout at the University Club, but not with his usual trainer Greg Raleigh. "To the last day," Merida wrote, "nobody was too small in Tom Foley's world. . . . Foley's big worry was that he had inadvertently bruised the feelings of someone he so valued. The gesture was a fitting metaphor for Foley's brand of tempered leadership. For, whatever his faults in the 5½ years he presided over the House, no one who observed him thought he was anything but a study in the art of graciousness."[52]

Foley's message was much the same in his final press conference in the other Washington. He was not leaving with bitterness over his defeat, he told the congressional press corps, but with "gratitude to my constituents who have given me what I think is one of the greatest honors in public life, to represent them here in the Capitol of the United States, in the House of Representatives. . . . If I have any regret, I guess it is a regret that somehow I was not able to communicate."

"Clearly," the *Washington Post's* Kevin Merida observed, "Foley is not of the Sound Bite Generation. And that explains, in part, the trouble many House

Democrats had with him, even as they cheered his best qualities—his decency, intellect, and commitment to public service." Quoting a junior Democratic congressman who admired Foley, Merida wrote "'He is not of this world of Rush Limbaugh and all the talk shows, and it hurt, especially when you have a leadership on the other side willing to use every tool at their disposal. He was part of a world of gentlemanly, cordial, bipartisan relationships.'"[53]

Speaker Foley's last day in the House came to an end when Republican Representative Robert H. Michel of Illinois, an old friend, equally out of step with the sound-bite generation, rose to offer a resolution praising Foley's "fair and impartial manner. You came to the Speaker's office at a time when our institution needed the kind of virtues you have for so long typified: integrity, decency and a commitment to crafting reasoned solutions to difficult problems."[54]

But Foley had the last word. As the retiring Republican Leader Michel ascended the rostrum, at Foley's invitation, to preside over the House, as he had hoped to do as Speaker for so many years, Foley spoke one last time. He urged members to value the House as "the voice of American democracy" and to make sure that Americans understood "the value and importance of this, their House of Representatives."[55]

> It was John McCormack who once said we should always feel very proud to be the representatives of half-a-million or so of our fellow Americans. That it was one of the great honors in American life to be a Representative in Congress. And that when we came to work in the morning, and when we first caught a glimpse of the Capitol from east or west, north or south, in rain or shine, in sun or shade, however it appeared, if it didn't give us a sense of thrill, a sense of not only personal satisfaction, but very deep gratitude to our constituents for the honor of letting us represent them, we should simply quit. Those members who no longer felt that thrill had stayed too long.[56]

Foley never served that long.

CHAPTER FOURTEEN

What Lies Ahead,
What's Left Behind

While I might have envied the new Speaker's ability to curb the independent agen-
das of committee chairs relative to the leadership . . . the price was too high.
—Thomas S. Foley, 1996

The 104th Congress and the "Contract with America"

A MONG THE MANY HALLMARKS which distinguished the 104th Congress was that its Republican majority had been elected to govern under an anti-government banner. In *Time* magazine's January 9, 1995 cover story, newly elected Speaker of the House Newt Gingrich was termed "the slayer of the Old Order."[1] He reportedly said that the 1994 congressional elections were the most portentous since Lincoln's 1860 election, which led to the formation of the Republican Party. With Washington, D.C.'s unabashed fixation with power, Speaker Gingrich was quickly being compared with such speakers of the past as Joseph Cannon and Thomas Brackett Reed. To be compared with the "czar" speakers was to be in powerful company.

It's an apocryphal story. I hope it's true. Some have suggested it might have been Speaker Cannon's story, but I'll stick with his predecessor for whom it makes more sense. Republican Speaker Reed, who represented the entire state of Maine, an at-large district, was supposedly asked by a constituent to please send him a copy of the rules and regulations of the House of Representatives, to which the Speaker charily replied by sending an autographed photograph of himself. Indeed, the Rules of the

House were known as Reed's Rules because he had implemented them with an autocratic enthusiasm, so much so that he was once asked by a Democratic member, "what is the function of the minority?" "The function of the minority, sir," the Speaker replied, "is to make a quorum and to draw its pay."

Looking back, *The New Yorker's* "Letter from Washington" in December 1996 described those early months of the 104th: "The Republicans, upon taking control of Congress in 1994 . . . proved to be even more intemperate than the Democrats had been two years earlier. They strutted about in triumph, appearing almost testosterone-addled. . . . In Washington, contentiousness had become a major industry. . . . Meanwhile, the rest of the country was—by any reasonable historical standard—remarkably placid and prosperous. . . . The public seemed perpetually appalled by the torrent of inconsequential vituperation."[2]

One long-term interpretation of the 1994 election was that it was an overdue reaction against "big," "intrusive" government starting in the 1960s with President Lyndon Johnson's "Great Society" programs. The shorter-term theory was that politics had become more volatile and the public more impatient. Voters had thrown the Democrats out for failing to be responsive, and could do the same to the Republicans. As leader of the change, Gingrich was worried about dangers in the short-term and interpreted the long-term as his party's legislative mandate. He didn't quarrel with the characterization of himself as "a self-styled revolutionary, bent on radical change—on fundamentally revising the role of government and overturning the established order."[3]

The freshman class, representing nearly a third of the Republican majority, arrived with considerable media hoopla which focused on its "Contract with America" campaign agenda on term limits, balancing the budget, the line-item veto, reforming welfare, reducing the federal government, and cutting taxes. Of the seventy-three freshmen, more than half had been endorsed by the Christian Coalition, but probably more important in the new leadership's view, most felt that they owed their election and new majority status to Gingrich. "A very large percentage of the freshmen felt that but for him they wouldn't be in the Congress at all."[4]

Gingrich had actively solicited many of them to run for the House, offered campaign advice and sometimes campaign contributions, and was "universally seen as the driving force behind the new Republican revolution." The 1994 freshman class stood in stark contrast to the last activist class. The Watergate class of 1974 had sought to disperse and decentralize power. The class of 1994 sought to strengthen the power of the leadership so as to enforce ideological unity.[5]

In the 103rd Congress, the Democratic Caucus had balked at significantly strengthening the prerogatives of Speaker Foley. The majority had been divided on key policy issues, had relied on the presidency to provide the cohesion of a legislative agenda, and preferred to center power in the committee system. But

Foley, and most of his previous Democratic predecessors as Speaker, would have felt a certain empathy with Gingrich in seeing some of the advantages in empowering the Speakership: it discouraged party defections, limited negotiating among committee chairs, pointed to a legislative agenda for the rank-and-file membership, and provided a clear focus for the press and the public.

"The major losers in the enhancement of Gingrich's office were the incoming committee chairmen and other influential Republicans," observed political science Congress-watchers Lawrence Evans and Walter Oleszek. "New to majority status, however, the committee leaders were not fully entrenched in their positions. Thus, they had somewhat less to lose from strengthening the Speakership than had their Democratic predecessors, who were used to exercising considerable autonomy."[6]

After four decades in the minority, the new Speaker felt the party had to deliver or voters would return the Democrats to power. However, it was Representative Newt Gingrich, the same driving force that had persuaded both moderate and conservative Republicans in the 1980s to adopt a confrontational stance toward the Democratic management of the House, and who had sought to foster public discontent with the institution of Congress, who was now the pivotal figure behind consolidating power in the office of the Speaker.[7]

Where Speaker Foley and the Democratic leadership had often been unable to exert tough, arm-twisting, aggressive guidance of the party's rank-and-file members, Gingrich had no such hesitancy or lack of punch. Intra-party discipline was backed by muscle. A September e-mail document slipped to the press reported on the new Speaker's threats against recalcitrant members of the Agriculture Committee: ". . . they would be knocked out of the line of succession for chairman, and would lose their chairmanships of other committees."[8]

By mid-April 1995, television networks, newspapers, and magazines were filled with stories taking Speaker Gingrich at his word and equating the Congress's first hundred days with those of President Franklin D. Roosevelt during the Great Depression. The media attention was such that on April 7, the day the House leadership officially completed action on their "Contract," Speaker Gingrich addressed the nation live in prime time on several television networks. Except to respond to a President, never before had a Speaker requested an opportunity to appear on national television to address the nation; never before would any television network likely have granted a Speaker time if he had in fact asked.[9]

The contrast between Gingrich's and Foley's leadership style was stark. Unlike Foley's effort to find a common basis of governing with Republican President George Bush, Gingrich expected his platform to rival or even supplant President Clinton's. Immediately after the election, Gingrich began to work through rules changes and other related mechanisms to assure himself something of the formal power in the Speakership that had characterized the classically strong Republican "czar" Speakers of the turn of the century.

I think it was an aberration. You can obviously get a Speaker who will pose himself as a counter to the President and lead a political contest against him, but I would still argue that these are all very individualistic situations. Speaker Gingrich came in without any pre-existing committee "barons." There weren't any real centers of power that were interested in protecting themselves against encroachment.

It was an ideal time for him. To some extent, he could define his powers and himself as Speaker pretty much as he wished. For a time he was reportedly summoning in the staff directors of various committees to sit down with his staff to receive their instructions. Where the Democratic leadership was frequently forced to deal with things indirectly, he was able to involve himself directly in the internal aspects of legislation.

The legacy of Democratic reforms of the 1970s had included the nomination of committee chairs by the Steering and Policy Committee in which the Speaker had a significant influence, but with final selection being made by the entire caucus. Although it involved no formal change in House rules, in the 104th Congress the Speaker informally assigned committee chairs, and Gingrich bypassed three senior members in line for chairs to give the seats to younger but more committed members.

It's another example of the difference between the law and the prophets. For Democrats, the law technically is that the Steering and Policy Committee has to recommend the naming of committee chairs. However, if Steering and Policy names any candidate other than the sitting committee chair, the incumbent can take the issue to the caucus and have an up-or-down vote. For a Democratic Speaker to have done what Speaker Gingrich did would have drawn a lot of blood and created a lot of controversy. It would have pitted the Speaker not only against that individual committee chairman, but the chairmen in general. They were a "union."

At one point in my Speakership a number of committee chairmen were informally meeting, in secret, under [Administration Committee chair] Charlie Rose's encouragement to consider "the welfare, feeding, discipline, and health of the committee chairmen system." Charlie was using it as a kind of power base for his own ends, but if the chairmen had felt threatened as a group, they would have been quick to say "no bishop no king." In the congresses before the 104th Congress there would have been no doubt that with the first committee chairman offered up on the block, the barons would have all gathered at Runnymede.

Under Gingrich's rule, there would be no "old barons" to challenge him. In essence, he would run the House with the assistance of the Speaker's Advisory Group, comprising the inner circle of the leadership. He would appoint "task forces" for dealing with various subjects that cut across committee jurisdiction, lessening the power of standing committee chairs. A "Contract" provision undergirded the transfer of power by limiting the terms of committee chairs to six years (the Speaker was limited to eight years in office). The new Speaker also assumed virtual control over committee assignments. Was this to be the way of things in future Houses, that the Speaker would single-handedly select committee chairs? Was there no continuing value in some degree of seniority or acquired expertise when it came to the progression of committee chairs?

> Seniority is extremely important in creating a presumed order of responsibility and leadership. It is something you deviate from occasionally, but what you expect to see in the normal course of events is the tradition of seniority continuing. I think if you had an open situation, where every two years we had a popularity contest in committees for who is going to be chair, there would be an awful stirring and role playing taking place six months before the end of a Congress. It ought to be a very high hurdle for the next person in line to become the chairman. It should take a major shift in normal practice for seniority not to be followed. It is a threshold that suppresses ambition, conspiracy, anarchy, and the creation of cabals.

It was clear that his prominence, power, and confrontational style would leave Gingrich constantly open to attacks from his adversaries and the investigative focus of reporters, with unknown implications for his future. The Speaker's decision at the beginning of the 104th Congress to open his daily press briefings to television immediately provided film footage of angry remarks and led to overexposure. The daily press briefings by Speaker Gingrich ceased several months into the first session.

> When the Speaker, as Mr. Gingrich has done, raises himself to a press figure of sufficient weight, then he can issue press releases and be pretty much guaranteed to be covered. That's not automatic with the Speakership. His notoriety as Speaker, if I can use that word, has been exceptional, receiving enormous publicity, both in coming into office with a new Republican majority and even to the point of his own personal difficulties guaranteeing daily coverage. He's been in the position to command press attention. How often it's been used to defend the institution of the House of Representatives is another question. I think the point is that there are times when the Speaker has to be able speak for the House, for the institution of Congress, because without him, or somebody like him, nobody else is likely to do it.

Under Gingrich's leadership during the first hundred days, House Republicans took a number of steps that suggested a partisan approach to running the

House. After years of adamant pressure to make the administration of the House bipartisan, the GOP leaders reversed course when they achieved a majority and moved to a structure firmly under the control of the Speaker. The House Administrator, created in the aftermath of the House "bank" scandal—to be hired and overseen by joint party leadership—was replaced and put under the sole control of the Speaker and his party. "To be sure," noted Congress-watcher Norm Ornstein, "having a tightly organized administrative structure in the House, with clear lines of responsibility and accountability, is an idea that has been endorsed over the years by a wide range of lawmakers in both parties. But the top officers put in place by the Republicans, while having strong credentials, tended to have highly partisan backgrounds, raising real questions about the future fairness of the House's operations."[10]

The Celebration of the First Hundred Days

"I don't know of any time since the New Deal and the Depression and the first 100 days of Franklin Roosevelt that you have seen the kind of effort and energy put into passing a set of commitments," Speaker Gingrich said of the Republican efforts to implement the Contract with America.[11]

Not one single Republican serving in the House in the 103rd Congress, or even in recent memory, had ever served in a Republican majority. For the Republicans it was a giddy, exciting, heart-palpitating experience with visions of the "new Jerusalem." Hyperbole was to be expected. Simply being in Washington, D.C., you could sense the excitement on the Republican side. Of course on the Democratic side there was deep depression. Committee chairmen had their staffs cut, their privileges stripped, and their pride pummeled.

The Contract with America proposed changes in the conduct of the House business and outlined ten legislative goals focused on cutting taxes, balancing the federal budget, and reducing the federal role in social welfare provisions. It served as both a means of extending the unfinished "Reagan Revolution" and a blueprint for a more definitive dismantling of the federal government than Reagan had contemplated. In one analyst's view, the Contract proposed that a Republican majority in the House would "transform the way Congress works. That historic change would be the end of government that is too big, too intrusive, and too easy with the public's money. It can be the beginning of a Congress that respects the values and shares the faith of the American family."[12] Taken together, the Contract proposals would move authority and resources away from Congress, the executive branch, the courts, and federal agencies, while enhancing the decision-making role of the market, state and local government, families, and religious and community associations.

Over the first hundred days of the 104th Congress, the leadership moved some thirty Contract-based bills with near total Republican unity and the selective support of a significant number of Democrats. However, the apparent bipartisanship was deceptive. In a number of cases the torrid pace of congressional action, Republican rhetoric, and extensive press treatment lavished on the Contract obscured reality. The areas of greatest bipartisan support for the Contract reflected a consensus reached previously in the 103rd Congress. Congressional accountability was an example. The Contract stated that "all laws that apply to the rest of the country [should] also apply equally to the Congress." When President Clinton signed the Congressional Accountability Act on January 22, 1995, it was not the first but simply the latest in a series of steps Congress had taken to comply with federal standards.[13]

By the end of 1995, only three of the ten Contract objectives had become law—congressional accountability, reduction of unfunded mandates, and a minor reduction in federal paperwork. All three bills were beneficiaries of the consensus formed in the 103rd Congress.

The Process

Unlike its predecessors over the previous four decades, the 104th Congress was seen as having overcome the "natural inertia of the institution" to draft, consider, debate, and pass legislation. At times there were as many as thirty or forty House and Senate committees and subcommittees meeting daily. In the process, any effective legislative, journalistic, or public scrutiny was virtually impossible and, in most cases, there was no Democratic alternative offered in debate. "The Democrats don't have a chance to organize a national opposition to any issue," one Gingrich aide observed, "because they're coming too fast. . . . The constant rat-a-tat-tat of our bills has put the Democrats in an extraordinarily difficult position where they can't marshal public support for opposition to any of our bills."[14]

The parliamentary tenor of the House in its first hundred days meant that deliberation in the classic sense—carefully thinking through alternatives, debating them, and then moving to a broader public judgment—was largely absent in the House, both in committees and on the floor. The populist character of the new House, combined with the new leadership's relentless schedule, meant that the emphasis was on processing legislation, not on debate and discussion.

If bipartisan interchange between the majority and minority was lacking, the role that lobbyists played in writing the Republicans' legislation was without precedent. The *Washington Post* reported that a lobbyist for the energy and petrochemical industries wrote the first draft of the bill placing a moratorium on federal regulations, and the *New York Times* indicated that a bill to weaken the Clean Water Act was written by a task force of lobbyists representing regulated polluters working alongside congressional sponsors on the Transportation and Infrastructure Committee.[15] Previous Democratic congressional majorities had their alliances with labor, minority advocates, the elderly, and children's rights and environmental groups, but sympathetic lobbyists now had unparalleled access to the Capitol.

I'm not convinced that interest groups were dominant in the 103rd Congress in terms of any active role in writing legislation. They were more effective than in recent congresses in being able to blunt, alter, or deny legislative initiatives. They had more of a negative veto effect. The most effective were those that had behind them, not so much the money power that people frequently allude to, but strong and well-organized constituency groups. The most effective lobbying today, in my view, is the organization of constituency opinion. If you can identify groups in the country that are responsive to concerns, and can be stimulated to communicate with Congress, very often you have an impact.

Gun owners, citizens concerned with home schooling, groups troubled about one foreign policy issue or another, are examples of interests that very often get the attention of members of Congress. Ironically, at a time of mass communication, it doesn't take very many telephone calls, letters, faxes, e-mails, or Internet postings before members of Congress begin to conclude that if they've seen the evidence of eighty faxes, there must be 80,000 or 200,000 people out there concerned about the same thing.

When I was chairman of the Agriculture Committee, I was asked by a prominent agricultural organization if it would be all right if they invited a subcommittee, which dealt with their particular sector of agriculture, to conduct a public hearing in the auditorium during their convention. I remember being shocked. "You mean you want me to authorize a subcommittee to hold an official hearing as part of your convention program? Absolutely not." I thought it was amazing hubris to request it. It was inconceivable to me that the Congress would permit its committee system to be an item on the program of a national agricultural organization and be vulnerable to an announcement that, "this is our captive committee."

I think to some degree some of the things that happened in the 104th Congress reflected that concern. There was some evidence that business organizations and other interest groups were given some extraordinary privileges in terms of participating in the actual drafting of legislation. Interest groups have always been criticized for having more than a desirable degree of influence or impact on legislation, but there have been only a few times in the past that charges were made that the "lobbyists" have been inside congressional offices using government-provided equipment, working with congressional staff, and actually drafting legislation on the spot. Someone might argue, "Well, what's the difference?" A group comes through and presents a member of Congress with a draft of a bill that they have produced in their downtown Washington, D.C., or New York offices, and that member incorporates some of the language and objectives of that proposal into legislation that he or she introduces or supports. Is this really any different than actually coming into a representative's office, sitting down at the office computer, and, with the representative's staff, collaboratively drafting the legislation?

I think there is a difference. There is a point at which the use of a member's office, equipment, and staff, crosses a line. Maybe it's only a degree of propriety or appearance, but there is a threshold that's been crossed when you have almost created a category of adjunct staff members recruited from the private sector.

When the new majority leadership found that time or votes were insufficient for floor action on bills, legislation was put into appropriation bills. Policies legislated through appropriations bills, so-called "riders," have the advantage of being attached to bills that must pass for the government to continuing functioning. Legislating in appropriations bills had long been a violation of House rules unless specific exceptions were made. However, the new House leadership had initiated a process of legitimizing such riders if the authorizing and appropriating committees agreed. This was a way of getting around the regular procedure of holding hearings, "marking up" a bill from subcommittee to committee, getting a rule, and taking a bill to the floor for debate and a vote. It frequently amounted to a kind of sleight-of-hand. Unlike bills which were scheduled on the calendar, riders were buried deep in the bowels of lengthy, complicated, appropriations bills.[16]

In the early months of 1995 Foley proved reluctant to offer any criticism of Speaker Gingrich. As the course of the 104th Congress proceeded, he privately shared the concerns of many of his former colleagues that centralization had gone too far and was coming at too great a cost. Foley had argued that some of what Gingrich had done to centralize direction in the office of the Speaker he would have liked to have done himself. But the cost, in part, was fewer hearings and more legislation crafted in back rooms by Gingrich's advisory group, all of which robbed the legislative process of real debate over new policy. The process also helped created a chamber characterized by bitter partisanship, interpersonal acrimony, and a general lack of civility.

I thought both the new Speaker's means and results went too far. I was critical of using a task force system to bypass the committee process. It not only denied the rights of the minority, but the public and press as well. It reversed the trend of past congressional reforms which attempted to move congressional operations toward a more open legislative process. From the fall of Republican "czar" Speaker Joe Cannon in 1910 to the reforms of the 1970s, there was a fairly steady divestment of power from the committee chairmen. But, even after those reforms, which were designed, in part, to streamline the Speaker's role and that of the new subcommittee chairmen, full committee chairmen still retained a critical legislative role.

Before the change to the Republican congressional party majority in 1994, one problem of the committee structure was that the chairs tended to operate with their own agendas, which might or might not have been congruent with a broader leadership agenda. The chairs were supported by an extremely competent, singularly loyal, obedient, and professional career committee staff. As Speaker, I very often felt that I had to battle not only the chairmen, but also these senior staff. I had thought at one point that Speaker Gingrich was endeavoring to secure a required leadership imprimatur for the hiring and promoting of these key committee staff as one means of influencing the committees toward the achievement of a centrally-approved agenda.

As a former Speaker, while I might have envied the new Speaker's ability to curb the independent agendas of committee chairmen relative to the leadership, this new authority appeared to be more the result of the novelty of the Republican new majority status than an orchestrated change in the structure of the House. The price was too high.

Unwilling to compromise with President Clinton—or even more moderate Republicans in the Senate—the House leadership in the fall of 1995 forced a confrontation with the President that resulted in a six-day shutdown of the government in November.

Most of the time you ought to be able to work out a common-ground solution. All-or-nothing confrontations are generally sterile. They don't produce a result, they lead to temporary gridlock, and somebody inherits the political blame. After the blame has been assigned, particularly if it goes dramatically in one direction, then there has to be a retreat.

I believe, in part, this has become a function of more recent times, and the more recent majority of the Republican Party's having a strong core of intellectually committed conservatives who are fundamentally anxious for confrontation and push the leadership into those positions. They seek to dominate the process from time to time, if not constantly. Their disappointment and defeats seem to have created an underlying bitterness which produces the next confrontation. By apparently boasting about the shutdowns of the federal government, congressional Republicans took political responsibility for what were almost universally unpopular vents. Those who believed that the government had a positive role to play were naturally alienated. Those who were extremely anti-government were frustrated by the fact that most government employees "were being paid for going to movies in the afternoon." The press always manages to find the little tow-headed, blue-eyed boy from Iowa, stranded in Washington, D.C., who can't visit the Smithsonian's Air and Space Museum or the dinosaurs at the Museum of Natural History.

It was a predictable political disaster, and by the spring of 1996 congressional Republicans were ruefully aware of the public damage and the need for repair.

It wasn't until January 1996 that Senate Majority Leader Robert Dole pushed through a continuing resolution to keep the government afloat. This was without much consultation with and despite resistance in the House.

The House Republicans also brought about confrontation on environmental policies—drawing the ire of many Americans who worried about a lessening of environmental safeguards. The usual majority party approach of packaging an issue and then selling it to the caucus or conference to ensure wide support once it reached the floor was not done on the environmental agenda. House Republicans' first year in the majority underscored what history indicated: major legislative reform almost invariably requires either unified government with substantial congressional majorities or bipartisan cooperation rather than one-party dogmatism.

As a Republican Congress and a Democratic President competed for the middle ground in the final months of the session, the 104th Congress managed to overhaul the nation's welfare system, undid New Deal-era farm programs and guaranteed farmers fixed and declining payments regardless of market prices, provided the next President with a line-item veto to strike specific items from spending bills, rewrote the ground rules for the country's telecommunications industry, raised the minimum wage, took steps to curb illegal immigration, created new environmental standards, and guaranteed most employees health insurance when they lost or left their jobs.[17]

As former Speaker Foley observed,

> I think both parties have found that positions that reflect the strong progressive wing of the Democratic Party or the very conservative wing of the Republican Party don't always have effective public support. The country tends to be quite centrist.[18]

For his part, Gingrich sounded almost Foleyesque in his own appraisal of the 104th Congress as he suggested that the past two years of bitter partisanship had been his own coming of age, and that harsh partisan politics bore little fruit. "All of us in the House have learned a little more about this process in the last two years. . . . Some days it is very frustrating, some days it is very partisan. And then occasionally it matures and it comes together and people listen to each other."[19]

When Foley had been the Number One Democrat in the House, he had frequently been caught between the liberal wing of his own party and a Republican President. That changed in 1993 when he found himself unquestionably cast in a more partisan role as legislative point-man for President Clinton. Yet even then, he continued to see his role as Speaker as demanding civility and fairness, ever in search of a legislative solution rather than stalemate.

> On occasion I've thought that if I were designing the system ideally I'd probably follow the model of European parliaments and create a very honorific and politically impotent role for the Speaker of presiding over the House, making rulings, and observing the protection of members. But one of the reasons that's difficult to do is the U.S. background where Speakers have real authority, power, and influence within political parties and they are not likely to be the first ones to want to vacate the position. The aura of the Speaker being third in line to the presidency would make it difficult to recreate a judicial office removed from the political system, but I think the model could have some advantages.

> But the House of Representatives probably needs to have a strong Speakership today as much as it has at any time in its history because the pressures on members, the diversity of influences from outside the Congress, and the complexity of legislative proposals is greater than in the past. I want to emphasize that there is need for a centralizing, organizing principle in the House of Representatives that is best expressed by the Speakership. It is much more fluid than it was before. The party structures are less highly organized, the regional interests are less centered. It's more complicated today than it was twenty-five or fifty years ago.

> If you don't have a Speaker who is able to bring some kind of organized pressures or discipline to the House it would be very chaotic, as it has from time to time, even in this latest period when Speaker Gingrich has been weakened or his authority has been questioned.

> You simply have to insure that when you're carrying out the role of presiding over the House that you're fair, that the votes are fair, and that the process is as fair as possible. Where it gets into difficulty is where you start elaborating legislative tactics and procedures that include using the Rules Committee for too many restrictive rules and encouraging extraordinary legislative remedies. In the past there has been some feeling, on the part of the minority, both in the current situation and before, that the Speaker had stepped over the line of fairness and impartiality by bringing his partisan attitudes too much down to the level of legislative operations. That's where it's hard.

Even in reflecting over the past, there was an oft-voiced refrain. When asked in November 1994 what advice he would give the new Republican Speaker, Foley said the recognition that "when one becomes Speaker of the House, you are the Speaker of the whole House and not just one party. You have the responsibility to be fair and impartial to all members, to enforce the rules without regard to party, and to uphold the traditions and honor of the institution." At the heart of the advice was his recognition of the Speaker's role in setting the legislative tone for the House of Representatives and the public's regard for the institution.

It had the ring of good advice then, and probably will as long as there is a Speaker and a House.

Foley relaxing in his Capitol office with Alice, the Foleys' Belgian Malinois, which they had rescued from the dog pound. For years Alice accompanied the Foleys to Capitol Hill and was even a 1988 feature in one of Foley's more famous campaign television spots, "Top Dog." *Washington State University Libraries.*

🏛

Return to Public Service

Not only will I be following a line of distinguished predecessors [as U.S. Ambassador to Japan] *but there's an opportunity to make a final contribution to public life. . . . A little bit of this is wanting to write another chapter beyond having been lost in the oblivion of the private sector or wandering aimlessly along the beaches of Barbados as the sun sets.*

—Thomas S. Foley, 1997

U NLIKE FORMER SPEAKERS THOMAS P. O'NEILL and Jim Wright who, in retirement, were frequently seen in the hallways of Congress or on the lecture circuit, Foley tended to view the successes and travails of the new Republican majority from afar.[1] He was occasionally interviewed by C-SPAN, participated on a public affairs roundtable such as CNN's *Capital Gang*, or was queried by a newspaper on the latest example of congressional turmoil, but, generally speaking, he had left thirty years of elective politics behind and felt uncomfortable playing any overly visible role as a former Speaker. In financial disclosure forms filed with the Office of Government Ethics in September 1997, and covering 1996 through May 1997, Foley had a paltry seven honoraria for public speaking, and four of those were before academic audiences.[2]

He had not lost interest in or lost touch with politics in general as suggested by his visits to The Thomas S. Foley Institute for Public Policy and Public Service which had been established at Washington State University in 1995,[3] or his assessment of the results of the 1996 presidential and congressional elections on Seattle and Spokane television after the November elections. In the nation's capitol, however, there were more than enough political pundits to go around, former members of Congress are easily forgotten, and Foley had no instinct to compete for television time.

Foley's one clear official government involvement was his uncompensated role as chairman of the President's Foreign Intelligence Advisory Board. Along with other business, academic, and former government officials, some with extensive intelligence backgrounds such as Admiral Elmo Zumwalt, Air Force General Lew Allen, and former New Hampshire Republican Senator Warren Rudman, the appointed members had the responsibility of assessing the quality, quantity, and adequacy of foreign intelligence collection and of counterintelligence activities undertaken by all government agencies, and of advising the President on matters concerning intelligence and national security. It was, however, a very low visibility role virtually unknown by the public and even most government employees.[4]

Although not an equity partner, Foley's $400,000-a-year salary with the powerhouse D.C. law and lobby firm of Akin, Gump, Strauss, Hauer, & Feld and his service on corporate boards including H.J. Heinz, Patriot American Hospital, RCM Technologies, Inc., and the Hanford Environmental Health Foundation, insured a comfortable life. "How does a longtime public servant adapt to life in the private sector?" asked the *Legal Times*. "Like a fish to water, if you're former House Speaker Thomas Foley."[5] It was a little too glib.

> The transition to the private sector is not as easy as it might appear. There are rewarding aspects including the salary levels, but the actual work doesn't seem to flow as easily as you might hope. You're learning a new kind of work in a new culture which seems to be more entrepreneurial and often more acquisitive on behalf of the firm or business than you're accustomed to. It takes a little while, and sometimes it doesn't come as quickly as you'd hoped, if at all.

Early in 1997 the *Washington Post's* "Federal Page" and Al Kamen's "The Loop" began to hint that he was under consideration to replace former Vice President Walter Mondale, who had left Tokyo as U.S. Ambassador in December 1996. As an unofficial White House sounding board, Kamen's "rumors" carried a special authenticity.[6] For those who knew Foley, it also made a good deal of sense. He was interested in and liked diplomacy, and, as a boy, had once considered the Foreign Service as a possible career path.

> I became interested in a diplomatic career when I was in grade school at twelve or thirteen. I don't know the occasion for that interest, but I was sufficiently focused on it that my father decided that I should talk to Judge [Lewis] Schwellenbach who was the U.S. Judge in Spokane, Washington. He was a former United States Senator who had accepted an appointment as a United States District Judge. He and his wife Anne were friends of my mother and father, and they lived about a block away from us, so we were virtually neighbors. My father thought that Judge

Schwellenbach[7] was the foundation of all knowledge and experience when it came to the federal government, so the idea of a career in the U.S. Foreign Service for me was a natural one to run by the Judge.

I went up to see him in his big, imposing, late-Victorian house, and was ushered into a wood-paneled library. As I remember, I was seated in a relatively low chair, towered over by the Judge at his desk. He looked something like J.P. Morgan. Not a comforting thing. I hardly got out of my mouth that I was interested in being a Foreign Service officer before he blurted out, "Bad idea. Choose another career." I must have looked totally perplexed, and he went on. "You don't have the money. Your family doesn't have nearly enough money. You have to have a lot of money to be in the foreign service. Tom, ambassadorships go to people with money. The principal and major ambassadorships go to people who have a great deal of personal money so that they can support the embassy, entertain lavishly, and carry on the affairs of the United States in a manner that's considered to be appropriate, and the government doesn't provide that. You should never undertake a career in which, if you're able to, and you have the talent to, you can't achieve the highest level of success. So, this is not a good career choice for you." That was the end of that chapter of my life.

Forgotten as a career path, perhaps, but not as an interest. Even though it might be considered primarily a Senate focus, Foley always thought that members of the House had an important international role as well as a legislative responsibility for international relations.

> I remember regretting that my constituent interests required me to be more attracted to seek positions on the Agriculture and Interior committees. Otherwise, one of the committees I would have sought would have been International Relations.

Over the course of thirty years in elective politics, Foley maintained a sustained involvement with Britain, Ireland, France, Germany, and the former Soviet Union, but at the top of the list was Japan. Not only was Japan a country of particular importance in U.S. trade and national security relationships, it had also loomed large in the Pacific Northwest for decades. Washington state was the largest exporter of wheat to Japan, and also exported timber and aircraft. Foley's identification with wheat exports was such that, as a Spokane guest of Foley's in the 1970s, Japanese Agriculture Minister, and later Prime Minister, Tsutomu Hata, awed by seeing huge piles of wheat stores outside grain elevators during a bumper-crop season, forever after called Foley "Mr. Wheat."

> In the late 1960s I began my involvement with the early Shimoda Conferences. They were named after the small fishing village where

Admiral Perry first landed, and every few years there were bilateral U.S.-Japanese meetings which included governmental, private sector, and academic representatives. Starting about the same time I also became engaged in the parliamentary exchanges between the Congress and the Japanese Diet. Although I've known some better than others, I think I've known every Japanese Prime Minister since the late '60s.

Not only because of the nature of Washington state's export-driven economy, but also in economic terms, Foley was never much attracted to government regulations, with exceptions in areas such as health and safety which he felt overrode solely economic interests. Foley was for years identified as a "free trader." His was a position that came with a political price, particularly with organized labor. Although the AFL-CIO had been an early participant in trade liberalization discussions, labor had become increasingly concerned about and resistant to liberalization policies, which labor leaders believed contributed to the export of jobs, particularly in the manufacturing sector. Foley's free trade advocacy also put him at odds with the rest of his leadership team during the congressional debate over the North American Free Trade Agreement (NAFTA) and was a factor in his 1994 congressional defeat.

I think my position on NAFTA had a negative impact on my campaign. It wasn't so much that it produced active resistance, but more that it led to a disenthralling reaction. Political alliances have their periods of tension, and I think the long ties I had with labor were put under strain by such things as the WTO [World Trade Organization] issues embodied in the agreement.

As it turned out, the press rumors of Foley's consideration for the ambassadorship to Japan were accurate. Toward the end of 1996, when it was clear that Ambassador Mondale would leave, Foley began to receive mid-level administration queries about his possible interest in the position.

At one point I tended to discourage the idea, and then changed course and said I might well be interested. It's not at all a problem if you don't get selected, but the problem is that, once you've set the process in motion of people recommending you for a post, if suddenly they call up and say, "If the President spoke to you about Japan, what would your answer be?" and you say, "Thank you very much, but I don't think I can do that." If you say that, then the people who have been working away trying to get that call made are left out on the end of a limb and you obviously create embarrassments for the people who recommended you. At some point in time, if you say, "Yes, you may recommend me," you'd better be 99 percent sure that you're going to say "yes" if the offer comes.

That offer came in February 1997 when Foley received a call from the President's National Security Adviser, Sandy Berger. The fact that the call came from Air Force One led to a reasonable assumption that the call was at the President's behest. While there was never a formal presentation by President Clinton, he did take Foley aside at a White House meeting and asked how the Japan business was going. "We sure want to get you over there," Foley remembered the President saying.

In 1994 Foley had gained an enormous lease of personal freedom. He was earning more money, he could spend it and invest it any way he chose, he could go where he wanted, he could accept invitations from whomever he wanted, he didn't have people looking over his shoulder, he was not being critiqued daily. It was a long list of personal freedoms he lacked as Speaker. Why was he prepared to give all that up?

> I think that's a good question. The greater part of my life has been spent in public life, public service if you will, and that's something for which I have more inclination, more interest, and more ability to do. I also wasn't satisfied with my ability to produce clients and business for the firm to the degree that I hoped to do. They've been unbelievably generous to me, never expressed any dissatisfaction or concern, and I couldn't have asked for a warmer or more generous environment.
>
> But big law firms of almost any character are businesses that have to meet the bottom line, and they have enormous expenses. They are businesses that generate constant expenses and the income of the partners is determined by the firm's success at the end of the year. They are associations of talented professionals, but they also have an entrepreneurial character which is undeniable.
>
> There's also a draw back into public life which people who have spent a long time in it have. It's a very high honor to be an ambassador, to represent the President and the country in a foreign nation of enormous importance, as is Japan. It is a post which has been filled by a former Vice President and Senate Majority Leader. Not only will I be following a line of distinguished predecessors, but there's an opportunity to make a final contribution to public life.

Between February 1997, when Foley told National Security Adviser Berger that he would accept the ambassadorship, and September 1997, when Foley's nomination was officially sent to the Senate, there was no official action on the nomination. The vacuum was filled by speculation. In May, *Business Week,* whose editors openly wondered if Foley was too "pro-Japan," ran an article entitled "The Wrong Man to Send to Tokyo?" "The Japanese couldn't be happier. They've been lobbying long and hard for his appointment. To Tokyo, the genteel, mild-mannered Foley would be a welcome relief from his two tough predecessors, Michael H. Armacost and Walter F. Mondale. . . . The Japanese have been cultivating Foley for years. At their behest, he led 13 congressional trips to Japan since the late 1960s. Since losing his House seat in 1994, he has visited Japan five times, once to troll for clients for his law firm . . . and another to pick up the highest decoration Japan bestows on foreigners who are not heads of state. Foley's Grand Cordon of the Order of the Rising Sun, Paulownia Flowers, awarded a year ago, is usually reserved for members of Japan's imperial family and former Japanese prime ministers. Only three other Americans have been so honored—former Secretary of State George Shultz and former ambassadors to Japan Douglas MacArthur II and Mike Mansfield. . . . All but one of Japan's living former prime ministers showed up at Foley's award ceremony." For the authors, Foley's expected selection was "a reward for past service to the Democratic Party" while it underscored "a softer White House stance toward Japan."[8]

> There were occasional mentions in the district, particularly among labor people who thought that maybe I was too friendly to the Japanese, but the only really explicit press comment that I can recall was in the May issue of *Business Week*. The article was written by a former bureau chief now resident in Tokyo. The article not only criticized the possibility of my appointment, it highlighted the possibility that Christopher Lefleur might be selected as DCM [Deputy Chief of Mission]. It suggested that the American trade hard-liners' worst nightmare would be Foley as ambassador and Lefleur as DCM. I didn't really know Christopher Lefleur prior to reading his name in the article, but he turned out to be one of the DCM candidates the State Department suggested I interview. I did and found him to be superbly qualified and ended up recommending his appointment as my DCM. In an ironic way, his name wasn't brought to my attention officially by *Business Week,* but the magazine's attack certainly didn't do him any harm.

> Actually, I think if you have a reputation for being unfriendly or harsh, then it's more difficult to deliver a diplomatic message with the same impact than if it comes from someone who is thought by the host country to be friendly in his or her attitude. It's too easy to brush aside the representations of someone thought to be hostile as simply reflecting a general attitude. On the other hand, coming from someone who's thought to be sympathetic, a tough message would probably be taken more seriously.

Foley was just one of many potential ambassadors caught in delay. In September 1997 a U.S. ambassador had finally arrived in Canada, a position which had been vacant since May 1996. There was no U.S. ambassador in Bonn for over a year, Tokyo since December, and the list went on to include the Republic of Korea, India, and a number of countries in Africa. Every administration came into office promising that it would renew the moral and ethical standards of government, implying that the last administration had allowed the standards to grow lax. So the ethical standards offices were charged with the responsibility of examining every nuance in the background of a potential appointee to make sure there was no basis for risk or embarrassment. There is always a justification for detailed scrutiny, but at times the process appeared to have run amuck.

I think the Japanese were wondering what was taking so long. Each country likes to think it has a particular relationship with the United States. Name an important country, a Britain, Brazil, Canada, France, Germany, Mexico, or a Japan. Each can usually lay claim to a special bilateral relationship with the U.S. and, conversely, each can all feel special offense. In the case of Japan there's also possibly a sense of, "Well, if Foley is such an important political figure, why doesn't the process move more quickly for him?" But this is more damaging to me than it is to the U.S. Part of the trouble is that the explanations aren't really very persuasive and Japan tends to read a slight in between the lines. I also think that the Japanese are sensitive to the fact that since I've been criticized for being too friendly to Japan, the last thing they feel they should do is appear to be too impatient. The absence of an ambassador is damaging. It leads to irritation, confusion, and wonderment.

Part of the trouble is that they have an active, and somewhat inventive, press. The Japanese practice is not to wonder in silence. It's always some sort of open wondering, and if there isn't a good reason, they'll sometimes invent one. There were stories going around as to whether maybe I was involved in the inquiries over campaign fundraising. It was totally untrue. There was no problem of that kind at all, but again, the inventive Japanese reporter, and his editor, could come up with some sort of speculative reason for the delay. If it proved to be wrong, well, so be it, let's look for another reason.

Even in the absence of anything official, however, preparations for a possible diplomatic life were not at a standstill in the Foley household. Both Foley and Heather enrolled in Japanese classes at the State Department's Foreign Service Institute (FSI) and participated in the Ambassadorial Seminar or so-called "Ambassador's School." Although unpaid, Heather had served for most of Foley's career in the highly responsible role of chief-of-staff. As the FSI described the role of ambassador's spouse, she would now have no official responsibilities, but would often be expected to host receptions and serve as "an aide and confidant to the ambassador." As Foley diplomatically indicated, Heather had "adjusted" to the idea of going overseas, but possibly not in the traditional FSI role.[9]

The two-week FSI program is given several times a year and the course covers such subjects as the role and responsibilities of an ambassador, the authority of an ambassador, managing an embassy, and the relationship to the American community and non-foreign service personnel.

Overall, it gives you a sense of how ambassadors are viewed by the Department, embassy personnel, the American community overseas, and by the foreign host government. It's useful. Because it's a "one size fits all" course whether you're going to Britain or Mongolia, it obviously doesn't answer every question, but the more I think about it, like many things, the more distant you get from it, the better it seems. It's a good program.

There were some interesting discussions on how the Department of State makes comments and what they expect from ambassadors in terms of clearing any statements that might confuse the press on what U.S. policy is. The simple answer they often give is, "what you do in Japan or Britain is one thing, but don't come back here [the U.S.] and go on 'Meet the Press' and start expounding on even the narrow range of issues dealing within your country without plenty of prior approval." This Secretary [Madeleine Albright], not atypically, is conscious that, as Secretary of State, she, along with the President, is the principal voice of U.S. foreign policy, and she does not want to have any competitors. That's very good policy, and I have no quarrel with it. They are more concerned with what happens in the American press. In other words, be careful before you give an interview to the *New York Times*.

Finally, the process which Foley described as slow-slow-rush-rush produced the presidential nomination and, within two weeks, Foley was scheduled for a September 24, 1997 confirmation hearing before the Senate Foreign Relations Committee with the Subcommittee on East Asian and Pacific Affairs acting on behalf of the full committee. To prepare the three ambassadorial nominees, Foley for Japan, Stephen W. Bosworth for the Republic of Korea, and Alphonse F. LaPorta for Mongolia, the State Department organized a so-called "murder board" to brief the nominees on the hearing.

I had thought they would be similar to what my congressional staff put me through before an appearance on a Sunday television interview program. I thought you would be "put through the paces" on the ten most important issues that might come up. I'm guessing now, trying to put myself in the Department's position, and I've concluded their motivation is more stylistic. Essentially, they want you to avoid saying, "Well, when I get to Japan I'm going to do this or I'm going to do that." They repeated the same advice innumerable times, "Keep remembering the phrase, 'If confirmed,' 'If confirmed,' 'If confirmed,' so you don't appear to be presuming your confirmation. Throw that phrase in every time you're asked a question of policy. Secondly, always express a little uncertainty about this or that issue, and always admit you're not fully informed on the matter yet, but you're going to give it a lot of attention."

Interestingly, they included former Labor Department Secretary Robert Reich's comments from his book [*Locked in the Cabinet*][10] about being briefed by congressional staffers. In his book there is a description about his preparation before his appearance before the Labor and Human Resources subcommittee. He's being briefed by a former Democratic and a former Republican staffer, and apparently he's giving extremely articulate answers to their questions; highly schooled answers to complex issues of labor mobility and marginal costs of job training, and so on. One of the staffers interrupts and says something like this, "Dr. Reich, with all respect, the Senate really doesn't care how much you know about this subject. They generally expect that you know quite a bit. They're much more interested in learning from you whether you know how much they know about this subject, and how likely you are to want to work with them on this important problem, keeping in mind their background, knowledge, and concern about this issue, that you will not forget their interest."

Foley was not without friends at the hearing. Washington state U.S. senators Republican Slade Gorton and Democrat Patty Murray presented him to the subcommittee. "Tom Foley was, for many years," noted Senator Gorton, "the number one citizen in the state that I represent. He is an individual who carries qualities that, when one sums them all up in a single word, that word is probably diplomatic. . . . Tom Foley is, in my opinion, not simply a good nominee for the post, but the best nominee for the post that the president could possibly have picked." Senator Murray echoed the praise. "In my opinion," she said, "no Member of Congress knows as much about Japan . . . he knows them well and they know him."[11]

If his former Washington state Senate colleagues' presence might have been expected, less so was his former House colleague, Republican Representative Henry Hyde of Illinois. He had not been asked to appear but, upon hearing of Foley's nomination, he had "thrust" himself upon the former Speaker. Having accompanied Foley on previous congressional delegations to Japan, Hyde was convinced there was no better person than Foley to serve as Ambassador. "I am confident," representative Hyde stated, that Tom Foley "will represent our country and our interests with the same brilliance he has conducted his previous public service career. I am proud to be here, even though I thrust myself on Speaker Foley, because I wanted to express . . . the fact that the man and the job are so perfectly matched."[12]

Representative Hyde's remarks provided Foley with an *ad lib* anecdote he inserted in his opening remarks to the subcommittee.

It's a story, which I hope is true, about Ambassador Mike Mansfield and Secretary of State George Shultz. I think Mansfield was one of the greatest ambassadors we ever sent abroad, and I think George Shultz was one of the great Secretaries of State in recent years. Mansfield had a great reputation as an American ambassador to Japan. He was revered by the Japanese people.

Shultz had a practice, I'm told, that when receiving American ambassadors in his office, he would twirl a large library globe and ask, "Mr. Ambassador, show me your country," meaning show me where you're going, or where you've been, representing the United States. When he did that with Mike Mansfield, instead of pointing to Japan, Mansfield stopped the globe at the United States, suspiciously close to a large state in the West [Montana], and said, "Mr. Secretary, this is my country."

Foley learned the lesson of his State Department briefers well. His prepared remarks to the subcommittee were scattered with "if confirmed" from the beginning.

Mr. Chairman, I am deeply honored that President Clinton has nominated me to be Ambassador to Japan. If I am confirmed by the Senate, I will undertake this assignment energetically and to the best of my ability and will effectively represent the President and our country in Japan, our key ally and friend in Asia. . . . Mr. Chairman, if I am confirmed by the Senate I will be returning to full-time public service, where I have spent the greater part of my professional life.[13]

In his five pages of prepared remarks, he thanked "my closest partner and colleague Heather," legendary Washington senators Henry Jackson and Warren Magnuson, and "the citizens of eastern Washington and . . . all of my colleagues in the House, both Democrats and Republicans."

Foley indicated his belief that "there is no bilateral relationship more important than that between the United States and Japan." He referred to the security relationship based in the Mutual Security Treaty of 1960 and Japan's position as the United States' second largest trading partner after Canada.

But a recitation of official connections between the United States and Japan ought not to conceal the personal ties between them. . . . There are over 40,000 Japanese students in the United States and about 1,800 American students in Japan. The shared heritage, the friendships, and the accumulation of experiences of Japanese in the United States and Americans in Japan add special strength and warmth to our relationship.

Foley concluded with what he saw as the bilateral challenges for the next few years, including the management of the security relationship and economic relations and the pursuit of a dialogue with Japan on deregulation.

The committee unanimously recommended Foley's confirmation, but action by the full Senate would take time. Foley's earlier "worst case scenario" prediction of his confirmation becoming the victim of some unrelated partisan squabble threatened to be a self-fulfilling prophecy. There were press reports that Senate Majority Leader Trent Lott had been slowing up a number of ambassadorial nominations, including Foley's, while wrangling with the Democrats over issues such as campaign finance reform.[14] The atmosphere also seemed to have led to an overly enthusiastic miscue.

I was called by the State Department in late October with the information and hearty congratulations that I had just been confirmed. That afternoon I was scheduled to attend a reception recognizing a group of "Mansfield Fellows" who had just returned from Japan. So I went to the Japanese Embassy reception, and Senator Mansfield, former U.S. Ambassador to Japan, was there, and asked, "What's the story on your confirmation?" I said, "Well, in fact, I've just been confirmed." "Congratulations," he said, and took me over to the Japanese ambassador and said, "Mr. Ambassador, Mr. Foley's just been confirmed." "Congratulations," he said, and asked whether I'd like to say anything to the group. "No, thank you," I responded.

It seemed like only a few minutes later that there was an urgent message for me at the embassy to call the Department of State. I dialed the number and was connected with the Department's Office of Legislative Affairs which had called to tell me how embarrassed they were. On the schedule of people to be confirmed there had apparently been six of us, and five had been confirmed, and one had not. Guess who? The ambassadors-designate to Korea, Italy, Mongolia, and several other places, had been confirmed, but I had not. I had to go back and tell, individually, the people who had been congratulating me, that there'd been a little slippage.

Without checking with the Department, the next day I called Trent Lott, and told him that I needed his help. He said, "Well, I tried to get it done last night, but you're too high profile. The place is kind of testy up here," he said. "[Democratic Leader] Tom Daschle is interrupting meetings of committees which is creating some problems for our guys. But I'll get it done, I'm not going to wait too long on this. We take care of our own. We were Whips together."

In fact, he had started the conversation by asking, "How many votes have you really got?" referring to an earlier vote-counting experience we'd had as Whips. "I think you're low-balling me," I responded. "How many votes have you got?"

That same day the Department had asked whether I wanted [Secretary of State] Madeleine Albright to call Senator Lott. I said I didn't think it was necessary and that we should give the process some time. I think they were getting a little worried that things might be hung up forever. But, Trent had said, "we take care of our own," and he did. Within a week I was confirmed.

On Monday, October 27, 1997, the full Senate unanimously approved Foley, 91 to 0, as U.S. ambassador to Japan. In the seventh-floor Benjamin Franklin Room of the Department of State on November 6, 1997, Thomas S. Foley was sworn in as U.S. ambassador to Japan. On the dais with Foley were Heather Foley and her sister Jill Strachan. Secretary of State Albright's remarks were affectionate, the words of a friend. Looking out over the multi-generational audience, she spoke of seeing "members, like myself, of the Tom Foley fan club":

> We Americans have traditionally sent to our mission in Tokyo only our very best. Today we ask Tom Foley to trade one distinguished title, Mr. Speaker, for another that's even sweeter to my ears, Mr. Ambassador. And in sending him to Japan, we honor our closest ally in Asia, and one of our closest friends in the world. President Clinton has not just selected a good choice, he has selected the single person best qualified to represent America, and American interests in "the land of the rising sun."
>
> I say this, not simply because of Ambassador Foley's 30 years in public service; not simply because of his political presence and his probing intellect which ranges across subjects as diverse as international trade, constitutional law, and the arcane procedures of our federal government; not simply because of his career-long fascination with Japan, his understanding of U.S.-Japan issues or his close acquaintance with Japanese political, economic, and civic leaders; and not even because Heather Foley is such a widely respected and accomplished contributor to the Foley Team. What makes it the perfect choice is how well all of these elements are combined.
>
> . . . . Our U.S. ambassador to Japan will have the full confidence of his President and his Secretary of State, and the full support of his former colleagues in the Congress and, judging from the comments last week of [Japanese] Prime Minister Hashimoto, the full respect and friendship of his interlocutors in Japan, and he will arrive in Tokyo armed with all the knowledge and powers and persuasion he needs to do the job, and what an important job that is.[15]

Foley spent much of his time in response thanking people, including the former U.S. ambassadors to Japan in the audience, Mike Mansfield and Brookings Institution president Michael Armacost. Foley admitted he would probably fail in his attempt to model his remarks on the famed brevity of former Ambassador Mansfield.

> One of my great predecessors, former Senate Majority Leader and Ambassador Mansfield, had a reputation for brevity. As we all know,

"Meet the Press" just celebrated its 50th anniversary. When the old "Meet the Press" met, they had three guest panelists, moderator Lawrence Spivak, and the guest to be interviewed. The object was to get around the panel and the guest twice in the 30-minute program. When the Majority Leader was the guest, they got around the circle six-and-a-half times. . . . When he first arrived in Tokyo, he greeted the entire embassy staff with the brief statement: "Hello. I'm the new boy in town. Shoot."[16]

On Saturday, November 15, Ambassador Foley arrived at Tokyo's Narita Airport following the longest vacancy in that job since World War II. Now 68, he replaced Ambassador Walter F. Mondale who left Japan eleven months earlier. He arrived at a time of relative harmony in the U.S.-Japan security relationship following the recently announced Clinton-Hashimoto guidelines redefining U.S.-Japanese security cooperation. But there were some difficulties as well, especially the rapidly increasing U.S. trade deficit with Japan. After declining for two years, sharp increases began in the last quarter of 1996 and continued to expand throughout 1997. In Foley's view, the prospects for the next several years were rather bleak.

There were additional economic crises that had plagued other Asian nations in the fall of 1997 and contributed to the Japanese stock market's greatest plunge in two years. While those were not problems with which Foley would grapple alone, "he will be pressing the United States' interests while the Japanese government is preoccupied with domestic problems," wrote a Tokyo-based *Washington Post* reporter.[17]

Although Foley had been criticized by some as an apologist for Japan,[18] former Ambassador Mondale saw Foley's understanding of Japan as "a tremendous asset." Negotiations with Japan, noted Mondale, move slowly because the country decides by consensus. That tends to strengthen those who hold out for the status quo. "Japanese businesses in an industry work together in ways that in this country would violate anti-trust laws," Mondale added. Foley emphasized patience and persistence.[19]

As he addressed a large gathering on his arrival, Foley outlined what he saw as a growing problem in U.S.-Japanese relations: increased political concentration on the trade deficit. Such an emphasis would bring stress to a bilateral relationship Foley considered almost singularly important:

Whatever field we consider—trade, security, research and technology, the sciences, the environment, education or economic development—there is, indeed, no cooperative bilateral partnership more important than that between the United States and Japan. . . . Our partnership is the key to a peaceful and prosperous 21st century in Asia and the rest of the world.[20]

At three o'clock on the afternoon of November 19, 1997, "Ambassador Extraordinary and Plenipotentiary" Thomas S. Foley presented his presidentially signed credentials to His Majesty, The Emperor of Japan, at the Emperor's Palace in Tokyo. The traditional ceremony had its full measure of expected pageantry; it was also preceded by a smaller measure of unexpected drama.

In January 1997 Foley was fitted with an artificial knee. On the evening after his arrival in Japan, as Foley returned from a reception, he heard a pop in his knee and fell to the floor. Although he thought he could hear the household staff down the hall, they couldn't hear his call for help. He dragged himself to the bedside phone, but it was put "on record" at night. His room also had an emergency direct line to the Marine Guard post at the embassy. He decided his situation qualified. Several Marines arrived, helped Foley into a car for a trip to the local hospital. After a series of Japanese physicians examined him it was determined that a piece of his artificial knee had slipped out of place. A splint and hospital cane would have to serve until Foley could undergo surgery. Foley now began to wonder about the traditional horse-and-carriage ride during the presentation of credentials ceremony.

His predecessors as ambassador to Japan had all urged him to go by carriage as an auspicious way to begin his tenure. The Prime Minister had emphasized to Foley that the privilege of riding in the imperial carriage was a once-in-a-lifetime opportunity. No Japanese officials are allowed to ride in the carriage. "Not even my good friend Bill [Clinton] may ride in the carriage," said Hashimoto. It was reserved for members of the Imperial Family. The single exception was foreign ambassadors, and only on the day that they presented their credentials.

Foley and his six accompanying embassy officers were met by the white-uniformed train master at Tokyo Central Station, and he was helped into the first of three imperial carriages with their matching teams of horses by "Master of The Ceremonies" Kimura. After a ten-minute procession through the palace grounds, attended by mounted police, they arrived at the palace. Passing through various halls and reception rooms, the party finally arrived at the ceremonial room, where an elaborately decorated throne was the only furniture. "Kimura-san," Foley said as he was about to enter the room, "I think I can walk without the cane." The Master of The Ceremonies replied, "Your Excellency, the Emperor has been told you will have a cane. You will have a cane."

A moment later, with the assistance of his hospital cane, Foley bowed, approached the Emperor, bowed again, and said, "Your Majesty, I have been appointed the Ambassador of the United States to Japan. I have the honor to present my letters of credence and my predecessor's letter of withdrawal, to your Majesty."

***

When asked much earlier in the process of becoming an ambassador why he was willing to forsake his newly-acquired independence, privacy, and significantly larger private sector income to re-enter public service and all its constraints, Foley had pondered long before answering.

> There is one other thing. Maybe it's not a big part of the decision, but I recognize it as being part of it. I'm not ashamed to have lost an election. I think that's part of the business of being in elective office. It's not a disgrace to lose. It's part of the system. However, you know, in a way I wish, if I'd had a choice, I might have retired voluntarily rather than to have been caught up in the great earthquake of 1994, and to have as a footnote to my career that this was only the third time that a Speaker was defeated, emphasizing with an asterisk that not only did the Democrats lose control of the House, but that Tom Foley, the forty-ninth Speaker of the House, suffered an almost unprecedented loss, period.
>
> So, a little bit of this is wanting to write another chapter beyond having been lost in the oblivion of the private sector or wandering aimlessly along the beaches of Barbados as the sun sets.

That new chapter had begun.

Notes

Endnote Abbreviations

CQWR—Congressional Quarterly Weekly Report
CSM—Christian Science Monitor
NYT—New York Times
Ore—The [Portland] *Oregonian*
PI—Seattle Post-Intelligencer
SC—Spokane Daily Chronicle
SR—Spokesman-Review (Spokane, Washington)
WP—Washington Post
WSJ—Wall Street Journal
WT—Washington Times
WWUB—Walla Walla [Washington] *Union Bulletin*

Notes for Chapter One

1. Writers' Program of the Work Projects Administration in the State of Washington, *Washington: A Guide to the Evergreen State* (Portland, Or.: Binfords & Mort, 1941).
2. Florence Boutwell, *The Spokane Valley: A History of the Growing Years* (Spokane: The Arthur H. Clark Co., 1995), vol. 2, p. 136.
3. David H. Stratton, ed., *Spokane & The Inland Empire* (Pullman: Washington State University Press, 1991), pp. 154-155; Eastern Washington State Historical Society, *Viewing the Past* (Spokane: Eastern Washington State Historical Society, 1977).
4. Stratton, *Spokane & The Inland Empire*, p. 13; Dorothy Rochon Powers, *Heritage from Heroes* (Spokane: Fairmount Memorial Association, 1993), p. 83.
5. Alan Ehrenhalt and Robert E. Healy, eds., *Politics in America* (Washington, D.C.: Congressional Quarterly Press, 1982), p. 1268.
6. Robert L. Rose, *SR*, December 7, 1986, p. A1; John Newhouse, "Profiles: The Navigator," *The New Yorker*, April 10, 1989.
7. *SR*, September 6, 1940; John J. Lemon, *SC*, March 27, 1974; Kathleen O'Sullivan, *SR*, March 19, 1961, p. 18.

8. Karen Dorn Steele, *SR*, April 2, 1989, p. A1.
9. "Judge Foley: A Long Distinguished Career," *SIGNUM of Gonzaga University*, May 1974, p. 9.
10. *Viewing the Past*, p. 50.
11. *Washington: A Guide to the Evergreen State*, p. 254.
12. John E. Yang, *WSJ*, August 23, 1989, p. A12.
13. Dorothy Powers, *SR*, May 12, 1985, p. A13.
14. Paul Turner, *SR*, June 7, 1989, p. A6.
15. Newhouse, "Profiles," pp. 48-50, 54, 56, 58-60, 62-63, 66-72, 74-76, 78-84. Newhouse spent a number of hours with Foley and friends and acquaintances both in Washington, D.C., and Spokane, and his profile, extending through the period Foley served as Majority Leader of the House, remains a model of insight and superb writing.
16. Jim Camden, *SR*, January 6, 1990, p. A1.
17. Timothy Egan, *NYT*, June 8, 1989, p. B11; Newhouse, "Profiles." See also *Current Biography Yearbook 1989*, p. 178.
18. Jim Lynch, *SR*, August 1, 1993, p. A1.
19. Jacqueline Trescott, *WP*, June 1, 1989, p. C13.
20. John E. Yang, *WSJ*, August 22, 1989, p. A12.
21. Paul Turner, *SR*, June 7, 1989, p. A1.
22. Louise Sweeney, *CSM*, February 22, 1990, p. 15.
23. Bill Whalen, *WT, Insight*, May 1, 1989, p. 21.
24. *SR*, September 3, 1983, pp. A1-2.
25. Newhouse, "Profiles," April 10, 1989, p. 62.
26. Robert L. Rose, *SR*, December 8, 1986, p. A1; *SR*, July 17, 1964, p. 5.

Notes for Chapter Two

1. *SC*, November 4, 1964, p. 5.
2. *SR*, November 5, 1964, p. 39.
3. *Current Biography Yearbook 1989*, p. 178.
4. John Newhouse, "Profiles: The Navigator," *The New Yorker*, April 10, 1989.
5. Janet Hook, *CQWR*, March 8, 1986, p. 550.
6. *SC*, November 4, 1964, p. 3.
7. Jacqueline Trescott, *WP*, June 1, 1989, p. C13.
8. Jim Wright, *Balance of Power: Presidents and Congress from the Era of McCarthy to the Age of Gingrich* (Atlanta: Turner Publishing, Inc., 1996), p. 110.
9. Newhouse, "Profiles," *The New Yorker*, April 10, 1989, p. 62.
10. Kevin P. Phillips, *The Emerging Republican Majority* (Garden City, New York: Anchor Books, 1970), pp. 452-460.
11. *SR*, October 7, 1966, p. A5.
12. *SR*, October 29, 1966, p. A5.
13. *SC*, October 24, 1966, p. 21.
14. *SR*, October 7, 1966, p. A5.
15. *SR*, October 13, 1966, p. A10; *SR*, October 19, 1966, p. 5.
16. *SC*, October 14, 1966, p. 10.
17. *SR*, October 28, 1966, p. 12.
18. *SC*, November 9, 1966, p. 5.
19. *SR*, October 24, 1969, p. A6.
20. *Ibid.*
21. *SR*, November 6, 1968.

22. Jack E. Fisher, *SR*, October 25, 1970, p. A8.
23. *SC*, November 4, 1970, p. A11.
24. *The Almanac of American Politics* (1972), pp. 866-867.
25. *SR*, November 9, 1972, p. 42.
26. *SR*, October 24, 1972, editorial.
27. Roger H. Davidson and Walter J. Oleszek, *Congress Against Itself* (Bloomington and London: Indiana University Press, 1977), pp. ix-x, 7. Davidson, chairman of the Political Science Department at the University of California, Santa Barbara, and Oleszek, specialist on Congress for the Congressional Research Service, served as staff members of the Select Committee on Committees.
28. Barbara Sinclair, *Legislators, Leaders, and Lawmaking: The U.S. House of Representatives in the Postreform Era* (Baltimore and London: The Johns Hopkins University Press, 1995), p. 20.
29. Richard Bolling, *House Out of Order* (New York: Dutton, 1965), p. 70.
30. Sinclair, Legislators, *Leaders, and Lawmaking*, pp. 20-21.
31. *SR*, December 20, 1968, p. 6.
32. *SC*, November 9, 1968.
33. Rick Bonino, *SR*, June 30, 1976, p. 23.
34. Karen Dorn Steele, *SR*, June 7, 1989, p. A2.
35. Lois Romano, *WP*, February 9, 1990, pp. D1-D2.
36. Newhouse, "Profile," p. 70.
37. Bill Whalen, "Mr. Nice Guy Under Fire," *WT, Insight*, August 19, 1991, p. 32.
38. Elizabeth Hicket with Cathryn Donohoe, *WT*, March 30, 1992, pp. D1-D2.
39. Lois Romano, *WP*, February 9, 1990, p. D2; Louise Sweeney, CSM, February 22, 1990, pp. 14-15.

Notes for Chapter Three

1. Richard F. Fenno, "The Internal Distribution of Influence: The House," in David B. Truman, ed., *The Congress and America's Future* (Englewood Cliffs, N.J.: Prentice-Hall, 1965), as cited in Barbara Sinclair, *Legislators, Leaders, and Lawmaking: The U.S. House of Representatives in the Postreform Era* (Baltimore and London: The Johns Hopkins University Press, 1955), p. 212.
2. Sinclair, *Legislators, Leaders, and Lawmaking*, pp. 22-28.
3. *Ibid.*, pp. 20, 34-35.
4. C. Lawrence Evans and Walter J. Oleszek, *Congress Under Fire: Reform Politics and the Republican Majority* (Boston and New York: Houghton Mifflin Company, 1997), p. 51.
5. Ronald M. Peters, Jr. *The American Speakership: The Office in Historical Perspective* (Baltimore and London: The Johns Hopkins University Press, 1990), p. 209.
6. Alan Ehrenhalt, ed., *Politics in America: Members of Congress in Washington and at Home* (Washington, D.C.: Congressional Quarterly Press, 1981), p. 98.
7. John Jacobs, *A Rage for Justice: The Passion and Politics of Phillip Burton* (Berkeley and Los Angeles: University of California Press, 1995), p. 181.
8. Jeremiah Baruch, "An Achieving Heart: Phil Burton, Practical Liberal," *Commonweal*, May 6, 1983, pp. 261-263.
9. Jacobs, *A Rage for Justice*, p. xix.
10. *Ibid.*, p. 252.
11. *Ibid.*, p. 267.
12. *Ibid.*, p. 258.
13. *Ibid.*

14. *Ibid.,* p. 268.
15. Michael Barone, Grant Ujifusa, Douglas Mathews, *The Almanac of American Politics 1974* and *1976* (New York: E.P. Dutton & Co., 1973, 1975), pp. 987-988, 833-834.
16. *Ibid., 1976,* pp. 833-834.
17. Janet Hook, *CQWR,* March 8, 1986, p. 550.
18. Alan Ehrenhalt, ed., *Politics in America, 1986* (Washington, D.C.: Congressional Quarterly, Inc., 1985), p. 1630.
19. *SC,* July 14, 1976, p. A6.
20. *SR,* October 30, 1976, editorial.
21. Karen Elliott House, *WSJ,* September 14, 1977, p. 1.
22. *SC,* September 14, 1977, p. A1.
23. Karen Elliott House, *WSJ,* September 14, 1977, pp. 1, 21.
24. Jim Dullenty, *SR,* July 18, 1978, p. 28; *SC,* July 18, 1978, p. 6.
25. *SC,* September 23, 1977, p. A5; Rob Allen, *SR,* July 28, 1977, p. A5.
26. *SC,* March 9, 1978, p. A3.
27. *SR,* March 3, 1978, p. A4.
28. *SR,* November 8, 1978, p. A1.
29. Rick Bonino, *SR,* October 31, 1978, p. A9.
30. *SR,* September 7, 1980, p. A3.
31. Robert Harper, *SR,* August 26, 1979, p. B4; Bill Morlin, *SC,* July 7, 1979, p. 3.

Notes for Chapter Four

1. Bill Morlin, *SC,* July 7, 1979, p. A3.
2. Doug Floyd, *SC,* September 9, 1980, p. 3.
3. *SC,* May 9, 1980, p. 32.
4. Dick Moody, *SC,* October 22, 1980, p. 3; Robert L. Rose, *SR,* October 19, 1980, pp. A1, A6.
5. Doug Floyd, *SC,* September 9, 1980, p. A-3.
6. *SR,* September 7, 1980, p. A3.
7. *SR,* October 31, 1980, p. 27.
8. *SC,* November 5, 1980, p. 6.
9. Dick Moody, *SC,* January 7, 1982, p. A1.
10. Christopher Madison, "The Heir Presumptive," *National Journal,* April 29, 1989, p. 1035.
11. Barbara Sinclair, *Legislators, Leaders, and Lawmaking: The U.S. House of Representatives in the Postreform Era* (Baltimore and London: The Johns Hopkins University Press, 1995), pp. 116-120.
12. Diane Granat, *CQWR,* November 30, 1985, pp. 2498-2502.
13. John Jacobs, *A Rage for Justice: The Passion and Politics of Phillip Burton* (Berkeley: University of California Press, 1995), p. 217.
14. Alan Ehrenhalt, ed., *Politics in America, 1984* (Washington, D.C.: Congressional Quarterly, Inc., 1985), p. 1630.
15. Jonathan Fuerbringer, *NYT,* December 9, 1986, p. B17.
16. Warren B. Rudman, *Combat: Twelve Years in the U.S. Senate* (New York: Random House, 1996), pp. 72-73.
17. Michael Barone and Grant Ujifusa, *The Almanac of American Politics 1982* (Washington, D.C.: Barone & Co., 1982), p. 1157.
18. Dick Moody, *SC,* January 7, 1982, p. A1; Bart Preecs, *SR,* August 9, 1981, p. B1.

19. *Ibid.*, and Alan Ehrenhalt, *Politics in America, 1982* (Washington, D.C.: Congressional Quarterly, Inc., 1983), p. 1606.
20. Dick Moody, *SC*, October 13, 1982, p. 1.
21. *Ibid.*
22. *SR*, November 18, 1981, p. A9.
23. Dave Workman, *SR*, October 17, 1982, p. B1.
24. *SR*, October 31, 1982, p. A20, editorial.
25. *SC*, October 29, 1982, editorial.
26. Rick Bonino, *SR*, November 4, 1982, p. A1.
27. Janet Hook, *CQWR*, March 8, 1986, p. 549.
28. Robert L. Rose, *SR*, November 1, 1983, p. 1; Robert Parry, *SC*, November 4, 1983, p. 1.
29. Rick Bonino, *SR*, October 15, 1984, p. A1.
30. Rick Bonino, *SR*, October 23, 1984, p. A1.
31. *SR*, October 21, 1984, p. A16, editorial.
32. Rick Bonino, *SR*, November 7, 1984, p. C1.
33. Ronald M. Peters, Jr., *The Speaker: Leadership in the U.S. House of Representatives* (Washington, D.C.: Congressional Quarterly, Inc., 1994), p. 258.
34. Diane Granat, *CQWR*, December 8, 1984, pp. 3051-3057; and February 11, 1984, pp. 246-249.
35. Janet Hook, *CQWR*, January 8, 1994, pp. 16-17.
36. Diane Granat, *CQWR*, December 28, 1985, pp. 2727-2747.
37. *Ibid.*, p. 2728.
38. Elizabeth Wehr, *CQWR*, October 12, 1985, pp. 2035-2042.
39. Rudman, *Combat*, pp. 92-93.
40. Elizabeth Wehr, *CQWR*, October 5, 1985, pp. 1975-1978.
41. Stephen F. Stine, *CQWR*, October 12, 1985, p. 2038.
42. Elizabeth Wehr, *CQWR*, December 14, 1985, p. 2605.
43. Elizabeth Wehr, *CQWR*, October 12, 1985, p 2036.
44. Janet Hook, *CQWR*, March 8, 1986, p. 552.
45. Elizabeth Wehr, *CQWR*, December 7, 1985, p. 2548.
46. Janet Hook, *CQWR*, March 8, 1986, p. 552.
47. Diane Granat, *CQWR*, December 28, 1985, p. 2728.
48. Janet Hook, *CQWR*, February 15, 1986, pp. 298-300; August 23, 1986, p. 1960.
49. Janet Hook, *CQWR*, March 8, 1986, pp. 549-552.
50. Phil Duncan, ed., *Politics in America, 1990* (Washington, D.C.: Congressional Quarterly, Inc., 1989), p. 1588.

Notes for Chapter Five

1. Jim Camden, *SR*, October 20, 1986, p. A1.
2. Jim Camden, *SC*, November 5, 1986, p. A3.
3. Gary L. Galemore, *The Grace Commission* (Washington, D.C.: Government Division 93-741 GOV, Congressional Research Service, Library of Congress, August 17, 1993).
4. *SR*, October 26, 1986, p. A16, editorial.
5. Robert L. Rose, *SR*, December 9, 1986, p. A6.
6. Jim Camden, *SC*, November 5, 1986, p. A3.
7. Charles Moritz, ed., *Current Biography Yearbook 1989* (New York: H.W. Wilson Co., 1989), pp. 199-203. The Gingrich quote cited was reported by David Osborne in *Mother Jones*, November, 1984.

8. Fred Barnes, "The Wright Stuff: Democrats Will Miss Him When He's Gone," *The New Republic*, May 15, 1989, pp. 13-16.

9. Ronald M. Peters, *The American Speakership: The Office in Historical Perspective* (Baltimore and London: The Johns Hopkins University Press, 1990), p. 267. With particular attention to the use of the Rules Committee, see also Roger Davidson, "The New Centralization on Capitol Hill," *Review of Politics* 50 (Summer 1988), pp. 346-364, and Stanley Bach and Steven S. Smith, *Managing Uncertainty in the House of Representatives: Adaptation and Innovation in Special Rules* (Washington, D.C.: Brookings Institution, 1988).

10. Bill Whalen, *WT*, *Insight*, September 18, 1989, pp. 26-27.

11. Barnes, "The Wright Stuff," p. 15. In an appraisal of Wright's Speakership just prior to his resignation, Barnes wrote that "Democrats are lucky. They benefited enormously from Wright's no-holds barred style. He gave them two wonderful years. And now they won't have to pay the consequences. My assumption is that Wright's ethics violations will force him to step down as Speaker. The most widely respected man in the House will replace him—Tom Foley. Wright was perfect for trumping Reagan. Foley fits nicely with the Bush era. He's cautious, conciliatory, reasonably bipartisan, and adept with the press. Bush likes him. He's trusted by Republicans. And he's not odd at all."

12. Margaret Carlson, "Fallen Angel: Tony Coelho's Deal with the Devil," *The New Republic*, June 12, 1989, p. 18.

13. Janet Hook, *CQWR*, March 8, 1986, p. 549.

14. Warren B. Rudman, *Combat: Twelve Years in the U.S. Senate* (New York: Random House, 1996), p. 103.

15. R.W. Apple, Jr., *NYT*, November 4, 1988, p. A20.

16. *Ibid.*

17. Jim Camden, *SR*, November 9, 1988, p. A1.

18. *SR*, October 7, 1988, p. A4, editorial.

19. Jim Camden, *SR*, November 9, 1988, p. A1.

20. *CQWR*, April 15, 1989, p. 795.

21. Jim Wright, *Reflections of a Public Man* (Fort Worth: Madison Publishing Co., 1984).

22. "Report of the Special Outside Counsel in the Matter of Speaker James C. Wright, Jr." Committee on Standards of Official Conduct, U.S. House of Representatives, 101st Congress, February 21, 1989, pp. 7-9.

23. *CQWR*, April 15, 1989, p. 796.

24. *Ibid.*

25. Janet Hook, *CQWR*, February 11, 1989, pp. 261-263.

26. *CQWR*, April 15, 1989, p. 795.

27. Janet Hook, *CQWR*, March 18, 1989, p. 563.

28. Janet Hook, *CQWR*, May 20, 1989, pp. 1165-1166.

29. Janet Hook, *CQWR*, April 8, 1989, p. 729.

30. *SR*, April 3, 1989, p. 1.

31. Janet Hook, *CQWR*, May 27, 1989, p. 1225.

Notes for Chapter Six

1. Gloria Borger, "The Rise of the Accidental Speaker," *U.S. News & World Report*, June 5, 1989, p. 38.

2. Louise Sweeney, *CSM*, February 22, 1990, pp. 14-15.

3. In an ironic reprise of Speaker Wright's language upon his resignation, Republican Whip Tom DeLay, in his January 21, 1997 defense against ethics sanctions levied

against Speaker Gingrich—the man who had launched the Wright attack—appealed "Let's stop this madness. Let's stop the cannibalism." Jackie Koszczuk, *CQWR*, January 25, 1997, p. 228.

4. Hayes Gorey, "Waiting for Opportunity to Knock: Tom Foley is the Accidental Tourist of American Politics," *Time*, June 5, 1989, p. 34.
5. Gloria Borger and Steven V. Roberts, "Who Won the Ethics War?: Now that Wright has Gone, the Republican Strategy is at Risk," *U.S. News & World Report*, June 12, 1989, pp. 18-20.
6. *Congressional Quarterly Almanac 1989*, p. 40, as quoted in C. Lawrence Evans and Walter J. Oleszek, *Congress Under Fire: Reform Politics and the Republican Majority* (Boston and New York: Houghton Mifflin Company, 1997), p. 34.
7. Jim Camden, *SR*, June 7, 1989, pp. A1, A4.
8. *SR*, June 7, 1989, p. B6, editorial.
9. Kathleen Hall Jamieson, Executive Summary of testimony by the Dean of the Annenberg School for Communication, University of Pennsylvania, before the Subcommittee on Rules and Organization of the House, April 17, 1997. The subcommittee was holding a hearing on "Civility in the House of Representatives."
10. David E. Rosenbaum, *NYT*, June 2, 1989, p. A1.
11. Borger, "Accidental Speaker," p. 38.
12. Karen Foerstel, "His Likely Successor Has Taken Different Path," *Roll Call*, June 1, 1989, p. 4.
13. Gorey, "Waiting for Opportunity," p. 36.
14. Borger, "Accidental Speaker," p. 39.
15. David Rogers and John E. Yang, *WSJ*, June 7, 1989, p. A34.
16. John E. Yang and David Rogers, *WSJ*, June 1, 1989, pp. A1, A23. The authors noted that "Ms. Cheney and her husband, Defense Secretary Dick Cheney, are close friends of Mr. Foley, despite strong ideological differences."
17. Dennis R. Still, "Ranking the Speakers: Congressional Scholars' Perceptions of the U.S. House Speakers," paper presented at Midwest Political Science Association annual meeting, April 23-25, 1998.
18. Foley received *Der Grosse Verdienst-Kruz* from the Federal Republic of Germany; the *Legion d'Honeur* from France; the *Knight of the British Empire* from Britain; and from Japan, the *Order of the Rising Sun*, which had previously been awarded to Gen. Douglas MacArthur and U.S. Ambassador Mike Mansfield.
19. Karen Dorn Steele, *SR*, June 7, 1989, p. A6.
20. Hon. Bill Richardson of New Mexico, *Congressional Record*, Extension of Remarks, April 10, 1991, p. E1180.
21. Louise Sweeney, *CSM*, February 22, 1990, p. 14.
22. David Rogers and John E. Yang, *WSJ*, June 7, 1989, p. A34.
23. Bernard Weinraub, *NYT*, June 8, 1989, p. A1, B11.
24. E.J. Dionne, Jr., *NYT*, June 9, 1989, p. A23.
25. Gloria Borger, "Anatomy of a Smear," *U.S. News & World Report*, June 19, 1989, pp. 40-41.
26. Hendrik Hertzberg, "TRB From Washington: Atwatergate," *The New Republic*, July 3, 1989, p. 4.
27. Bernard Weinraub, *NYT*, June 8, 1989, p. B11.
28. Charles Moritz, ed., *Current Biography Yearbook 1987* (New York: H.W. Wilson Co., 1988), pp. 200-204; Phil Duncan, ed., *Politics in America 1992: The 102nd Congress* (Washington, D.C.: Congressional Quarterly Inc., 1991), pp. 846-849.
29. David Rogers, *WSJ*, August 5, 1993, p. A14.

30. Fred Barnes, "Musical Chairs: The House Democrats After Jim Wright," *The New Republic,* June 12, 1989, pp. 14-15.
31. Alan Ehrenhalt, ed., *Politics in America: The 100th Congress* (Washington, D.C.: Congressional Quarterly Inc., 1987), pp. 1283-1286.
32. Duncan, *Politics in America 1992,* pp. 439-443, 766-769, 1440-1443.
33. Gary Hymel, "What is a Congressional Staffer," included in Jeffrey B. Trammel and Steve Piacente, *The Almanac of the Unelected: Staff of the U.S. Congress 1993* (Washington, D.C.: The Almanac of the Unelected, Inc., 1993).
34. Jim Lynch, *SR,* March 27, 1994, p. A1.
35. *Ibid.*
36. Steven V. Roberts with Michael Barone, "After Wright's Fall: The Bush-Foley-Mitchell Team will Thrive on Coalition Politics," *U.S. News & World Report,* June 5, 1989, pp. 34-35.
37. William McGurn, "On the Scene," *National Review,* November 10, 1989, pp. 22-23.
38. *Current Biography,* September 1989, p. 8.
39. Alan Ehrenhalt, *CQWR,* September 12, 1986, pp. 2131-38; see also Barbara Sinclair, *Legislators, Leaders, and Lawmaking: The U.S. House of Representatives in the Postreform Era* (Baltimore and London: The Johns Hopkins University Press), p. 261.
40. Sinclair, *Legislators, Leaders, and Lawmaking,* p. 261.
41. Roberts with Barone, "After Wright's Fall," p. 35.
42. Katharine Q. Seelye, *NYT,* June 1, 1994, pp. C1, C7.
43. Tom Kenworthy, *WP,* June 16, 1991, p. A7.
44. Sinclair, *Legislators, Leaders, and Lawmaking,* p. 270.
45. Ronald M. Peters, Jr., ed., *The Speaker Leadership in the U.S. House of Representatives* (Washington, D.C.: Congressional Quarterly, Inc., 1994), in foreword by Thomas S. Foley, p. *xii.*

Notes for Chapter Seven

1. Joan Biskupic, *CQWR,* September 2, 1989, pp. 2255-2258.
2. Joan Biskupic, *CQWR,* July 1, 1989, p. 1622.
3. *Ibid.*
4. Press Conference with the Speaker of the House, Tuesday, September 12, 1989, 11:52 a.m.-12:02 p.m.
5. Press Conference with the Speaker of the House, April 3, 1990, 12:28 p.m.-12:32 p.m.
6. Louise Sweeney, *CSM,* February 22, 1990, p. 15.
7. "Bushwaterism," *The New Republic,* July 17 & 24, 1989, p. 5, editorial.
8. Press Conference with the Speaker of the House, Wednesday, September 13, 1989, 9:47 a.m.-10:02 a.m.
9. Ronald M. Peters, Jr., *The American Speakership: The Office in Historical Perspective* (Baltimore and London: The Johns Hopkins University Press, 1990), pp. 294-295.
10. Bill Whalen, "A Powerful Brood on Capitol Hill," *Insight,* November 20, 1989, pp. 20-21.
11. Peters, *American Speakership,* p. 297.
12. Jacob Weisberg, "On the Hill: Cat Scam," *The New Republic,* October 30, 1989, pp. 11-12.
13. Barbara Sinclair, *Legislators, Leaders, and Lawmaking: The U.S. House of Representatives in the Postreform Era* (Baltimore and London: The Johns Hopkins University Press, 1995), pp. 174-175, 212-214, 236-237.

14. Christopher Hanson, "On the Hill: Pay Dirt," *The New Republic*, December 25, 1989, pp. 10-11. Hanson, a Washington correspondent for the *Seattle Post-Intelligencer* and other Hearst papers, noted the extraordinary non-aggression pact between Democratic and Republican leaders which involved the opposing party coming to the defense of any member attacked for his or her pro-raise vote.

15. Robert S. Miller and Donald O. Dewey, *Glendale Law Review*, v. 10, nos. 1-2, 1991, pp. 91-109. The House was in full compliance with the Madison amendment to the Constitution which finally received the required three-fourths of states' ratification in May 1992. On June 8, 1789, James Madison had introduced thirty-three proposed amendments to the Constitution. These were narrowed down to twelve amendments by Congress. The ten amendments which were ratified by 1791 were known as the Bill of Rights. The other two amendments did not receive the ratification of the required three-fourths of the states. The first was a technical amendment regarding the apportionment of representatives in Congress. The second stated that "[n]o law varying the compensation for the services of the senators and representatives shall take effect until an election of representatives shall have intervened." Madison himself considered this one of the "lesser cases enumerated" among the amendments he proposed. He did not believe that "the power of the legislature to ascertain its own emolument . . . is likely to be abused, perhaps of all the powers granted it is least likely to abuse." Speaking in support of the Madison amendment some two hundred years after it was proposed, and in defense of the process by which the House had passed a salary increase, Foley said: "Despite all the nonsense that people have written about midnight payraises, the pay raise of the House of Representatives was enacted in early November of 1989 and became effective . . . over a year and two months later, and after an election."

16. Phil Duncan, ed., *Politics in America 1992* (Washington, D.C.: Congressional Quarterly, Inc., 1991), p. 470; Sinclair, *Legislators, Leaders, and Lawmaking*, pp. 252-254.

17. Chris Harvey, "A Speaker Who Is Well-Spoken Of," *Insight*, December 18, 1989, p. 22.

18. John R. Crawford, *CQWR*, July 21, 1990, p. 2277.

19. Press Conference with the Speaker of the House, May 15, 1990, 11:53 a.m.-12:01 p.m.

20. Pamela Fessler, *CQWR,* May 12, 1990, pp. 1457-1463.

21. Press Conference with the Speaker of the House, Thursday, May 24, 1990, 10:48 a.m.-11 a.m.

22. Pamela Fessler, *CQWR,* June 30, 1990, pp. 2029-2032.

23. The core negotiators included Speaker Foley, House Minority Leader Michel, House Majority Leader Gephardt, Senate Majority Leader Mitchell, Senate Minority Leader Dole, Treasury Secretary Brady, White House Chief of Staff Sununu, and Office of Management and Budget Director Darman.

24. George Hager, *CQWR*, September 29, 1990, p. 3096.

25. *Ibid.*, pp. 3093-3100.

26. Janet Hook, *CQWR*, October 6, 1990, p. 3191.

27. Duncan, *Politics in America 1992*, pp. 846-847.

28. George Hager, *CQWR,* October 6, 1990, pp. 3183-3188. "It took remarkable boldness, even recklessness, for Gingrich to break with his own president in 1990. But it is lost on no one that you can draw a straight line from that audacious act to his ultimate ascension to the Speakership." George Hager, *CQWR*, February 8, 1997, p. 390.

29. Janet Hook, *CQWR*, October 6, 1990, pp. 3189-3191.

30. Duncan, *Politics in America 1992.*

31. *SR*, August 4, 1990, p. A8.

32. *SR*, August 7, 1990, p. B4, editorial.

33. Jim Camden, *SR*, September 20, 1990, p. B2.

34. Jim Camden, *SR*, November 2, 1990, p. B1.
35. *SR*, November 1, 1990, p. B6, editorial.
36. Timothy Egan, *NYT*, June 8, 1989, p. B11.
37. Robin Toner, *NYT*, August 21, 1989, p. A10.
38. Eric Sorensen, *SR*, November 8, 1990, p. A1.

Notes for Chapter Eight

1. Mary Cohn, ed., *Congressional Quarterly's Guide to Congress* (Washington, D.C.: Congressional Quarterly, Inc., 1991), pp. 209-214.
2. *Ibid.*, p. 210-211.
3. Carroll J. Doherty, *CQWR*, December 8, 1990, pp. 4082-4085.
4. Joan Biskupic, *CQWR*, December 8, 1990, p. 4084.
5. Janet Hook, *CQWR*, January 5, 1991, p. 5.
6. Joan Biskupic, *CQWR*, January 12, 1991, p. 70.
7. Carroll J. Doherty, *CQWR*, January 12, 1991, p. 66.
8. *Ibid.*, pp. 65-66.
9. *Ibid.*, p. 69.
10. Jeffrey Frank, *CQWR*, October 29, 1983, pp. 2231-2234.
11. Chuck Alston, *CQWR*, January 19, 1991, p. 182.
12. Carroll J. Doherty, *CQWR*, January 19, 1991, p. 179.
13. *CQWR*, December 28, 1991, p. 3763.
14. Chuck Alston and *Congressional Quarterly* staff, *CQWR*, December 7, 1991, pp. 3563-3564.
15. "A Mensch," *Roll Call*, January 17, 1991, p. 4, editorial.
16. Richard E. Cohen, "Faulting Foley," *National Journal*, August 10, 1991, p. 1968.
17. *Congressional Quarterly* staff, *CQWR*, December 28, 1991, p. 2776. One of the most complete treatments of the Family and Medical Leave Act, including an epilogue which assesses its impact after becoming law, is Ronald D. Elving's *Conflict and Compromise: How Congress Makes the Law* (New York: Simon & Schuster Touchstone Books, 1996). In the tradition of Eric Redman's 1970s account of the creation of the National Health Services Corps, *The Dance of Legislation*, Elving provides a vivid account of the legislative process in the 1990s.
18. Ronald M. Peters, *The American Speakership: The Office in Historical Perspective* (Baltimore and London: The Johns Hopkins University Press, 1990), p. 284.
19. Cohen, "Faulting Foley," p. 1968.
20. "Now, Govern," *The New Republic*, April 1, 1991, pp. 7-9, editorial.
21. John R. Cranford, *CQWR*, April 21, 1990, pp. 1175-1178.
22. Sidney Blumenthal, "Flatliners," *The New Republic*, May 20, 1991, pp. 16-18.
23. Michael Barone, "Wright, Coelho and the S & L fiasco," *U.S. News & World Report*, June 12, 1989, pp. 21-22.
24. John R. Cranford, *CQWR*, March 16, 1991, pp. 653-656.
25. Cohen, "Faulting Foley," p. 1967.
26. Chuck Alston, *CQWR*, November 2, 1991, pp. 3177-3178.
27. *Ibid.*, p. 3178.
28. John Newhouse, "The Navigator," *New Yorker*, April 10, 1989, pp. 67-68.
29. "Tom Foley, Gun Nut," *The New Republic*, January 28, 1991, pp. 7-8, editorial. In its criticism of the failure of the 101st Congress to pass the Brady Bill, the magazine noted that "in this disgraceful drama the NRA, as usual, played the villain. But in shooting down the Brady Bill the country's most sanguinary special interest lobby had an unlikely

sidekick. Speaker of the House Thomas P. [sic] Foley, rightly renowned for his civility and decency, has an almost instinctive aversion to passionate enthusiasm. Yet he went far out of his way, flouting the will of the House Democratic Caucus and the likely majority of the House as a whole, to display an unwonted zealotry in a dubious cause."

30. Joan Biskupic, *CQWR*, May 11, 1991, pp. 1196-1202; Janet Hook, *CQWR*, May 11, 1991, pp. 1198-1199.

31. Joan Biskupic, *CQWR*, March 9, 1991 pp. 604-607.

32. Joan Biskupic, *CQWR*, May 4, 1991, pp. 1134-1135.

33. Janet Hook, *CQWR*, May 11, 1991, pp. 1198-1199.

34. Joan Biskupic, *CQWR*, June 8, 1991, pp. 1500-1501.

35. Joan Biskupic, *CQWR*, June 8, 1991, pp. 1498-1503.

36. *CQWR*, December 28, 1991, pp. 3763-3771.

Notes for Chapter Nine

1. "The Keating Five Hearings: A Special Report," *Congressional Quarterly's Guide to Congress* (Washington, D.C.: Congressional Quarterly, Inc., 4th ed., 1991), p. 817.

2. "New Procedures in Place After Bank Audit," *Roll Call*, February 8, 1990; *WP*, February 8, 1990.

3. Phil Kuntz, *CQWR*, November 2, 1991, pp. 3179-3181.

4. Kelly D. Patterson and David B. Magleby, "Public Support for Congress," *Public Opinion Quarterly* (Winter 1992), pp. 543-44 and C. Lawrence Evans and Walter J. Oleszek, *Congress Under Fire: Reform Politics and the Republican Majority* (Boston and New York: Houghton Mifflin Company, 1997), p. 35.

5. Chuck Alston, *CQWR*, October 26, 1991, pp. 3106-3107.

6. *Ibid.*

7. Phil Kuntz, *CQWR*, November 2, 1991, p. 3181.

8. Press Conference with the Speaker of the House, February 5, 1992, 1:32 p.m.-1:49 p.m.

9. Former Republican Representative Mickey Edwards of Oklahoma observed, "I told him [Gingrich] at the time it was he who was whipping up the system, creating the anger. . . . When you start turning the public into a mob you've got a real problem." Quoted in a profile of Speaker Gingrich by Connie Bruck, "The Politics of Perception," *The New Yorker*, October 9, 1994, p. 74.

10. S. Robert Lichter and David R. Amundson, "Less News Is Worse News: Television News Coverage of Congress, 1972-1992," in Thomas E. Mann and Norman J. Ornstein, eds., *Congress, the Press, and the Public* (Washington, D.C.: American Enterprise Institute and the Brookings Institution, 1994).

11. Paul S. Runquist, Paul E. Dwyer, John S. Pontius, and Mildred Amer, *CRS Report for Congress, House of Representatives' Management: Background and Current Issues* (Washington, D.C.: Congressional Research Service, The Library of Congress, April 17, 1992). Much of the narrative on the "House Bank" is drawn from Jeffrey R. Biggs, "The Changing Landscape of Congress," in Elaine S. Povich, *Partners & Adversaries: The Contentious Connection Between Congress & the Media* (Arlington, Va.: The Freedom Forum, Inc., 1996), pp. 71-75.

12. "The Gang of Seven," *Roll Call*, August 17, 1992, p. 4.

13. Richard S. Dunham, "The Hill's Young Turks," *Business Week*, June 1, 1992, p. 79.

14. Press Conference with the Speaker of the House, Wednesday, March 11, 1992, 1:45 p.m.-2 p.m.

15. Phil Kuntz, *CQWR*, March 28, 1992, pp. 782-784; Phil Kuntz, *CQWR*, December 19, 1992, pp. 3877-3879.
16. Janet Hook, *CQWR*, June 6, 1992, pp. 1579-1585.
17. Janet Hook, *CQWR*, August 8, 1992, p. 2332.
18. George Bush, "Remarks and a Question-and-Answer Session in Lafayette, Louisiana, October 24, 1992," *George Bush: Public Papers of the Presidents of the United States* (Washington, D.C.: Government Printing Office, 1993), vol. 2, 1992-1993, p. 1966.
19. Barbara Sinclair, *Legislators, Leaders, and Lawmaking: The U.S. House of Representatives in the Postreform Era* (Baltimore and London: The Johns Hopkins University Press, 1995), p. 192.
20. Evans and Oleszek, *Congress Under Fire*, p. 42.
21. Sinclair, *Legislators, Leaders, and Lawmaking*, p. 192.
22. Press Conference with the Speaker of the House, April 8, 1992, 10:48 a.m.-11:01 a.m.
23. Janet Hook with Beth Donovan, *CQWR*, April 4, 1992, p. 857. It was to prove ironic that, among a number of broadly supported rules changes proposed by the new Republican majority in the House of Representatives for the 104th Congress, the bipartisan character of the House Administrator was transformed into a politically appointed role under the supervision of the Speaker.
24. Richard Morris and Helen Dewar, *WP,* March 20, 1992, A16.
25. The term "feeding frenzy" is derived from University of Virginia Political Science Professor Larry J. Sabato's book, *Feeding Frenzy: How Attack Journalism Has Transformed American Politics* (New York: Free Press, 1991). See also Norman J. Ornstein and Amy L. Schenkenberg, "Congress Bashing: External Pressures for Reform and the Future of the Institution" in James A. Thurber and Roger H. Davidson, *Remaking Congress: Change and Stability in the 1990s* (Washington, D.C.: Congressional Quarterly Inc., 1995).
26. Tom Kenworthy, *WP*, April 26, 1992, p. C5.
27. Runquist, et. al., *CRS Report for Congress.*
28. Between 1986 and 1992, *The Times Mirror* Center for the People and the Press measured "public attentiveness to major news stories." Those events followed most closely included the explosion of the space shuttle *Challenger* (80 percent of the public followed the story), the 1989 San Francisco earthquake (73 percent), and the 1992 Los Angeles riots after the Rodney King verdict (70 percent). Of the 294 high-interest stories tracked, only twenty-one were about Congress, with the "House Bank" ranking highest in sixty-second place, followed by 31 percent of the public. It ranked higher than the 1986 major revision of the U.S. tax code, the Clean Water Act, congressional action on the Iran-Contra scandal, and the savings-and-loan banking crisis, all of which arguably impacted the nation and the average citizen more importantly. For more detail see Stephen Hess, "The Decline and Fall of Congressional News" in Mann and Ornstein, *Congress, The Press, and the Public.*
29. Charlotte Hays, "Women Who Scare Men: In Washington, It's Easy," *The Washingtonian*, April 1992, pp. 66-69.
30. Karen Dorn Steele and Jim Camden, *SR*, April 8, 1992, p. A1.
31. Lois Romano, *WP*, February 9, 1990, pp. D1-D2.
32. Ronald M. Peters, Jr., *The American Speakership: The Office in Historical Perspective* (Baltimore and London: The Johns Hopkins University Press, 1990), p. 254.
33. Janet Hook with Beth Donovan, *CQWR*, April 4, 1992, pp. 856-857.
34. Richard Blow, "Foley Flexes," *Mother Jones*, July/August 1993, p. 40.
35. Clifford Krauss, *NYT*, January 9, 1993, p. A1.
36. *Congressional Quarterly* staff, "Profile: Thomas S. Foley—Heavy Weather," *American Caucus*, April 13-April 26, 1992, pp. 6-8.

37. Jim Lynch, *SR*, October 18, 1992, p. A1.
38. Blow, "Foley Flexes," p. 42.
39. Jim Lynch, *SR*, October 18, 1992, p. A12.
40. Janet Hook, *CQWR*, August 15, 1992, p. 2429.
41. David S. Broder, *WP*, August 26, 1992, p. A2.
42. Blow, "Foley Flexes," p. 40.
43. *Ibid.*, p. 42.
44. Evans and Oleszek, *Congress Under Fire*, pp. 54-55.
45. Stephen Pizzo, "Lions Into Lambs: Perks and Plum Assignments Muted Freshmen's Call to Reform," *Mother Jones*, July/August 1993, p. 40.
46. Kenneth J. Cooper, *WP*, November 9, 1992, p. A8.
47. Evans and Oleszek, *Congress Under Fire,* pp. 52-53.
48. *Ibid.*
49. Cooper, "House Democratic Leaders," p. A8; and Blow, "Foley Flexes," pp. 40-41.

Notes for Chapter Ten

1. Jim Camden, *SR*, May 8, 1992, p. B1.
2. Jim Lynch, *SR*, August 23, 1992, p. B1.
3. Jim Lynch, *SR*, October 20, 1992, p. A1.
4. Jim Lynch, *SR,* October 19, 1992, p. A1.
5. Timothy Egan, *NYT*, October 31, 1992, A6.
6. *SR*, October 20, 1992, p. B6, editorial.
7. Joel Connelly, *PI*, April 24, 1992, p. A1.
8. *Ibid.*
9. Ronald M. Peters, Jr., *The American Speakership: The Office in Historical Perspective* (Baltimore and London: The Johns Hopkins University Press, 1990) pp. 285-86.
10. Adam Clymer, *NYT*, November 16, 1992, p. A1.
11. David Rogers, *WSJ*, December 4, 1992, p. A10.
12. Fred Barnes, "Hill Potatoes," *The New Republic*, May 20, 1991, pp. 26-27.
13. Steven S. Smith and Christopher J. Deering, *Committees in Congress*, (Washington, D.C.: *Congressional Quarterly* Press, 1984), pp. 250-258; and Steven S. Smith, *Call to Order: Floor Politics in the House and Senate* (Washington, D.C.: The Brookings Institution, 1989), pp. 197-232.
14. Stephen Gettinger, "Committees at Work: The New Milieu," *Congressional Quarterly Committee Guide*, May 1, 1993, pp. 7-8.
15. C. Lawrence Evans and Walter J. Oleszek, *Congress Under Fire: Reform Politics and the Republican Majority* (Boston and New York: Houghton Mifflin Company, 1997), p. 40.
16. Calvin J. Mouw and Michael B. Mackuen, "The Strategic Agenda in Legislative Politics," *American Political Science Review*, Vol. 86, No. 1, March 1992, pp. 87-105.
17. Barbara Sinclair, *Legislators, Leaders, and Lawmaking: The U.S. House of Representatives in the Postreform Era* (Baltimore and London: The Johns Hopkins University Press, 1995), pp. 182-183.
18. Adam Clymer, *NYT*, January 6, 1993, p. A16.
19. Beth Donovan, *CQWR*, January 9, 1993, pp. 57-58. After being characterized by Minority Whip Newt Gingrich as "an abuse of power," U.S. District Judge Harold H. Greene found the rules change constitutional with the added provision requiring an immediate, members-only revote on any issue decided by delegate participation. See Beth Donovan, *CQWR*, March 13, 1993, p. 57.
20. Beth Donovan, *CQWR*, p. 57.

21. Janet Hook, *CQWR* and Kitty Cunningham, *CQWR*, October 9, 1993, pp. 2714-2718; David W. Brady and Craig Volden, *Revolving Gridlock: Politics and Policy from Carter to Clinton* (Boulder, Co.: Westview Press, 1988), p. 176.

Notes for Chapter Eleven

1. Jill Zuckman, *CQWR,* February 6, 1993, p. 267.
2. Blaine Harden, *WP,* September 8, 1996, p. A14.
3. Clifford Krauss, *NYT,* February 22, 1993, p. A14.
4. Anthony King, "Running Scared," *The Atlantic Monthly*, January 1997, pp. 41-61. In reviewing the impact of our electoral system on members and dismissing many of the over-arching panaceas, King concludes that the real difficulty "is the hyper-responsiveness of American politicians that is induced by their having to run scared so much of the time. . . .The American people cannot govern themselves. They therefore need to find appropriate means of choosing representatives who can do a decent job of governing on their behalf, and that means giving the people's representatives space, time, and freedom in which to make decisions, knowing that if they get them wrong, they will be punished by the voters. . . .What America needs today, though it does not seem to know it, is a more realistic and down-to-earth form of division-of-labor democracy."
5. Martin Schram, *Speaking Freely: Former Members of Congress Talk About Money in Politics* (Washington, D.C.: Center for Response Politics, 1995), pp. 9-11, 47-48, 56. Schram, a nationally syndicated columnist for the Scripps Howard News Service, interviewed twenty-five recently retired members of Congress including Foley, Mitchell, House Minority Leader Robert Michel, and others, about the appearances and actual abuses of the current campaign process. The study grew out of the notion that senators and representatives who have recently left office, or are just about to leave office, would feel they could speak freely about the true role of political money in the making of public policy.
6. Milton S. Gwirtzman, *WP*, January 12, 1997, p. C3.
7. Ilyse J. Vernon, *CQWR*, June 19, 1993, p. 1538.
8. Schram, *Speaking Freely*, p. 130.
9. Beth Donovan, *CQWR*, February 6, 1993, p. 250.
10. *CQWR*, March 13, 1993, p. 573.
11. Beth Donovan, *CQWR,* June 19, 1993, pp. 1533-1540.
12. Beth Donovan, *CQWR,* August 14, 1993, pp. 2215-2218.
13. Beth Donovan, *CQWR,* September 25, 1993, pp. 2523-2526.
14. Beth Donovan, *CQWR,* May 8, 1993, pp. 1121-1122.
15. Beth Donovan, *CQWR,* March 20, 1993, p. 646.
16. Janet Hook and the *Congressional Quarterly* staff, *CQWR,* October 2, 1993, pp. 2613-2618.
17. Beth Donovan, *CQWR,* November 27, 1993, pp. 3246-3249.
18. Clifford Krauss, *NYT,* November 23, 1993, pp. A1, B8.
19. Thomas Galvin, *CQWR,* February 20, 1993, pp. 287-288. In recognition of rank-and-file freshman sentiment for reform, Speaker Foley stated that "I do not think that anyone would think it fair if Congress were exempt from cuts."
20. George Hager, *CQWR,* August 7, 1993, pp. 2130-2131.
21. David S. Cloud, *CQWR,* August 7, 1993, pp. 2132-2133.
22. Janet Hook, *Congressional Quarterly Weekly Report*, August 7, 1993, p. 2128.
23. Jon Healey and Chuck Alston, *CQWR,* March 20, 1993, pp. 652.

24. Richard E. Cohen, "Foley Shows a Firm Hand at the Helm," *National Journal*, August 14, 1993, p. 2044.
25. George Hager and David S. Cloud, *CQWR*, August 7, 1993, pp. 2122-2129.
26. Jon Healey, *CQWR*, April 24, 1993, pp. 1001-1004.
27. Cohen, "Foley Shows a Firm Hand," p. 2044.
28. David S. Broder, *WP*, March 14, 1993, pp. A1, A6.
29. Elizabeth Drew, *Showdown: The Struggle Between the Gingrich Congress and the Clinton White House* (New York: Simon & Schuster, 1996), pp. 64-65.
30. David S. Cloud and George Hager, *CQWR*, July 31, 1993, pp. 2023-2028.
31. *CQWR*, August 14, 1993, p. 2243.
32. David S. Cloud, *CQWR*, October 16, 1993, pp. 2791-2796.
33. Jon Healey and Thomas H. Moore, *CQWR*, November 20, 1993, pp. 3181-3183.
34. Janet Hook, *CQWR*, November 20, 1993, pp. 3184-3185; the vote count is listed on p. 3224.
35. Steve Langdon, *CQWR*, September 25, 1993, p. 2527; Janet Hook and the *Congressional Quarterly* staff, *CQWR*, December 11, 1993, pp. 3355-3357.

Notes for Chapter Twelve

1. Janet Hook and the *Congressional Quarterly* staff, *CQWR*, January 8, 1994, pp. 5-14.
2. Janet Hook, *CQWR*, January 29, 1994, pp. 153-156.
3. Dave Kaplan, *CQWR*, February 19, 1994, pp. 382-415.
4. Janet Hook, *CQWR*, April 2, 1994, pp. 785-789.
5. Janet Hook, *CQWR*, March 5, 1994, p. 517.
6. *CQWR*, February 12, 1994, p. 342.
7. Holly Idelson, *CQWR, October 15*, 1994, pp. 2969-2971.
8. Timothy Egan, *NYT*, February 11, 1994, p. A20.
9. Timothy Egan, *NYT,* January 12, 1994, p. A10.
10. Jim Camden, *SR*, April 27, 1988, p. B1; Les Blumenthal, Associated Press, *SC*, May 26, 1988; Les Blumenthal, *SR*, March 7, 1989, p. A1.
11. Glenn R. Simpson, *Roll Call*, reprinted in *SR,* July 25, 1993, p. A17.
12. Jim Lynch, *SR*, August 3, 1993, p. B1. Two years later the Securities and Exchange Commission, in a civil action, fined and censured Peter de Roetth and his partner in Account Management Corporation for a violation of fiduciary trust disclosing its help to favored clients to its other account holders. de Roetth indicated that the firm had allocated the stock offerings at its own discretion and the friends were "predominantly school teachers and artists." The SEC found no wrongdoing by the favored clients. *SR*, October 4, 1995, p. A-1; Mary Jacoby, "Foley Investment Adviser Fined by SEC," *Roll Call*, October 5, 1995.
13. Janet Hook, *CQWR*, June 25, 1994, p. 1679.
14. Holly Idelson, *CQWR*, October 1, 1994, pp. 2802-2806.
15. Janet Hook, *CQWR,* January 19, 1994, pp. 153-156.
16. *Ibid.*
17. Beth Donovan, *CQWR*, February 26, 1994, pp. 475-478.
18. C. Lawrence Evans and Walter J. Oleszek, *Congress Under Fire: Reform Politics and the Republican Majority* (Boston and New York: Houghton Mifflin Company, 1997), pp. 85-86.
19. Alissa J. Rubin, *CQWR*, July 30, 1994, pp. 214-216.
20. David Rogers, *WSJ*, July 27, 1994, pp. A2, A5.
21. Phil Kuntz, *CQWR*, August 13, 1994, p. 2311.

22. Adam Clymer, *NYT*, September 14, 1994, p. A13.
23. Ceco Connolly, *CQWR*, October 1, 1994, pp. 2753-2755.
24. Jennifer Babson, *CQWR*, August 20, 1994, p. 2454.
25. Holly Idelson, *CQWR*, August 13, 1994, pp. 2340-2343.
26. Holly Idelson with Beth Donovan, *CQWR*, October 1, 1994, p. 2754.
27. Beth Donovan, *CQWR*, October 1, 1994, pp. 2757-2758.
28. *NYT*, October 12, 1994, editorial.
29. Phil Kuntz, *CQWR*, September 24, 1994, pp. 2656-2657.
30. "The October Massacre," *The New Republic*, October 24, 1994, p. 7.
31. Evans and Oleszek, *Congress Under Fire*, p. 62.
32. David S. Cloud, *CQWR*, October 8, 1994, pp. 2854-2855.
33. Richard Scammon, *CQWR*, October 8, 1994, p. 2855.
34. Bob Benenson, *CQWR*, October 8, 1994, p. 2856.
35. David R. Mayhew, *Divided We Govern: Party Control, Lawmaking, and Investigations, 1946-1990* (New Haven, Ct.: Yale University Press, 1991) pp. 132-133.

Notes for Chapter Thirteen

1. Dave Kaplan, *CQWR*, October 8, 1994, pp. 2901-2905.
2. For general background on the long-term Democratic majority in the House: David R. Mayhew, *Divided We Govern: Party Control, Lawmaking, and Investigations, 1946-1990* (New Haven, Ct.: Yale University Press, 1991); Peter F. Galerisi, ed., *Divided Government: Change, Uncertainty, and the Constitutional Order* (Lanham, Md.: Rowman & Littlefield Publishers, 1996); James A. Thurber, ed., *Divided Democracy: Cooperation and Conflict Between the President and Congress* (Washington, D.C.: Congressional Quarterly Press, 1991).
3. David W. Brady, John F. Cogan, and Douglas Rivers, *How the Republicans Captured the House* (Stanford: Hoover Institution Press, 1955).
4. Gary C. Jacobson, *The Electoral Origins of Divided Government: Competition in U.S. House Elections, 1946-1988* (Boulder, Co.: Westview Press, 1990), p. 135.
5. Joel Connelly, *PI*, May 24, 1994, p. A1.
6. Gary C. Jacobson and Samuel Kernell, *Strategy and Choice in Congressional Elections* (New Haven, Ct.: Yale University Press, 2d ed., 1983).
7. David Ammons, "Incumbents Feel Heat," *Clark County Columbian*, October 4, 1994.
8. Joel Connelly, *PI*, May 24, 1994, p. A1.
9. Ed Rollins with Tom Defrank, *Bare Knuckles and Back Rooms: My Life in American Politics* (New York: Broadway Books, 1996), pp. 303-304.
10. Joel Connelly, *PI*, October 6, 1994, p. A1.
11. Rollins, *Bare Knuckles and Back Rooms*, p. 305.
12. Linda Killian, *The Freshmen: What Happened to the Republican Revolution?* (Boulder, Co.: Westview Press, 1998), p. 19.
13. Rollins, *Bare Knuckles and Back Rooms*, p. 324.
14. Victor Gold, "George Bush Speaks Out," *The Washingtonian*, February 1994, v. 29, p. 129.
15. Sabato quoted in Michael Rust, "Manipulating the Candidate," *Insight*, March 10, 1997, pp. 10-11.
16. James A. Thurber, "Political Consultants: A Self-Portrait of the Profession: Survey Reveals They Blame Voters, Media, Candidates for the Ills of Campaign System," *Roll Call*, July 23, 1998, p. 18. Sponsored by a grant from the Pew Charitable Trusts to American University's Center for Congressional and Presidential Studies, director of the

Center Thurber coordinated the first in-depth national survey of political consultants through interviews with 200 top-level campaign professionals. The consultants were disproportionately white (98 percent), male (82 percent), highly educated (94 percent graduated from college and 40 percent had graduate degrees), relatively young (75 percent were under the age of fifty and 40 percent under the age of forty), and had extensive prior experience working in government or party politics. More than 70 percent of the consultants earned more than $100,000 annually and 30 percent more than $200,000 a year.

17. Rollins, *Bare Knuckles and Back Rooms*, pp. 306, 324.
18. Timothy Egan, *NYT,* October 29, 1994, p. A7.
19. Christopher Hanson, *PI*, September 15, 1994, p. B1.
20. *WWUB*, July 24, 1994, p. 3.
21. Jim Camden, *SR*, September 22, 1994, p. A1.
22. "Congress Daily's Hill Briefs," *National Journal*, September 23, 1994, p. 3.
23. Jim Camden, *SR*, September 11, 1994, p. Ca.
24. George Nethercutt received $10,900 directly in NRA PAC money in 1994 and 1995, but the NRA independently spent an additional $70,000 in the 1994 race against Foley. On March 22, 1998, the House voted 239-173 to repeal the assault weapons ban with only six of the seventy-three GOP freshmen from 1994 voting against the repeal, and "only one of those six, Jon Fox of Pennsylvania, had received any PAC money from the NRA." See Killian, *The Freshmen*, p. 285.
25. Timothy Egan, *NYT,* October 29, 1994, p. A8.
26. David Rogers, *WSJ*, October 27, 1994, p. A22.
27. Kenneth J. Cooper, *WP*, November 5, 1994, pp. A1, A9.
28. Mike Prager, *SR*, October 13, 1994.
29. *Spokane Valley Herald*, September 15, 1994; Joel Connelly, *PI*, October 6, 1994, p. A1.
30. Foster Church, *Ore*, October 31, 1994, pp. A1, A8. Jim Camden, *SR*, October 27, 1994; Mike Prager, *SR*, October 13, 1994.
31. Jim Camden and Jess Walter, *SR*, November 5, 1994, pp. A1, A6; Christopher Hanson, *PI*, November 5, 1994, p. A1; David Rogers, *WSJ*, October 27, 1994, p. A22.
32. Christopher Hanson, *PI*, November 5, 1994, p. A1.
33. Kevin Merida, *WP*, November 9, 1994, p. A5.
34. Timothy Egan, *NYT*, October 29, 1994, pp. A1, A9; Chris Peck, *SR*, October 9, 1994.
35. Adam Clymer, *NYT,* August 29, 1993.
36. Timothy Egan, *NYT*, October 29, 1994.
37. Joel Connelly, *PI*, October 6, 1994, p. A1.
38. "George Nethercutt for Congress, Republican Gathering in Pomeroy, Washington," April 1994.
39. Timothy Egan, *NYT*, October 29, 1994, p. A9.
40. *Ibid.*, p. A1.
41. *Ibid.*, p. A9.
42. Eric Sorensen, *SR*, October 26, 1994, p. A1.
43. Rollins, *Bare Knuckles and Back Rooms*, p. 330.
44. Timothy Egan, *NYT*, October 26, 1994, p. A26.
45. Katharine Q. Seelye, *NYT*, October 27, 1994, p. A1, A26.
46. *WWUB*, October 23, 1994, editorial endorsement.
47. *SR*, October 2, 1994, p. A1.
48. Jess Walter, *SR*, October 15, 1994, p. A1.
49. John Webster for the editorial board, *SR*, November 13, 1994.
50. Anthony King, "Running Scared," *The Atlantic Monthly*, January 1997, p. 52. King quotes fiscal conservative Democrat Timothy J. Penny of Minnesota who retired in

1994 rather than run for reelection and, with journalist Major Garrett, wrote a 1995 book *Common Cents*. "Voters routinely punish lawmakers who try to do unpopular things, who challenge them to face unpleasant truths about the budget, crime, Social Security, or tax policy. . . ."

51. Jess Walter, *SR*, November 10, 1994, pp. A1, A17.
52. Kevin Merida, *WP*, December 2, 1994, p. F1.
53. *Ibid.*
54. Adam Clymer, *NYT*, November 30, 1994, p. A10.
55. *Ibid.*, p. A11.
56. Foley had recounted the McCormack story two years earlier to one of a handful of the true veteran political correspondents of Foley's career, *Seattle Post-Intelligencer* national correspondent Joel Connelly. Connelly included the anecdote and Foley's response in his article "Foley Still Up to Challenges of Office," *PI*, April 24, 1992, p. A1.

Notes for Chapter Fourteen

1. Karen Tumulty, "Man with a Vision," *Time*, January 5, 1995, p. 23.
2. Joe KIein, "Letter from Washington: The Hug," *The New Yorker*, December 16, 1996, p. 54.
3. Elizabeth Drew, *Showdown: The Struggle Between Gingrich, Congress, and the Clinton White House* (New York: Simon & Schuster, 1996), pp. 21, 24.
4. *Ibid.*, pp. 27, 29.
5. Norman J. Ornstein and Amy L. Schenkenberg, "The 1995 Congress: The First Hundred Days and Beyond," *Political Science Quarterly*, v. 10, no. 2, Summer 1995, pp. 183-206.
6. C. Lawrence Evans and Walter J. Oleszek, *Congress Under Fire: Reform Politics and the Republican Majority* (Boston and New York: Houghton Mifflin Company, 1997), pp. 85-86.
7. *Ibid.*, p. 108.
8. Drew, *Showdown* , p. 180.
9. Ed Gillespie and Bob Schellhas, eds., *Contract with America: The Bold Plan by Rep. Newt Gingrich, Rep. Dick Armey and the House Republicans to Change the Nation* (New York: Time Books, 1994).
10. Drew, *Showdown* , p. 37.
11. Ornstein and Schenkenberg, "The 1995 Congress," pp. 183-206.
12. Norman Ornstein, "A Progress Report on GOP Reforms," *Roll Call*, December 5, 1994, p. 5.
13. Donna Cassata, *CQWR*, April 1, 1995, pp. 909-912.
14. David Plotke, "Against Government: The Contract with America," *DISSENT*, v. 42, Summer 1995, pp. 348-353.
15. Louis Fisher, "The 'Contract with America': What It Really Means," *New York Review of Books*, v. 42, June 22, 1995, pp. 20-24.
16. Drew, *Showdown*, p. 100.
17. *Ibid.*, pp. 116-117.
18. *Ibid.*, p. 260.
19. Donna Cassata, *CQWR* , November 2, 1996, pp. 3123-3124.

Notes for Epilogue

1. Adam Clymer, *NYT*, November 2, 1997.
2. "What's an Ex-Speaker Worth?" *Legal Times*, October 13, 1997, p. 13.
3. *The Foley Institute Report* (Pullman, Wa.: The Thomas S. Foley Institute for Public Policy and Public Service, Washington State University, Spring 1997).
4. Paul McClure, ed., *Washington Information Directory 1996-1997* (Washington, D.C.: Congressional Quarterly, Inc., 1996), p. 384.
5. "What's an Ex-Speaker Worth?," p. 13. According to Laurie Snyder, *SR*, October 28, 1997, p. A1, accepting an ambassadorship would be a "financial hit" as Foley's salary would drop to $123,100 from the $393,940 he made at Akin Gump. His $123,800 government pension would be suspended, and he would have to resign from positions on corporate boards from which he earned $50,000 in 1996.
6. Paul Starobin, "An Ear for Gossip," *National Journal*, October 4, 1997, p. 1949. White House press secretary Michael D. McCurry was quoted as saying that "if the Administration has an important personnel announcement, we generally give it to Al Kamen because everyone will read it before we announce it."
7. Schwellenbach later became Secretary of Labor in President Truman's cabinet.
8. Robert C. Neff and Amy Borrus, "The Wrong Man to Send to Tokyo?" *Business Week*, May 12, 1997, p. 56.
9. Laurie Snyder, *SR*, October 28, 1997, p. A1.
10. Robert B. Reich, *Locked in the Cabinet* (New York: Alfred A. Knopf, 1997). Included in his description of his Senate confirmation hearings for Labor Secretary, Reich describes cramming for the hearing as akin to "a prizefighter getting ready for the big one. . . . 'Time out,' says my chief interrogator, a rotund, middle-aged Hill staffer with graying red hair and decades of experience at this sort of thing. 'Let's stop here and critique your performance so far'. . . . 'Look,' he says, stepping out from behind the table which serves as a mock committee rostrum. 'This hearing isn't designed to test your knowledge. Its purpose is to test your respect for them'. . . . 'You don't have to come up with the right answer,' he continues, pacing around the room. 'You've got a big handicap. Your whole life you've been trying to show people how smart you are. That's not what you should do on Thursday. You try to show them how smart you are, you're in trouble. . . . This is all about respect,' he says. 'Your respect for them. The President's respect for them. The executive branch's respect for the legislative branch. . . .'", pp. 37-39.
11. Tape recorded by Jeffrey Biggs; in possession of Jeffrey Biggs.
12. Tape recorded by Jeffrey Biggs; in possession of Jeffrey Biggs.
13. Laurie Snyder, *SR*, October 28, 1997, p. A1.
14. Tape recorded by Jeffrey Biggs; in possession of Jeffrey Biggs.
15. Tape recorded by Jeffrey Biggs; in possession of Jeffrey Biggs.
16. Tape recorded by Jeffrey Biggs; in possession of Jeffrey Biggs.
17. Al Kamen, *WP*, October 27, 1997, p. A23.
18. *WP*, October 28, 1997, p. A4.
19. Kevin Sullivan, *WP*, November 16, 1997, p. A25.
20. Alan Tonelson of the U.S. Business & Industrial Council, a lobbying group for the manufacturing industry, reportedly said Foley was no different than other people who have directed American policy toward Japan over the last fifty years. "Their highest priority is to maintain the U.S.-Japan security alliance. . . . They won't jeopardize this by bringing up trade issues too aggressively." See Laurie Snyder, *SR*, October 28, 1997, p. A1.

Bibliography

Allen, Rob, "Goal: Unseat Foley—Republicans Gird for '78 Campaign," *The Spokesman-Review*, July 28, 1977, p. A5.

Alston, Chuck and *Congressional Quarterly* staff, "Year Begins with Bang Abroad, Ends with Whimper at Home," *Congressional Quarterly Weekly Report*, December 7, 1991, pp. 3563-3564.

_____, Bombers Heading for Baghdad as Hill Leaders Got Word," *Congressional Quarterly Weekly Report*, January 19, 1991, p.182.

_____, Bush Takes Congress to Task; Democrats Fire Right Back," *Congressional Quarterly Weekly Report*, October 26, 1991, pp. 3106-3107.

_____, "The Speaker and the Chairmen: A Taoist Approach to Power," *Congressional Quarterly Weekly Report*, November 2, 1991, pp. 3177-3178.

"America's Angry voters," *The Economist*, November 2, 1996, p. 22.

Ammons, David, "Incumbents Feel Heat," *Clark County Columbian*, October 4, 1994.

Apple, R.W., Jr., "Foley Assesses Presidential Elections and Tells Why He Wouldn't Run," *The New York Times*, November 4, 1988, p. A20.

Babson, Jennifer, "Gun Ban 'Energized' NRA Members," *Congressional Quarterly Weekly Report*, August 20, 1994, p. 2454.

Bach, Stanley and Steven S. Smith, *Managing Uncertainty in the House of Representatives: Adaptation and Innovation in Special Rules* (Washington, D.C.: Brookings Institution, 1988).

Barnes, Fred, "Hill Potatoes," *The New Republic*, May 20, 1991, pp. 26-27.

_____, "Musical Chairs: The House Democrats after Jim Wright," *The New Republic*, June 12, 1989, pp. 14-15.

_____, "The Wright Stuff: Democrats Will Miss Him when He's Gone," *The New Republic*, May 15, 1989, pp. 13-16.

Barone, Michael and Grant Ujifusa, *The Almanac of American Politics 1984* (Washington, D.C.: *National Journal*, 1983), p. 1244.

Barone, Michael, Grant Ujifusa, and Douglas Matthews, *The Almanac of American Politics 1974* and *1976* (New York: E.P. Dutton & Co., 1973, 1975), pp. 987-88, 833-34.

_____, *The Almanac of American Politics 1978* (New York: E.P. Dutton & Co., 1977), pp. 75-76.

Barone, Michael, "Wright, Coelho and the S & L Fiasco," *U.S. News & World Report*, June 12, 1989, pp. 21-22.

Barrett, Paul M. and David Rogers, "A Timely Measure Gains Ratification after Two Centuries," *The Wall Street Journal*, May 8, 1992, p. A10.

Barry, John M., *The Ambition and the Power: The Fall of Jim Wright: A True Story of Washington* (New York: Penguin Books, 1989).

Baruch, Jeremiah, "An Achieving Heart: Phil Burton, Practical Liberal," *Commonweal*, May 6, 1983, pp. 261-263.

Benenson, Bob, "House Postpones GATT Vote in Last-Minute Drama," *Congressional Quarterly Weekly Report*, October 8, 1994, p. 2856.

Biggs, Jeffrey R., tape recordings of the *Statement by the Honorable Thomas S. Foley before the Senate Foreign Relations Committee*, September 24, 1997; and November 6, 1997 State Department swearing-in ceremony.

_____, "The Changing Landscape of Congress," in Elaine S. Povich, *Partners & Adversaries: The Contentious Connection Between Congress & the Media* (Arlington, Va.: The Freedom Forum, Inc., 1996), pp. 71-75.

Biskupic, Joan, "Constitutional Questions Remain," *Congressional Quarterly Weekly Report*, January 12, 1991, p. 70.

_____, "Civil Rights: Bill Passes House, not Muster; Next Chance is in Senate," *Congressional Quarterly Weekly Report*, June 8, 1991, pp. 1498-1503.

_____, "Letter-Writing and Campaigns," *Congressional Quarterly Weekly Report*, March 9, 1991, p. 605.

_____, "NRA, Gun-Control Supporters Take Aim at Swing Voters," *Congressional Quarterly Weekly Report*, March 9, 1991, pp. 604-607.

_____, "Sponsors of Gun-Control Bills Vie for Procedural Edge," *Congressional Quarterly Weekly Report*, May 4, 1991, pp. 1134-1135.

Blow, Richard, "Foley Flexes," *Mother Jones*, July/August 1993, pp. 30-43.

Blumenthal, Les (Associated Press), "Foley Success as a Speaker," *The Spokane Daily Chronicle*, May 26, 1988, p. A1.

Blumenthal, Sidney, "Flatliners," *The New Republic*, May 20, 1991, pp. 16-18.

Bolling, Richard, *House Out of Order* (New York: Dutton, 1965).

Bonino, Rick, "At Least (Nice Guys) Foley, Hebner Agree on One Item," *The Spokesman-Review*, October 15, 1984, p. A1.

_____, "Foley Claims Another Term on Solid Win," *The Spokesman-Review*, November 7, 1984, p. C1.

_____, "Foley, Morrison Predict Reagan Changes," *The Spokesman-Review*, November 4, 1982, p. A1.

_____, "Foley, Alton Ask Probe of Campaign 'Low Blows,'" *The Spokesman-Review*, October 31, 1978, p. A9.

_____, "Foley: 11th Election," *The Spokesman-Review*, October 23, 1984, p. A1.

_____, "Washington Wives Brief Democrats," *The Spokesman-Review*, June 30, 1976, p. A23.

Borger, Gloria, "Anatomy of a Smear," *U.S. News & World Report*, June 19, 1989, pp. 40-41.

_____. "The Rise of the Accidental Speaker," *U.S. World & News Report*, June 5, 1989, p. 39.

Borger, Gloria and Steven V. Roberts, "Who Won the Ethics War?: Now that Wright has Gone, the Republican Strategy is at Risk," *U.S. News & World Report*, June 12, 1989, pp. 18-20.

Boutwell, Florence, *The Spokane Valley: A History of the Growing Years* (Spokane: The Arthur H. Clark Co., 1995), Vol. 2.

Broder, David S., "Foley Calls Spendthrift Charge Against Congress a 'Big Lie,'" *The Washington Post*, August 26, 1992, p. A2.

_____, "Hill Democrats Vote as One: New Era of Unity or Short-Term Honeymoon?" *The Washington Post*, March 14, 1993, pp. A1, A6.

Brooks, David, "The New Bleeding Hearts: Will 'Compassionate' Conservatives Succeed in Reinventing the Right?" *The Washington Post*, February 16, 1997, p. C1.

Brown, Lynne P., and Robert L. Peabody, "Patterns of Succession in House Democratic Leadership: The Choices of Wright, Foley, Coelho, 1986" paper presented at the annual meeting of the American Political Science Association, Chicago, 1987.

_____, "Patterns of Succession in House Democratic Leadership: Foley, Gephardt, and Gray, 1989," in Robert L. Peabody and Nelson W. Polsby, eds., in *New Perspectives on the House of Representatives* (Baltimore: Johns Hopkins University Press, 4th ed., 1992).

Bruck, Connie, "The Politics of Perception," *The New Yorker*, October 9, 1994, p. 74.

Calmes, Jackie, "Countdown to Vote on Clinton Plan: Negotiators Will Forgive Mitchell if he Delivers Senate," *The Wall Street Journal*, August 5, 1993, p. A14.

_____, "Reagan's Address Repeats Familiar Themes," *Congressional Quarterly Weekly Report*, February 8, 1986, p. 260.

Camden, Jim, "Foley Crushes Wakefield in 3-to-1 Victory," *The Spokane Daily Chronicle*, November 5, 1986, p. A3.

_____, "Foley, Old Pal in Glare of Spotlight," *The Spokesman-Review*, April 27, 1988, p. B1.

_____, "Foley Praises Congress' Victories while Derby Says 'Fire the Coach,'" *The Spokesman-Review*, November 2, 1990, p. B1.

_____, "New Speaker Urges Colleagues to Decide Issues without Rancor," *The Spokesman-Review*, June 7, 1989, pp. A1, A4.

_____, "On Nearly All Debate Topics, Foley, Wakefield Disagree," *The Spokesman-Review*, October 20, 1986, p. A1.

_____, "Tom Foley Rolls to Easy House Wins," *The Spokesman-Review*, November 9, 1988, p. A1.

_____, "Tom Foley's Mother, Helen, Dies in Spokane at Age 88," *The Spokesman-Review*, January 6, 1990, p. A1.

_____, "Tom Foley's Approval Rating Slips," *The Spokesman-Review*, May 8, 1992, p. B1.

_____, "Write-in GOP Candidates Likely to Join Foley on Ballot," *The Spokesman-Review*, September 20, 1990, p. B2.

Carlson, Margaret, "Fallen Angel: Tony Coehlo's Deal with the Devil," *The New Republic*, June 12, 1989, p. 18.

Cassata, Donna, "Agenda for 105th Unlikely to Follow that of 104th," *Congressional Quarterly Weekly Report*, November 2, 1996, pp. 3123-3124.

_____, "Swift Progress of 'Contract' Inspires Awe and Concern," *Congressional Quarterly Weekly Report*, April 1, 1995, pp. 909-912.

Cheney, Richard B. and Lynne V. Cheney, *Kings of the Hill: Power and Personality in the House of Representatives* (New York: Continuum, 1983).

Cloud, David S., "GOP and Interest Groups Dig in to Dump Gift Ban in Senate," *Congressional Quarterly Weekly Report*, October 8, 1994, pp. 2854-2855.

_____, "New Levies on Gas and the Rich Would Yield $240 Billion," *Congressional Quarterly Weekly Report*, August 7, 1993, pp. 2132-2133.

Clymer, Adam, "Clinton Discusses Legislative Moves with Congressmen," *The New York Times*, November 16, 1992, p. A1.

_____, "Democrats Set Up Priorities as 103rd Congress Convenes," *The New York Times*, January 6, 1993, p. A16.

_____, "Foley Urges Republicans to Meet with Democrats on Health Care," *The New York Times*, September 14, 1994, p. A13.

_____, "Problems Are Harder Now, House Speaker Says," *The New York Times*, August 29, 1993, p. A6.

_____, "The Revolution is Dead, Long Live the Revolution," *The New York Times*, November 2, 1997, p. A1.

_____, "A Toppled Foley Gives Up the Gavel: After 30 Years in the House, Farewell and a Message of Gratitude," *The New York Times*, November 30, 1994, p. A10.

Cohen, Richard E. and William Schneider, "Epitaph for an Era," *National Journal*, January 14, 1995, p. 83.

Cohen, Richard E., "Faulting Foley," *National Journal*, August 10, 1991, p. 1967.

_____, "Foley Shows a Firm Hand at the Helm," *National Journal*, August 14, 1993, p. 2044.

Congressional Quarterly Staff, "Profile: Thomas S. Foley—Heavy Weather," *American Caucus*, April 13-April 26, 1992.

Congressional Quarterly Weekly Report staff:

    —"Campaign Finance: Public Funding Fading Fast," March 13, 1993, p. 573.

    —"Key Votes: Economy, Events Overseas, Drive '91 Confrontations," December 28, 1991, pp. 3763-3771.

    —"Term Limits: Opponents Win First Round," February 12, 1994, p. 342.

Connelly, Joel and Michael Paulson, "Gung-ho Democrats Slam GOP Contract," *The Post-Intelligencer*, October 15, 1994, p. A1.

Connelly, Joel, "Foley Displays Clout as He Prepares to Run for 16th House Term," *The* (Seattle) *Post-Intelligencer*, May 24, 1994, p. A1.

_____, "Foley Still Up to Challenges of Office," *The* (Seattle) *Post-Intelligencer*, April 24, 1992, p. A1.

_____, "Nethercutt Keeps His Focus on Foley," *The* (Seattle) *Post-Intelligencer*, October 6, 1994, p. A1.

_____, "Region to Feel Energy Tax Bite, Foley Warns," *The* (Seattle) *Post-Intelligencer*, April 13, 1993, p. A1.

Connolly, Ceci, "Legislation Goes Overboard as Members Eye the Exits," *Congressional Quarterly Weekly Report*, October 1, 1994, pp. 2753-2755.

Cook, Rhodes, "From Mentors to Self-Promotion," *Congressional Quarterly Weekly Report*, March 12, 1994, p. 577.

Cook, Timothy E., *Governing with the News: The News Media as a Political Institution* (Chicago and London: The University of Chicago Press, 1998).

_____, *Making Laws and Making News: Media Strategies in the U.S. House of Representatives* (Washington, D.C.: Brookings Institution, 1989).

Cooper, Kenneth J., "House Democratic Leaders Travel to Freshman Class," *The Washington Post*, November 9, 1992, p. A8.

Corn, David, "The Battle for the House" *The Nation*, November 11, 1996, p. 12.

Cranford, John R., "House Approves Bill to Refill Coffers for Bailout Effort," *Congressional Quarterly Weekly Report*, May 16, 1991, pp. 653-656.

Cunningham, Kitty, "Good-bye 'Generational Gap,'" *Congressional Quarterly Weekly Report*, October 9, 1993, pp. 2714-2718.

Davidson, Roger H. and Walter J. Oleszek, *Congress Against Itself* (Bloomington and London: Indiana University Press, 1977).

Davidson, Roger H., Susan Webb Hammond, and Raymond W. Smock, eds. *Masters of the House: Congressional Leaders over Two Centuries* (Boulder, Co.: Westview Press, 1998).

Davidson, Roger, "The New Centralization on Capitol Hill," *Review of Politics* 50 (Summer 1988), pp. 346-364.

Dionne, E.J., Jr., "President Supports Atwater in Furor over Foley Memo," *The New York Times*, June 9, 1989, p. A23.

Doherty, Carroll J., "Bush is Given Authorization to Use Force Against Iraq," *Congressional Quarterly Weekly Report*, January 12, 1991, p. 66.

_____, "Congress Applauds President from Sidelines of War," *Congressional Quarterly Weekly Report*, January 19, 1991, p. 179.

Donovan, Beth, "Black Caucus: PAC Funds a Must for Minorities," *Congressional Quarterly Weekly Report*, September 25, 1993, pp. 2523-2526.

_____, "Campaign Finance: Clinton Courts Fellow Democrats in Drive for Major Overhaul," *Congressional Quarterly Weekly Report*, February 6, 1993, p. 250.

_____, "Clinton's Appeal to the People Carries. . . Short-Term Gains, Long-Term Risks," *Congressional Quarterly Weekly Report*, August 20, 1994, pp. 2450-2451.

_____, "Constitutional Doubts Bedevil Hasty Campaign Finance Bill," *Congressional Quarterly Weekly Report*, August 14, 1993, pp. 2215-2218.

_____, "Democrats as Divided as Ever on Eve of First Markup," *Congressional Quarterly Weekly Report*, February 26, 1994, pp. 475-478.

_____, "Democrats' Overhaul Bill Dies on Senate Procedural Votes," *Congressional Quarterly Weekly Report*, October 1, 1994, pp. 2757-2758.

_____, "House Takes First Big Step in Overhauling System," *Congressional Quarterly Weekly Report*, November 27, 1993, pp. 3246-3249.

_____, "Maverick Chairmen Forgiven as Clinton Reworks Bill," *Congressional Quarterly Weekly Report*, June 12, 1993, p. 1451-1452.

_____, "A New-Look Congress Begins with a Shadow of the Old," *Congressional Quarterly Weekly Report*, January 9, 1993, pp. 57-58.

_____, "Partial Victory for Democrats on Delegate Voting," *Congressional Quarterly Weekly Report*, March 13, 1993, p. 573.

_____, "Power in the Twilight," *Congressional Quarterly Weekly Report*, March 12, 1994, p. 578.

_____, "Republicans Plan Filibusters, Imperiling Senate Schedule," *Congressional Quarterly Weekly Report*, September 24, 1994, p. 2655.

_____, "Senate Passes Campaign Finance by Gutting Public Funding," *Congressional Quarterly Weekly Report*, June 19, 1993, pp. 1533-1540.

Drew, Elizabeth, *Showdown: The Struggle Between the Gingrich Congress and the Clinton White House* (New York: Simon & Schuster, 1996).

Dullenty, Jim, "Power in Washington: Foley on the Brink of National Leadership," *The Spokesman-Review*, July 18, 1978, p. 28; *Spokane Daily Chronicle*, July 18, 1978, p. 6.

Duncan, Phil, ed., *Politics in America 1992* (Washington, D.C.: *Congressional Quarterly* Inc.,1991), pp. 439-443, 766-769, 846-849, 1440-1443.

Dunham, Richard S., "The Hill's Young Turks," *Business Week*, June 1, 1992, p. 79.

Eastern Washington State Historical Society, *Viewing the Past* (Spokane: Eastern Washington State Historical Society, 1977).

Egan, Timothy, "Federal Judge Strikes Down Law Limiting the Terms of Lawmakers," *The New York Times*, February 11, 1994, p. A20.

_____, "Foley, Behind in Polls, Plays Gingrich Card," *The New York Times*, October 26, 1994, p. A26.

_____, "Foley's Lawyers Argue Against Limits on Terms," *The New York Times*, January 12, 1994, p. A10.

_____, "Foley's Roots: Of Thin Pork, Thick Wheat," *The New York Times*, June 8, 1989, p. B11.

_____, "The No. 1 Congressman and His No. 1 Test," *The New York Times*, October 29, 1994, p. A7.

_____, "Poor Showing by Foley Hints at Trouble on Nov. 8," *The New York Times*, September 22, 1994, p. A1.

_____, "The Speaker Facing Well-Financed Rival," *The New York Times*, October 31, 1992, p. A6.

Ehrenhalt, Alan, ed. and Robert E. Healy, assoc. ed., *Politics in America* (Washington, D.C.: *Congressional Quarterly* Press, 1982).

Ehrenhalt, Alan, ed., *Politics in America: Members of Congress in Washington and at Home* (Washington, D.C.: *Congressional Quarterly* Press, 1981).

_____, *Politics in America: The 100th Congress* (Washington, D.C.: *Congressional Quarterly* Inc., 1987), p. 1283.

Ehrenhalt, Alan, "Media, Power Shifts Dominate O'Neill's House," *Congressional Quarterly Weekly Report*, September 13, 1986, pp. 2131-2138.

_____, "Media, Power Shifts Dominate O'Neill's House," *Congressional Quarterly Weekly Report*, September 13, 1986, pp. 2131-2138.

Elliott House, Karen, "Quiet Persuader: How Rep. Foley Played a Key Role in Shaping Disputed Farm Bill," *The Wall Street Journal*, September 14, 1977, p. 1.

Elving, Ronald D., *Conflict & Compromise: How Congress Makes the Law* (New York: Simon & Schuster, 1995).

_____, "The Quiet Climb to Leadership," *Congressional Quarterly Weekly Report*, March 18, 1989, p. 558.

Evans, C. Lawrence and Walter J. Oleszek, *Congress Under Fire: Reform Politics and the Republican Majority* (Boston and New York: Houghton Mifflin Company, 1997).

Fenno, Richard F., Jr., *Home Style: House Members in Their Districts* (Boston: Little, Brown, 1978).

_____, "The Internal Distribution of Influence: The House," in David B. Truman, ed., *The Congress and America's Future* (Englewood Cliffs, N.J.: Prentice-Hall, 1965).

Fessler, Pamela, "Bush's Sudden Shift on Taxes Gets Budget Talks Moving," *Congressional Quarterly Weekly Report,* June 30, 1990, pp. 2029-2032.

_____, "Read My Lips: No Conditions, Bush Tells Democrats," *Congressional Quarterly Weekly Report*, May 12, 1990, pp. 1457-1463.

Fiorina, Morris, and Kenneth Shepsle, "Formal Theories of Leadership: Agents, Agenda-Setters, and Entrepreneurs," in Bryan D. Jones, ed., *Leadership and Politics* (Lawrence: University of Kansas Press, 1989).

Fisher, Jack E., "Foley, Gamble Square Off," *The Spokesman-Review*, October 25, 1970, p. A8.

Fisher, Louis, "The 'Contract with America': What It Really Means," *The New York Review of Books*, June 22, 1995, pp. 20-24.

Floyd, Doug, "Candidates Crowding Foley for 5th District Seat," *The Spokane Daily Chronicle*, September 9, 1980, p. 3.

Foerstel, Karen, "His Likely Successor Has Taken Different Path," *Roll Call*, June 1,1989, p. 4.

Foley, Thomas S., *Press Conference with the Speaker of the House*, The Capitol, U.S House of Representatives, Foley Archives, Washington State University Library, Pullman, Washington:
> —September 12, 1989, 9:46 a.m. - 12:02 p.m.
> —September 13, 1989, 9:47 a.m. - 10:02 a.m.
> —November 1, 1989, 9:46 a.m. - 10:00 a.m.
> —April 3, 1990, 12:28 p.m. - 12:32 p.m.
> —May 15, 1990, 11:53 a.m.- 12:01 p.m.
> —May 24, 1990; 10:48 a.m. - 11:00 a.m.
> —February 5, 1992, 1:32 p.m. - 1:49 p.m.
> —February 27, 1992, 9:48 a.m.- 10:00 a.m.

—March 11, 1992, 1:45 p.m.- 2:00 p.m.

—March 25, 1992, 1:49 p.m. - 2:01 p.m.

—April 8, 1992, 10:48 a.m.- 11:01 a.m.

—June 29, 1992, 11:45 a.m.-12:01 p.m.

Follett, Mary Parker, *The Speaker of the House of Representatives* (New York: Bert Franklin Reprints, 1974; originally published 1896).

Fuerbringer, Jonathan, "Men in the News: 3 Democrats Rise in 100th," *The New York Times*, December 9, 1986, p. B17.

Galvin, Thomas, "Pressed by Clinton's Example, Leaders Promise Cutbacks," *Congressional Quarterly Weekly Report*, February 20, 1993, pp. 287-288.

Gettinger, Stephen, "Committees at Work: The New Milieu," *Congressional Quarterly Committee Guide* (Washington, D.C.: *Congressional Quarterly* Inc., May 1, 1992), pp. 7-8.

Gillespie, Ed and Bob Schellhas, eds., *Contract with America: The Bold Plan by Rep. Newt Gingrich, Rep. Dick Armey and the House Republicans to Change the Nation* (New York: Time Books, 1994).

Gorey, Hayes, "Waiting for Opportunity to Knock: Tom Foley is the Accidental Tourist of American Politics," *Time*, June 5, 1989, p. 34.

Granat, Diane, and *Congressional Quarterly* staff, "Democratic and GOP Leaders Named for the 99th Congress," *Congressional Quarterly Weekly Report*, December 8, 1984, pp. 3051-3057.

_____, "On Balance, A Year of Taking the Initiative," *Congressional Quarterly Weekly Report*, December 28, 1985, pp. 2727-2747.

_____, "Six Seeking House Democratic Whip Position," *Congressional Quarterly Weekly Report*, November 30, 1985, pp. 2498-2502.

_____, "Televised Partisan Skirmishes Erupt in House," *Congressional Quarterly Weekly Report*, February 11, 1984, pp. 246-249.

Gwirtzman, Milton S., "The Supreme Problem: Why the Court's Previous Rulings Prevent Real Change," *The Washington Post*, January 12, 1997, p. C3.

Hager, George and David S. Cloud, "Democrats Tie Their Fate to Clinton's Budget Bill," *Congressional Quarterly Weekly Report*, August 7, 1993, pp. 2122-2129.

Hager, George, "Arm-Twisting Yields House Win for Spending-Control Bill," *Congressional Quarterly Weekly Report*, May 1, 1993, p. 1069.

_____, "The Budget Package: 1993 Deal—Remembrance of Things Past," *Congressional Quarterly Weekly Report*, August 7, 1993, pp. 2130-2131.

_____, "Defiant House Rebukes Leaders; New Round of Fights Begins," *Congressional Quarterly Weekly Report*, October 6, 1990, pp. 3183-3188.

_____, "Finding Political Gain in a Budget Revolt," *Congressional Quarterly Weekly Report*, February 8, 1997, p. 390.

_____, "Just Hours from Fiscal Chaos, Summit Strained for a Deal," *Congressional Quarterly Weekly Report*, September 29, 1990, pp. 3093-3100.

Hanson, Christopher, "Foley May Fear GOP Foe: Nethercutt Appeals to Crossover Voters, If He Wins Primary," *The* (Seattle) *Post-Intelligencer*, September 15, 1994, p. B1.

_____, "On the Hill: Pay Dirt," *The New Republic*, December 25, 1989, pp. 10-11.

_____, "Perot Hits Spokane, Lights into Foley," *The* (Seattle)*Post-Intelligencer*, November 5, 1994, p. A1.

Harden, Blaine, "Campaign '96: Dole—Family Leave is Anti-Business," *The Washington Post*, September 8, 1996, p. A14.

Harper, Robert, "Republicans Back Off from Campaign to Unseat Foley," *The Spokesman-Review*, August 26, 1979, p. B4.

Harvey, Chris, "A Speaker Who is Well-Spoken Of," *INSIGHT* (*Washington Times*), December 18, 1989, p. 22.

Healey, Jon and Chuck Alston, "Stimulus Bill Prevails in House, but Senate Battle Awaits," *Congressional Quarterly Weekly Report*, March 20, 1993, pp. 652.

Healey, Jon, "Democrats Look to Salvage Part of Stimulus Plan," *Congressional Quarterly Weekly Report*, April 24, 1993, pp. 1001-1004.

Hertzberg, Hendrik, "TRB from Washington: Atwatergate," *The New Republic*, July 3, 1989, p. 4.

Hicket, Elizabeth, with Cathryn Donohoe, "Woman of the House: Why Hill Insiders are Hell-bent for Heather, the Speaker's Wife," *The Washington Times*, March 30, 1992, pp. D1-D2.

Higgins, H. Henry, "Party Chairmen Voice Final Pleas," *The Spokane Daily Chronicle*, November 4, 1966, p. A18.

Hook, Janet and *Congressional Quarterly* Staff, "Democrats Hail 'Productivity,' but Image Problems Remain," *Congressional Quarterly Weekly Report*, December 11, 1993, pp. 3355-3357.

_____, "Reforms Are Hard to Come by As 'Reform Month' Looms," *Congressional Quarterly Weekly Report*, October 2, 1993, pp. 2613-2618.

_____, "A Year of Big Decisions Looms after Year of Big Promises," *Congressional Quarterly Weekly Report*, January 8, 1994, pp. 5-14.

Hook, Janet with Beth Donovan, "A Beleaguered Speaker Seeks Quick Reforms in Operations," *Congressional Quarterly Weekly Report*, April 4, 1992, p. 857.

Hook, Janet, "Anatomy of a Budget Showdown: The Limits of Leaders' Clout," *Congressional Quarterly Weekly Report*, October 6, 1990, p. 3191.

_____, "Arkansas Case a Crucible in Term Limit Debate, *Congressional Quarterly Weekly Report*, June 25, 1994, p. 1679.

_____, "Clinton Sets Get-Tough Agenda, Hard Line on Social Reforms," *Congressional Quarterly Weekly Report*, January 19, 1994, pp. 153-156.

_____, "Conference Without Walls," *Congressional Quarterly Weekly Report*, August 7, 1993, p. 2128.

_____, "Congress Heads for Grand Legislative Finale," *Congressional Quarterly Weekly Report*, August 23, 1986, p. 1960.

_____, "Court Ruling on Budget Law Puts Spotlight on GAO Role," *Congressional Quarterly Weekly Report*, February 15, 1986, pp. 298-300.

_____, "Foley Caught Between His Party. . . and His Constituency on Gun Control," *Congressional Quarterly Weekly Report*, June 8, 1991, pp. 1198-1199.

_____, "Foley: Rising to Top by Accident and Design," *Congressional Quarterly Weekly Report*, March 8, 1986, p. 549.

_____, "House GOP Hones a Sharper Edge as Michel Turns in His Sword," *Congressional Quarterly Weekly Report*, October 9, 1993, pp. 2714-2718.

_____, "Mitchell's Retirement Roils Senate Outlook," *Congressional Quarterly Weekly Report*, March 5, 1994, p. 517.

_____, "O'Neill Changed Speaker's Role and Helped Remake House," *Congressional Quarterly Weekly Report*, January 8, 1994, pp. 16-17.

_____, "Pay Raise is Killed, but the Headaches Persist," *Congressional Quarterly Weekly Report*, February 11, 1989, pp. 261-267.

_____, "Speaker Foley's Fortunes Rise as Clinton Gains Momentum: Challenges to His Power Position Have Faded Though He has Kept His Low-Key Style," *Congressional Quarterly Weekly Report*, August 15, 1992, p. 2429.

_____, "The State of the Union: Clinton Sets Get-Tough Agenda, Hard Line on Social Reforms," *Congressional Quarterly Weekly Report*, January 29, 1994, pp. 153-156.

————, "Voters' Hostility is Shaping the Business of Congress," *Congressional Quarterly Weekly Report*, April 2, 1994, pp. 785-789.

Hymel, Gary, "What is a Congressional Staffer," included in Jeffrey B. Trammel and Steve Piacente, *The Almanac of the Unelected: Staff of the U.S. Congress 1993* (Washington, D.C.: The Almanac of the Unelected, Inc., 1993).

Idelson, Holly with Beth Donovan, "The Foley Factor," *Congressional Quarterly Weekly Report*, October 1, 1994, p. 2754.

Idelson, Holly, "Candidates Seeing Term Limits as a Top Vote-Getting Tactic," *Congressional Quarterly Weekly Report*, October 15, 1994, pp. 2969-2971.

————, "Clinton, Democrats Scramble to Save Anti-Crime Bill," *Congressional Quarterly Weekly Report*, August 13, 1994, pp. 2340-2343.

————, "For Some Republicans, a Tough Call," *Congressional Quarterly Weekly Report*, August 13, 1994, p. 2341.

————, "Review to be Turning Point for Term Limits Issue," *Congressional Quarterly Weekly Report*, October 1, 1994, pp. 2802-2806.

Jacobs, John, *A Rage for Justice: The Passion and Politics of Phillip Burton* (Berkeley and Los Angeles: University of California Press, 1995).

Jacobson, Gary C. and Samuel Kernell, *Strategy and Choice in Congressional Elections* (New Haven, Ct.: Yale University Press, 2nd ed., 1983).

Jacobson, Gary C., *The Electoral Origins of Divided Government: Competition in U.S. House Elections, 1946-1988* (Boulder, Co.: Westview Press, 1990).

Jacoby, Mary, "Foley Investment Adviser Fined by SEC," *Roll Call*, October 5, 1995, p. 1.

Jamieson, Kathleen Hall, *Executive Summary of Testimony by the Dean of the Annenberg School for Communication, University of Pennsylvania, before the Subcommittee on Rules and Organization of the House, April 17, 1997.*

Jehl, Douglas, "Battle on Crime Bill Tests Clinton's Strategic Skills," *The New York Times*, August 23, 1994, pp. A1, A14.

Johnson, David, "Foley Denies His Wife Focus of Inquiry," *The New York Times*, March 26, 1992, reprinted in *The Spokesman-Review*, March 26, 1992, p. A1.

"Judge Foley: A Long Distinguished Career," *SIGNUM of Gonzaga University*, May 1974, p. 9.

Kamen, Al, "A Farewell Curveball for State's Spokesman," *The Washington Post*, October 27, 1997, p. A23.

Kaplan, Dave, "House Democrats in Danger: The Question is How Much," *Congressional Quarterly Weekly Report*, October 8, 1994, pp. 2901-2905.

————, "Incumbents Call It Quits at Record Clip," *Congressional Quarterly Weekly Report*, February 19, 1994, pp. 382-415.

Kenworthy, Tom, "Keep the Bums In!," *The Washington Post*, April 26, 1992, p. C5.

————, "Trimmed Down, Pumped Up: The Dawn of a New Tom Foley," *The Washington Post*, June 16, 1991, p. A7.

King, Anthony, "Running Scared," *The Atlantic Monthly*, January 1997, pp. 41-61.

Klein, Joe, "Letter from Washington: The Hug," *The New Yorker*, December 16, 1996, pp. 53-54.

Koszczuk, Jackie, "Republicans Struggle to Leave Ethics Probe Behind Them," *Congressional Quarterly Weekly Report*, January 25, 1997, p. 228.

Krauss, Clifford, "Clinton's Point Men Face Doubts about Their Edge," *The New York Times*, February 22, 1993, p. A14.

————, "House, 255 to 175, Votes to Restrict Campaign Spending," *The New York Times*, November 23, 1993, pp. A1, B8.

————, "Oklahoman Who Opposed Foley to Lose House Intelligence Post," *The New York Times*, January 9, 1993, p. A1.

Kuntz, Phil, "Defensive Members Move to Cut Special Breaks for Congress," *Congressional Quarterly Weekly Report*, November 2, 1991, p. 3181.

_____, "Democrats' Defeat Raises Specter of Gridlock," *Congressional Quarterly Weekly Report*, August 13, 1994, p. 2311.

_____, "Hard-Fought Crime Bill Battle Spoils Field for Health Care," *Congressional Quarterly Weekly Report*, August 27, 1994, p. 2485.

_____, "Stiff Limits on Gifts to Members Will Ride on Final Lobby Bill," *Congressional Quarterly Weekly Report*, September 24, 1994, pp. 2656-2657.

Langdon, Steve, "Clinton Prevails on Capital Hill Despite Poor Showing in Polls," *Congressional Quarterly Weekly Report*, September 25, 1993, p. 2527.

Lemon, John J., "Foley to Leave Court Post," *The Spokane Daily Chronicle*, March 27, 1974.

Lichter, S. Robert and David R. Amundson, "Less News is Worse News: Television News Coverage of Congress, 1972-1992" in Thomas E. Mann and Norman J. Ornstein, eds., *Congress, the Press, and the Public* (Washington, D.C.: American Enterprise Institute and the Brookings Institution, 1994)

Lynch, Jim, "Foley Counters Charge He's Out of Touch," *The Spokesman Review,* October 19, 1992, p. A1.

_____, "Foley Says Stock Deals Didn't Violate Rules," *The Spokesman-Review*, August 3, 1993, p. B1.

_____, "Foley's Army Carries Clout: Aides Silent but Powerful," *The Spokesman-Review*, March 27, 1994, p. A1.

_____, "4 GOP Candidates Dueling to Be the One to Challenge Foley," *The Spokesman-Review*, August 23, 1992, p. B1.

_____, "Keeping House: Tom Foley Stands Above Tumult," *The Spokesman-Review*, October 18, 1992, p. A1.

_____, "An Old Friend's Loyalty Pays Off Big for Foley," *The Spokesman-Review*, August 1, 1993, p. A1.

_____, "Sonneland Only Foe to Give Foley a Race," *The Spokesman-Review*, October 20, 1992, p. A1.

Madison, Christopher, "The Heir Presumptive," *National Journal*, April 29, 1989, p. 1035.

Mayhew, David R., *Divided We Govern: Party Control, Lawmaking, and Investigations, 1946-1990* (New Haven and London: Yale University Press, 1991).

McClure, Paul, ed., *Washington Information Directory 1996-1997* (Washington, D.C.: Congressional Quarterly Inc., 1996).

McGurn, William, "On the Scene," *National Review*, November 10, 1989, pp. 22-23.

Miller, Robert S. and Donald O. Dewey, *Glendale Law Review*, v. 10, nos. 1-2 (1991), pp. 91-109.

Moody, Dick, "Foley Battling Same Charges," *The Spokane Daily Chronicle*, October 13, 1982, p. 1.

_____, "Foley Blasts 'Falsehoods' in Sonneland Ad Claims," *The Spokane Daily Chronicle*, October 22, 1980, p. 3.

_____, "Foley in Bulls-eye," *The Spokane Daily Chronicle*, January 7, 1982, p. 1.

_____, "Foley Survives Mutiny," *The Spokane Daily Chronicle*, November 5, 1980, p. 36.

Moritz, Charles, ed., *Current Biography Yearbook 1960, 1987, 1989* (New York: H.W. Wilson Co., 1960, 1987, 1989).

Morlin, Bill, "Foley Starts Sprint Toward '80," *The Spokane Daily Chronicle*, July 7, 1979, p. 3.

Morris, Richard and Helen Dewar, "Approval of Congress Hits All-Time Low, Poll Finds," *The Washington Post*, March 20, 1992, p. A16.

Mouw, Calvin J. and Michael B. Mackuen, "The Strategic Agenda in Legislative Politics," *American Political Science Review*, Vol. 86, No. 1 (March 1992), pp. 87-105.

Neff, Robert C. and Amy Borrus, "The Wrong Man to Send to Tokyo?" *Business Week*, May 12, 1997, p. 56.

The New Republic, editorials:

—"Bushwaterism," July 27 & 24, 1989, p. 5.

—"Tom Foley, Gun Nut," January 28, 1991, pp. 7-8.

—"Now, Govern," April 1, 1991, pp. 7-9.

Newhouse, John, "Profiles: The Navigator," *The New Yorker*, April 10, 1989, pp. 48-50ff.

O'Neill, Tip (Thomas P.) with William Novak, *Man of the House: The Life and Political Memoirs of Speaker Tip O'Neill* (New York: Random House, 1987).

O'Sullivan, Kathleen, "Judge Ralph E. Foley: Veteran Jurist Firm, but Gentle," *The Spokesman-Review*, March 19, 1961, p. 18.

Oleszek, Walter J., *Congressional Procedures and the Policy Process* (Washington, D.C.: Congressional Quarterly Press, 1984).

Ornstein, Norman J. and Amy L. Schenkenberg, "The 1995 Congress: The First Hundred Days and Beyond," *Political Science Quarterly*, V. 10, No. 2 (Summer 1995), pp. 183-206.

Ornstein, Norman, "A Progress Report on GOP Reforms," *Roll Call*, December 5, 1994, p. 5.

Parry, Robert (Associated Press), "Foley Fact-Finding Mission Leaves for Grenada," *The Spokane Daily Chronicle*, November 4, 1983, p. 1.

Patterson, Kelly D. and David B. Magleby, "Public Support for Congress," *Public Opinion Quarterly* (Winter 1992), pp. 543-544.

Peabody, Robert L., *Leadership in Congress: Stability, Succession, and Change* (Boston: Little, Brown, 1976).

Peck, Chris, "The Fifth Will Have the Final Say on Foley," *The Spokesman-Review*, October 9, 1994.

Peters, Ronald M., Jr., *The American Speakership: The Office in Historical Perspective* (Baltimore: Johns Hopkins University Press, 1990).

Phillips, Kevin P., *The Emerging Republican Majority* (Garden City, N.Y.: Anchor Books, 1970).

Pizzo, Stephen, "Lions into Lambs: Perks and Plum Assignments Muted Freshmen's Call to Reform," *Mother Jones*, July/August 1993, p. 40.

Plotke, David, "Against Government: The Contract with America," *DISSENT*, v. 42 (Summer 1995), pp. 348-353.

Polsby, Nelson W., "The Institutionalization of the U.S. House of Representatives," *American Political Science Review*, 1968, Vol. 62 (March 1968), pp. 144-169.

Powers, Dorothy Rochon, *Heritage from Heroes* (Spokane: Fairmount Memorial Association, 1993).

————, "Judge Foley Remembered as a 'Gentle Man' of Courage, Fairness," *The Spokesman-Review*, May 12, 1985, p. A13.

Prager, Mike, "NRA Commits $50,000 for Ads Against Foley: Assault Rifle Ban Angers Group," *The Spokesman-Review*, October 13, 1994, p. A1.

Preecs, Bart, "Walking Political Tightrope, Foley's Set to Battle Again," *The Spokesman-Review*, August 9, 1981, p. B1.

Price, David E., "From Outsider to Insider," in Lawrence C. Dodd and Bruce I Oppenheimer, eds., *Congress Reconsidered* (Washington, D.C.: Congressional Quarterly Press, 4th ed., 1989).

Rapp, David, "Farm Bill Conferees Accept New Target-Price Programs," *Congressional Quarterly Weekly Report*, December 14, 1985, p. 2656.

Reich, Robert B., *Locked in the Cabinet* (New York: Alfred A. Knopf, 1997).

Richardson, Representative Bill of New Mexico, Extension of Remarks, *Congressional Record*, April 10, 1991, p. 1180.

Roberts, Steven V. with Michael Barone, "After Wright's Fall: The Bush-Foley-Mitchell Team Will Thrive on Coalition Politics," *U.S. News & World Report*, June 5, 1989, pp. 34-35.

Rogers, David and John E. Yang, "Foley Steps in as New Speaker of the House, Casting Himself as a Healer for 2 Parties," *The Wall Street Journal*, June 7, 1989, p. A34.

Rogers, David, "After Years of Gridlock and Scandals, Foley Appears Poised to Fulfill Potential as Speaker," *The Wall Street Journal*, December 4, 1992, p. A10.

_____, "Foley Says GOP Aims to Scuttle Any Health Bill," *The Wall Street Journal*, July 27, 1994, pp. A2, A5.

_____, ". . . While Foley-Gephardt 'Tag Team' Tries to Keep House Members in Line," *The Wall Street Journal*, August 5, 1993, p. A14.

Roll Call, editorials:

—"The Gang of Seven," August 17, 1992, p. 4.

—"A Mensch," January 17, 1991, p. 4.

—"New Procedures in Place after Bank Audit," February 8, 1990, p. 4.

Rollins, Ed with Tom Defrank, *Bare Knuckles and Back Rooms: My Life in American Politics* (New York: Broadway Books, 1996).

Romano, Lois, "Tom Foley's Right Hand: Behind the Scenes in the House, Wife and Top Aide Heather," *The Washington Post*, February 9, 1990, pp. D1-D2.

Rose, Robert L., "Eastern Label Untrue, Foley Says," *The Spokesman-Review*, October 19, 1980, pp. A1, A6.

_____, "Foley Labels First Race a Mad Scheme: Looking Back at 64's Adventure in Politics," *The Spokesman-Review*, December 8, 1986, p. A1.

_____, "Foley to Lead Fact Finders in Grenada," *The Spokesman-Review*, November 1, 1983, p. 1.

_____, "Knickered Schoolboy to House Leader: Tom Foley's Political Ascent has been by Accident and by Design," *The Spokesman-Review*, December 7, 1986, p. A1.

_____, "Reagan Fall Would Be 'Disaster'," *The Spokesman-Review*, December 9, 1986, p. A6.

Rosenbaum, David E., "A Politician Outside the Mold: Thomas Stephen Foley," *The New York Times*, June 2, 1989, p. A1.

Rubin, Alissa J., "Leaders Using Fervent Approach to Convert Wavering Members," *Congressional Quarterly Weekly Report*, July 30, 1994, pp. 214-216.

Rudman, Warren B., *Combat: Twelve Years in the U.S. Senate* (New York: Random House, 1996).

Runquist, Paul S., Paul E. Dwyer, John S. Pontius, and Mildred Amer, *CRS Report for Congress, House of Representatives' Management: Background and Current Issues* (Washington, D.C.: Congressional Research Service, The Library of Congress, April 17, 1992).

Rust, Michael, "Manipulating the Candidate," *INSIGHT* (*The Washington Times*), March 10, 1977, pp. 10-11.

Sabato, Larry J., *Feeding Frenzy: How Attack Journalism Has Transformed American Politics* (New York: Free Press, 1991).

Scammon, Richard, "Senate Demurs on Labor Rules, but House Acts on Its Own," *Congressional Quarterly Weekly Report*, October 8, 1994, p. 2855.

Schram, Martin, *Speaking Freely: Former Members of Congress Talk About Money in Politics* (Washington, D.C.: Center for Responsive Politics, 1995).

Seelye, Katharin Q., "A Veteran Logroller Works on His Triceps," *The New York Times*, June 1, 1994, pp. C1, C7.

_____, "With Fiery Words, Gingrich Builds His Kingdom," *The New York Times*, October 27, 1994, p. A1, A26.

SIGNUM of Gonzaga University, May 1974, p. 9, "Judge Foley: A Long Distinguished Career."

Simpson, Alan K., *Right in the Old Gazoo: A Lifetime of Scrapping with the Press* (New York: William Morrow and Co., Inc., 1997).

Simpson, Glenn R., "Foley Stocks were Innocent Giving," *Roll Call*, reprinted in *The Spokesman-Review*, July 25, 1993, p. A17.

Sinclair, Barbara, "The Congressional Party: Evolving Organizational, Agenda-Setting, and Policy Roles," in L. Sandy Maisel, ed., *The Parties Respond* (Boulder, Co.: Westview Press, 1990).

_____, *Legislators, Leaders, and Lawmaking: The U.S. House of Representatives in the Postreform Era* (Baltimore and London: The Johns Hopkins University Press, 1995).

_____, *Majority Leadership in the U.S. House* (Baltimore: Johns Hopkins University Press, 1983).

Smith, Hedrick, *The Power Game* (New York: Ballantine Books, 1988).

_____, "Majority Party Leadership in the House of Representatives: A Reassessment," paper presented at the annual meeting of the American Political Science Association, Washington, D.C., 1988.

_____, "Strong Party Leadership in a Weak Party Era—The Evolution of Party Leadership in the Modern House," in Ronald Peters and Allen Herzke, eds., *The Atomistic Congress* (Armonk, N.Y.: M.E. Sharpe, 1992).

Smith, Steven S. and Christopher J. Deering, *Committees in Congress* (Washington, D.C.: *Congressional Quarterly* Press, 1984).

Snyder, Laurie, "What's an Ex-Speaker Worth?" *The Spokesman-Review*, October 28, 1997, p. A1.

Sorensen, Eric, "Farmers are Hot in Dusty, Where Foley Vote Dried Up," *The Spokesman-Review*, November 8, 1990, p. A1.

Starobin, Paul, "An Ear for Gossip," *National Journal*, October 4, 1997, p. 1949.

Steele, Karen Dorn and Jim Camden, "Foley's Interests and Experience Span the Globe," *The Spokesman-Review*, June 7, 1989, p. A6.

_____, "Heather Foley Rebuts Criticism," *The Spokesman-Review*, April 8, 1992, p. A1.

_____, "Majority Leader Commands Respect," *The Spokesman Review*, April 2, 1989, p. A1.

_____, "Practicing Politics by Sharing Power: Foley's Reputation Built on Consensus and Careful Moves," *The Spokesman-Review*, June 7, 1989, p. A3.

_____, "Quietly, Heather Foley Manages," *The Spokesman-Review*, June 7, 1989, p. A2.

Stine, Stephen F., "Controlling the Budget: An Old Idea," *Congressional Quarterly Weekly Report*, October 12, 1985, p. 2038.

Stratton, David H., ed., *Spokane & The Inland Empire* (Pullman: Washington State University Press, 1991).

Streitfeld, David, *The Washington Post*, September 5, 1966, p. C6.

Sullivan, Kevin, "Foley's Arrival Ends 11-Month Vacancy," *The Washington Post*, November 16, 1997, p. A25.

Sutton, Lorna, "Farmers Ask Closer Ties with Foley," *The Spokesman-Review*, November 9, 1978, p. A9.

Sweeney, Louise, "King of the Hill: Speaker Tom Foley is a Cautious Man Who's Not Afraid to Face Down a Political Stampede," *The Christian Science Monitor*, February 22, 1990, p. 15.

"Texas Radio Covers De-Foley-Ate Project," *Spokane Valley Herald*, September 15, 1994, p. 1.

The Thomas S. Foley Institute for Public Policy and Public Service, *The Foley Institute Report*, Washington State University, Spring 1997.

Toner, Robin, "Foley Showing Fight on Some Partisan Issues," *The New York Times,* as reprinted in *The Spokesman-Review*, July 3, 1989, p. A1.

_____, "Foley Shows He is Speaker for both Washingtons," *The New York Times*, August 21, 1989, p. A10.

Trescott, Jacqueline, "Tom Foley and the Changing of the Guard: The Gentleman from Washington, True to Form," *The Washington Post*, June 1, 1989, p. C13.

Tumulty, Karen, "Man with a Vision," *Time,* January 5, 1995, p. 23.

Turner, Paul, "The Speaker from Spokane," *The Spokesman-Review*, June 7, 1989, p. A6.

Vernon, Ilyse J., "A History of Spending Limits," *Congressional Quarterly Weekly Report*, June 19, 1993, p. 1538.

Webster, John, "Our View: Voters Must Focus on NW Issues," *The Spokesman-Review*, editorial, October 11, 1994, p. A8.

Wehr, Elizabeth, "Budget-Balancing: Decisiveness vs. Caution," *Congressional Quarterly Weekly Report*, October 26, 1985, p. 2149.

_____, "Budget Conference Leaders Agree on Key Points," *Congressional Quarterly Weekly Report*, December 7, 1985, p. 2548.

_____, "Congress Enacts Far-Reaching Budget Measure," *Congressional Quarterly Weekly Report*, December 14, 1985, p. 2605.

_____, "House Centrist Bloc: Still Waiting to Happen," *Congressional Quarterly Weekly Report*, May 25, 1985, p. 972.

_____, "Senate Passes Plan to Balance Federal Budget," *Congressional Quarterly Weekly Report*, October 12, 1985, pp. 2035-2042.

_____, "Support Grows for Balancing Federal Budget," *Congressional Quarterly Weekly Report*, October 5, 1985, pp. 1975-1978.

Weinraub, Bernard, "President Rebukes Key Election Aide for Foley Attack," *The New York Times*, June 8, 1989, p. B11.

Weisberg, Jacob, "On the Hill: Cat Scam," *The New Republic*, October 30, 1989, pp. 11-12.

Whalen, Bill, "Foley is Taking his Time to Get to the Top of the Hill," *INSIGHT (Washington Times)*, May 1, 1989, p. 21.

_____, "In Texas, Mighty Big Boots to Fill," *INSIGHT (Washington Times)*, September 18, 1989, pp. 26-27.

_____, "Mr. Nice Guy Under Fire," *INSIGHT (Washington Times)*, August 19, 1991, p. 32.

_____, "A Powerful Brood on Capitol Hill," *INSIGHT (Washington Times)* , November 20, 1989, pp. 20-21.

"What's an Ex-Speaker Worth?", *Legal Times*, October 13, 1997, p. 13.

Workman, Dave, "Politics Means Money. . . Big Money!" *The Spokesman Review*, October 17, 1982, p. B1.

Wright, Jim, *Balance of Power: Presidents and Congress from the Era of McCarthy to the Age of Gingrich* (Atlanta: Turner Publishing, Inc., 1996).

Writers' Program of the Work Projects Administration in the State of Washington, *Washington: A Guide to the Evergreen State* (Portland, Or.: Binfords & Mort, 1941).

Yang, John E. and David Rogers, "Quiet Speaker: Thomas Foley, in Line to Succeed Wright, is Worldly, Thoughtful," *The Wall Street Journal*, June 1, 1989, pp. A1, A23.

Yang, John E., "House Speaker Foley, Very Much the Product of his State, Hasn't Fallen Far from the Tree," *The Wall Street Journal*, August 23, 1989, p. A12.

Zuckman, Jill, "As Family Leave is Enacted, Some See End to Logjam," *Congressional Quarterly Weekly Report*, February 6, 1993, p. 267.

Acknowledgments

A MONG THE MANY FRIENDS and colleagues who provided insights and direction, heartfelt thanks are extended to those who read early versions of the manuscript and whose wisdom and helpful criticism is reflected throughout this book: Ron Elving, then political editor of *Congressional Quarterly Weekly Reports*, currently political editor of *USA Today* and author of *Conflict & Compromise: How Congress Makes the Law;* Barbara Sinclair, Marvin Hoffenberg Professor of American Politics at UCLA, whose books such as *Majority Leadership in the U.S. House* and *Legislators, Leaders, and Lawmaking: The U.S. House of Representatives in the Postreform Era* have set a benchmark for scholarship on the Congress; Walter J. Oleszek, senior specialist in American national government for the Library of Congress's Congressional Research Service, whose understanding of the institution is only hinted at in his books, including *Congress and Its Members* and *Congress Against Itself* (with Roger H. Davidson); two scholars of Congress, Norman Ornstein of the American Enterprise Institute and Thomas Mann of the Brookings Institution, who together are close to unrivaled among their generation in informing the American public about the Congress and whose jointly-authored book, *Congress, the Press and the Public*, places Congress in an important societal context; James Thurber, professor of government and director of the Center for Congressional and Presidential Studies of American University; and senior specialist in American national government of the Congressional Research Service, Stanley Bach, who, along with Elving, Sinclair, Ornstein, Mann, and Thurber, is a former American Political Science Association (APSA) Congressional Fellow. The staff of the APSA was invariably supportive, particularly executive director Catherine E. Rudder, a former Congressional Fellow and director of the program, and Sheilah Mann, APSA director of education and professional development.

A number of former Foley staffers and astute observers of politics in eastern Washington were equally generous in their critiques of early versions of the manuscript. In particular, the authors express sincere thanks to Werner Brandt, former executive assistant to the Speaker and former House Sergeant-at-Arms; Janet Gilpatrick, director of Foley's Fifth Congressional District Spokane office; and Jess Walter, former *Spokesman-Review* political reporter and author of *Every Knee Shall Bow: The Truth and Tragedy of Ruby Ridge and the Randy Weaver Family*. And, while the effort was made to make the book relevant to a scholarly community, the authors were ambitious enough to try to make it of interest to a larger community with less of an appetite for politics. The down-to-earth readings of Janice Erzinger Biggs, Victoria Biggs Johnson, and Donald Johnson were borne out of love and common sense and helped strip away any undue scholarly artifice.

Many former Foley staffers, campaign workers, House and Senate colleagues, and friends—unnamed in the text—contributed to the meaning of this book, as did many journalists and scholars who helped document congressional activity from 1964-1994. We particularly recognize the staff of the *Congressional Quarterly Weekly Reports*, whose writing continues to achieve an unrivaled standard for those seeking the facts, the insights, and an understanding of the first branch of government.

For first-time authors the transformation from manuscript to book is a wondrous and humbling process. The authors offer heartfelt appreciation to *The Spokesman-Review* managing editor Chris Peck and his staff; Larry Stark of Washington State University's Manuscripts, Archives, and Special Collections; the thoroughly professional staff of Washington State University Press including director Tom Sanders, associate director Mary Read, marketing coordinator Sue Emory, book designer Dave Hoyt, and proofreader Jean Taylor, all of whom smoothed out a wealth of rough edges; and most particularly WSU Press editor Keith Petersen. With tenacity and just enough diplomacy, Keith eliminated the extraneous, turned the rambling into the concise, and kept the entire narrative on target. While the thanks to all these people is manifold, any errors are solely ours.

And, at the head of a long line of people to whom we owe thanks stand our parents, Ralph and Helen Foley and Wallace and Janice Biggs, whose love, nurture, and respect for public service always pointed us in the right direction, and our families Heather Foley and Janet, Jennifer, and Jessica Biggs, who lived through the entire process. Their love, patience, support, good humor, comradeship, and willing sacrifices have always been beyond price, book or no book.

Jeffrey R. Biggs
Thomas S. Foley

About the Authors

Jeffrey R. Biggs grew up in Laramie, Wyoming, and was educated at Harvard (BA), Victoria University of Wellington, New Zealand (MA) on a Fulbright, and George Washington University (PhD). His twenty-one years in the Foreign Service included assignments as a cultural center director in Brazil, press attaché in Portugal, and deputy chief of mission in Bolivia. He also was an American Political Science Association Congressional Fellow. Biggs was press secretary/spokesman to Representative Thomas S. Foley from 1987-1994, a visiting fellow at the Freedom Forum, and served on the faculty of the Parliamentary Institute at the Congressional Research Service of the Library of Congress while researching this book. Currently he is director of the American Political Science Association's Congressional Fellowship Program. He and his wife Janet live in Bethesda, Maryland, and have two daughters, Jennifer and Jessica.

Thomas S. Foley was born in Spokane where he attended Gonzaga High School. He graduated from the University of Washington and the University of Washington School of Law. Admitted to the bar in 1957, he practiced law in Spokane and was appointed deputy prosecuting attorney for Spokane County in 1958. He served as assistant attorney general for the State of Washington and assistant chief clerk and special counsel of the Committee on Interior and Insular Affairs of the United States Senate. Foley won election as a Democrat to the House of Representatives in 1964, and represented Washington's Fifth District for thirty years. In the House he served as chairman of the Committee on Agriculture, majority whip, majority leader, and Speaker. He currently is the United States Ambassador to Japan, where he lives with his wife Heather.

Index